SYMBOLIC INTERACTION
and
ETHNOGRAPHIC RESEARCH

SYMBOLIC INTERACTION

and

ETHNOGRAPHIC RESEARCH

*Intersubjectivity and the
Study of Human Lived Experience*

ROBERT PRUS

STATE UNIVERSITY OF NEW YORK PRESS

Published by
State University of New York Press, Albany

© 1996 State University of New York

For information, address State University of New York Press,
State University Plaza, Albany, N.Y., 12246

Production by Cathleen Collins
Marketing by Dana Yanulavich

Library of Congress Cataloging in Publication Data

Prus, Robert C.
    Symbolic interaction and ethnographic research : intersubjectivity
and the study of human lived experience / Robert Prus.
        p.   cm.
    Includes bibliographical references and index.
        ISBN 0-7914-2701-3. — ISBN 0-7914-2702-1
        1. Symbolic interactionism.   2. Sociology—Methodology.   3. Social
sciences—Philosophy.   I. Title.
    HM291.P727   1996
    302—dc20   94-49571
                                                                             CIP

10 9 8 7 6 5 4 3 2

This book is dedicated to my wife, Lorraine:
Elegant and enchanting,
Warm and witty,
Interested and insightful,
"The Contessa," as I affectionately call her,
has been of invaluable assistance in helping me put this manuscript together!

And in memory of:
Wilhelm Dilthey (1933–1911)
George Herbert Mead (1863–1931)
Charles Horton Cooley (1864–1929)
Pioneers in the quest for an intersubjective social science

Beyond their love, the greatest gift
that one generation can give to the next,
in the human struggle for existence,
is their stock of knowledge.

Contents

Foreword

In the following pages, Robert Prus provides an erudite treatise of the recurring theoretical and methodological debates now evident throughout the social sciences. These debates challenge the status of theory and method more generally and more forcefully than any in the last half century. Yet within them, old theoretical tensions between determinism and human agency arise anew. For Prus, any theory about the human condition must assume that human beings are active, reflective agents who construct their lives and, in turn, this assumption must systematically inform any method designed to study them.

As he examines the development of theory and method, Prus charts a trail through the forests of debates in the social sciences. He takes us from the thickets of early positivism through the tangles of current postmodernism. Throughout this journey, he makes an impassioned call to follow and to develop realist ethnography in the tradition of Herbert Blumer. He aims to redirect social science to gain congruence between theory and method and actual human experience. To do so, Prus advocates immersing ourselves in the research process, respecting our research participants and their worlds, and sharing their lived experience. Hence, Prus seeks to recast social science squarely in the interpretive tradition, and he speaks with strength, courage, and compassion.

Although Prus's analysis centers upon symbolic interactionism, the implications of his book are much wider. For that matter, this book represents more than a single volume or an isolated study. It represents the theoretical culmination of an odyssey of ethnographic adventures, intellectual explorations, and methodological reflections. In short, this book contains the knowledge and wisdom gained over an entire career by a social scientist who dared to question and who had the courage to grow. Robert Prus gives us the mature thoughts of an ethnographer whose earlier field research sparked him to delve deeply into the theoretical underpinnings of the social scientific enterprise. Thus, this book reflects much more than just another voice in the current noisy fray about theory, method, and the future of social science.

The argument that Prus makes is fourfold: (1) the debates in social scientific theory are far from over, (2) people create reality and their lived experience as they reflect on, interact with, and respond to others; thus, reality is fundamentally *intersubjective*, (3) only theories that take into account this intersubjective nature of human experience can understand, explain, and illuminate how people create their social and personal realities, and (4) therefore, we need a radical reconstruction of social science to develop a method that respects and captures lived experience.

Prus portrays the debates in theory as continuous and ongoing. He's right. To comprehend why dominant theoretical paradigms emerged, he reviews the development of sociological theory. He expertly traces the intellectual roots, methodological beginnings, and epistemological implications of the interpretive tradition. What should be the purpose of social scientific research? For Prus, the answer is unequivocable. Its purpose is to study and to understand human group life. To realize this purpose, he contends that we must learn how people make sense of their experience and construct meaningful activities in their daily worlds. From Prus's interpretive position, failing to attend to these social processes ignores the quintessential nature of social science. Thus, positivism is basically flawed as it does not account for the human production of meaning and action.

Adopting the interpretive tradition necessitates viewing individuals as inherently *social* actors who act in social worlds and live within human communities, no matter how diffuse and seemingly ephemeral. Here, Prus's position draws upon Meadian and Blumerian symbolic interactionism and, for that matter, coincides with Durkheimian sociological realism. He puts forth a fundamentally social view of human existence. At essence, we are social beings. We interact within society and are influenced by our interpretations of our interactions with others. We strive to develop shared definitions of our worlds and of our experiences with these others. I use "we" quite intentionally, for including ourselves gets at the core of Prus's theoretical insight and method: in Prus's image of social science, the scientist is part of the studied collectivity. We do not simply study the other, as *Other*. Rather, to the extent that we enter their worlds, we become the other, and perhaps they in some part become us. Hence, a profoundly humanistic and egalitarian view of the research process comes through in Prus's argument. We enter our research participants' worlds to understand their thoughts, feelings, and actions. But we do so as genuine participants ourselves, not as distanced, unbiased observers who dispassionately record the doings of others, like scientists attending to specimens in a laboratory. Yes, our curiosity might superficially resemble that of an "unbiased" observer. But it is a curiosity born through authentic interest, aimed toward understanding, and tempered by compassion. True, we record notes and render voices. However, we do so to portray our research participants' meanings with depth, openness, and appreciation. Of course, we may enter worlds where people think, feel, and act in ways that we reject. Still, we try to understand their worlds and seek to learn how they create them. Our involvement can produce altered views of those we study and sobering realizations about ourselves.

Prus's treatment of Mead and Blumer is insightful, accurate, and articulate. However, bringing Wilhelm Dilthey back into the center of epistemological discourse is this book's major theoretical contribution. According to Prus, we must go back to Dilthey to retrieve our intrepretive roots. Dilthey provides the fundamental groundwork for understanding human reality as intersubjective and for developing a social science based upon this premise.

The way we conduct research not only makes intersubjectivity more visible, but also contributes to it. By building on Dilthey, Prus makes the strongest case I have seen since that of Alfred Schutz for viewing social and individual reality as inherently intersubjective. Such intersubjectivity develops as people interact and come to view and treat their worlds in common ways. Prus's intersubjectivity does not merely occur; it is created through human action and shared meanings. He views intersubjectivity explicitly as an ongoing *accomplishment*. Thus, reality is not a given; nor is it entirely predictable. In contrast, Prus argues that people together construct and reconstruct meaning, as they act and interact. Essentially then, meanings arise, are maintained, and change as people pursue daily activity. Through unexpected events and, more often, mundane routines, meanings emerge and become shared. Intersubjectivity depends upon sharing language and symbols. People accomplish intersubjectivity through *mutually* constructing actions, interactions, and meanings. However, their intersubjectivity is not an entirely conscious or strategic response. They develop intersubjectivity as they take-for-granted and view these meanings as the natural way to think, feel, and act. In this way, people elevate their intersubjective reality founded in mutuality to "objective" reality. (I might add that the same process occurs in scientific discourse.) To the extent that people reify their taken-for-granted shared definitions and mutual understandings, their intersubjective reality will gain the obdurate force of objective reality.

Through his explication of intersubjectivity, Prus makes clear that positivists err when they claim that symbolic interactionism is a subjectivist approach. Positivists have dismissed symbolic interactionist research because it emphasizes meanings and because these meanings are not readily amenable to statistical procedures using standardized measures.

From one vantagepoint after another, Robert Prus eloquently reminds us throughout his book that human experience is intersubjective. As a result, he also finds qualitative studies that do not attend to intersubjectivity wanting. He takes exception to a narrow interactionism that uses only observation without engaging the research participants. We must learn what their intersubjective meanings are. Prus insists that we can do that only by involving ourselves in their language and symbols and by discovering how they view and reflect upon their actions. Purely observational studies cannot begin to understand or to capture intersubjectivity. Further, such studies do not and cannot involve the empathetic understanding of lived experience. Thus, Prus objects to those studies that impute dramaturgical meanings through actions and expressions given off rather than reflectively acknowledged. To understand what people intend and why they act as they do we must enter into their experience. We must share it. As he explicates his notions of intersubjectivity and builds support for his position, Prus then tells how to discover intersubjectivity and why we should become part of it. Without prescribing techniques, he provides a research agenda that directs and shapes our work.

Therefore, Prus's proposal for radically restructuring scientific inquiry logically follows his quest to understand and to analyze human lived experience as intersubjective. Social science cannot rely on objectivist methods—whether they are qualitative or quantitative. Moreover, we cannot abandon empiricism completely as the most cynical postmodernists conclude. This brings us to ethnographic research: only through sustained involvement and attention to shared meanings and activities can we understand human experience.

Integrating Dilthey's use of intersubjectivity with Mead and Blumer's emphasis on meaning and process in symbolic interactionism gives Prus a highly consistent, well-reasoned stance toward theory and research. His methodological approach flows logically and consistently from his theoretical perspective. Both distinguish him significantly from the postmodern turn in the social sciences. Prus takes a long view of both the human condition and social science theory. First, he observes that the existential problematics of contemporary human life resemble those of prior centuries. Second, he argues that current theoretical inquiries hearken back to earlier debates. The first point supports his view that we must study the human struggle for existence as it actually occurs in daily life. The second point reaffirms his position that we not be distracted from our study by theoretical fads and fashions.

Over the past decade, Robert Prus has steadfastly insisted that we study the mutual construction of intersubjectivity among living, thinking, feeling, and acting human beings. As a result, he has emerged as one of the clearest voices to oppose the postmodern turn in the social sciences. He sees the postmodern turn as a temporary fad that obfuscates our theoretical mission and muddles our research agenda. Nonetheless, his is a measured critique. While he realizes that postmodernism has leveled significant criticisms of positivistic science, he recognizes that postmodernism takes social science away from the empirical world. In this sense, Prus discerns the conservative bent in cynical postmodernists' proposals to abandon ethnographic research altogether. When Prus turns his critical eye to the postmodernist reliance on structural variables such as class, race, and gender, he finds that postmodernists mistakenly assume that meanings of these variables remain fixed, stable, and shared. Prus's entire approach rests on studying social processes. Thus, he refuses to leave structural variables unanalyzed and demands that we examine the processes that construct them. Prus levels compelling criticisms at postmodernism. What might postmodernists say about his approach to research? Ironically, Prus may provide the most workable answers to date to resolve postmodern critiques of qualitative research. Taking Prus's position seriously dissolves some of the most trenchant postmodern criticisms of qualitative research as voyeuristic, authoritarian, and imperious. If so, the force of postmodernist criticism about authorial representation also substantially weakens. Through joining social worlds as participants ourselves and by understanding the people within them, our representations will portray them as human beings striving to live in the ways they know while moving along the routes they take. Their voices will rise—strong, yet even—throughout our written pages. Our mirrors of their lives will reflect measured images, evanescent empirical truths, perhaps, but ones well-told and rich in enduring larger meaning.

In summary, one could not gain the kind of perspective Prus has developed from simply reading the classical theorists he has elegantly discussed. Rather, this perspective comes from having grappled with research dilemmas firsthand, and then seeking to make intellectual and theoretical sense of them. Prus's model of doing research is neither easy nor quick. It means making our best effort to look at the world from the eyes of those we study and to record it faithfully from their view. It also means reflexively examining our interpretations at every stage of the research process. Thus, it means approaching the world with wonder, pursuing new intellectual and experiential paths, sensing nuances of feeling and meaning, and sharing our lives as well as theirs.

This book may be read as a historical chronicle of theoretical debates, as an interpretation of theoretical hegemony, as a statement of the status of the discipline, and as a call to renew the vitality of our research by radically reconstructing it. I think Prus makes his most significant contribution when he calls for the reconstruction of social scientific research. Yes, Robert Prus has an agenda for symbolic interactionists specifically and social scientists, more generally. He calls us to return to the field, to share the worlds of those we study to, understand their realities, and to develop compassionate analyses of how they produce these realities. And while we do so, Prus enjoins us to hear the echoes of our theoretical predecessors and to see the imprint of their ideas on the pages we write. Only then will the current noisy, and often fruitless, theoretical fray grow distant, and for us turn quiet and still. Only then will we deepen our theoretical insight and refine our research craft. His book is a major step in this direction. Read it. Use it. Dare to question and have the courage to grow.

Kathy Charmaz
Sonoma State University

Preface

All our knowledge of the world, in common-sense as well as in scientific thinking, involves constructs, i.e., a set of abstractions, generalizations, formulations, idealizations specific to the respective level of thought organization. Strictly speaking, there are no things as facts, pure and simple. . . . They are, therefore, always interpreted facts. . . . This does not mean that, in daily life or in science, we are unable to grasp the reality of the world. It just means that we grasp merely certain aspects of it, namely those which are relevant to us for carrying on our business of living or from the point of view of a body of accepted rules of procedure of thinking called the method of science. (Schutz, 1962:5)

Because they are historical products of human activity, all socially constructed universes change, and the change is brought about by the concrete actions of human beings. . . . Reality is socially defined. But the definitions are always embodied, that is, concrete individuals and groups of individuals serve as definers of reality. (Berger and Luckmann, 1966:116)

This is a book about people. It focuses on the human quest for intersubjectivity (or mutuality of understanding) and the development of meaningful activity amidst the ambiguities entailed in the human struggle for existence. More specifically, it considers the implications of intersubjectivity and the social essences of action for those in the social sciences.

This volume centrally builds on, and takes its vitality from, the works of a great many scholars who have been interested in understanding the human condition. At the same time, this book is a critique of the ways in which the study of human behavior or the study of human group life has been approached in the social sciences. It is not a critique of the sincerity or dedication of those in the social sciences (although there is the matter of motivated resistances to be considered), nor is it a critique either of "science" as a human endeavor (but some reconceptualization of the notion of science may be in order). I do contend, however, that mainstream social scientists are fundamentally mistaken in the ways in which they have approached the study of the human condition. As opposed to the postmodernists, though, who are inclined to reduce human lived experience to textuality, I emphasize the necessity of developing a social science that is conceptually informed and intimately and rigorously grounded in the (intersubjective) world of human lived experience (and practical accomplishment).

This means, in part, that what is proposed here is a shift from a variable-oriented social science, one in which the emphasis is on uncovering the factors, forces, and structures thought to cause or produce certain kinds of human behavior and conditions, to a social science that is, first and foremost, concerned with developing an understanding of the ways in which human group life is accomplished from the viewpoint of those engaged in its production.

In contrast to those who would try to reduce the study of the human condition to "individual properties" or "social structures" of sorts, the orientation taken here is both intersubjective and activity-based to the core. This perspective not only reflects the necessity of establishing intimate familiarity with the (intersubjective) other through the "role-taking" processes (Mead, 1934) implied in ethnographic research (observation, participant-observation, and extended intercommunication with the other), but also acknowledges and attends to the ongoing accomplishment of everyday life in the "here and now" (while mindful of the evershifting present within people's experiences with the past and their anticipations of the future).

The approach taken here is also characterized by an emphasis on relevancy and correspondence; an insistence that the theory and methods of the social sciences respect "the actualities of human group life." The objective, thus, is to establish a greater (epistemological) coherence between the theory, methods, and research that typify the social sciences, and the actual day-to-day practices and experiences of the people involved in the (human) production of action.

There will always be those in the social sciences who proclaim that we need a "new theory" or a "new approach" for comprehending the human condition in each new decade, era, or century, and they will promote a variety of viewpoints for this purpose. This attentiveness to temporally situated developments may inform as well as entertain in certain respects. However, we should not become unduly preoccupied with the fads and fashions (intellectual and otherwise) of the moment. Although human group life does change and flow in a substantive sense, it has a more fundamental, enduring quality. Contemporary group life is not different in more foundational respects from human group life in the nineteenth century, the fifteenth century, or any other period in which people (as linguistically interacting beings) exist(ed).

All people (past, present, and future) must come to terms with developments in technologies, shifts in fashions and worldviews, and the ongoing struggle for existence amidst ambiguous social relations and a problematic physical environment. Matters of developing perspectives on the world, becoming involved in situations, acquiring identities, doing activities, developing relationships, and experiencing emotionality are nothing new to humankind. Likewise, observations to the effect that "things are always changing," that "things are really different now," or that "we have outgrown the past," are by no means novel, although perhaps certain disjunctures may never have been so acutely appreciated by particular observers.

Rather than proposing something "new," I want to draw attention to a perspective that is as integral to the human condition as is humankind's first experience with the symbol; to a phenomenon that takes place every time a parent or other caretaker attempts to interact with a child in a meaningful fashion and continues for as long as that person has consciousness of self and other. I want to emphasize the necessity of attending to the human quest for intersubjectivity and the minded accomplishment of human activity. Ironically, this means centrally acknowledging aspects of the human condition that mainstream social scientists have almost entirely ignored. In attempting to be "scientific," to apply the methods of the physical sciences to the study of human group life, a great many social scientists have neglected the essential features of human lived experience. Moreover, they have pushed these essences of human group life so far from active consideration that their theories and methods have lost essential relevance with respect to the lives of those they purport to study. As active participants in their own social arenas, these scholars have maintained a sense of intersubjectivity and envision themselves to engage in meaningful activity on a more or less sustained basis. However, they have not accorded the same capabilities to those they study.

The proposal that social scientists attend to intersubjectivity and human activity in a more concerted manner necessitates radically reorienting our images of science. It involves reconceptualizing the ways in which physical science is accomplished in practice, but most particularly it entails a redefinition of the "scientific method" as this pertains to the study of the human condition.

Although this volume lays out the central features of an intersubjective social science and considers a number of major debates in the field, I can take very little credit for the ideas presented herein. The premises undergirding this statement are rooted in the works of Wilhelm Dilthey, George Herbert Mead, Charles Horton Cooley, Herbert Blumer, and Alfred Schutz, amongst others. This statement has also been vitally informed by those ethnographers (particularly

Chicago-style interactionists) who have actively pursued the intersubjective objective by attempting to learn about the life-worlds of others in an extended, intimate manner. I've not met the early pioneers of intersubjective social science, nor those (of course) on whose insights they've built. Fortunately, some of their central thoughts have been recorded in books and journals, and I have tried to do their ideas justice by working with them in the ways in which they had intended.

While indebted to these scholars of years past, I owe a great deal, as well, to a more contemporary set of others, both inside and outside academia, for teaching me about the worlds that they know and for encouraging (and challenging) me to pursue the study of human lived experience in a more sustained manner. Thus, I thank first the great many people who over the years have shared their experiences and taught me about their life-worlds in the course of the various ethnographic research projects on which I've embarked.

In addition, I very much appreciate the collegiality and intellectual stimulation generated by others who shared my interest in the study of the human condition. With apologies to those who have been inadvertently missed, I am grateful to the following people for examining parts of this manuscript and otherwise sharing their thoughts, concerns, stocks of knowledge, and insights with me: Patricia and Peter Adler, Cheryl and Daniel Albas, Leon Anderson, Hans Bakker, Eleen Baumann, Joel Best, Herbert Blumer, Craig Bryson, Robert A. Campbell, Carl Couch, Jim Curtis, Norman Denzin, Mary Lorenz Dietz, Bob Farmer, Scott Grills, Jack Haas, Rick Helmes-Hayes, Dick Henshell, Nancy Herman, Rosanna Hertz, Styllianoss Irini, John Johnson, Ron Lambert, John Lofland, Helena (Znaniecki) Lopata, Stan Lyman, David Maines, Elizabeth McNulty, Gail Miller, Richard Mitchell, Tom Morrione, Adie Nelson, Larry Reynolds, Howard Robboy, Clint Sanders, Stan Saxton, Marvin Scott, William Shaffir, C. R. D. Sharper, Charlie Smith, Eldon Snyder, John Stratton, Graham Tomlinson, Audrey Wipper, and Daniel Wolf. My colleague, Lorne Dawson, with whom I have coauthored chapter 8, deserves special recognition as an invaluable source of assistance and dialogue on a day-to-day basis.

As well, I would very much like to thank Kathy Charmaz for her contributions to this volume. Beyond writing a particularly thoughtful foreword, Kathy has reviewed and commented on the entire manuscript.

I have learned a great deal about human intersubjectivity through field research and can see no viable alternative to ethnographic research in the quest for understanding the human condition. However, I also found it very instructive to examine in closer detail the ways in which our predecessors had attempted to come to terms with intersubjectivity and the accomplishment of human group life. Increasingly, I've become aware that unless we build on both kinds of insights, we will not be in a position to offer very much to those who follow us. It is my hope that this material will represent a set of resources to which people interested in the world of human lived experience may turn in their quest for developing a social science that is genuinely attentive to the inter-subjective other.

Acknowledgments

I would like to express may appreciation to Christine Worden (Acquisitions editor), Cathleen Collins (Production Editor), and the staff at SUNY Press both for their interest in the intersubjective dimension of human lived experience and for their assistance in enabling me to make this book available.

PERMISSIONS

I would like to acknowledge permission from the following publishers to reprint selected portions of the works listed below:

Anderson, Nels. 1983. "A Stranger at the Gate: Reflections on the Chicago School of Sociology." *Urban Life* 11:396–406. Copyright (c) 1983 by Sage Publications, Inc.. Extract reprinted by permission of Sage Publications, Inc.

Blumer, Herbert. 1962. "Society as Symbolic Interaction" Pp. 179–192 in Arnold Rose (editor) *Human Behavior and Social Process*. Boston: Houghton-Mifflin. Copyright (c) 1962 by Houghton-Mifflin Company. Extract reprinted by permission of Houghton-Mifflin Company.

———. 1966. "Sociological Implications of the Thought of George Herbert Mead." *American Journal of Sociology* 71: 535–548. Copyright (c) 1966 by the University of Chicago. Extracts reprinted by permission of the University of Chicago Press.

———. 1969. *Symbolic Interactionism*. Englewood Cliffs, N.J.: Prentice-Hall. Copyright (c) 1969 by Prentice-Hall, Inc.. Extracts reprinted by permission of Prentice-Hall, Inc.

Couch, Carl. 1984. "Symbolic Interaction and Generic Sociological Principles." *Symbolic Interaction* 7 (1):1–14. Copyright (c) 1984 by JAI Press Inc. Extract reprinted by permission of JAI Press Inc.

Dawson, Lorne L., and Robert C. Prus. 1993. "Interactionist Ethnography and Discourse Postmodernist Discourse: Affinities and Disjunctures in Approaching the Study of Human Lived Experience." Pp. 147–177 in Norman K. Denzin (editor) *Studies in Symbolic Interaction*, Volume 15, 1993. Copyright (c) 1993 by JAI Press Inc. Extract reprinted by permission of JAI Press Inc.

———. "Human Enterprise, Intersubjectivity, and the Ethnographic Other: A Reply to Denzin and Fontana. Pp. 193–200 in Norman K. Denzin (editor) *Studies in Symbolic Interaction*, Volume 15, 1993. Copyright (c) 1993 by JAI Press Inc. Extract reprinted by permission of JAI Press Inc.

Denzin, Norman K. 1993. "The Postmodern Sensibility." Pp. 179–188 in Norman K. Denzin (editor) *Studies in Symbolic Interaction*, Volume 15. copyright (c) 1993 by JAI Press Inc. Extract reprinted by permission of JAI Press Inc.

Ermarth, Michael. 1978. *Wilhelm Dilthey: The Critique of Historical Reason*. Chicago: University of Chicago Press. Copyright (c) 1978 by the University of Chicago. Extracts reprinted by permission of the University of Chicago Press.

Lofland, Lyn. 1980. "Reminiscences of Classic Chicago: The Blumer-Hughes Talk." *Urban Life* 9:251–281. Copyright (c) 1980 by Sage Publications, Inc.. Extract reprinted by permission of Sage Publications, Inc.

Mead, George Herbert. 1934. *Mind, Self and Society*, edited by Charles W. Morris. Chicago: University of Chicago Press. Copyright (c) 1934 by the University of Chicago. Extracts reprinted by permission of the University of Chicago Press.

1

STUDYING HUMAN LIVED EXPERIENCE

An Introduction to the Intersubjective Enterprise

Hooks, that's what you use to hook an audience into an act.[1] *It can be anything that attracts them, sex, money, power, greed, mystery. Anything to get their attention and hopefully hold on to it. . . . The importance of the hook goes back, it all has to do with the performance of magic. And the hook is, "Why would someone be interested in watching me do a magic trick?" This is the question we have to ask. And once hooked, "Why would they continue to be interested?". . . You have to assume that magic is inherently boring. It's like juggling, you can only watch it for about four minutes and then you really get sick, "Yeah, it's amazing, so what?" Yeah, the guy spent fifteen years (practicing). . . . It's boring because you're watching it, you're not involved in it. . . . The hook has to be, "How do you make what you're doing interesting to the audience?" And, this applies to magic, anything! Why is the audience interested? You have to figure out how to hook them into it, how to keep them hooked. Well, magic, the way I do it is, I have certain rules. I try to appeal to one of the seven deadly sins. Greed, that's a good one for me, and gambling and fate. . . . So a lot of my tricks have to do with gambling, that sort of thing. . . . The hook is, finding something the spectator is interested in, and relating the trick to what he's interested in. If you can't do that, you don't have a good trick or you don't have a good presentation. . . . You don't want the question to arise, "How did you do that?", until you've finished performing.*

1. *Sharper: He's [magician] talking about the hook here. The hook for hustlers was the fast buck gambling, the game of chance. That was our hook, everyone wants to make a buck, you know what I mean. If they've seen us gambling, and fast money, money changing hands, the game looked good. You were comfortable with the people around the room, people at the table. That was the hook. We didn't have to use a hook, the hook was there. The hook is the money, obviously. You know people, they want to make a fast buck, an easy dollar. (Prus and Sharper, 1991:252, 253)*

1

At the heart of the sociological enterprise is the idea that human behavior is the product of community life; that people's behaviors cannot be reduced to individual properties. A major task facing sociologists (and social scientists more generally), therefore, revolves around the study of *the accomplishment of intersubjectivity*; that is, indicating how people become social entities and how they attend to one another and the products of human endeavor in the course of day-to-day life.

Part of the reason that magicians and hustlers are so intriguing to many people may reflect the notions that we "live in a world of images" and that anyone able to manipulate these images can shape the realities experienced by other people. As the preceding statements from a magician and a card and dice hustler indicate, however, those attempting to do influence work are always dependent on those with whom they interact. Although anyone may be able to generate a little "magic" when the other accepts the images or viewpoints one promotes, there can be no "magic" without the other. One can improvise and rehearse routines on one's own, but without someone to experience the mutuality of the encounter, without someone to accept (however temporary) one's definitions of the situation, there is no magic, no sharing of one's creativity with the other.

Magicians and hustlers may be seen as somewhat unique in that they deliberately, systematically, and more or less continuously attempt to create illusions,[1] but since they must relate to others in ways that those people find meaningful to encourage them to take certain lines of action, their work is of interest across the realm of human association. Despite their varying interests and intentions, concerns with "image work" (and the ensuing interpretations and adjustments on the part of the other) are central not only to magicians and hustlers, but also to politicians, religious leaders, union leaders, advertising agents, salespeople, entertainers, journalists, scientists, counsellors, teachers, friends, parents, children, work associates, enemies, and anyone else who endeavors to influence, or even communicate with, anyone else. All constructions of reality, all notions of definition, identification, and explanation, all matters of education, enterprise, entertainment, interpersonal relations, organizational practices, cultic involvements, collective behavior, and political struggles of all sorts are rooted in the human accomplishment of intersubjectivity.

Once one accepts the dictum that a major objective of any "science" (or the concerted study of some phenomenon) is to achieve intimate familiarity with one's subject matter, then concern with developing a social science centers on the pursuit of a theory and a methodology sensitive to the interpretive and interactive features of human group life.

Over the past century, the social sciences have been dominated by "positivist" (structuralist) approaches to the study of human behavior. Although positivism will be discussed in more detail as this volume unfolds, positivist

(positivist/structuralist) approaches tend to assume that people can be studied in manners paralleling the methods used to study physical objects. This viewpoint has been challenged in many ways over time, but the major debate in the social sciences has been between the positivists and the interpretivists. Some scholars have tried to blend the two approaches in various ways, but no viable syntheses have been sustained. As will become more evident in the chapters following, the development of an interpretivist social science has run somewhat concurrently with a critique of positivist social science.[2]

Since the 1980s, the positivist-interpretivist debate has become complicated somewhat by the introduction of postmodernism (poststructuralism, deconstructionism) to the social sciences. The intellectual roots and some major variants of postmodernist thought are considered in chapters 7 and 8, wherein the approaches falling under both the positivist/structuralist tradition and the postmodernist/poststructuralist umbrella are compared and contrasted with the intersubjectivist approach taken in this volume. In the interim, it is useful to appreciate that (a) the essential theoretical and methodological foundations of an interpretivist approach to the study of human group life were developed long before concerns with postmodernist agenda were introduced to the social sciences, and (b) positivism has represented the major obstacle to the development of an interpretive social science for the past century. As well, (c) while postmodernism has yet to contribute a major or consequential epistemological legacy to the social sciences, the deeply entrenched positivist tradition seems apt to dominate the study of human behavior for some time to come. Thus, although the current intellectual context has become complicated somewhat by the introduction of postmodernist thought, the issues raised by those embarking on postmodernist agendas are best examined later in this volume. Regardless of the significance one attributes to the "postmodernist impulse,"[3] it is important to attend first to the more enduring debates surrounding the study of human behavior as these pertain to matters of theory, methods, and ongoing research, and to examine the intersubjectivist approach in more detail. Only in these ways may one be in a more appropriate position to contextualize and assess contemporary lines of thought as these relate to the quest for understanding the human condition.

SOCIAL SCIENCE AND AN INTRODUCTION TO THE POSITIVIST-INTERPRETIVIST DEBATE

"When you cannot measure ◉ your knowledge is ◉ meager ◉ and ◉ unsatisfactory ◉" Lord Kevin (Bulmer, 1984:151)

The positivist-interpretivist debate revolves around the ways in which human behavior should be conceptualized and studied. Extended discussions of matters pertaining to epistemology (a consideration of the relationships of theory and methods of knowing about the world) are discouraged in many programs in the social sciences, wherein an emphasis on observable phenomena and the operationalization of variables has preempted many considerations of the premises undergirding the study of the human condition. Nevertheless, except in the most extreme cases, virtually all academics in the social sciences find themselves attempting to deal with issues revolving around (positivist) determinism and (interpretivist) human agency. As a result, almost everyone will be thrust into at least occasional debates regarding "the most pertinent theoretical and methodological directions for the studying the human element."

Some social scientists may prefer to avoid such issues, contending that they have no time for or interest in "philosophical issues," or claiming that such groundwork has already been established by those initiating or promoting the positivist agenda. In part, their position is justified by concerns with "getting on with the tasks at hand" and related reservations that discussions of this sort will take them into endless realms of metaspeculation or various moral issues. At the same time, however, these viewpoints are somewhat academically remiss. Considerations of the baseline assumptions that inform the social sciences provide scholars with important opportunities to assess the viability of the very foundations of their claims about the nature of the world, their methods of approaching the study of the world, and often a very substantial portion of their (hopefully) productive life's work.

While there is much variation within each approach, those adopting a *positivist* (or positivist/structuralist) orientation generally take the viewpoint that human behavior is a product of the forces, factors, or structures (internal and external) that act on people to generate particular outcomes. The intellectual foundations of positivism are considered in more detail later,[4] but it may be useful to observe that the canons of contemporary positivism in the social sciences were most centrally formulated in Auguste Comte's *Cours de Philosophie Positive* (1830–1842) and John Stuart Mill's *System of Logic* (1843). While differing somewhat in their emphasis on the primacy of sociology vs. psychology (respectively) in their systems, both scholars argued for a human science that would follow the compelling successes, logic, and methods that they associated with the physical sciences.

Auguste Comte (1798–1857) who coined the terms "positive philosophy" and "sociology" (Giddens, 1976:131), extended and crystallized many of the ideas with which his mentor, Saint-Simon, had worked. Like Saint-Simon,

Comte was concerned with employing the methods and insights of (physical) science to establish a vital new (moral) order. Comte, however, envisioned an even more vital role for sociology or "social physics" in the development of that new order. Although Comte's concerns with fashioning a new community orientation were inconsistent with large parts of his positivist philosophy, his commitments to scientific practices resonated with the position of others, perhaps most notably John Stewart Mill, who also argued for the development of a social science grounded rigorously in the images of the physical sciences. While somewhat persuaded by Comte's arguments regarding the unique features of human societies, Mill (1843) concentrated on developing the laws of individual psychology and emphasized experimentation and observation. Comte's approach was considerably more ambiguous (and confused) conceptually and methodologically, but his insistence on the study of society as a unique, irreducible configuration (which displayed an affinity with the models invoked in the biological sciences) was integral in carving out and legitimating "the human group" as a realm of intellectual focus.

Viewing science as a form of emancipation from theology and metaspeculation, Comte argued that the scientific method, which he envisioned as directly adaptable from the natural sciences, would provide the fundamental means for both developing knowledge about, and ways of more effectively dealing with, the human condition. Human society, Comte posited, could and should be studied scientifically, using the methods that had shown themselves to be so successful in the natural sciences. Likewise, he argued for the desirability of developing a series of lawlike generalizations, which would enable social scientists to predict and control (direct, shape) the human condition. Given his centrality in defining the field of sociology at its inception, Comte's notions of science and knowledge—causation and determinism, and structuralism and objectivism—became highly consequential in shaping the elementary theoretical and methodological directions of the field. As Bryant (1985:29–30) observes, Comte was not especially concerned about the precise techniques of positivist social science, but nonetheless saw the development of observation, experimentation, and comparison as essential to the scientific enterprise, with mathematics as the fundamental tool for the development of all science.

In complementary fashion, Emile Durkheim's (1897) quantitative or rate-data analysis of suicide and Wilhelm Wundt's efforts to establish the first experimental psychological laboratory (1879) are especially noteworthy with respect to the development of a positivist methodology in the social sciences. Although Wundt (see chapter 2) also encouraged his colleagues to pursue a form of social ("folk") psychology informed by interpretive analysis, this was largely ignored in the quest for methodological rigor and scientism. The die was cast. Inspired by Mill and Wundt, psychology was to become a "science of experimentation," while sociology was to become largely dominated by "survey research." In both cases, and across the social sciences more generally, a positivist "methodology" was invoked.

Although Comte and Durkheim were clearly not intersubjectivists, their emphasis on the necessity of explaining human behavior by reference to group life is most notable. Indeed, in discussing Comte's work, Mead (1936: especially 465–466) contends that Comte's primary contribution to the field is his insistence on maintaining the notion that society was a reality *sui generis*, a unique, but essential element in the study of the human condition. This emphasis (with its concomitant refusal to engage in psychological reductionism), likewise, may be the most enduring sociological contribution of Emile Durkheim who, like those instructing others in architectural design, also left his mark on the contemporary foundations of sociology and the directions that survey research has taken more generally.

Like Comte, Durkheim fully intended to apply the methods of the physical sciences to the study of the human condition. In contrast to the vagueness with which Comte left the field, however, Durkheim proposed a specific methodological orientation for examining and detailing "the forces shaping society."

Durkheim's (1897) study of *Suicide* provided a model that, much like Wundt's psychological laboratory, prominently encouraged positivist research in social sciences. No less importantly, though, Durkheim's (1895 [1938]) *The Rules of Sociological Method*, which built upon the thinking of Auguste Comte, provided a statement that was intended to (*a*) outline the appropriate subject matter for sociology, (*b*) establish the field as a "science" in its own right, and (*c*) establish the methodology of the natural sciences as the method for the social sciences:

> *Our principle, then, implies no metaphysical conception, no speculation about the fundamental nature of beings. What it demands is that the sociologist put himself in the same state of mind as the physicist, chemist, or physiologist when he probes into a still unexplored region of the scientific domain. When he penetrates the social world, he must be aware that he is penetrating the unknown; he must feel himself in the presence of facts whose laws are as unsuspected as were those before the era of biology. . . . (Durkheim, 1938 [trans.] author's preface to the second edition: xlv)*

A social fact is every way of acting, fixed or not, capable of exercising on the individual an external constraint; or again, every way of acting which is general throughout a given society, while at the same time existing in its own right independent of its individual manifestations. (Durkheim, 1895 [1938]: 13). . . . The determining cause of a social fact should be sought out among the social facts preceding it and not among the states of individual consciousness. (Durkheim, 1895 [1938]: 110)

Durkheim's visions of applying the highly successful models of the physical sciences to the human condition quickly became widely acknowledged in the fledgling social sciences. Clearly, too, it was a methodological approach that Durkheim intended to have envisioned as beyond epistemological debate.[5] However, as becomes more evident in the following quotation (see the references to philosophy, free will, determinism, and causation), Durkheim's (positivist) approach is self-contradictory:

Our method. . . . is entirely independent of philosophy. . . . Sociology does not need to choose between the great hypotheses which divide metaphysicians. It needs to embrace free will no more than determinism. All that it asks is that the principle of causality be applied to social phenomena. . . . Since the law of causality has been verified in other realms of nature, . . . we are justified in claiming that is equally true of the social world. . . (Durkheim, 1895 [1938]: 141)

Despite its epistemological flaws, Durkheim's methodology has had a major impact on both sociology more specifically and the social sciences more generally. Not only have mainstream social scientists (particularly those favoring survey research) used Durkheim's statement on methods as a foundational justification for perpetuating a positivist social science (and discounting alternative approaches), but they have further objectified its tenets by embarking on research modelled after *Suicide* and many have employed his model(s) of social order as foundational themes with which to develop their own interpretations of the data they have gathered.

Although Durkheim's theoretical (functionalist) viewpoint has fallen into some relative disfavor among positivist/structuralist researchers over the past few decades, his (survey) methodological orientation has maintained a strong following in mainstream social sciences. As a consequence of computer-aided technology, quantitative analysis has become more sophisticated since Durkheim's time, but Durkheim's essential rationale has maintained currency in present day positivist/structuralist research in the social sciences. Like Durkheim, those working in the positivist/structuralist tradition have accepted the notion that human behavior should be studied in manners similar to the ways in which one might study physical or nonminded objects (ergo, the referent, "billiard ball determinism").

Emphasizing the (causal) relations between certain structures or conditions and particular outcomes, those adopting a positivist approach leave little room in their models for human agency in the production of action. For these scholars, the operationalization (and quantification) of "variables" or "factors" is extremely consequential and provides essential grist for their statistical procedures. Using data from experiments, surveys (questionnaires, census data), and other counting practices, these researchers are concerned with uncovering and specifying the structures, forces, or conditions that (they assume) cause people to act in this or that manner. Focusing on outcomes and variable correlates, they typically portray human behavior in terms of dependent (outcome conditions), independent (causal), intervening (mediating conditions), and control (possibly confounding) variables. Aspects of the human condition are then represented in the statistical relationships by which these researchers define particular sets of (rate-based) data.

While most researchers in the social sciences are quantitative in their emphasis, not all positivists or structuralists are particularly concerned with the operationalization of variables, measurements, and statistical analysis. Much topical historical analyses, as well as a great deal of the discourse inspired by Weberian, Freudian, Marxist, feminist, and postmodernist emphases, invoke baseline variants of structural determinism, even though those adopting these viewpoints need show little inclination toward, or reverence for, statistical portrayals of the human condition. Unlike their more quantitatively oriented counterparts, most of these structuralists do not strive to be defined (nor are they apt to be envisioned as) "scientific" in their work. Some of these people may be quite precise in developing aspects of their analysis, but often the key concepts with which they work are more vaguely developed (e.g., Marxist notions of social class, feminist notions of gender). Consequently, while these analysts often disavow positivist (quantitative) identification, they rather commonly employ baseline notions of structural determinism in the models and images they promote. The pursuit of secondary agendas (e.g., the ideologies implied in Marxist and feminist analysis) as well as some mixing of positivist and interpretivist orientations often serve to obfuscate or conceal an underlying emphasis on structural determinism (e.g., economic determinism, biological determinism).[6]

By contrast, the *interpretivists* contend that people are different from other objects and that the study of human behavior, consequently, requires a methodology that is attentive to those differences. The interpretivists envision human group life as actively constituted by people in interaction with others. Human behavior is seen as denoting an interpretive, interactive process. The primary methodological procedures are ethnographic (participant-observation, observation, and open-ended interviews) in nature. Human life is studied as it is experienced and accomplished by the very people involved in its production. The interpretivists are centrally concerned with the meanings people attach to their situations and the ways in which they go about constructing their activities in conjunction with others.

The positivists have been highly critical of the interpretive approach. One of the most central lines of criticism alleges that the interpretivist approach is subjective and unscientific because (*a*) the interpretivists emphasize the meanings that people attach to their behaviors and (*b*) these meanings are not readily operationalized (observed, counted, and statistically processed). The positivists argue that they are much more scientific in the ways in which they study human behavior because they develop "objective" (i.e., standardized) measurements of causes and effects (or independent and dependent variables) and use statistical procedures to analyze the data that they've collected through experiments, surveys, and other measurement strategies.

In response, the interpretivists observe that the *study of human behavior is the study of human lived experience and that human experience is rooted in people's meanings, interpretations, activities, and interactions.* These notions, they posit, are the essential substance of a social science. Likewise, the interpretivists contend that, in disattending to the interpretive, interactive processes by which human behavior is developed, the positivists overlook the fundamental social essences of human behavior. Thus, one might ask if an approach (positivism in this case) that disregards or disattends to the essence of its own subject matter should be envisioned as a "scientific" approach. Because of this fundamental flaw, the interpretivists do not accord positivist social science the scientific status its practitioners claim.

However, insofar as positivist approaches presently dominate the social sciences (departments, journals, publishing houses, granting agencies), the interpretive critique has not fallen on welcome ears. Most social scientists have developed their careers acknowledging, pursuing, and promoting positivist research. Many have achieved considerable levels of personal competence and recognition within academic circles because of their (structuralist) work. Insofar as these scholars see their position or competencies jeopardized in some manner by the interpretive critique, some may reject or even refuse to carefully consider the interpretive approach on grounds quite other than its intellectual merits.[7]

SYMBOLIC INTERACTION AND THE STUDY OF HUMAN LIVED EXPERIENCE

Although symbolic interaction (Mead, 1934; Blumer, 1969) represents only one of several interpretive approaches to the social sciences, it may be useful to provide a preliminary overview of this particular approach to the study of human group life before examining more fully the roots, variations, issues, and debates cutting across the study of human lived experience. People more familiar with the interactionist tradition will find much that they recognize in this immediate discussion, but this material may be particularly helpful to those newer to the field, since it outlines some very basic features of both the interactionist and interpretivist approaches to the social sciences.

Developed most explicitly by George Herbert Mead (1934) and Herbert George Blumer (1969),[8] symbolic interaction may be envisioned as the study of the ways in which people make sense of their life-situations and the ways in which they go about their activities, in conjunction with others, on a day-to-day basis. It is very much a "down to earth" approach, which insists upon rigorously grounding its notions of the ways in which human group life is accomplished in the day-to-day practices and experiences of the people whose lives one purports to study. Although Herbert Blumer very much envisioned himself as a student of George Herbert Mead, the interactionist tradition may be seen to build more broadly on four subtraditions (discussed in detail later): (1) the hermeneutics (interpretive understanding) of Wilhelm Dilthey, (2) American pragmatism (which emphasized the practical accomplishment of human activity), (3) Cooley's (1909) method of "sympathetic introspection" or what more commonly has become known as ethnographic research or field research, and (4) the body of ethnographic research, which was developed primarily at the University of Chicago.

Central to the interactionist approach is the notion that human life is community life; that *human life is thoroughly intersubjective in its essence*. At base is the recognition that humans (and human behavior) cannot be understood apart from the community context in which people live. *Humans derive their (social) essences from the communities in which they are located, and human communities are contingent on the development of shared (or intersubjectively acknowledged) symbols or languages*. This means that there can be no self without the (community) other. People may be born with physiological capacities of sorts, but people's awarenesses of the world (their abilities to learn, think, and create) are contingent on the acquisition of a (community-based) language. It is only in the process of acquiring a language (and interacting with others) that humans may begin to acquire "stocks of knowledge" or develop minds. Only on this basis may individuals begin to distinguish and make sense of the objects (including themselves) that they envision as constituting their worlds.

It is in the course of developing familiarity with the language of a community that people are able to approximate rudimentary understandings of, or perspectives on, human life-worlds. Only once people develop some fundamental conceptualizations of "the world" may they begin to exhibit some sort of reflectivity and meaningful human agency. Only with the acquisition of a language-based set of understandings or perspective are people able to take themselves into account in developing and pursuing particular lines of action. As Mead (1934) observes, it is the attainment of language that makes the possession of a "self" possible.

Language acquisition and use is at the core of human intersubjectivity. Only when people share sets of symbols are they able to communicate with one another and act in other ways that are mindful of the viewpoints of the other. Accessing or sharing a common language does not presuppose that people will automatically act in cooperative ways or in manners that others might deem rational. However, language provides the basis on which people establish common (community) understandings and it is through ongoing (symbolic) interaction with the other that one may establish more precise levels of intersubjectivity or more comprehensive understandings of the viewpoints of the other as well as more intricate senses of self.

While human worlds are symbolically or linguistically constructed (i.e., effectively denoting multiple symbolic realities), *the human world is also a world of activity*. Thus, just as one cannot reduce the study of human behavior to the study of individual qualities, similarly one cannot reduce human behavior to symbolic or linguistic realities, even though people's activities are meaningful only within the symbolic frameworks that humans collectively develop in the course of their existence.[9] While some human activity is directly predicated on the human struggle for existence in an environment that can resist human definition and enterprise in some very basic manners, by no means is the human condition limited to the struggle for existence. In fact, the areas to which human attention may be directed seem infinite. The diverse meanings that people are able to attach to any [objects] of their awareness require a particular attentiveness on the part of those studying human behavior to the ways in which people assign (and alter the) meanings to [objects].[10]

Rather than endowing [objects] with inherent meanings or assuming that certain shapes, colors, masses, sizes, and the like, exist in predefined terms, the position taken here (Mead, 1934:78) is that *people bring [objects] into existence by the ways in which they attend to, distinguish, define, and act toward these [experiential essences]*. This is not to deny that [things] are "out there" or that particular [objects] may impinge on people or resist people's efforts to perform actions. Indeed, the capacity for [things] to act on (and resist) people are central to Blumer's (1969) notion of an "obdurate reality" and the human struggle for existence. However, people's awarenesses of [things], the ways in which they view (delineate, categorize, appreciate) these [objects], and the manners in which people act toward the [objects] they've distinguished from other [things] are all problematic in scope, emphasis, and particulars.

Moreover, insofar as people develop conceptualizations of the world in the course of achieving a mutuality (or sharing) of experience (through linguistic or symbolic interchange), the [objects] of human awareness reflect a community or intersubjective base. As people acquire a language and a sense of object relations through association with particular human groups, they develop capacities for self-reflectivity. By adopting the viewpoint of the (community-based) other, people begin to distinguish themselves from other things in their environment; they acquire selves (or more accurately, images or senses of self). In the process of becoming "objects unto themselves," people achieve capacities for thought and action on a more solitary or independent basis.

Working with stocks of knowledge (and conceptual schemes) gleaned through interaction with others, but now applying these in particular or situated contexts, in familiar and in different ways, people formulate thoughts, achieve unique experiences, experience novelty, and pursue creativity. Indeed, given the limitations of their existing (linguistic) stocks of knowledge on a collective basis as well as individual variants within, people's experiences may well outstrip their abilities to retain and formulate more precise or lasting images of these events. People may sometimes retain particularly vivid images of events even when they are unable to define and classify these within their current linguistic terms, but it is only when people are able to find ways of sharing their experiences with others that they achieve the potential of turning these experiences into more enduring (i.e., community objectified or signified) features of reality. Thus, the processes of "indicating" (pointing to, drawing attention to, or signifying [things]) and "representing" (illustrating, imitating, describing in word or gestures, writing about, photographing, or recording) become exceedingly consequential in the matter of sharing experiences with others. As Mead (1934) observes in his discussion of the *symbol*, successful sharing is contingent on one's ability to invoke the sensations that one experiences in the mind of the other. Better approximations of shared experiences are dependent, therefore, not only on the sender's attempts and abilities to formulate or portray experiences to the other in manners that the other would comprehend, but also on the recipient being willing and able to adopt the viewpoint of the sender in interpreting these messages.

The pre-existence of human communities, each with its prevailing stocks of knowledge, means that individuals do not have to bring most objects of their awareness into existence on their own, at least on a foundational level. Thus, *to a very large extent, the world of (delineated, meaningful) objects precedes (and "object-ifies") one's (existence and) experience.* In the process of providing newcomers with a language and a set of practices for making sense of, and coming to terms with, the world at hand, others in the community not only inform newcomers about the nature of [reality] as they know it, but also enable newcomers to make sense of the experiences they have with people, themselves, and the other objects and situations they encounter. It is on this basis that people achieve foundations for embarking on meaningful activity.

As interacting, self-reflective beings, people not only develop ways of viewing and acting toward other objects (including other people and themselves), but they also can direct, monitor, assess, and adjust their own behaviors over time. This recognition, that *people do not merely act toward objects, but also can make self-indications (i.e., attend to, consider, and alter their own behaviors) in the process of developing particular lines of action toward things*, has profound implications for the study of human behavior. While people seem amenable to some forms of learning by means of object association or conditioning, these can be dramatically affected by any symbolic or linguistic linkages that people establish between (alleged) "stimuli" [object 1] and "responses" [objects 2, 3, etc.]. On the flip side, the intersubjective nature of the human condition also enables humans to greatly transcend the modes of learning associated with other mammal species. *The human capacity for intersubjectivity*, as indicated by language and cultural development, meaningful interaction, self-reflectivity, and minded behavior, *introduces complexities that require an entirely different theoretical and methodological approach than those that may be appropriate for studying other animals* (including the most sophisticated nonhuman mammals).[11]

Likewise, it is not enough to ask about people's attitudes or backgrounds and to try to correlate these in some manner with people's behaviors (or the consequences of their behaviors). It is, as Blumer (1969) so cogently argues, a fundamental error to view people as mediums through which various structures may find expression. *People not only think, anticipate, act, interact, assess, and adjust; but they do so by invoking intersubjectively derived languages and they operate most fundamentally within intersubjectively sustained symbolic realities.* This is why it is so unproductive to endeavor to explain human behavior by invoking "factors," "variables," or "structures" at either the level of group properties or individual characteristics. Although people need not act wisely or in manners considered desirable from this or that perspective, it is most inappropriate to embark on studies of the human condition without attending centrally to the very features that are distinctively human. Any "science of human behavior" should respect, both conceptually and methodologically, the intersubjective features of the human condition.

This emphasis on intersubjectivity is best appreciated within the context of human activity. People are not perpetually or uniformly active, but human group life is characterized by activity. As reflective entities, people may pursue activities on their own on a meaningful basis, but are also commonly faced with the tasks of coordinating (cooperation, competition, conflict) their activities with those of others. Further, human activity does not simply involve someone invoking behavior of some sort, but more accurately entails several subprocesses. Most notably, these include: defining the situation at hand, considering and anticipating both particular lines of action and potential outcomes, implementing behavior, monitoring oneself along the way, assessing situations both in process and in retrospect, and adjusting or modifying one's behavior both during immediate events and following earlier episodes.

This means that [objects] not only take on meanings as people initiate activity mindful of these [things], but in the process of acting toward [objects] people may revise the meanings they had earlier attached to those [objects]. More is involved, though. Even as they (*a*) develop lines of action (anticipating, manipulating, adjusting their behavior) toward particular [objects], people are also faced with (*b*) the task of managing the constituent parts of activities (e.g., capacities, motions, timing) that those activities entail. Consider something as simple as bouncing a ball off the wall and catching it; finding the washroom at night in darkened, especially unfamiliar, living quarters; or going for a walk in the woods ("Watch your step!").

When other people are involved, activity often entails (*c*) the matter of coming to terms with these others. Frequently, this means attending and making adjustments to others in the contexts of cooperation, competition, or conflict of various sorts. As well, insofar as people realize that they have limited stocks of knowledge with which to work, are unable to anticipate all eventualities, are dependent on the cooperation of other people, and are faced with the prospects of coming to terms with the resistances implied in encounters with other objects in their environment, it becomes apparent that a great deal of human behavior is characterized by ambiguity. Thus, in addition to attentiveness to the diversity of meanings that people may attach to [objects] at one point in time, social scientists also need to be mindful of people's capacities for adjustive reflectivity and the practical human matter of developing lines of action in nebulous contexts.

Recognizing the centrality of these concerns, it may be instructive to specify a set of assumptions that people working within an interactionist/interpretive tradition normally make (sometimes explicitly, sometimes implicitly) as they approach the study of human lived experience:

1. *Human group life is intersubjective.* Human group life reflects a shared linguistic or symbolic reality that takes its shape as people interact with one another. Human group life is community life, and human behavior cannot be reduced to individual properties. All meaningful essences, including the more solitary experiences of (linguistic) members of human groups, derive from or are built on comprehensions of "the reality of the other."

2. *Human group life is (multi) perspectival.* Rather than posit the existence of a singular or objective reality that people would experience in some uniform manner, it is recognized that people distinguish and develop meanings for [objects] as they interact with one another and develop styles of relating to those objects. Both the identification of [things] as "objects" and the meanings attached to objects are problematic in their existence and directions. However, when groups of people establish consensus among themselves on the existence and meanings of particular objects, they tend to envision their definitions of situations as "real" or "objective."[12] While the adoption of certain world views may enable a group of people to do things that others may not, it is essential to attend carefully to the realities of the groups under consideration. It is these viewpoints that represent the paramount realities for understanding people's participation in the situations at hand. Thus, people are seen to operate in versions of (multiple) realities, which they share (albeit imperfectly) with others at an "intersubjective" level.

3. *Human group life is reflective.* Through interaction with others and by taking the viewpoint of the other with respect to oneself, people develop capacities to become objects of their own awareness. By attending to the viewpoint of "the other" (what Mead [1934] terms "role-taking"), people are able to attribute meanings to their own "essences" and to develop lines of action that take themselves (and other objects) into account. Enabling people to see themselves from

the standpoint of the other and to "converse with themselves about themselves," the acquisition of (self-) reflectivity fosters meaningful initiative (i.e., human agency, enterprise, intentionality) as people develop their activities in manners that take themselves into account. As reflective entities, people may pursue activities on their own as well as resist unwanted input from others.

4. *Human group life is activity-based.* While human behavior is meaningful only within intersubjectively constructed, conveyed, and mediated contexts, and implies an ongoing interpretive process with respect to behaviors invoked in both solitary and collective instances, human group life is organized around the doing, constructing, creating, building, forging, coordinating, and adjusting of behavior. There is no requirement that the activity in question be successful as intended, nor it be viewed as wise or rational by others, or even by the actors themselves, over time. Activity draws our attention to the matter of ongoing enterprise, to the constituent notions of defining, anticipating, invoking, encountering resistance, accomplishing, experiencing failure, reassessing and adjusting, on both interactive as well as more solitary behavioral levels.

5. *Human group life is negotiable.* Acknowledging the abilities of people to influence and resist the influences of others, this premise makes the interactive dimension of human reflectivity especially explicit. Thus, the activities implied in cooperation, competition, conflict, and compromise are recognized as central to human interaction. Although all matters of interaction may be quite uneven, some element of mutuality, sharedness, or intersubjectivity is evident whenever people attend to, endeavor to shape the behaviors of, or attempt to "get their own way" in dealing with others.

6. *Human group life is relational.* People do not associate with one another in random or undifferentiated manners but tend to associate somewhat selectively with others as they develop more particularistic bonds or affiliations with other members of the communities in which they find themselves. This premise not only acknowledges the differing identities (i.e., self and other definitions) that people attach to one another, but it is also mindful of the loyalties, disaffections, and other interactional styles that emerge between people in the course of human interaction. Thus, in addition to the perspectives characterizing the community at large, many of the activities in which people engage are made particularly meaningful and shaped in certain manners

because of people's attentiveness to specific others in the setting. Ensuing definitions and negotiations of reality (including language), thus, depend centrally on people's involvements and embeddedness in particular groups within the broader community of others.

7. *Human group life is processual.* Human lived experiences are viewed as emergent or ongoing social constructions or productions. The emphasis is on how human group life is shaped by people as they go about their activities at this, that, and other points in time. While notions of intersubjectivity, particularized worldviews, reflectivity, activity, negotiated interchange, and relationships are all central to the ways in which the interactionists approach the study of human lived experience, so is the matter of process. Referring to the emergent or ongoing nature of group life, process is basic to an understanding of these other themes. Intersubjectivity (and the sharing of symbolic realities) is an ongoing process. Perspectives are also best approached in process terms, as the meanings that people attach to objects are developed, acted upon, and changed over time. Likewise, reflectivity is not only a product of ongoing association, but assumes its significance as "human agency" when people go about their activities. Reflectivity is dialectically experienced and expressed as people engage in instances of definition, interpretation, intentionality, assessment, and minded activities over time. Representing the implementation of the perspectives that people acquire through association with others and their senses of (reflective) self-agency, activity is also fundamentally tied to process. Denoting (experiential and behavioral) sequences of definitions, anticipations, implementations, assessments, and adjustments, which build up over time (techniques, practices, skills, stocks of knowledge and manners of engaging objects), activity provides a very powerful sense of emergence, transition, or process. Negotiation or interchange also assumes a processual dimension as people define situations (and selves), work out tentative lines of action, make indications to others, interpret the indications of others, and make ensuing adjustments to others in the form of subsequent definitions, plans, and indications. Relationships, as well, are best understood in processual terms (or as having natural histories) with respect to their emergence, intensification, dissipation, and possible reconstitution, as people attend to specific others and attempt to adjust their activities mindful of those with whom they associate. The primary conceptual and methodological implication of this processual emphasis

is this: since all aspects of group life take place in process terms or take their shape over time, *it is essential that the human condition be conceptualized and studied in manners that are acutely mindful of the emergent nature of human lived experience.*

ETHNOGRAPHIC RESEARCH: THE QUEST FOR INTIMATE FAMILIARITY

Although it is beyond the scope of the present volume to provide a detailed statement on the practices involved in conducting ethnographic research, people newer to the field may find it useful to briefly consider some rudimentary features of an interactive examination of the way of life of a group of people. Much of the ensuing discussion presupposes some familiarity with the ethnographic tradition.[13] Following a brief discussion of the hermeneutic essence of the human condition and its implications for research in the social sciences, attention is directed to some baseline practices and concerns associated with field research.

Since people differ from other objects of study by virtue of their interpretive (and interactive) capacities, it is essential that those embarking on studies of human life-worlds be sensitive to the "double hermeneutic" (or the task of interpreting entities that themselves interpret the worlds they experience), at the outset.[14] The "objects" (people [and their activities]) that social scientists study not only interpret other aspects of their worlds, but they also exchange (and recast) their interpretations as they interact with others and reflect upon their experiences in the course of their daily routines. Further, not only may people attempt to make sense of researchers' attempts to study them, but, as skilled interactants in their own right, people can act back on researchers. They can help researchers understand their situations by their openness, tutelage, and other modes of sharing aspects of their worlds with these researchers. However, people can also withhold cooperation, engage in purposive deception, and embark on other types of evasive and concealing activity. In contrast to the physical scientists who study nonminded or noninterpreting objects, *those in the social sciences require a methodology that is sensitive to the human capacity for "symbolic interaction."* To ignore any of the earlier discussed features of group life (intersubjectivity, multi-perspectives, reflectivity, activity, negotiability, relationships, and processes) is to violate central qualities of this subject matter.

The research implications of these assumptions are highly consequential. It means that people studying people should attend to: (1) the intersubjective nature of human behavior; (2) the viewpoints of those whose worlds they purport to examine; (3) the interpretations or meanings that people attach to themselves, other people, and other objects of their experiences; (4) the ways in which people do things on both a solitary and interactive basis; (5) the attempts that people make to influence (as well as accommodate and resist the inputs and behaviors of) others; (6) the bonds that people develop with others over time and the ways in which they attend to these relationships; and (7) the processes, natural histories or sequences of encounters, exchanges, and events that people develop and experience over time.

While each ethnography will assume somewhat different emphasis from the next, ethnographers generally rely on three sources of data (observation, participant-observation, and interviews) in their attempts to achieve intimate familiarity with the life-worlds of those they study.

Observation encompasses not only those things that one witnesses through one's visual and audio senses, but also includes any documents, diaries, records, frequency counts,[15] maps, and the like that one may be able to obtain in particular settings. While the materials thusly gathered can be valuable, it is imperative to recognize that the worth of any observation (or artifact) is contingent on researchers' abilities to achieve clear and accurate definitions of how that phenomenon or aspect of the situation was experienced and constructed by those participating in the situations under consideration. Even richly detailed, observational material, on its own, is much too limited (i.e., intersubjectively inadequate as) a basis on which to build an ethnographic study because one would have to make extensive inferences regarding people's meanings (and intentions). However, observational materials (particularly those that are more detailed, more descriptive in essence) can be very valuable in helping researchers formulate questions to be pursued in interviews as well as in providing a means of assessing and contextualizing the information one obtains through interviews and participant-observation.

Participant-observation adds an entirely different and vital dimension to the notion of observation. Although the practice of describing and analyzing one's own experiences has often been dismissed as "biased" or "subjective" by those who think that researchers should distance themselves from their subject matters, the participant-observer role allows the researcher to get infinitely closer to the lived experiences of the participants than does straight observation. Their experiences as participants may afford researchers with invaluable vantage points for appreciating certain aspects of particular life-worlds. As well, it may enable them to access the experiences of others in these settings in much more meaningful fashions than can be accomplished through questionnaires or experiments, for instance. Still, researcher-participants in the field should strive for as much balance in representation as possible in attending to the experiences of those who constitute the setting under consideration. In particular, it is critical that researchers develop a thorough appreciation of where and in what ways one's own experiences may approximate and differ from those of others in the setting.

Like those doing straight observation, researchers engaged in participant-observation normally try to remain fairly unobtrusive or nondisruptive in the setting being studied. However, participant-observation entails a more active (and interactive) and ambiguous role as researchers attempt to fit into the (dynamic) settings at hand. Insofar as more sustained participant-observation typically allows researchers to experience on a firsthand basis many aspects of the life-worlds of the other, it offers a rather unique and instructive form of data to those able and willing to assume the role of the other in a more comprehensive sense. Additionally, since it typically puts researchers in close, sustained contact with others, participant-observation generates further opportunities for researchers to gain insight into the viewpoints and practices of the other through ongoing commentary and other interactions. Participant-observation, thus, may provide researchers with a doubly privileged form of contact with the other.

Interviews represent the third major method of gathering ethnographic data, and under some circumstances may provide the primary source of data for field researchers. By inquiring extensively into the experiences of others, interviewers may learn a great deal about the life-worlds of the other. Interviews should not be seen as substitutes for extensive involvements as participant-observers, but it is not always feasible for researchers to participate in all settings in all membership manners. When researchers are able to establish extended levels of trust and openness with people who are willing to share their experiences and teach them about their life-worlds, extended, open-ended interviews may be used to obtain much insight into the life-situations of the other.

Ethnographers sometimes develop fairly extensive interview formats, but these normally take shape in the field as researchers learn more about the situations and the participants involved. The ethnographic interview is characterized by careful and receptive listening, open-ended queries, and extensive probing. It reflects an intense curiosity about the situation of the other and questions that develop as the researcher spends more time in the life-world of the other. Researchers in the field vary greatly in the ways in and extent to which they pursue interview materials, but a fuller openness to the other or greater receptiveness to letting the other "talk back" to the researcher is fundamental in achieving a more viable sense of intersubjectivity. Indeed, without this opportunity to uncover, ascertain, and qualify the meanings that others hold for objects in their life-worlds and the ways in which people go about accomplishing their activities in practice, it would make little sense to talk about studying human lived experience.

Although each research setting is somewhat different from the next (as is each encounter with the same person), and may necessitate some change in one's practices, there is little doubt about the generally enhanced quality (amount and depth) of the data one may obtain by spending more time in the setting and more fully participating in the life-worlds of the other. When researchers are able to gather observational, participant-observation, and interview data on a more or less simultaneous basis, this generally leads to a more complete understanding of the other. Researchers who become more completely immersed in the setting are not only more apt to be exposed to a wider and more intricate range of materials, but they are typically in a much better situation to inquire about, pursue, and assess incoming information gleaned in all of these manners.

OVERVIEW OF THE VOLUME

The recognition that intersubjectivity is at the core of the human essence implies that any viable theory of human behavior would necessarily be interpretive, hermeneutic, or reflexive in its thrust. It would be based explicitly on ongoing reflective interchange. There are a variety of interpretive viewpoints (see chapters 2 and 3) that one might invoke to meet the criterion of intersubjectivity at a theoretical level. However, one also faces the matter of developing a methodology that both respects the intersubjective nature of human group life and maintains a coherence with one's hermeneutic viewpoint. There may be many ways of learning things about people, but to qualify as an intersubjective method, one would have to employ some variant of an ethnographic approach: an approach that opens the researcher to the life-world of the other through interpersonal exchange. In this same schema, one would anticipate that the ensuing analysis also would reflect a relativistic appreciation of the (intersubjective) context in which the research has emerged. Thus, the analysis would likely be somewhat comparative, as well as descriptive, as researchers attempt to uncover and examine both the more unique and more mundane experiences and practices of the ethnographic other and consider these against a background of literature that scholars working in an intersubjective tradition have developed around the studies of other life-worlds that they have had opportunities to examine on a firsthand basis. Further, to pursue an intersubjectively informed social science, it would be expected that the theory and the method employed would be sufficiently flexible that they could be adjusted, more or less continuously, to accommodate ongoing inquiries (and the resistances encountered) into the life-worlds of the other. Minimally, then, it is proposed that the study of human behavior requires the blending of (a) an interpretive viewpoint with (b) the practice of ethnographic inquiry, (c) a comparative-adjustive style of analysis, and (d) an ongoing appraisal and adjustment of existing theoretical and methodological positions to actual studies of experiences and practices of the (ethnographic) other.

A number of other interpretive viewpoints will be addressed in subsequent chapters, but for our purposes *Chicago-style (or Blumerian) symbolic interaction* is particularly compelling. Not only does this tradition emphasize the thoroughly intersubjective nature of community life, but it also draws attention to the active dimensions (human struggles and enterprise) of the accomplishment of inter-subjectivity. As well, since it is steeped in ethnographic inquiry, Chicago-style interactionism both lends itself to a comparative-reflective mode of analysis and insists that theory and methods be adjusted to researchers' experiences in their encounters with the other.

Interactionism is sometimes portrayed (by positivist/structuralist critics) as a subjective social science or a microlevel sociology, but both these images are quite mistaken. Symbolic interaction is *inter*subjective to the core and envisions the development of language or ongoing symbolic interchanges as fundamental to the human essence (and the human struggle for existence). People are seen to develop (multiple) worldviews or definitions of reality as they interact with one another and attempt to incorporate particular objects of their awareness into their activities. Notions of community, self, action, reflectivity, symbolic realities, human interchange, and collective behavior are fundamental to inter-actionism, as are the processes of conflict, cooperation, and compromise. Like-wise, while interactionism builds on situated definitions and interchanges, and insists on the pursuit of research grounded rigorously in human lived experience and the ongoing production of action, it is quite able to deal with more molar matters such as fashion, the media, social problems, industrialization, economic development, law and policy formation, and other political processes.

At first glance, the methodology (open-ended inquiry, participant-obser-vation, and observation) of ethnographic research may seem less rigorous or scientific than some other approaches in the social sciences, especially to those who have been encouraged to envision positivist structuralism and quantification as synonymous with scientific progress. However, this inference is highly in-accurate. Ethnographic inquiry is a singularly powerful technique for studying the ways in which human behavior takes its shape. Ethnographic research requires an openness to the other. Indeed, it is only through "role-taking" (Mead, 1934) and interpersonal inquiry (or what Cooley [1909] termed, "sympathetic introspection") that one may attempt to achieve intersubjectivity with "the (human) other." It is only through conversing with the other and attempting to experience the situation of the other through extended role-taking activity that one may tap into the life-worlds of the other on a more adequate (accurate, sustained, and comprehensive) basis. Attempting to achieve an insider-level working knowledge of the other by opening oneself to the lived experiences of the other by direct, sustained contact, ethnography is the technique in the social sciences that most readily enables researchers to respect the nature of human group life. Envisioning people as having capacities for human agency; to think, act, and interact within a community (intersubjective) context, ethnographic research is the method in the social sciences which is most attentive to the manners in which people define their situations and accomplish their activities on an ongoing, day-to-day basis.

While ethnographic inquiry uniquely fosters the pursuit of an intersubjectively informed, activity-based study of community life, the approach taken in this volume is also concerned with developing concepts that enable scholars to both appreciate the idiographic features of particular contexts and transcend the particular contexts in which inquiries are conducted. Approaching ethnographic research in a more transcontextual or transsituational manner not only fosters the development, elaboration, and assessment of generic or basic social processes, but also suggests a framework that may be used as conceptual inspiration for future inquiry as well as a forum around which dialogue pertaining to diversely contextualized inquiry may be more productively (i.e., conceptual cross-fertilization) focused and developed.

Focusing on the "doing" or "accomplishing" of everyday life, the chapters in this volume examine a series of theoretical and methodological issues entailed in an interpretive/ethnographic study of human group life. Drawing heavily on the works of scholars who have contributed most centrally to the development of symbolic interaction and other interpretive approaches to the study of human lived experience, the material considered in this volume is essential to a wider appreciation of the social or human sciences. The chapters developed here deal with the historical roots, assumptions, variants, concepts, and literature characterizing an interpretive/ethnographic approach to the study of human behavior and address many of the major issues and obstacles facing those embarking on the study of human lived experience.

Chapter 2, *"Interpretive Roots: Experience as Intersubjective Reality,"* focuses on what was to become the intellectual foundation of symbolic interaction, but in the process traces the broader origins of the interpretive tradition in the social sciences. This chapter begins by examining the hermeneutics (interpretive understanding) of Wilhelm Dilthey and considers the contributions of Georg Simmel, Max Weber, and Wilhelm Wundt to the development of the interpretive paradigm, before turning to American pragmatism, as represented by the works of Charles Horton Cooley and George Herbert Mead. Despite some variation in overall emphasis, these scholars envisioned the social sciences as a study of human lived experience: as the interpretive or hermeneutic understanding of the self and the other within an interactive community context. They were concerned with ascertaining the ways in which people make sense of their worlds, mindful of the others with whom they jointly constitute a community. From this viewpoint, language or the development of a shared set of symbolic meanings is seen as both the product of human interchange and the essential foundation on which human community life exists.

Chapter 3, *"Contemporary Variants of the Interpretive Tradition"* elaborates on the notions of intersubjectivity outlined in chapter 2, showing how these took root in the social sciences and the ways in which they have been pursued and reformulated within the contexts and debates in which a more contemporary set of scholars found themselves. While the work of Herbert Blumer (who most thoroughly epitomizes Chicago-style symbolic interactionism) is singularly consequential in this respect, a number of other noteworthy offshoots are presented. Thus, attention is given to the Iowa school of symbolic interaction, dramaturgical analysis, labeling theory, social construction theory, ethnomethodology, structuration theory, and the new sociology of science. These variants will be compared and contrasted with the symbolic interactionism of George Herbert Mead and Herbert Blumer, but together they provide a body of concepts and resources that people pursuing the study of everyday life will find exceedingly important.

"The Ethnographic Research Tradition," chapter 4, is concerned with the development of the research traditions, in anthropology and sociology, which focus on the life-styles or human lived experiences of particular groups of people. Although it does not offer the conceptual tools provided in the earlier chapters, chapter 4 is especially valuable for understanding the intellectual heritage of contemporary ethnography. Some attention is given to the anthropological literature, but particular emphasis is placed on the development of ethnographic research in sociology as it took root at the University of Chicago. Consideration is given to "the classics" in this area and to the scholars (such as W. I. Thomas, Ernest Burgess, Robert Park, Everett Hughes, and Herbert Blumer) who played such vital roles in the development of field research. As well, by considering the objectives, dilemmas, and tentative early steps of these inquiries, this chapter

provides a frame of reference with which to approach and assess subsequent efforts in this direction.

The fifth chapter, *"Generic Social Processes,"* builds on many of the theoretical concerns and ethnographic considerations discussed in the preceding chapters, but more explicitly addresses the matter of conceptual development through ongoing ethnographic inquiry. Emphasizing a series of action-based concepts, such as acquiring perspectives, achieving identities, getting involved, doing activities, and developing relationships, *generic social processes* provide trans-situational reference points that enable scholars to compare and contrast ethnographic studies in many contexts. For instance, by focusing on a particular generic social process, such as "acquiring perspectives," and attending to people's participation in settings seemingly as diverse as deviant subcultures, hospitals, religious groups, schoolrooms, and the marketplace, we may begin to obtain a fuller appreciation of how people develop orientational frameworks or world-views regardless of the contexts in which they find themselves. Likewise, the notion of "getting involved" not only allows us to compare the recruiting practices of biker gangs, shuffleboard clubs, fund-raisers, and political parties, but also the ways in which people pursue involvements with respect to ballet, medical school, or tattoos. By attending to the analytical grids represented by these transcontextual, action-oriented processes, one may acquire the major conceptual tools for embarking on research in any setting involving human behavior.

Providing an interactionist statement on *"Experiencing Emotionality,"* chapter 6 might well have been included within the preceding discussion of generic social processes; for it not only acknowledges and builds upon the other generic social processes discussed therein, but also contributes to a more comprehensive appreciation of the subprocesses entailed in acquiring perspectives, doing activity, developing relationships, and the like. Still, since the topic of emotionality has been less explicitly addressed in the interactionist literature than the other themes discussed in chapter 5, it requires a more extended discussion than was possible to achieve in a style keeping with the more succinct formulations of the other processes. While people may only be able to partially control and direct their emotional experiences, this does not differentiate emotional activity from other realms of human involvement and activity, for in the struggle for human existence there is much that people cannot control or direct on either an individual or a collective basis. The inability to entirely direct and control emotional experiences, therefore, does not remove emotional experience from the realm of human enterprise or intersubjective accomplishment. Indeed, and to the contrary, there is much to be gained by approaching the study of emotion in process terms, as a matter of human endeavor and intersubjective accomplishment (and frustration). In this chapter, three processes central to emotion work are delineated: (1) learning to define emotional experiences; (2) developing techniques for expressing and controlling emotional experiences; and (3) experiencing emotional episodes and entanglements. Although "emotional activities" may be seen as sufficiently unique to justify development as another generic social process, it should be recognized that this consideration of affective involvements very much builds on the preceding generic social processes.

Chapter 7, *"Betwixt Positivist Proclivities and Postmodernist Propensities,"* locates a number of themes pertinent to the study of human lived experience within the context of some major issues (and dilemmas) facing contemporary social scientists. Consequently, consideration is given to the positivist/structuralist–interpretivist/interactionist debate and to interactionist/ethnographic encounters with postmodernism. While the social sciences appear to have derived considerable early impetus from concerns with moral reform and social control, and an emphasis on "appropriate" moral orders continues to define the agenda for the social sciences in some respects (e.g., funding and researcher moralities), this chapter focuses primarily on the problematics of pursuing an intersubjective social science within (*a*) the context of a deeply entrenched set of positivist paradigms, (*b*) an emergent postmodernist thrust, and (*c*) the ongoing demands of ethnographic inquiry. It may be tempting, and even appropriate in certain respects, to locate the intersubjectivist or interactionist approach as a midpoint of sorts on a continuum between positivism and postmodernism, but a more extended consideration of these three approaches suggests that this would be inaccurate and impractical for a great many purposes. This statement indicates realms of conceptual and methodological overlap as well as the epistemological discrepancies characterizing interactionism and positivism on the one hand and interactionism and postmodernism on the other. Thus, particularly mindful of the sorts of resistances and challenges facing scholars who take seriously the task of studying human lived experience, this chapter situates the pursuit of an intersubjective social science within the context of these developments. Of the various chapters in this volume, readers may find chapter 7 the most controversial. Rather than attempt to fuse or synthesize the intersubjectivist approach with either positivist or postmodernist approaches, this chapter lays out the baseline assumptions of each and endeavors to assess the relative merit of each for developing a social science that is genuinely attentive to human lived experience and the human struggle for existence. Those who wish to avoid academic debate for one reason or another or those who (optimistically) hope for an eclectic blending of sorts may find this material somewhat polemical or purist in thrust. However, the view taken here is one of insisting on a rigorous attentiveness to the world as known and acted toward by human beings in a community context. Only in this way may one maintain an integrity or coherence of theory, methods, and research as this pertains to the ongoing accomplishment of everyday life.

The last chapter, *"Obdurate Reality and the Intersubjective Other,"* represents an extension of some of the issues developed in chapter 7, but focuses more directly on the task of generating a social science that builds on the intersubjective essence of community life and the ongoing production of action. In contrast to postmodernist sociologists who tend to reduce human experience to textual reality and the positivist social scientists who tend to reduce human lived experience to structuralist reality, it is argued that human existence is predicated on people coming to terms with the day-to-day situations in which they find themselves. What is required is a pragmatic appreciation of the human life-world as it is accomplished by people acting and interacting with others in community settings, on a day-to-day, moment to moment basis. This active participation "in the world out there" necessitates a pronounced appreciation of the "obdurate reality" to which Blumer (1969) referred. By attending to Blumer's notion of a resistant, objectified, intersubjectively sustained, and processually oriented reality in which the human struggle for existence takes place on the one hand, and being mindful of the ethnographic implications of the "privilege of presence" on the other, we may more effectively pursue a thoroughly intersubjective social science—one that is rigorously grounded in the study of human lived experience.

Addressing a series of theoretical and methodological concerns of central consequence to people studying human group life, this volume fosters a fuller sense of the research tradition in which the emphasis on studying human lived experience emerged. This book is not intended as a formula or recipe for doing ethnographic research. Instead, it is anticipated that these statements, along with the bibliography at the end, may serve as a part of the ethnographer's "tool kit," a set of conceptual and methodological resources that one may use in approaching "the study of the other."

NOTES

1. It matters not whether the illusions are intended to convey the impression that "something unusual is happening" when it is not, or whether they are designed to indicate that "nothing unusual is happening" when it

is. In actual practice, card and dice hustlers try to maintain an overall impression of an unexceptional context ("just a regular game") and magicians specialize in producing dramatic effects; but both sets of performers often engage in both types of effects (something is happening, nothing is happening) in the process of shading (distracting, covering) and enhancing their intended overall (natural or exceptional appearing) effects. (See Prus and Sharper 1991.)

2. As indicated later in this chapter, but developed more fully in chapters 2, 3, and 4, the interpretivist or intersubjectivist tradition is very much rooted in the works of scholars such as Wilhelm Dilthey, George Herbert Mead, Charles Horton Cooley, Herbert Blumer, Alfred Schutz, Peter Berger and Thomas Luckmann, Harold Garfinkel, and T. S. Kuhn.

3. In postponing a fuller discussion of postmodernism until a later point in the volume, no attempt is made to avoid direct consideration of the postmodernist critique. At the risk of attempting to address rather complex issues in a highly truncated fashion, the essential position taken on post-modernism is this: while people may view postmodernism in many ways, what is most compelling from the point of view of developing a social science grounded in (theoretical and methodological) intersubjectivity is the postmodernist recognition of relativism and the linguistically mediated nature of reality. Although postmodernism offers some novelty of ex-perience in the ways in which these notions are expressed, these themes are far from unique to postmodernism. Conversely, what is most prob-lematic about the postmodernist enterprise is (1) its baseline, debilitating, totalistic (Nietdschean) skepticism; (2) its inattentiveness to (a) "obdurate reality," (b) the human struggle for existence, (c) the human production of action and the products of human endeavor, and (d) human interaction and its processual features; (3) its lack of conceptual discipline and epistemological integrity; (4) the tendency for postmodernist thinkers to lapse into structuralist explanations; and (5) the tendency of those invoking a postmodernist frame to use "scholarly text" as vehicles for promoting a variety of other agendas (e.g., morality, consciousness-raising, self-expressionism) that subvert a more careful, rigorous study of human lived experience. Postmodernism has attracted a great deal of attention in academic circles but, as indicated in chapters 7 and 8, it does not have much to offer to those already working in the interpretivist tradition.

4. While comparisons and contrasts of positivist and intersubjectivist approaches to the social sciences are made throughout this volume, a more sustained examination of the premises that undergird positivist approaches to the physical and social sciences is developed in chapters 7 and 8.

5. Viewing pragmatism as somewhat of a threat not only to the sociology he had been developing but also to French civilization more generally, Durkheim prepared a series of lectures on pragmatism and sociology in 1913–1914 (Durkheim, 1983). While he found a number of features of pragmatism (via Peirce, James, Dewey, and Schilling) rather intriguing, Durkheim was clearly bothered by what he envisioned as James's (whom Durkheim defines as the major spokesperson for the tradition) tendencies toward psychological reductionism. Durkheim also tended to locate relativist orientations in the philosophies of Nietzsche and Bergson. Had Durkheim encountered the writings of Charles Horton Cooley and George Herbert Mead or been more familiar with the writings of Wilhelm Dilthey, his reactions to pragmatism might have been quite different. For a very insightful discussion of Durkheim's consideration of pragmatism and his possible receptivity to the writings of George Herbert Mead, see Stone and Farberman (1967).

6. I apologize for this highly cryptic rendering of a wide assortment of literature. There are extensive variations in the positions adopted by Weberians, Marxists, and feminists, for example. Indeed, as in the case of "feminist scholarship," the arrays of theoretical and methodological orientations and practices are so far ranging, that the term "feminist" obscures much more than it reveals on an epistemological level (see Reinharz, 1992; Oleson, 1994). Readers interested in an interactionist position on gender and sexuality should see Kuhn (1954), who takes issues with the biological determinism implied in research along the lines of the Kinsey reports.

   Unless one wishes to argue that one needs a special theory of human association for each subgroup that someone may identify in the broader population (e.g., young-old, rich-poor, male-female, black-white-oriental; and every sub-subgroup, such as young, rich, university-educated, females of color), then it seems essential to attend to more generic features of human association. Likewise, scholars able to divest themselves of secondary agendas (e.g., moralism, consciousness-raising) may concentrate more clearly on the task of developing an appreciation of the lived experiences of all peoples. Otherwise, these same academics risk objectifying (and encouraging grand narratives that perpetuate) the very "structures" (and modes of analysis) that they seem at times interested in eliminating from sociological analysis (e.g., biological determinism, racial accentuation). Scholars who wish to privilege themselves by involving certain moral or popular agendas as a means of fostering their scholarship, should recognize that their work is apt to become identified with, and subject to, criticisms directed toward those modes of analyses. People sometimes make important contributions to the understanding of the human condition while pursuing secondary agendas, but their overall products are likely to be weakened as a result.

7. A consideration of personal and culturally motivated resistances to new developments in academia is developed somewhat more fully in chapter 7.

8. Chapters 2, 3, and 4 of this volume provide a much more detailed account of both the roots of symbolic interaction and the varieties of interpretive approaches to the study of human group life. For other statements on symbolic interaction, see Mead, 1934; (especially) Blumer, 1969, as well as Shibutani (1961), Laurer and Handel (1977), Charon (1979), Karp and Yoels (1979), and Morrione (forthcoming). Those more familiar with symbolic interaction will quickly recognize that the approach taken here is very consistent with, and centrally builds on, Blumerian or "Chicago-style" symbolic interaction. While Mead (1934) referred to this approach as "social behaviorism," the term, "symbolic interactionism," which Blumer (1937) rather casually struck, has become the more enduring referent.

9. As indicated in chapters 7 and 8, this attentiveness to the human production of action represents a vital point of divergence between interactionist and postmodernist approaches to the human condition.

10. An object is any item, thing, distinction, concept, behavior, or image to which people may refer (i.e., become aware of, attend to, point to, acknowledge, consider, discuss, or otherwise act toward).

11. The experiences of preverbal (normally) infants pose particular problems for social scientists. Not only (in the absence of shared gestures) is it virtually impossible to ascertain any meanings that preverbal children may assign to [objects], but it is also most difficult to define the point(s) at which infants cease to be "preverbal." Although reflectivity seems most evident when the child begins making generally acknowledged indications to oneself or others, an inability to communicate outwardly does not mean that some minimalist internal verbal comprehension or reflectivity may not be taking place. As well, insofar as verbally astute others are organizing their routines and those of the child around certain (linguistically informed) practices and modes of relating to the preverbal other, they may be endowing even preverbal beings with qualities that they may be quite unable to achieve or sustain on their own. Readers interested in the relationship between language, thinking, and self are apt to find Don

Evan's (Evans and Falk, 1986; Evans, 1987, 1988, 1994) ethnographic work with deaf children both fascinating and highly insightful.

12. See Schutz (1962, 1964) and Berger and Luckmann (1966) for particularly valuable elaborations of the "objectification" (and typification) process as this pertains to people's sense of reality and their "stocks of knowledge."

13. Chapter 4 in this volume provides an account of the development of ethnographic research in anthropology and sociology (especially with respect to interactionist ethnography). For materials dealing a little more squarely with ethnographic research in the field, see Palmer (1928), Paul (1953), Becker (1970), Wax (1971), Bogdan and Taylor (1975), Lofland and Lofland (1984), Jorgensen (1989), Shaffir and Stebbins (1991).

14. Although Giddens (1974, 1976, 1984) appears to have been the first person to use the term, "double hermeneutic," notions of this sort have long been deemed fundamental to an interactionist viewpoint.

15. Although frequency counts are usually so highly abstracted that much of their contextual value is lost, they may be useful in providing researchers with a certain kind of information about the situation at hand. Unfortunately, most (positivist) social science is built on these highly decontextualized "observations." Attempts to explain human behavior are often further confounded when researchers embark on the process of correlating two or more sets of these (highly abstracted, decontextualized) frequency counts, and then endeavor (however "learnedly") to speculate on the relevance of these (now increasingly nebulous) "findings."

2

INTERPRETIVE ROOTS

Experience as Intersubjective Reality

Like all realms of science and knowledge, theory in the social sciences is very much a *social product* and a *social process*. Social theory, or ideas about how group life takes place, involves some creativity and initiative on the part of particular thinkers, but it is fundamentally rooted in the social, interactive contexts in which these people find themselves.

Social theory as presented in textbooks often appears to have a rather definitive, objective, if not forbidding, quality to it, but the production of people's ideas about group life takes on a very human quality when we begin to consider the ways in which the scholars involved have attempted to come to terms with the situations they encountered. Theory involves creativity, but it also denotes human enterprise and is often fraught with ambiguity as well as resistance on the part of other scholars whose viewpoints are being challenged.

The ensuing discussion attempts to piece together, in detective-like fashion, the key players and their interlinkages in what constitutes an "interpretive approach to the study of human group life." This discussion is necessarily abbreviated; it simply is not possible to fill in all of the gaps one encounters in detailing some of the more direct lines of influence and inspiration.

The scholars we will be considering were much more concerned about sorting out their understandings of group life than leaving us easy trails to follow regarding the development of their ideas. As well, academic community life has taken directions they would not have been able to anticipate, even had they so desired. While textbook authors sometimes discuss theorists with great certainty, the people producing "theory" do not know how their efforts will be received by others, especially over time.

The debates surrounding theory within the social sciences are far from over. The following material attempts to trace the development of the interpretive paradigm, but it should be appreciated that by examining this perspective, readers enter into the interpretive-positivist debate and begin to experience some of the ways in which the interpretive viewpoint challenges mainstream social science.

THE HERMENEUTIC (INTERPRETIVE) TRADITION

The term "hermeneutics" was originally used to refer to the interpretive study of the Greek classics and religious texts. It reflects an awareness that recorded statements are inevitably subject to interpretation, as well as a recognition of the interpretive work performed by the Greek messenger god, Hermes (whose task it was to communicate between the other Greek gods and the Greeks). Those undertaking the tasks of studying and deciphering the Greek classics and other religious statements were, thus, labeled "hermeneutic scholars." Interestingly, while the interpretive frame has long been rather rigorously applied, mostly by theologians, to the study of texts, it was not until much later that these notions were systematically considered with respect to other instances of human behavior.[1] And, rather ironically, while people are more or less continuously engaged in hermeneutic or interpretive activity in their day-to-day routines (e.g., in the course of general conversation, attending class, watching television), these "meaning-making" practices have largely been overlooked or dismissed as inconsequential by many students of human behavior. This peculiar omission adds an element of intrigue to the development of "social theory."

In what follows, we first examine the contributions of Wilhelm Dilthey, who played a much overlooked but exceedingly consequential role in developing the interpretive paradigm in German social theory in the late 1800s and early 1900s. Next, consideration is given to the contributions of Georg Simmel, Max Weber, and Wilhelm Wundt, before shifting attention to American Pragmatism, the intellectual precursor to symbolic interactionism. Here, an appreciation of the works of Charles Horton Cooley and George Herbert Mead is essential in establishing the foundation on which Chicago-style symbolic interaction was developed (and most notably expressed in the works of Herbert Blumer). In addition to delineating the historical roots underlying the interpretive approach to the study of human lived experience, these scholars provide an exceedingly valuable conceptual scheme with which to approach the entire collection of materials assembled in this volume. Thus, this chapter introduces many of the essential theoretical issues of interpretive/ethnographic analysis by attending to the scholars who played the most central roles in the early development of the interpretive study of everyday life.

Wilhelm Dilthey: Interpretation as Intersubjectivity

Every word, every sentence, every gesture or politeness, every work of art, and every historical action are only comprehensible because of a community that binds the expresser with the interpreter; every person lives, thinks, and acts constantly in a sphere of community and only in such a sphere does he understand. (Dilthey, in Ermarth, 1978:278)

Wilhelm Dilthey (1833–1911) might most appropriately be considered the founder of contemporary interpretive social science. Although others (most notably the theologian Friedrich Schleiermacher and the philosopher Friedrich Trendelenburg) had helped pioneer the hermeneutic concepts upon which Dilthey built many of his formulations,[2] it was Dilthey who most explicitly extended the hermeneutic or interpretive insight or *versteben* (interpretive understanding) beyond textual interpretations to all other instances of human behavior. Dilthey's range of scholarship was remarkably broad, encompassing disciplines such as history, mathematics, music and literary criticism, as well as psychology and sociology, and his work was far from consistently focused on the interpretive paradigm. However, more than anyone else, Dilthey appears to be pivotal in explicating the conceptual foundations of a hermeneutic social science and precipitating the interpretive critique that positivism faces (see Rickman, 1976:246–263; Ermarth, 1978).

The quotes selected for inclusion here do not begin to represent the full range of Dilthey's scholarship nor do they convey some of the inconsistencies in his works. Further, while Dilthey's links to *American pragmatism* and *symbolic interaction* have not yet been investigated very fully, it is difficult to deny strong affinities of Dilthey's hermeneutical human science with the two traditions that played the most central roles in the development of ethnographic research in sociology.

As the introductory quote indicates, Dilthey stressed the fundamentally *intersubjective* nature of human behavior: that human life is group life and is built on a *sharedness of understandings*. Interpretation, thus, depends pivotally on making sense of the other by reference to the *community context* in which the actions of the other are embedded.

Given the interpretive nature of human life, Dilthey contended that the human sciences (*Geisteswissenschaften*) require a conceptual and methodological approach which is very different from that used in the study of physical (nonminded) objects (*Naturwissenschaften*).[3] Although both social scientists and physical scientists are seen as engaging in interpretive activity, the subject matter of the human sciences is notably different. In contrast to the other objects one might study, Dilthey observed that humans have the capacity for intentional, meaningful activity (i.e., human agency) as well as an awareness of self as an object (i.e., self-reflectivity):

> *In the human sciences there prevails a special fundamental relation . . . such that we are living in society at once as an active agent . . . and are also aware of our effects. (Dilthey, in Ermarth, 1978:107)*

Interpretation, human agency, and self-awareness, these are key features in Dilthey's notions of a social science, but so, too, is *the inseparability of the self from the other*. The self is rooted and thoroughly grounded in people's experiences in the interactive community of others:

> *A self without an other, or an outer without an inner—these are merely senseless words. All this finally boils down to the fact that there is no such thing as an "enclosed self" from which the other or the outer could arise. (Dilthey, in Ermarth, 1978:101)*

> *The whole framework of the mental [experiential, perceptual] is permeated with this basic experience of community, in which the consciousness of the self and that of similarity with others, of the identity of human nature and yet of individuality, are linked together. (Dilthey, in Ermarth, 1978:285)*

For Dilthey, as well, the paramount reality is *the world of human lived experience*. In contrast to those positivist social scientists who tend to dismiss human lived experience as subjective, epiphenomenal, or inconsequential, Dilthey observed that human reality could not exist other than through people's experiences of the world:

> *Life is a thoroughly empirical reality—the human reality which all of us "live through" and constantly refer to in ordinary speech; it is the human condition itself, not a transcendental Idea. There is no reality outside or beyond life, for everything we think, perceive, or imagine is ultimately woven in our existence. (Ermarth, 1978:109, paraphrasing Dilthey)*

The world of lived experience entails a more or less ongoing set of interpretations of the here and now, but these interpretations are rooted in the stocks of knowledge that people accumulate through associations with others. For Dilthey, *language* is both the base on which, and the medium through which, human experience is formulated. Language is both the foundation on which all human knowledge (conceptualization) is generated and the means of conveying cultural (substantive) understandings and practices. Thus, Dilthey insists that the human sciences attend to the culturally (and linguistically) mediated community contexts in which human behavior takes place. Using the term, "objective mind" to refer to the "social atmosphere" (or the taken for granted set) of meanings in which we live (Ermarth, 1978:278),[4] Dilthey is very much attuned to the *shared* conceptual features of human interchange:

> *From earliest childhood on, our self receives its sustenance from this world of objective mind. It is also the medium in which the understanding of other persons and their expressions takes place. For everything in which mind has objectified itself contains something common to the I and the Thou. . . . The child grows up in the order and way of the life of the family, which it shares with other members; the guidance of the mother is absorbed in this coherence. Before it learns to speak, the child is already emerged in this medium of common forms. . . . It learns to understand the gestures and miens, movements and exclamations, words and sentences only because they reappear constantly in identical form and in the same relationships to that which they mean and express. Thus the individual orients itself in the world of objective mind. (Dilthey, in Ermarth, 1978:277–278)*

Envisioning language as both shaping and being shaped by human experience, Dilthey contends that language is at the core of human existence:

> *Man fulfills himself only in the perception of all forms of human existence— and no other organ is provided for this [perception] than language and writing. (Dilthey, in Ermarth, 1978:278)*

Dilthey never found any of the prevailing disciplinary boundaries or thrusts satisfactory as a home base for the development of a hermeneutic social science. He had great respect for the conceptual rigor of philosophy, but felt that philosophers paid far too little attention to the actualities of human lived experience to develop an appropriately informed (interpretive) human science. Likewise, while Dilthey insisted on the importance of a historical-cultural dimension to help establish a community context in which to locate human behavior, he observed that most historians not only disattended to the her-meneutical nature of their subject matters, but also overlooked the interpretive (or self-reflective) essence of their own constructions. Dilthey was critical of history that did not encompass philosophy, theory, and concepts, or did not acknowledge the importance of generalizing, typifying, and using comparative methods (Ermarth, 1978:25–27, 317–322, 350–355). To be viable, Dilthey contended, history has to appreciate the dynamic, interactive, intersubjective nature of community life and has to develop concepts attentive to these notions. Although Dilthey saw the development of a hermeneutic social science as something of an art form in itself, he appeared most reluctant to ever seriously consider relegating hermeneutic social science to the (nonempirical) realm of literary expressions. Dilthey had long hoped that a hermeneutic social science might be located in the disciplines of psychology, anthropology, or (later) sociology; realms of study that he felt offered the most potential for the sustained, philosophically informed examination of human lived experience. Even here, however, his assessments were mixed. Many of his reservations revolved around notions of positivism and grand philosophies that dominated these disciplines, especially psychology and sociology. Dilthey clearly articulated his disenchantment not only with the positivist notions of determinism, causation, and reductionism that were already rampant in psychology at the time, but also with what he felt was the misplaced emphasis and general irrelevancy of their inquiries to human lived experience (see Ermarth, 1978:148, 170, 185). He was particularly troubled by the failure of psychology to recognize the culturally mediated (intersubjective) nature of human experience. Likewise, he could not find much of relevance to human lived experience in the positivist philosophy (sociology) of Auguste Comte (Ermarth, 1978:298) or the grand materialism of Karl Marx. Nonetheless, Dilthey hoped that a discipline somewhat along the lines of "descriptive (or introspective) psychology," "philosophical anthropology," or the sociology of Georg Simmel, might provide the base for a detailed hermeneutic social science.

Methodologically, Dilthey had developed a strong appreciation for "introspective psychology" and *verstehen*, as well as the methods of textual interpretation developed by the hermeneutic scholars. He also appears to have searched for, but never quite anticipated, ethnographic research of the type that was to emerge at the University of Chicago in the 1920s. It should be appreciated that the anthropologists of Dilthey's era engaged in very little direct ethnographic research themselves. The closest approximations were those ethnologists or folk psychologists (see Wilhelm Wundt, following) who relied on missionaries' and other travellers' (secondhand) accounts of encounters with foreign cultures. Some scholars in academia at that time were engaged in survey research of sorts and might make other inquiries of those whom they encountered, but little in the way of sustained involvement (participant-observation) in particular settings or the recordings of open-ended interviews was evident in Dilthey's era (Oberschall, 1965).

Despite the pivotal nature of Dilthey's work for the interpretive tradition, only recently have sociologists begun to attend to Dilthey's writings. However, some of the ideas with which Dilthey (and his associates) worked may be noted in the works of Georg Simmel, Max Weber, and Wilhelm Wundt, and even more centrally in the writings of George Herbert Mead and Herbert Blumer.

Georg Simmel: Form and Content

The motive which is responsible for the constitution of "pure sociology" as a specific problem area. . . derives from two propositions. One is that in any human society one can distinguish between its content and its form. The other is that society, itself, in general refers to the interaction among individuals. (Simmel, 1950:40)

Georg Simmel (1858–1918) is best known for his pronounced emphasis on sociology as the study of the *forms* of human association.[5] Simmel encouraged sociologists to envision group life as sets of *ongoing social processes*; to look past the particular content of situations to the more abstract or generic forms of association that human interchanges entail. Conflict, cooperation, compromise, mediation, domination and subordination, secrecy, sociability, and exchange— these were only some of the forms to which Simmel attended as he attempted to portray the manner in which people interacted with others.

Although Georg Simmel is often considered one of the founders of sociology, Simmel's affinities with Wilhelm Dilthey have been almost entirely overlooked. However, the two scholars were colleagues at the University of Berlin. As Oakes (1980:57–59) observes, shifts in (the senior scholar) Dilthey's works were often followed by parallel shifts in Simmel's work. In contrast to most other German scholars at the time, however, Simmel was somewhat remiss in his documentation. Thus, we are not able to gain as complete a sense of their interdependencies as one would hope.[6] Noteworthy in this regard is Dilthey's observation (Ermarth, 1978:298), while endorsing the sociology of Georg Simmel, that he might have been credited for having anticipated aspects of Simmel's analysis of social life. Still, their works differed in important respects. Simmel was much more concerned about detailing the "forms of association" than was Dilthey. However, Simmel was considerably less appreciative of the interpretive essence of human interchange. Both scholars were fundamentally attuned to the notion of intersubjectivity, but Simmel appears much less concerned with the ways one might pursue the study of human lived experience than was Dilthey.[7] In these regards, Dilthey is even more a scholar of note for those working in the interpretive tradition than is Georg Simmel.

However, whereas sociologists have generally been unaware of Dilthey's works, Georg Simmel achieved considerable stature in early American sociology. This was in large part due to Albion Small (who edited the American Journal of Sociology for the first thirty years of its existence), W. I. Thomas, and Robert Park, each of whom taught at the University of Chicago after having studied with Simmel. Simmel published several articles in the *American Journal of Sociology*, and fragments of ten of these were reprinted in Park and Burgess's (1921) classic collection of readings, *Introduction to the Science of Sociology*. The statements that appeared in the *American Journal of Sociology* helped to establish a conceptual frame for the ethnographic research that emerged in the early 1900s in Chicago.

Max Weber: Emphasizing and Obscuring Verstehen Sociology

While many sociologists would likely attribute the concept of *verstehen* or interpretive understanding to Max Weber (Jr.) (1864–1920), it appears that Weber contributed comparatively little to either *verstehen* sociology or the emergence of ethnographic research (which assumes interpretive understanding) in a direct or unique sense. In developing his notions of social theory, Weber built on aspects of Dilthey's work on verstehen (hermeneutics), but Dilthey's materials are developed much more extensively and consistently than are Weber's. Further, whereas Dilthey attempted to develop an entire approach to the social sciences around the notion of verstehen, Weber pursued a rather different set of agendas.

Although incorporating some important features of Dilthey's thought into his own theory, Weber was also significantly influenced by Wilhelm Windelband and Heinrich Rickert (see Coser, 1971:244–247; Bryant, 1985:64–76). Windelband's and Rickert's conceptualizations of the human sciences shared many affinities with Dilthey's viewpoints, but they attempted to disregard the *Naturwissenschaften-Geisteswissenschaften* (physical–social science) dichotomy that Dilthey stressed. Instead, they posited that the differences between scientists revolved not around their subject matters but reflected the objectives of the researchers. Scientists taking a nomothetic approach or pursuing the study of generalized laws of human behavior, they argued, would approximate the methodologies of the natural sciences; those assuming a more idiographic approach would be more concerned with achieving descriptive accounts of the unique circumstances in this or that instance. This position seems somewhat dubious in the practical accomplishment of scientific knowledge (which implies an ongoing exchange between conceptual developments and cases in point), but more importantly, for our purposes, it fails to appreciate the fundamentally intersubjective essence of human group life. Nevertheless, Weber (along with many others) attempted to work within this framework. Thus, while maintaining claims about the centrality of *verstehen* for the human sciences, Weber proposed to incorporate verstehen within a causal, albeit qualified positivist framework:

> *Sociology. . . is a science which attempts the interpretive understanding of social action in order thereby to arrive at a causal explanation of its course and effects. (Weber, 1947:88)*

On the surface, Weber's synthetic approach to sociology appeared to resolve the intense debates that had arisen from the hermeneutic challenge to the already deeply entrenched positivist (following August Comte and John Stuart Mill) viewpoints and practices of the social sciences. Finally, it seemed, there was a way out. Social scientists could acknowledge the interpretive features of human group life and yet proceed relatively undaunted by the otherwise devastating hermeneutic critique levelled by Dilthey and others. In recognizing the centrality of interpretive understanding for the social sciences, Weber had implicitly accepted Dilthey's *Naturwissenschaften-Geisteswissenschaften* distinction; but he did not recognize this distinction at a more explicit level. Much of his work, consequently, displays this uneven or mixed emphasis.

Although his attempted reconciliation of interpretive and positivist paradigms likely contributed considerably to Weber's popularity as a scholar, his synthesis was far from successful (Giddens, 1974; Alexander, 1983) and his sociology became obscured as a result. On the one hand, Weber emerges as a champion of sorts for the interpretive tradition, but at the same time, he effectively muted its more fundamental relevance to the study of human lived experience.

While professing to incorporate *verstehen* in his baseline assumptions, Weber only partially attended to the interpretive essence of human group life in the course of pursuing his "empirical" work.[8] Along with others buying into this sort of synthesis, Weber generated an intellectual stance in which the hermeneutic thrust was largely dismissed from a more active consideration in social research. By striking a cross-section of popular intellectual chords (particularly among those favoring conceptual and methodological syntheses of sorts), Weber (perhaps inadvertently to some extent) diverted people's attention away from the more profoundly hermeneutic (sociological) insights that Dilthey developed.

As indicated both by his definition of sociology and in his work more generally, Weber's orientations are characterized by much ambiguity if not also considerable confusion and contradiction. Thus, it is a matter of some debate not only as to whether Weber's theoretical leanings (while allegedly interpretivist) were ultimately positivist in thrust (e.g., Dawe, 1970; Giddens, 1974; Hollis, 1977; Alexander, 1983, especially 33; 128–129),[9] but how Weber's sociology might be best characterized in other terms as well (see Alexander, 1983, especially 10–16; 128–135). Even Weber's notion of "ideal types" is of minimal assistance in these matters (Bryant, 1985:91–95). While Weber implies a concern with the practical accomplishment of action, his usage of "ideal types" not only moves the analytical focus some distance from the actualities of human behavior but (as Alexander, 1983:27, observes) may effectively preclude voluntaristic dimensions of human behavior. One could, it seems, debate rather endlessly (and learnedly) about Weber's relative positions on interpretivism and positivism (as well as his notion of ideal types and other central thrusts of his work), but for our purposes, it may be most useful to recognize that Weber's *verstehen soziologie* was not well developed in essential respects.

Perhaps, one might envision Weber as pursuing a mixed set of conceptual and methodological agendas. Thus, Weber sought to develop "objective," causal statements about group life while simultaneously claiming an intellectual primacy in the foundations of "subjective experience." At the same time, Weber appears intent on using modes of historical-cultural-legalistic analysis to formulate more generic statements on the religious, political, and economic orderings of human societies. In particular, Weber seemed concerned with stipulating the historical and material conditions that fostered particular world views and the ways in which these collectively established beliefs or group mind-sets might find expression in the forms of association and practices characterizing particular societies. Although Weber is quite aware that actions of particular individuals might change the directions of community life in highly significant manners, his analysis tends to remain at a more abstract level and is more along the lines of considering the options and restrictions that rational beings in particular cultural-temporal eras might encounter. Within Weber's contextual analysis (e.g., studies in the sociology of religion), *verstehen* tends to be largely implicit and group-oriented, as opposed to denoting an attentiveness to the viewpoints of particular people and to the ways in which they go about accomplishing their activities on a "here and now" basis. As a consequence, Weber can only *speculate* both about the ways in which people actually take things into account and develop particular lines of action as well as any (active) causes (and restrictions) he *imputes* to people's behaviors.

Despite claims about maintaining *verstehen* as the centerpiece of his model of sociology (Weber 1947:87–115), Weber's conceptualization of the *intersubjective* nature of human lived experience is much less compelling and comprehensive than is Dilthey's. Somewhat mindful of Dilthey's works, Weber realized that *verstehen* was fundamental to the study of human group life. However, he did not realize just how very fundamentally this was the case.

First and most centrally, although he claims to have dispensed with the *Naturwissenschaften-Geisteswissenschaften* distinction on which Dilthey insisted, Weber was unable to avoid entirely the uniqueness of the human condition. Weber's work on religion, politics, and even bureaucracy and rationality, is contingent on the implicit acknowledgement that people *(unlike other objects of study)* develop diverse worldviews and take these viewpoints into account in developing their lines of action. Indeed, it is largely because of his recognition of the diverse social worlds that people create over time and the linkages of these historical creations with people's (albeit general) practices, that Weber's work achieves value, sociologically speaking. However, because he did not more fully pursue the hermeneutic distinction that Dilthey stresses, Weber had to resort to a more speculative social science. Instead of developing a social science that was more carefully and thoroughly grounded in interpretive practices and in the ongoing activities of people on a situated basis, Weber's work becomes particularly problematic because he invokes causal statements (factors) to account for both the emergence of particular life-worlds and people's behaviors therein. While this is consistent with the positivist features of Weber's sociological agenda, it greatly distances the analysis from the situations at hand (and rather ironically defeats the very notion of an empirically grounded science to which Weber subscribed). Weber, thus, partially—but only partially—appreciates that *the study of human group life* (denoting the ongoing actions and interactions of linguistic, self-reflective entities) *requires a theory and a methodology that respects the unique features of the human condition (vs. other objects of study)*.

Secondly, but also quite centrally, Weber appears to have had rather limited insight into the significance of *language* (versus Dilthey, Cooley, Mead, Blumer) or symbolic communication *as the enabling feature of human group life* as we know it. Thus, in reference to Weber's (1947:104) claim that, *"There is no priori reason to suppose that our ability to share the feelings of primitive men is much greater"* [than our abilities to understand animals—RP], Talcott Parsons (editor; Weber, 1947:104) observes:

> *Weber apparently does not adequately take account of the fundamental fact that no non-human species has even a primitive form of language; whereas no human*

group is known without a 'fully developed' one. The ability to use language is on the one hand a fundamental index of the state of development of the individual himself, so far as it is relevant to the theory of action. On the other hand, language is perhaps the most crucially important source of evidence for subjective phenomena.

Perhaps most ironic, in this rather telling commentary on Weber, is the fact that Parsons is not known for his sensitivities to the interpretive paradigm.

Third, Weber's use of the term *verstehen* appears to rely heavily on inferences and imputations of meanings to the observed or hypothetical other (see Schutz's [1932] and Abel's [1948] critiques). As Schutz (1932) goes to great length to establish, Weber does not acknowledge adequately the problematic, processual, and interactive nature of *verstehen*. Likewise, despite an insistence on "verification of subjective interpretation" (Bryant, 1985:88), Weber's notion of verification is more on the order of observers ascertaining congruent instances of interpretation across a range of cases than on "an interactive achievement of intersubjectivity with the (participant-actor) other." Weber evidences minimal concern with ethnographic inquiry or what Cooley (1909) termed *sympathetic introspection*. Quite simply, Weber fails to comprehend the extent to which *verstehen* or the accomplishment of intersubjectivity entails an interactive process. This is why Weber is so vulnerable to both Schutz's and Abel's criticisms.

Thus, although much of the sociological community's awarenesses of the concept of *verstehen* was generated through the works of Max Weber, Weber represents one of the weaker, more elusive, exemplars of the interpretive paradigm. Even the translation of Weber's statement on *verstehen* (Weber, 1947: 88–118) emerged not as a consequence of the centrality of these notions for his work but rather as part of a more sweeping interest generated in the comparative-historical-organizational works of Max Weber by Talcott Parsons and other functionalists.[10] Still, coming from a highly respected European scholar, Weber's statement on *verstehen* likely helped legitimate interpretive analysis and ethnographic inquiry within sociology. This seems to have been particularly important in departments with heavier functionalist and quantitative emphases. Further, while Weber's notion of *verstehen* shares some affinities with the ethnographic research that had been developed by the symbolic interactionists and anthropologists, there is very little evidence to suggest that Weber's work directly stimulated or fostered the development of ethnographic research (see Platt, 1985; Kivisto and Swatos, 1990).[11] Thus, references to Weber's work are sometimes encountered in discussions of ethnographic research, but these generally come from people who have noted some intellectual affinities but who have not sorted out the historical linkages (or lack thereof) of Weber and those who developed the ethnographic tradition.[12]

Still, regardless of the ambiguities and multidimensional (Alexander, 1983), if not contradictory, nature of much Weberian analysis, many sociologists appear to have derived considerable inspiration from the hermeneutical expressions found in Weber's work and have struggled to maintain an interpretive thrust in the discipline over the years. Indeed, it may be rather indirectly, through the efforts of these scholars valiantly attempting to defend the discipline from a more thoroughgoing positivism, that Weber's notion of *verstehen* has had its greatest impact on the sociological community.[13]

Wilhelm Wundt: Intersubjective Dimensions of Folk Psychology

Wilhelm Wundt (1832–1920) may be best known for his work on experimental (laboratory) psychology, but he was also centrally involved in the development of what was termed, *Volkerpsychologie* or "folk psychology." Although Wundt was only one of many scholars in this era involved in this tradition, folk psychology was to provide a significant source of stimulation for a number of scholars working within the interpretive and (emergent) ethnographic traditions.

Folk psychology (also psychical anthropology) was built on the recognition of the centrality of language and culture for human behavior, but was focused primarily on "primitive" culture rather than the "western culture" of the day. Several variants of folk psychology emerged in Germany, with some scholars more closely approximating mythologists or folklorists and others more akin to the anthropologists (archaeologists, ethnologists) of that era (Thomas, 1906; Wundt, 1916). Few, if any, folk psychologists had direct contact with the primitive cultures about which they wrote and most of their theories were based on accounts obtained from other travellers.

Importantly, as with many others working within this tradition, Wundt argued for the centrality of intersubjectivity, that human group life could *not* be reduced to psychological processes:[14]

> *A philosopher and a psychologist, Lazarus and Steinthal, may claim credit for having introduced the term, 'folk psychology' to designate this new area of knowledge. All phenomena with which mental sciences deal are, indeed, creations of the social community. Language, for example, is not the accidental discovery of an individual; it is the product of peoples, and generally speaking, there are*

> *as many different languages as there are originally distinct people. The same is true of the beginnings of art, of mythology, and of custom.* . . . *To-day, doubtless, folk psychology may be regarded as a branch of psychology concerning whose justification and problem there can no longer be any dispute. Its problem relates to those mental products which are created by a community of human life and are, therefore, inexplicable in terms merely of individual consciousness, since they presuppose the reciprocal action of many. (Wundt, 1916:2–3)*

> *In an account of the total development of mental life, however—and this is the decisive consideration, the 'folk' is the most important collective concept and the one with which all others are associated. The 'folk' embraces families, classes, clans, and groups. These various communities are not excluded from the concept 'folk' but are included within it. The term 'folk psychology' singles out precisely the folk as the decisive factor underlying the fundamental creations of the community. (Wundt, 1916:4–5)*

While Wundt envisioned folk psychology as an essential component of the field of psychology, the notions of community (intersubjectivity) to which Wundt referred are not very much in evidence in contemporary psychology. However, as much as anyone, Wundt served as a nucleus for attracting and exposing other scholars to *gemeinshaftpsychologie* (Wundt, 1916:4) or the study of elementary (primitive) forms of group life.[15] Although many of these students were interested in Wundt as a consequence of his work in the (then very popular) field of physiological psychology, some (such as William James and George Herbert Mead) would also be exposed to aspects of folk psychology and interpretive social thought.

AMERICAN PRAGMATISM: PRACTICAL ACCOMPLISHMENT

The pragmatist tradition took inspiration from the philosophies of Charles Peirce, William James, John Dewey, and George Herbert Mead. These scholars, and c￼￼ ￼f this ilk, were disenchanted with what they envisioned as the general r￼￼￼evance of philosophy and the prevailing social sciences for the everyday ￼ved situations in which people found themselves. The pragmatists' emphases were somewhat diverse, but they were generally opposed to "rationalist" or "determinist" (i.e., positivist) philosophy and wanted to develop conceptualizations of human behavior that attended to the actualities and practices of people.[16] The pragmatist "method" was initiated by Charles Peirce, but it was popularized by William James (1977:376–390, "What Pragmatism Means"). For James, pragmatism involved hypothetical questions, such as: What differences would arise if this line of action as opposed to this or that alternative were invoked? The value of any option hinged on the relative perceived consequences of that option for the situation at hand. However, as the term pragmatism became more popular in its usage, it became increasingly diffuse and difficult to define,[17] except that it implied a practical utility approach to knowledge and reflected the notion that practical utility as consensually defined would provide the most viable approximations of the truth. In practice, however, this postulate proved much less viable than it first seemed, for perceived utilities always reflected the viewpoints and interests of various people (and groups) involved in particular situations.

Despite the vagueness of pragmatism and the moral leanings of these scholars, the pragmatists shared a somewhat common objective, and insistence, in *developing an understanding of social life "in the making"* (see Meltzer et al. 1975; Shalin, 1986; Reynolds, 1993). They had somewhat differing notions of how and in what respects human conditions might be improved, but they were centrally interested in how things were accomplished at a practical level. Thus, they began to attend to the socially constituted (and relativistic) nature of human group life. They asked about the social processes by which community life took its shape. People were seen as reflective beings who possessed capacities to act mindfully of their own situations and in conjunction with others.

As well, the pragmatists placed considerable emphasis on the role that education could play in better preparing people for the obstacles they would face in life. While the pragmatists may be seen to be overly optimistic about the value of education as a means of alleviating personal and social disorganization, they directed people's attention to the importance of socialization processes and the dynamics of group association.

Pragmatism is typically deemed an American, if not distinctively American, production, but it appears to be rooted much more in German social thought than the term *American pragmatism* would imply. Indeed, James, Dewey, and Mead had all studied in Germany. Given their limited fluency in German,[18] their encounters with German philosophical and social sciences issues and literature of the day seem rather uneven. But minimally they were exposed to fragments of some of the ideas with which Dilthey, Wundt, and others worked, as well as to some of the more pronounced debates taking place around matters of positivism, Darwinism, and interpretive inquiry.

In this respect, and although recast and perhaps formulated anew, it should not be too surprising to find that many aspects of American pragmatism resonate with the positions of the German interpretivists. There was shared focusing on *human agency, communication, and social process*. People were seen to act toward things in terms of the meanings they held for those objects, but the meanings people attributed to objects were seen as socially constituted. Meanings of objects derived not from the objects themselves, but in the manners by which people acted toward (and interacted with respect to) those objects. There was also an explicit recognition of the socially embedded, emergent self and of language (especially by Cooley and Mead) as the central feature of human existence. Pragmatism was also characterized by a strong emphasis on achieving solutions to practical problems. Still, concerns with moral reform were by no means limited to the pragmatists, and were relatively commonplace in academic circles in America and Europe.[19]

Many of the pragmatist insights about human behavior (especially as formulated by Dewey, Cooley, and Mead) are as viable today as they were around the turn of the century and have been absorbed by and recast into what was to become known as "symbolic interaction." This shift took place primarily at the University of Chicago and is reflected in developments in theory, methods, and substantive research. While William James (psychology) and John Dewey (education) appear to have facilitated this dialogue with their work, it was Charles Horton Cooley and George Herbert Mead who made the most direct and sustained contributions to the development of symbolic interactionism.

EARLY INTERACTIONISM: THEORY AND METHODS

The term *symbolic interaction* was coined by Herbert Blumer in 1937, but is so appropriate for identifying many of the interpretive themes in the works of Charles Horton Cooley and George Herbert Mead, that it may be used to refer to these earlier scholars as well. Rather than attempt to define symbolic interaction at the present time, however, it may be instructive to consider the ways in which Cooley and Mead approached the study of human behavior.

Charles Horton Cooley: Language, Process, and Sympathetic Introspection

> *Records of behavior without interpretation are like a library of books in a strange tongue. They come from minds and mean nothing until they find their goal in other minds. (Cooley, 1926:70)*

Charles Horton Cooley (1864–1929), who studied primarily with John Dewey, maintained one of the most consistently sociological thrusts of all of the pragmatists. Like most other writers in early American sociology, Cooley's work is steeped in both morality and eclecticism. Still, his statements on group life, the social self, and the method of sympathetic introspection were most consequential.[20]

Cooley's focus on the study of group life as a *social process* was quite noteworthy, as was his emphasis on the role that *interaction* assumed in bonding people together within groups. Indeed, Cooley contended that an examination of these bonding practices or processes was central to the study of society:

> *(T)he ideal for sociology is to extend the behavior record to all the essential acts of man, making them intelligible, imaginable, predictable. We aim to see human life as an actual dramatic activity, and to participate also in those mental processes which are a part of human function and are accessible to sympathetic observation by the aid of gesture and language. (Cooley, 1928:316)*

> *I presume that our aim is to understand what part the form of life we have before us plays in the social process, and also, perhaps to foresee its operation, know how to influence it, and, by comparison, extend our knowledge to other forms more or less similar. (Cooley, 1928:319)*

Similarly, although he never pursued the idea very fully or rigorously, Cooley contended that an appreciation of *language* was fundamental to understanding human society. Cooley envisioned language to be as indispensable as the brain for matters of human perception, interpretation, and action:

> *Language is itself a form of social behavior, one of the latest achievements of evolution, and as indispensable as the brain itself to the higher kinds of life. Its function is to define, organize, and guide the subtler forms of human activity, and it is natural that social science, which aims to extend and perfect this function, should find in language its main instrument. (Cooley, 1928:316)*

In another insight, which goes largely undeveloped, Cooley alerts us to the centrality of *images* for human society and for people's experiences with their social worlds. The implication is that since we live in a world of images, it is essential that we consider the ways in which these images take their shape, become transformed, and are taken into account in the course of human group life:

> *In order to have a society it is evidently necessary that persons should get together somewhere; and they get together only as personal ideas in the mind. Where else? What other possible locus can be assigned for the real contact of persons, or in what other form can they come in contact except as impressions formed in this common locus (Cooley, 1922:119). . .*

I conclude, therefore, that the imaginations which people have of one another are the solid facts of society, and that to observe and interpret these must be the chief aim of sociology. (Cooley, 1922:121)

Although Cooley may be best known for the concept of *"the looking-glass self,"* this concept centrally reflects the idea that people live in a world of images. Here, Cooley emphasizes the socially rooted essence of the self; or establishes *the intersubjective foundations of the self:*

A social self of this sort might be called the reflective or looking-glass self:
"Each to each a looking-glass
Reflects the other that doth pass."
[The looking-glass self] *seems to have three principal elements: the imagination of our appearances to the other person; the imagination of his judgement of that appearance, and some sort of self-feeling, such as pride or mortification. (Cooley, 1922:184)*

Unfortunately, Cooley did not connect the concept of the looking-glass self to his statement on the primary group in any sustained manner. Still, *the primary group* represents another important element in Cooley's conceptualization of both the self and one's sense of morality:[21]

By primary groups I mean those characterized by intimate face-to-face association and cooperation. They are primary in several senses, but chiefly in that they are fundamental in forming the social nature and ideals of the individual. The result of intimate association, psychologically, is a certain fusion of individualities into a common whole, so that one's very self, for many purposes, at least, is the common life and expression of the group. (Cooley, 1909:23)

This point receives consideration, as well, in Cooley's discussion of the ideal self:

It would always be found, I think, that our ideal self is constructed chiefly out of ideas about us attributed to us by other people. We can hardly get a distinct view of ourselves except in this way, that is by placing ourselves at the standpoint of some one else. The impressions thus gained are worked over and over, like other mental material, and, according to the imaginative vigor of the mind, more or less reorganized, and projected as an ideal. (Cooley, 1922:397)

Cooley also contributed to the study of group life through his emphasis on *sympathetic introspection*, a methodology that was intended to gain access (through observations, interviews and participation) to the meanings and interpretations of the people involved in this or that setting. The term sympathetic introspection has been replaced by other referents, such as participant-observation, field research, naturalistic inquiry, and ethnographic research, but the methods Cooley endorsed were much akin to those that would become central to the development of ethnographic research in sociology at the University of Chicago. Thus, in describing this practice, Cooley distances himself from the "self absorbed philosopher" and encourages students of human behavior to reach out to the other in a process of:

> (S)ympathetic introspection, putting himself in intimate contact with various sorts of persons and allowing them to awake in himself a life similar to their own, which he afterwards to the best of his ability, recalls and describes. In this way he is more or less able to understand—always by introspection—children, idiots, criminals, rich and poor, conservative and radical—any phase of human nature not wholly alien to his own.
>
> This I conceive to be the principal method of social psychology. (Cooley, 1909:7)

It should also be noted that Cooley did not intend to confine this mode of analysis to small groups and proposed that one could use the same methods in the study of organizational life. His discussion of the case-study as applied to local institutions is especially pertinent here:

> (The) case study. . . gets at behavior directly and not by an indirect and abstract approach. If we can have enough of it and of sufficiently varied types to be representative of the social process, it will go far to enable us to understand that process, and perhaps to foresee its course.
>
> While persons and families are the usual objects of case study, the method may be extended to other constituents of the social process, to the life-histories of groups and institutions not too large to be treated in this direct and total fashion. These also are live things and offer a field of behavioristic study which, by no means unknown, has been relatively neglected. Nothing can take its place; it is a distinct and indispensable method. (Cooley, 1928:317–318)

It is not apparent that Charles Horton Cooley fully appreciated either the significance of the theory of self he had developed or the centrality of social process in the study of human lived experience. Still, as Mead (1930) acknowledged, Cooley's material on the self was groundbreaking in American social thought.[22] And, as Blumer (1928) observed, Cooley's method of *sympathetic introspection*, despite its limitations, was the essential method for the study of human group life.

George Herbert Mead: Mind, Self, and Society in Action

Although George Herbert Mead (1863–1931) taught in the philosophy department at the University of Chicago, he was to have a profound influence on what was to become known as *symbolic interaction*. Mead published little of his own work on social psychology, but three books on this subject—*The Philosophy of the Present* (1932), *Mind, Self, and Society* (1934), and *The Philosophy of the Act* (1938)—were published posthumously by students working primarily with notes from his classes. Of these volumes, the material dealt with in *Mind, Self, and Society* clearly has had the greatest impact on the sociological community.

Mead's thinking appears to have derived much inspiration from ongoing interaction with other pragmatists of that era (particularly Dewey, Cooley, and James), but it was Mead who provided the major conceptual foundations with which students and faculty (most notably Ellsworth Faris and especially Herbert Blumer) at the University of Chicago forged a unique interpretive tradition: symbolic interaction. Thus, as a means of comprehending symbolic interaction, it is essential to consider the "social behaviorism" of George Herbert Mead.

One finds very few references to Dilthey in Mead's work, but the social psychology that Mead developed is remarkably parallel with Dilthey's hermeneutic social science in several key respects.[23] Like Dilthey, Mead's notions are *intersubjective* (interactive and interpretive) to the core, with a strong insistence on recognizing the interrelatedness (and irreducibility) of "mind," "self," and "society." For both scholars, as well, *language* was considered absolutely fundamental to the human essence.[24] Although both a product and a process of human expression, language—or the symbolic means of achieving a sharedness of perspectives—was envisioned as the medium that made interaction possible and accounted for the development of mind, the dynamics of the self, and the production of action. Viewed thusly, mind, self, and society are rooted in, and sustained through, symbolically—mediated interaction. Even while recognizing the overlap between the ideas of Dilthey and Mead, one must appreciate that Mead's statements are approached, formulated, and presented so differently from those of Dilthey that it is difficult to deny the creativity of Mead's conceptualizations. One may fault Mead for not being explicitly more attentive to the parallels between his views and Dilthey's works, but simultaneously remain impressed with Mead's ingenuity and persistence in resolving issues pertinent to intersubjectivity in fields (e.g., physiology, instinct, evolution) that seem somewhat removed from those that Dilthey addressed.

To provide readers with an appreciation of the basis of Mead's thoughts, some extracts (primarily) from *Mind, Self and Society* are presented. In attending to these statements, however, it is most important that readers not only consider the interdependencies of Mead's concepts of mind, self and society, but also view these concepts as fundamentally intersubjective in their essences.

For Mead, the concept of *mind*, or an internalization of the perspective of the (interactive) community in which one is located, is viewed as an ongoing process by which one makes sense of the world as encountered. Although the mind provides a basis for organizing one's experiences,[25] Mead does not accept the idea of the mind as a given. The mind is a symbolic or linguistic essence and arises out of, and takes its (emergent) shapes from, the communication process. Mind develops through interaction with others. Thus, Mead spends considerable time establishing the centrality of the *shared gesture or significant symbol* as the foundation for human communication, conceptualization, and reflection:

> *Where the gesture reaches that situation [shared awareness -RP], it has become what we call "language." It is now a significant symbol and signifies a certain meaning. . . .*
> *The gesture is that phase of the individual act to which adjustment takes place on the part of other individuals in the social process of behavior. (Mead, 1934:46)*

> *Only in terms of gestures as significant symbols is the existence of the mind or intelligence possible; for only in terms of gestures which are significant symbols can thinking—which is simply an internalized or implicit conversation of the individual with himself by means of such gestures—take place. (Mead, 1934:47)*

From Mead's viewpoint, reality is a symbolic experience. Realities are created and transmitted, in the course of human interaction, through the development of shared sets of symbols:

> *Symbolization constitutes objects not constituted before, objects that would not exist except for the context of social relationships wherein symbolization occurs. Language does not simply symbolize a situation or object which is already there in advance; it makes possible the existence or appearance of that situation or object, for it is a part of the mechanism whereby that situation or object is created. (Mead, 1934:78)*

While individually "possessed," minds are community products that are more or less continuously in the making as people interact with others:

> *Mind arises through communication by a conversation of gestures in a social process or context of experience—not communication through mind. (Mead, 1934:49)*

Out of language emerges the field of mind. . . . We must regard mind, then, as arising and developing within the social process, with the empirical matrix of social interactions. (Mead, 1934:133)

Our contention is that mind can never find expression, and could never have come into existence at all, except in terms of a social environment; that an organized set or pattern of social relations and interactions (especially those of communication by means of gestures functioning as significant symbols and thus creating a universe of discourse) is necessarily presupposed by it and involved in its nature. (Mead, 1934:223)

From Mead's viewpoint, mind is not simply a passive receptacle. Mind involves an active sense of participation in the community of others. Hence, the ability to make (meaningful) indications to self and to others is essential for even rudimentary notions of "minded behavior":

"Imitation" depends on the individual influencing himself as others influence him, so that he is under the influence not only of the other but also of himself insofar as he uses the same vocal gesture. (Mead, 1934:65)

Mentality [minded behavior] in our approach simply comes in when the organism is able to point out meanings to others and to himself. (Mead, 1934:132)

If the mind might be viewed as an emergent, interpretive frame, which develops as people interact with others and work out lines of action with respect to the objects to which people attend in this or that manner, a stronger, fuller sense of the mind becomes apparent with the recognition of *the self* as an object of one's own awareness. Like the mind more generally, people's images of the self are predicated on interaction with others and involve people "taking the role" (adopting the viewpoint) of the other. As with mind, interaction (made possible through language) is essential if people are to develop a sense of self:

(S)elves must be accounted for in terms of the social process, and in terms of communication; and individuals must be brought into essential relation within that process before communication, or the contact between the minds of different individuals, becomes possible. The body is not a self, as such; it becomes a self only when it has developed a mind within the context of social experience. (Mead, 1934:49)

(T)he language process is essential for the development of the self. The self has a character which is different from that of the physiological organism proper. The self is something which has a development; it is not initially there at birth,

but arises in the process of social experience and activity, that is, arises in the process of social experience and activity. (Mead, 1934:135)

Mead clearly recognized the initiative capacity of humans for action (which he terms the "I"). However, the (more) social self or the focused or contextually meaningful self, is predicated on the recognition of oneself as an object (the "me") in a world of other (symbolic) objects.[26] Self-reflectivity or the recognition of self as an object, only comes about by taking the role (viewpoint) of the other. Thus, there can be no self without a prior recognition of the other:

It is the characteristic of the self as an object unto itself that I want to bring out. This characteristic is represented in the word "self," which is reflexive, and indicates that which can be both subject and object. (Mead, 1934:138)

The individual experiences himself as such, not directly, but only indirectly, from the particular standpoint of other individual members of the same social group, or from the generalized standpoint of the social group as a whole to which he belongs. . . .

The importance of what we term "communication" lies in the fact that it provides a form of behavior in which the organism or the individual may become an object unto himself. (Mead, 1934:138)

Where the self does appear it always involves an experience of another; there could not be an experience of a self simply by itself. (Mead, 1934:195)

Humans may be born with the physiological capacity for thought, but thinking (interpreting, defining, contemplating, assessing, selecting, creating) is a reflective process that develops only by attending to the other and envisioning the self as an object from the viewpoint of the other:

Thinking is a process of conversation with one's self when the individual takes the attitude of the other, especially when he takes the common attitude of the whole group, when the symbol that he uses is a common symbol, so that it has a meaning common to the entire group, to everyone who is in it and anyone who might be in it. It is a process of communication with participation in the experience of other people. (Mead, 1936:380–381)

Now, this inner thought, this inner flow of speech and what it means—words with their meanings—that call out intelligent response; it is this that constitutes the mind, insofar as that lies in the experience of the form. But this is only a part of the whole social process, for the self has arisen in that social process; it has its being there. Of course, you could carry such a self as that over to a Robinson

Crusoe island and leave him by himself, and he could carry that social process on by himself and extend it to his pets. He carries that on by himself, but it is only because he has grown up in society, because he can take attitudes and roles of others, that he can accomplish this. (Mead, 1936:381)

The reflective essence of self is rooted in a community of others, or what Mead termed *the generalized other:*

The organized community or social group that gives the individual his unity of self may be called "the generalized other." The attitude of the generalized other is the attitude of the whole community. . . . Thus, for example, in the case of such a social group as a baseball team, the team is the generalized other in so far as it enters—as an organized process or social activity—into the experiences of any of the individual members of it. (Mead, 1934:154)

Only by taking the attitude of the generalized other toward himself, in one or another of these ways, can he think at all; for only thus can thinking or the internalized conversation of gestures which constitutes thinking—occur. (Mead, 1934:156)

I want to be sure that we see that the content put into the mind is only a development and product of social interaction. It is a development which is of enormous importance, and which leads to complexities and complications of society which go almost beyond our power to trace, but originally it is nothing but the taking over of the attitude of the other. (Mead, 1934:191)

Further clarification of the notions of mind and self emerge when Mead focuses more squarely on *society.* Society or community, from Mead's viewpoint, consists of people interacting with one another in ways made meaningful as a consequence of *shared* symbolic representations of the generalized other. Human societies consist of communities of minded individuals who possess selves and who act and interact with one another in reflective (meaningful) manners:

Human society as we know it could not exist without minds and selves, since all its most characteristic features presuppose the possession of minds and selves by its individual members; but its individual members would not possess minds and selves if these had not arisen within or emerged out of the human social process in its lower stages of development. (Mead, 1934:227)

A human individual is able to indicate to himself what the other person is going to do, and then to take his attitude on the basis of that indication. He can analyze his act and reconstruct it by means of this process. The sort of intelligence he has is based not on physiological differentiation, nor based on herd instinct, but upon the development of the social process which enables him to carry out his part in the social reaction by indicating to himself the different possible reactions, analyzing them, and recombining them. It is that type of individual which makes human society possible. . . . In man [as opposed to other species—RP] the functional differentiation through language gives an entirely different principle of organization which produces not only a different type of individual but also a different society. (Mead, 1934:244)

The principle which I have suggested as basic to human social organization is that of communication involving participation in the other. This requires the appearance of the other in the self, the identification of the other with the self, the reaching of self-consciousness through the other. (Mead, 1934:253)

As people develop minds and selves (and indeed begin to realize the potential for thought and creativity by taking the viewpoint of the other), so do they also acquire (and internalize) notions of the moral orders of the communities in which they participate by taking the role of the other:

It is in the form of the generalized other that the social process influences the behavior of the individuals involved in it and carrying it on, i.e., that the community exercises control over the conduct of its individual members. (Mead, 1934:155)

(S)elf criticism is essentially social criticism, and behavior controlled by self-criticism is essentially behavior controlled socially. . . . Hence, social control, so far from tending to crush out the human individual or to obliterate his self-conscious individuality, is, on the contrary, actually constitutive of and inextricably associated with that individuality; for the individual is what he is, as a conscious and individual personality, just in as far as he is a member of society, involved in the social process of experience and activity and thereby socially controlled in his conduct. (Mead, 1934:255)

Mead (1934:269) clearly recognizes the differing "universes" of discourse that one may encounter as one moves from group to group, community to community, and the like. But insofar as the people involved establish shared means of communication, then there is a "potential universality" to the process of communication:

It is in terms of this mechanism of universals (or universally significant gestures or symbols) by means of which thinking operates, that the human individual

transcends the local social group to which he immediately belongs, and that his
social group accordingly (through its individual members) transcends itself and
relates itself to the whole larger context or environment of organized social relations
and interactions which surrounds it and of which it is only one part. (Mead,
1934:269, fn 13)

A fuller appreciation of Mead's work, however, hinges on the notion of
"action." So integral is *action* to Mead's formulation of social behaviorism, that
his book might better have been retitled, *Mind, Self and Society in Action*:

Social psychology studies the activity or behavior of the individual as it lies within
the social process; the behavior of an individual can be understood only in terms
of the behavior of the whole social group of which he is a member, since his
individual acts are involved in larger, social acts which go beyond himself and
which implicate the other members of that group.

We are not, in social psychology, building up the behavior of the social group
in terms of the behavior of the separate individuals composing it; rather, we are
starting out with a given social whole of complex group behavior, into which
we analyze (as elements) the behavior of each of the separate individuals composing
it. We attempt, that is, to explain the conduct of the individual in terms of the
organized conduct of the social group, rather than to account for the organized
conduct of the social group in terms of the individuals belonging to it. (Mead,
1934:6–7)

Social psychology is behavioristic in the sense of starting off with an observable
activity—the dynamic, ongoing process, and the social acts which are its component
elements—to be studied and analyzed scientifically. But it is not behavioristic
in the sense of ignoring the inner experience of the individual—the inner phase
of that process or activity. On the contrary, it is particularly concerned with the
rise of such experience within the process as a whole. (Mead, 1934:8)

While Cooley contributed some valuable insights to the theory of the socially
constituted self, Mead pursued the concept of the intersubjectivity much more
extensively and developed the basis for a full-fledged social psychology of human
lived experience. For Mead, as with Dilthey, human group life was viewed as
an *intersubjective* process. They saw human lived experience as an ongoing, interpretive, interactive enterprise. Clearly, they are not subjectivists![27] Nor are they
psychological reductionists. They stand in sharp opposition to those who would
reduce human behavior to individual or physiological factors. Likewise, these
scholars are very much at variance with those who would dismiss human lived
experience in favor of sweeping historical, cultural, or structural properties.

Thus, they are not historical, cultural or structural reductionists. Rather, they insist that the human or social sciences focus on human society as it is *intersubjectively constituted* in the course of everyday life.

CONCLUSION

Although Wilhelm Dilthey remains a relatively unknown figure within the social science community, his work is exceedingly central both to an appreciation of the roots of symbolic interaction and for the development of a *hermeneutic social science* more generally. This chapter, thus, begins with an examination of Dilthey's work on hermeneutics and its implications for the study of human group life. Dilthey has been extensively overlooked by scholars in the sociological community, who instead have focused on, and been diverted by, the writings of Max Weber; but Dilthey's hermeneutical insights are fundamental to a sociological appreciation of human group life. Although Weber incorporated aspects of Dilthey's work on *verstehen* into his conception of sociology and thereby helped sustain the interpretive tradition in some respects, his work lent itself to a variety of conceptual applications, only some of which may be seen as congruent with the intersubjective insights Dilthey provided.

Fortunately, many of the other ideas with which Dilthey worked were incorporated (albeit somewhat obscurely) into the writings of Georg Simmel and George Herbert Mead. Still, it was not until some time later that the essential groundwork that Dilthey laid for an intersubjective (social) science would be developed by Herbert Blumer (next chapter). Not only did Blumer draw out the fuller implications of a social science grounded in human lived experience, but he also was pivotal in integrating the interpretive and ethnographic traditions. While very much a student of George Herbert Mead, Blumer was also fundamentally attentive to Cooley's notion of *sympathetic introspection*. As indicated in the next chapter, it is through Blumer, and his insistence on the necessity of achieving intimate familiarity with the ethnographic other through close, sustained, firsthand interaction, that Dilthey's conception of an intersubjective (social) science receives its most adequate expression.

NOTES

1. See Dilthey (translation) in Rickman (1976:247–263) for a fuller historical account of hermeneutics. Ermarth (1978:15–62) provides valuable back-

ground on Dilthey's own introduction to hermeneutics and especially on the roles that Schleiermacher and Trendelenburg played in this process.

2. Anyone interested in the development of early social theory would likely find Ermarth's (1978) historically oriented portrayal of Dilthey's work of considerable value. In addition to providing much insight into Dilthey's work in a more direct sense, Ermarth attempts to locate Dilthey's productions within the sociocultural intellectual climate of the time (1800–1900). Although readers interested in Dilthey's contributions to the social sciences may also find it instructive to examine the works of Makkreel (1975), Rickman (1976, 1988), and Platinga (1980), Ermarth's (1978) statement was found especially valuable and is referenced more extensively as a consequence.

3. The argument is not that people studying humans do things differently from people studying other phenomenon, for both sets of scientists are seen to engage in *interpretive* enterprise. Rather, Dilthey's concern is that social scientists recognize that the "subject matter" they are studying (i.e., people) are also engaged in interpretive activities and that this notion be centrally incorporated into the agenda of the social sciences (ergo, the science of interpreting the interpreters). In this regard, Dilthey seems to have anticipated the "new" (constructionist or postMertonian) sociology of science discussed in chapter 3.

4. Readers may well note the affinities of Dilthey's "objective mind" with Mead's (1934) concept of "the generalized other."

5. See Oakes (1980) and Frisby (1984) for other statements on Simmel and his contributions to the study of human group life.

6. Frisby (1984) indicates that Simmel considered Hermann Steinthal and Moritz Lazarus, the founders of *Volkerpsychologie* (folk psychology), to be his two most important teachers in his student days. Here, as well, Simmel appears to share some intellectual affinities with Wilhelm Dilthey and Wilhelm Wundt.

7. Of all Simmel's works, it is the *Philosophy of Money* that best epitomizes the rich commonalities of these two scholars' systems of thought with respect to notions of intersubjectivity, interpretation, and social process.

8. As Alexander (1983:33) observes, "Weber's empirical sociology becomes a historical and comparative study of presuppositional rationality."

9. Only by stressing the idiographic emphasis Weber placed on historical analysis (determinism) is Bryant (1985:57–108, especially 78–98) able to make a case for Weber's rejection of certain aspects of positivism (invariant laws). Clearly, this does not deny Weber's concerns with causality or

historical determinism, or his tendency to ignore the *Naturwissenschaften-Geisteswissenshaften* distinction that Dilthey envisioned as central to the development of a genuine (hermeneutic) social science.

10. As a case in point, Bendix's (1960) rather detailed and widely acclaimed "intellectual portrait" of Max Weber makes remarkably few sustained references to *verstehen* (or other interpretive dimensions) as an important feature of Weber's work.

11. Although Weber spent some time doing research in a factory setting, this work should not be construed as ethnographic in any significant respect. Rather, he spent most of his time examining accounting practices and production registers in an attempt to correlate worker production curves with their social backgrounds (Oberschall, 1965:111–125).

12. Many European and North American sociologists (including many so-called, "theorists") lack viable familiarity with the works of Wilhelm Dilthey, George Herbert Mead, and Herbert Blumer. In part, this may reflect a failure to define Dilthey as a "sociologist" and a lack of appreciation of the intellectual links of German social theory and American pragmatism, as well as a "smug" intellectual unwillingness to define Mead and Blumer as sufficiently "classical" (i.e., in the European tradition) to qualify as "genuine theorists." Lacking a more adequate awareness of the works of Dilthey, Mead and Blumer, Weber's materials might well have represented the major notions of interpretive sociology with which these sociologists worked, at least until Giddens began reintroducing a more explicit hermeneutically informed sociology into the literature. However, even the seemingly well read Anthony Giddens (1976; 1984), who appears to have derived considerable inspiration from Dilthey and whose "new rules of the sociological method" and whose central thrust ("structuration") so clearly parallels Blumerian symbolic interaction, makes exceedingly few references to either Blumer or Mead.

13. In this regard, Weber's most consequential contribution to the social sciences may be represented in the works of Alfred Schutz. Largely disattending to Weber's substantive, methodological forays, Schutz (1932; 1962; 1964) derived central inspiration from Weber's consideration of *verstehen* and the pursuit of an interpretive sociology. While pointedly critical of Weber's limited and contradictory conceptualizations of meaningful action, Schutz's life project was very much one of establishing the foundations of meaningful behavior for those embarking on studies of the human condition. Schutz's own writings, along with those of Peter Berger and Thomas Luckmann (1966), which Schutz so directly inspired,

have profound significance for the sociology of knowledge and the study of human lived experience.

14. While inspired by aspects of Wundt's work, Mead (1904, 1906) argued that Wundt had violated his own contentions about the irreducibility of group processes by invoking unfounded psychological explanations for group processes.

15. In part, Wundt's hope was that by understanding the evolution of culture in more primitive societies one would understand the basis of contemporary society. Along the way he and others of this persuasion assumed notions of parallelism (in development) between various societies.

16. Morris (1970) provides one of the best accounts of the pragmatist movement, but readers may also wish to consult Rucker (1969:133–140) who also provides some valuable material on the sociology department at Chicago, Mills (1969) who oddly omitted Mead from his discussion, and Scheffler (1974). Konvitz and Kennedy (1960) provide a collection of statements extracted from ten scholars they identify as American Pragmatists. For valuable summary statements on the American Pragmatists, including Charles Peirce, William James, John Dewey, Charles H. Cooley, and George Herbert Mead, with respect to the development of symbolic interactionism, see Meltzer et al. (1975), Shalin (1986), Hammersley (1989), and Reynolds (1993).

17. Despite Peirce's initial formulation of pragmatism as a method of "how to make things clear," Peirce's attempts to formulate the pragmatic maxim (see Peirce in Konvitz and Kennedy, 1960:119–127, or Morris, 1970: 16–23) are themselves far from clear in intention or significance! Also of note is Peirce's contention (see Morris, 1970:25–32) that James, who most centrally promoted the pragmatist viewpoint, had significantly misrepresented Peirce's position!

18. Although James, Dewey, Mead, and many other American scholars of the day read German and spoke some German, it is not apparent that their comprehension of German (especially spoken German) was especially good. Present day scholars might also appreciate that these early scholars did not have at their disposal the vast array of translations and commentaries that are presently available to English-speaking scholars.

19. It is also worth noting the theological or religious roots of a great many nineteenth and early twentieth century social scientists. This was certainly the case for the American pragmatists, but also seems to have been true for many of the German social theorists, including Wilhelm Dilthey. Here,

too, the views of the American pragmatists coincide with the emphasis on praxis or the practical applications Dilthey sometimes expressed:

> *The meaning of the human sciences and their theory lies first and foremost in helping us with what we have to do in the world—with what we want to make of ourselves, with determining what we can undertake in the world and likewise what influence the world has upon us. (Dilthey, in Ermarth, 1978:108)*

20. Cooley (see 1926:63) attributes some of his insight on the social essence of the self to Baldwin's (1897) work and the "dialectics of personal growth." Readers may also be interested in Blumer's (1928) appraisal of Baldwin's social psychology. Blumer identifies Baldwin as the first distinctive American social psychologist, within the context of the conceptual and methodological development of the field of social psychology.

21. Although he does not make extended reference to Cooley, Sutherland's (1937) classic, *The Professional Thief*, and his later theory of "differential association" build centrally on the significance of primary group contacts for the learning of attitudes and behaviors conducive to criminal involvements.

22. While a very productive scholar at Michigan, Cooley's contributions would likely have been much more consequential had he been located at the University of Chicago. Thus, while Mead read and incorporated aspects of Cooley's thought into his own work and Cooley served as a literary inspiration of sorts for the students at Chicago who played such an important role in developing the ethnographic tradition, much of Cooley's potential may have gone unrealized by virtue of his location.

23. Apparently, Mead (see Joas, 1985:18–19), who had originally gone to Germany to study with Wundt, subsequently had some contact with Dilthey. During the two years Mead was registered at the University of Berlin (1889–1891), he took two courses from Dilthey (one on ethics and one on the history of philosophy) and started working on a dissertation on eye-hand coordination under Dilthey's supervision. While he returned rather abruptly to Michigan to take a job offered to him by John Dewey, Mead was in Germany during some of the major interpretive-positivist debates. It is not at all clear how attentive Mead was to Dilthey's works or the particular issues that Dilthey was examining at the time, but Mead appears minimally to have had some rudimentary exposure to Dilthey's ideas.

Perhaps no less revealing is this quote from Dewey in a paper prepared for Mead's (1931) memorial service:

> *In my earliest days of contact with him, as he returned from his studies at Berlin forty years ago, his mind was full of the problem which has always occupied him, the problem of individual mind and consciousness in relation to the world and society. (Dewey, 1931:311)*

As well, Mead (1904, 1906) had some familiarity with Wundt's folk psychology. Although Mead saw Wundt as moving beyond associational psychology, he was disenchanted with Wundt's tendencies to fall back into associationist modes of analysis (also see Joas, 1985:95–96). Thus, while Mead appears to have been inspired by Wundt's concept of the gesture and its implications for an intersubjective theory of language, Mead seemed to derive more direct impetus from Dilthey, and subsequently James, Dewey, and Cooley.

24. Despite the great importance they attached to language, neither Mead nor Dilthey was willing to divorce language from its intersubjective (community) context. Mead seems quite unwilling to separate language from the human formulation of action (and interaction); indeed, language is very much a part of this process. Language, for Dilthey, somewhat similarly, is a part of the historical-cultural mediated context that enables people to define (and experience) intersubjective reality on a here and now basis.

25. While mind implies a stock of knowledge about the world, it is much more than an accumulation of information. It represents a means of orienting oneself toward the world on an ongoing basis. We may envision the mind as representing an interpretive framework, but that should be qualified. This framework is typically multifaceted and may encompass a plurality of variants on a single perspective shared more generally within one's community or it may also entail a plurality of rather diverse viewpoints that people may encounter through association with an assortment of others whose life-styles are quite different from one another. The notion of "changing one's mind" signifies people's abilities to invoke alternative interpretations of a common theme as well as people's abilities to switch more completely the frameworks from which they view aspects of situations. Further, while people may change their minds "on their own," as they reflect upon situations from differing viewpoints over time, others may also encourage people to "change their minds" by challenging particular interpretive frameworks and/or promoting other viewpoints that they hope these people will take into account in developing their

lines of action. Likewise, "an inability to make up one's mind" would appear to denote situations in which people are torn between competing interpretations of particular situations.

26. Mead's (1934:173–178) discussion of the "I" and the "me" is much more complex than implied here. In part, these terms draw our attention to the dynamic, acting nature of the self: as an actor ("I") and an audience of one's own actions ("me"). Acknowledging people's abilities to be both objects unto themselves (as the "me") and active participants or agents (as the "I") in their presently unfolding situations, Mead envisioned the self as involving a process unto itself, whereby people may sequentially and simultaneously attend to themselves and the lines of action they are developing along the way.

27. In his review of *Mind, Self and Society*, Faris (1936) observes that this title significantly understates the priority that Mead assigned to "society" in the development of mind and self. Readers may also wish to refer to Faris's (1937b) and Blumer's (1966) statements on the social psychology of George Herbert Mead.

3

Contemporary Variants
of the Interpretive Tradition

Symbolic Interaction et al.

The interpretive tradition generated by Wilhelm Dilthey, Georg Simmel, Charles Horton Cooley, and George Herbert Mead has been most thoroughly and explicitly developed by Herbert Blumer. This chapter, thus, begins with an examination of Blumer's work. Not only did Blumer draw out the fuller implications of the works of George Herbert Mead for a social science grounded in human lived experience, but he also was pivotal in developing the interlinkages of the interpretive and ethnographic traditions. Exceedingly rich theoretically and methodologically, Blumer's work represents the major conceptual frame around which a great deal of interpretive/ethnographic inquiry has been conducted over the past several decades. However, other significant variations of interpretive analysis have emerged over the years as well. To this end, statements on the Iowa school of symbolic interaction, dramaturgical analysis, labelling theory, phenomenological sociology (reality construction and ethnomethodology), structuration theory, and the sociology of science are presented in this chapter.[1]

Chicago-Style Symbolic Interaction: Herbert Blumer

Symbolic interaction rests in the last analysis on three simple premises. The first premise is that human beings act toward things on the basis of the meanings they have for them. . . . The second premise is that the meaning of such things is derived from, or arises out of, the social interaction that one has with one's fellows. The third premise is that these meanings are handled in, and modified through, an interpretative process used by the person in dealing with the things he encounters. (Blumer, 1969:2)

A student of George Herbert Mead, Herbert George Blumer (1900–1987) continually emphasized the importance of Mead's work for the social sciences. However, in the process of elaborating upon the theoretical and methodological implications of symbolic interaction for the study of group life, Blumer also became the scholar who most effectively represented and developed the hermeneutic social science that Dilthey had introduced. Blumer was much more consistently focused on the production of social activity than was Dilthey, and there is little doubt that Blumer benefitted enormously from his absorption of Mead's social behaviorism; but it is Blumer who most cogently and forcefully emphasized the intersubjective foundations of human group life in twentieth century social science.

Herbert Blumer could not have envisioned the role he was to play in the development of interpretive social science or the approach he so aptly termed *symbolic interaction* in 1937. Still, his role as both a critic of positivist social science and a champion of the interpretive tradition began to take its shape in his (1928) doctoral dissertation ("Method in Social Psychology") at the University of Chicago. Ellsworth Faris chaired Blumer's dissertation and George Herbert Mead was on his committee, but the thesis Blumer wrote very much resonates with the tones he would develop in his later writings. The thesis surveyed the field of social psychology as it had been developed in America to that point. It is worth noting, as well, that most of the basic themes had been well established by then. Examining the methods used by social psychologists in the study of human behavior, Blumer asked whether the study of human behavior, as conceived in any of these manners, might be viewed as a scientific enterprise.[2] Blumer appears doubtful that the human sciences can meet the objectives and methodological rigor he associates with the physical sciences. The problem, he argues, is not one of intensity of application, but rather reflects the unique nature of the subject matter with which social scientists work.

Blumer's notions of symbolic interaction had not been extensively formulated at the time he wrote his dissertation, but Blumer (through contact with Mead) was most cognizant of the complex (reflective, interactive, emergent) nature of human behavior and concluded that the prevailing practices in the physical sciences were inadequate for capturing the fundamental features of human group life. Indeed, Blumer observed that Cooley's *sympathetic introspection* was the only methodology that seemed capable of approximating these essences. Thus, despite the liabilities Blumer attributes to this method (he was particularly concerned about differing levels of researchers' interpersonal skills and abilities to access the viewpoints of the other, as well as the problems of developing inquiries that readily lent themselves to comparisons), Blumer concluded that sympathetic introspection was the most viable method available to those doing social science:

> As used by social psychology [sympathetic introspection] becomes the essential method for the understanding of contemporary problems and life. Wherever any event, individual act, social situation, or cultural phenomenon is to be understood in its full social significance, sympathetic introspection must obviously be employed. (Blumer, 1928:343)

Blumer's own statements on symbolic interaction would appear only later (1937b; 1962; 1966; 1969), but here (1928) Blumer begins to develop an explicit interlinkage of theory and methods in the interpretive tradition. While Blumer clearly built on Mead's notions of social behaviorism, it was Blumer who most explicitly established *the vital link of the interpretive tradition with ethnographic research*. Blumer never used the term *hermeneutics*, but the task that Blumer accomplished, in relating the interpretive approach to a method for studying human lived experience, was one that had been of central concern to Dilthey.[3]

The significance of the interpretive/ethnographic link was made even more consequential by Blumer's criticisms of core features of positivist social science. Here, again, Blumer's position is more reminiscent of Dilthey's concerns than those of Mead (who appears only partially to have appreciated the methodological implications of his theory of human behavior):

> The prevailing practice of psychology and sociology is to treat social interaction as a neutral medium, as a mere forum for the operation of outside factors. Thus psychologists are led to account for the behavior of people by resorting to elements of the psychological equipment of the participants—such elements as motives, feelings, attitudes, or personality organization. Sociologists do the same sort of thing by resorting to societal factors, such as cultural prescriptions, values, social roles, or structural pressures. Both miss the central point that human interaction is a positive shaping process in its own right. The participants in it have to build up their respective lines of conduct by constant interpretation of each other's ongoing lines of action.... Factors of psychological equipment and social organization are not substitutes for the interpretive process; they are admissible only in terms of how they are handled in the interpretive process. (Blumer 1966:538)

In a series of papers, "Science without Concepts" (1931), "The Problem of the Concept in Social Psychology" (1940), "Public Opinion and Public Opinion Polling" (1948), "Psychological Import of the Human Group" (1953), "What's Wrong with Social Theory?" (1954), "Attitudes and the Social Act" (1955), and "Sociological Analysis and the 'Variable' " (1956), Blumer directs attention to the very weak foundations and misplaced emphasis of mainstream (positivist) social science.[4] He points out the folly of (both) psychological and sociological determinism and the simplistic and misleading nature of attitude research and variable analysis.

Blumer, it should be emphasized, is not quibbling with minor interpretations of these pursuits, but challenges these practices at the level of fundamental assumptions (and misrepresentations) pertaining to theory, methods, and research. The central problem, he observes, is that mainstream social science does not respect the nature of human group life. In not adequately acknowledging the interpretive, interactive essences of people's lived experiences, these approaches fail to achieve intimate familiarity with their subject matter. Thus, despite claims of a scientific enterprise, conventional (positivist) social science contributes little understanding of the ways in which human group life is accomplished. The following quote, which deals with "variable analysis," the mainstay of methodological (positivist) practice in the social sciences, illustrates Blumer's position:

> (T)he crucial limit to the successful application of variable analysis to human group life is set by the process of interpretation or definition that goes on in human groups. This process, which I believe to be at the core of human action, gives a character to human group life that seems to be at variance with the logical premises of variable analysis. (Blumer, 1956:685)

While Blumer attributes his theoretical notions largely to George Herbert Mead, it is Blumer who synthesized and developed the theoretical and methodological significance of Mead's ideas for the social sciences. The following discussion of symbolic interaction is built primarily around extracts from Blumer's superb (and remarkably succinct) rendering of the thought of George Herbert Mead.

For Blumer, as with Mead, the study of group life is the study of the ongoing production of action:

> The essence of society lies in an ongoing process of action—not in the posited structure of relations. Without action, any structure of relations between people is meaningless. To be understood, a society must be seen and grasped in terms of the action that comprises it. (Blumer 1966:541)

> *A society is seen as people meeting the varieties of situations that are thrust on them by their conditions of life. These situations are met by working out joint actions in which participants have to align their acts to one another. Each participant does so by interpreting the acts of others and, in turn, by making indications to others as to how they should act. (Blumer, 1966:541)*

Social behavior, through which society is constituted, is possible only because people (through association with others) come to develop selves and are able to make meaningful indications to themselves and others:

> *The possession of a self converts the human being into a special kind of actor, transforms his relation to the world, and gives his action a unique character. In asserting that the human being has a self, Mead simply meant that the human being is an object to himself. The human being may perceive himself, have conceptions of himself, communicate with himself, and act toward himself. . . . I wish to stress that Mead saw the self as a process and not as a structure. (Blumer, 1966:535)*

> *Human action acquires a radically different character as a result of being formed through a process of self-indication. Action is built up in coping with the world instead of merely being released from a pre-existing psychological structure by factors playing on that structure. By making indications to himself and by interpreting what he indicates, the human being has to forge or piece together a line of action . . . The fact that the human act is self directed or built up means in no sense that the actor necessarily exercises excellence in its construction. Indeed, he may do a very poor job in constructing his act. . . Such deficiencies in the construction of his acts do not belie the fact that his acts are still constructed by him out of what he takes into account. (Blumer, 1966:536–537)*

It is in this respect that the term *symbolic interaction* is so appropriate for designating the process of human interchange and intersubjectivity:

> *Symbolic interaction involves* interpretation, *or ascertaining the meaning of the actions or remarks of the other person, and* definition, *or conveying indications to another person as to how he is to act. Human association consists of a process of such interpretation and definition. Through this process the participants fit their own acts to the ongoing acts of one another and guide others in doing so. (Blumer, 1966:537–538)*

Noteworthy, too, is the relevance of this mode of analysis across the entire range of human association:

(S)ymbolic interaction is able to cover the full range of the generic forms of human association. It embraces equally well such relationships as cooperation, conflict, domination, exploitation, consensus, disagreement, closely knit identification, and indifferent concern for one another. The participants in each of such relations have the same common task of constructing their acts by interpreting and defining the acts of each other. The significance of this simple observation becomes evident in contrasting symbolic interaction with the various schemes of human interaction that are to be found in the literature. Almost always such schemes construct a general model of human interaction or society on the basis of a particular type of human relationship. (Blumer, 1966:538–539)

Whereas the positivists allege that their approach is "empirical" because they gather standardized "sense" data and use statistical analysis in processing this material, Blumer (1969:21–60) challenges these notions by questioning the viability of both their baseline assumptions and the "data" they take to represent human group life. Thus, Blumer insists that a genuine social science would be attentive to the empirical social world, the world of human lived experience:

Let me begin by identifying the empirical social world in the case of human beings. This world is the actual group life of human beings. It consists of what they experience and do, individually and collectively, as they engage in their respective forms of living; it covers the large complexes of interlaced activities that grow up as the actions of some spread out to affect the actions of others; and it embodies the large variety of relationships between the participants. . . . The empirical world, in short, is the world of everyday experience . . . Ongoing group life, whether in the past or the present, whether in the case of this or that people, whether in one or another geographical area, is the empirical social world of the social and psychological sciences. (Blumer, 1969:35)

In this respect, Blumer insists as well on researchers achieving "intimate familiarity" with their subject matter:

(T)he empirical social world consists of ongoing group life and one has to get close to this life to know what is going on in it. If one is going to respect the social world, one's problems, guiding conceptions, data, schemes of relationship, and ideas of interpretation have to be faithful to that empirical world. This is especially true in the case of human group life because of the persistent tendency of human beings in their collective life to build up separate worlds, marked by an operating milieu of different life situations and by the possession of different beliefs and conceptions for handling these situations. (Blumer, 1969:38)

No theorizing, however ingenious, and no observance of scientific protocol, however meticulous, are substitutes for developing a familiarity with what is actually going on in the sphere of life under study. (Blumer, 1969:39)

An appreciation of the socially constructed, interpretive, and processual features of human group life, as Blumer observes:

. . . raises the most serious question about the validity of most of the major approaches to the study and analysis of human group life that are followed today— approaches that treat social interaction as merely the medium through which determining factors produce behavior. . . These approaches grossly ignore the fact that social interaction is a formulative process in its own right—that people in interaction are not merely giving expression to such determining factors in forming their respective lines of action but are directing, checking, bending, and transforming their lines of action in the light of what they encounter in the action of others. . . It is necessary to view the given sphere of life under study as a moving process in which the participants are defining and interpreting each other's acts. (Blumer, 1969:52–53)

This emphasis on interpretive social processes can also be applied to the study of organizations, institutions and societies. However, it must be first recognized that these larger organizational units are made up of people engaged in interaction with one another in interpretive, emergent contexts. Thus, here as well, one requires a methodology attentive to these basic features of human group life:

Symbolic interaction sees these larger societal organizations or molar units in a different way. It sees them as arrangements of people who are interlinked in their respective actions. The organization and interdependency is between such actions of people stationed at different points. . . Instead of accounting for the activity of the organization and its parts in terms of organizational principles or system principles, it seeks explanation in the way in which the participants define, interpret, and meet the situations at their present points. . . (L)arge scale organization has to be seen, studied, and explained in terms of the process of interpretation engaged in by the acting participants as they handle the situations at their respective positions in the organization. (Blumer, 1969:58)

These notions are extended in Blumer's (1971) insightful statement on the study of "Social Problems as Collective Behavior":

Sociologists have erred in locating social problems in objective conditions. Instead, social problems have their being in a process of collective definition. This process determines whether social problems will arise, whether they become legitimated, how they are shaped in discussion, how they come to be addressed in official policy, and how they are reconstituted in putting planned action into effect. Sociological theory and study must respect this process. (Blumer, 1971:298)

In developing this statement on social problems, as well as in his work on race relations (Blumer, 1958; Blumer and Duster, 1980), industrialization (Blumer, 1947, 1960, 1990) and labor-management relations (Blumer, 1958), Blumer indicates not only that symbolic interaction is capable of dealing with what may be defined as molar or macro societal analysis, but that symbolic interaction provides the essential viewpoint for understanding human social process regardless of the setting or complexity of the context under consideration (see Maines, 1989; Maines and Morrione, 1990; Morrione, forthcoming). Further, while Blumer encourages scholars to be sensitive to the horizontal or lateral linkages that people develop with one another, he is concerned that analysts attend to the vertical and temporal dimensions of human association as well. Like Dilthey, Blumer envisioned all levels of individual and collective action to be rooted in, and developed through an interpretive, interactive community process. However, it is Blumer who, even more clearly than Dilthey, provides us with the conceptual and methodological directions with which to undertake a study of human group life as ongoing accomplishment.

Herbert Blumer's contributions to the social sciences are threefold. First, building on the works of George Herbert Mead, Blumer develops a clearer, more coherent and sociologically focused statement pertaining to the implications of the interpretive paradigm for the study of human lived experience than Dilthey, Cooley, or Mead had been able to generate. Furthermore, by emphasizing Cooley's notion of sympathetic introspection, Blumer helps establish the relevance of the interpretive approach for the ongoing study of human group life. Second, Blumer challenges the prevailing positivist (quantitative) traditions that dominate the social sciences. While his work here parallels Dilthey's earlier efforts, Blumer forcefully and clearly lays bare the central weaknesses of mainstream social science. Blumer is not quibbling about minor issues, but indicates that mainstream social science fails to attend to its subject matter: namely, that it neglects human lived experience and the processes by which people work out (all) aspects of their lives in conjunction with others. To be true to its subject matter, Blumer contends, social science has to respect the lived experiences of people. Any conceptual or methodological approach to the study of human behavior, thus, has to recognize human beings as living, thinking, acting, and interacting entities. Third, Blumer provides a conceptual framework which not only theoretically undergirds ethnographic research (see the next chapter) in the social sciences, but which also encourages the development of generic or transsituational social processes. While Blumer clearly builds on the works of others (as indicated both in this chapter and in the following chapter on ethnographic research), he has represented these positions so prominently and forcefully over a fifty-year period that he justly deserves (as Lyman and Vidich [1988] contend) to be acknowledged as the single most important social theorist of the twentieth century.

OTHER VARIANTS OF THE INTERPRETIVE APPROACH

Although Herbert Blumer provides us with a very powerful set of statements on the theoretical and methodological implications of a hermeneutic social science, there have been other important developments within the broader interpretive tradition. Particularly noteworthy here are materials pertaining to the Iowa school of symbolic interaction, dramaturgical sociology, labeling theory, phenomenological (social construction and ethnomethodology) sociology and the new sociology of science.[5] Central features of a number of these variants have been absorbed by (Chicago-style) symbolic interaction, but since students will encounter references to these other frameworks, it is important to give some attention to each. It also should be noted that the discussions of these variants of the interpretive tradition are presented mindful of the similarities and contrasts they represent with respect to Chicago-style (Mead, Blumer) interactionism. Consequently, while the presentation may appear critical at points, it enables us to maintain a more consistent (epistemological—i.e. the interlinkage of theory and method) orientation to the study of human group life. These other varieties of the interpretive tradition will be presented more or less in the chronological order of their introduction into the North American social sciences. Thus, it should not be assumed that the approaches discussed earlier or later are more or less consequential by virtue of their ordering. As well, their roots may be more intertwined than first seems. However, it is hoped that this discussion will foster a fuller appreciation of the interpretive tradition, as well as enable students to become generally more conversant with the paradigm.

The Iowa School of Symbolic Interaction

Manford Kuhn (1911–1963), the principal architect of what was to become known as the Iowa school of symbolic interaction, studied with Kimball Young at the University of Wisconsin. Young had some exposure to the social psychology of George Herbert Mead while at the University of Chicago, but

Young was much more eclectic (attempting to blend history, psychology, and sociology) and positivist in his approach to social psychology than was Mead.

While Manford Kuhn (Hickman and Kuhn, 1956; Kuhn, 1964) subscribed to many aspects of symbolic interaction as formulated by Mead (e.g., matters pertaining to language, role-taking, creativity, and the importance of the self), Kuhn's overall position appears much more akin to that of Max Weber than to George Herbert Mead. Like Weber, Kuhn contended that social scientists had to recognize the interpretive nature of human lived experience. However, both approached the study of human behavior in manners that approximated the methods used for comprehending other (nonminded, noninteracting) phenomena.

Building on Young's social psychology, Kuhn sought to generate an interactionist tradition that was much more structuralist in its thrust than the perspective being developed in Chicago. Concerned with emulating the methods of the physical sciences, Kuhn wanted to develop a theory of self and interaction that was quantitative, objective (standardized measurements), and lent itself to the causal statements regarding the emergence (self as a dependent variable) and direction (self as an independent variable) of the self.

In attempting to operationalize the self, Kuhn (see Spitzer, Couch, and Stratton, 1994:70–75) viewed the self as a relatively enduring, transsituational set of definitions that reflect not only people's statuses in society but also the ways in which others acted toward them over time. This set of identities, values, and definitions that people applied to themselves was seen to constitute an organized structure of "self-indications," which would be invoked in regulating one's activities and interactions with others. Kuhn also argued that the self could be articulated to others through a series of self-statements, which could be systematically coded and treated as variables in the production of behavior.

The instrument which Kuhn developed to access and operationalize these self-structures was the "Twenty Statements Test" (TST). Here, one asks respondents to provide twenty statements about the self (along the lines, "I am _____ ."). Although the TST was to prove a relatively fruitless venture, Kuhn, his students, and others who wanted to measure the self, spent a great deal of time attempting to infer structures of the self from masses of these self descriptions.

A very instructive way to conceptualize the Iowa school of symbolic interaction (sometimes referenced as "self theory" because of Kuhn) is to contrast it with the Chicago school in respect to matters of methodology, human agency, and process (see Meltzer and Petras, 1972; Meltzer, Petras, and Reynolds, 1978; Maines, 1986, 1989; and Reynolds, 1993).

While the two traditions claimed to be rooted in the work of George Herbert Mead, major differences arise between them with respect to the ways in which one might study human group life. Herbert Blumer, the major proponent of the Chicago tradition, insisted on a methodology (Cooley's "sympathetic introspection;" ethnography) that was attentive to the unique features of human lived experience. In contrast, Manford Kuhn argued for a methodology that was common to other scientific inquiry. Kuhn wanted to develop standardized measures of human behavior and derive causal statements concerning human conduct, with the eventual goal of predicting and controlling human behavior. Whereas Blumer prioritized notions of interaction and interpretation in the study of human behavior, Kuhn subordinated matters of interaction and interpretation to concerns with operationalization and measurement. Secondly, while Blumer emphasized the centrality of human agency or the study of people actively defining, shaping, and intersubjectively linking their behaviors in a community of others, Kuhn promoted a deterministic viewpoint in which people's behaviors were seen as caused by the sets of the self-attitudes they had internalized with respect to this or that role. Third, while Blumer stressed the necessity of developing a processual or emergent approach to the (active and interactive) formulation of human behavior, Kuhn argued that human behavior was the product of a self structured by a set of attitudes that reflected the positions (roles) one held in society.

Over the years a rather bitter rivalry developed between the Iowa and Chicago traditions. While the positivistically oriented Iowa school was subject to many of the general criticisms that Blumer levelled against mainstream social science, the Chicago people spent very little time criticizing the Iowa tradition in any specific sense. However, Kuhn and his students argued, variously, that ethnography was unscientific, that Blumer misrepresented Mead's work, and that a more astute awareness of Mead's work would indicate its greater affinity with the Iowa tradition.[6] While Blumer pointedly indicated the inappropriateness of positivist notions of science for the study of human behavior, he also challenged the integrity of these Iowa claims by referring to Mead's work. The more recent recognition of the linkages of Mead to Dilthey (who largely founded the hermeneutic social science) make the allegations of Kuhn and his students appear particularly unfounded. Still, these skirmishes may well have distracted Blumer from pursuing tasks of greater consequence for the interpretive tradition. They also created major rifts within symbolic interactionism. Although the Iowa-style interactionists accorded attention to human behavior, they failed to develop a methodology that was sensitive to human agency (reflectivity, enterprise) and human interchange (community, process, relationships).[7]

Since the mid 60's, the Iowa school has been dominated largely by Carl Couch (1925–1994) and his students (see Couch and Hintz, 1975; Couch et al., 1986a, b; Couch, Katovich and Buban, 1994).[8] After many frustrating setbacks, Couch set aside interests in the TST and other measurements of the self and had been conducting processual analyses of interchanges between people using videotape recordings as the data base. The typical approach for these analysts involves coding the exchanges of those they view on video screens in attempts to define the sequences by which people assemble their actions with respect to one another.

In contrast to Kuhn's earlier methodological emphasis on operationalizing the self-structure and its consequences for behavior, Couch (following Georg Simmel's attentiveness to the "forms" of association) has put the focus more squarely on process. Still, Couch and his associates have given relatively little attention to the ways in which the people they study interpret or make sense of the situations in which they find themselves (as they work through the tasks the researchers have assigned them). Thus, although those adopting this methodology have moved closer to the world of human lived experience than earlier Iowa attempts to measure the self, there is still limited appreciation of the significance of human agency (via ongoing reflectivity and interpretation). As they are presently used, videotaped recordings may provide researchers with some "data," but this material is largely observational in nature. In the absence of interviews or other participant-based accounts of their experiences, it is the researchers who assign meanings to the practices being considered. Thus, while Couch and his students have engaged in painstaking attempts to establish the behavioral features of elementary social forms, the epistemological (i.e., theory-methods linkage) integrity of these analyses (with respect to human reflectivity and agency) would be greatly enhanced had the Iowa scholars attended more fully to the participants' interpretations of the events that they jointly construct with each other.

Nevertheless, the emphasis on generic social process that Couch (1984) has forged clearly put the Iowa scholars in much closer harmony with those working in the Chicago tradition. Social process denotes the essential link for an assimilation of the two sets of scholars.[9]

Dramaturgical Sociology

All the world's a stage and all the men and women merely players. (Shakespeare [circa 1600], 1988:40)

When an individual enters the presence of others, they commonly seek to acquire information about him or to bring into play information about him already possessed. . . . Although some of this information may be sought almost as an end in itself, there are usually quite practical reasons for acquiring it. Information about the individual helps to define the situation, enabling others to know in advance what he will expect of them and what they may expect of him. (Goffman, 1959:1)

Erving Goffman's (1959) *The Presentation of Self in Everyday Life* sparked intensified interest in the interpretive paradigm.[10] Focusing on "impression management" and emphasizing "the dramaturgical metaphor," the Chicago-trained Erving Goffman (1922–1982) likened everyday life to theatrical performances. However, as Goffman observed, dramaturgical performances in everyday life represent much more than a means of entertaining audiences. They may have powerful implications for the performers' subsequent opportunities to achieve (and maintain) desired identities in a community setting. Insofar as people (as audiences or agents) act toward others (performers or targets) according to how they view these others, performers may gain considerably when they are able to shape the images (identities) that others attribute to them. It is in this regard that Goffman argues for the centrality of *impression management* for the study of ongoing community life:

Regardless of the particular objective which the individual has in mind and of his motive for having this objective, it will be in his interest to control the conduct of others, especially their responsive treatment of him. This control is achieved largely by influencing the definition of the situation which the others come to formulate, and he can influence this definition by expressing himself in such a way as to give them the kind of impression that will lead them to act voluntarily in accordance with his own plan. Thus, when an individual appears in the presence of others, there will usually be some reason for him to mobilize his activity so that it will convey an impression to others which it is in his interests to convey. (Goffman, 1959:3–4)

The others, in their turn, may be suitably impressed by the individual's efforts to convey something, or may misunderstand the situation and come to conclusions that are warranted neither by the individual's intent nor by the facts. In any case, in so far as the others act as if the individual had conveyed a particular impression, we may take a functional or pragmatic view and say that the individual has "effectively" projected a given definition of the situation and

*"effectively" fostered the understanding that a given state of affairs obtains.
(Goffman, 1959:6)*

Examining everyday life as theatre, Goffman rivetted readers' attention to the
human capacity for *self-reflectivity* in a much more compelling fashion than did
Cooley, Mead, or Blumer. Goffman's actors are alive, very much in an interactionist sense. They think, they watch, define and try to anticipate the other;
they plan, they perform. They make mistakes, and they readjust, sometimes
individually and sometimes with the cooperation of others. As objects of their
own awareness, people have images of themselves and they may pursue their
interests in conjunction with one another. They experience pride and they know
shame and embarrassment. They are aware, too, that others can experience
these feelings as well. In reading *The Presentation of Self in Everyday Life* (1959)
and *Stigma* (1963b), people see themselves in a mirrorlike (or "looking glass"—
Cooley, 1922:184) fashion. Readers relive their own ambitions and vulnerabilities
through the interpersonal other. Even in *Asylums* (1961), which focuses on the
underlife of total institutions, Goffman illustrates the persistence and presentation
of the *self* and the human enterprise entailed in the development and maintenance
of a *community* under conditions of extensive control and enforced deprivation
of freedom:

*(A)ny group of persons—prisoners, primitives, pilots, or patients—develop a life
of their own that becomes meaningful, reasonable, and normal once you get
close to it. . . . a good way to learn about any of these worlds is to submit oneself
in the company of the members of the daily round of petty contingencies in which
they are subject. (Goffman, 1961:ix–x)*

Likewise, Goffman portrays in strikingly vivid detail the ways in which
people take images of themselves and others into account in constructing their
day-to-day interchanges with one another. Goffman elaborates on front-stage
activity, addressing settings, props, and publicly presented characters. He also
takes readers into the back regions to examine preparations, teamwork, and
deception. And he shows how people move back and forth, sometimes abruptly,
between the two settings by discussing mistakes, embarrassment, and remedial
interchanges. Daily interaction is likened to the theatre, but the script is a much
more emergent one. People can and often do attend to the frameworks implied
by the settings and roles in which they find themselves, but they have to
formulate their own lines of action in a processual, interactive manner.

Although Goffman's earlier (1959, 1961, 1963a,b) work indicates considerable affinity with that of George Herbert Mead, Everett Hughes, and

Herbert Blumer, Goffman's overall style of inquiry seems most singularly reminiscent of Georg Simmel, who was also especially concerned about depicting the *forms* of association.[11] However, building on later developments in Chicago-style sociology and anthropology, Goffman achieves much more conceptual detail in his depictions of the interactional order than Simmel was able to develop.

Still, as with Simmel (and in contrast to Blumer), Goffman never provided an explicit statement on his methodology or the ways in which he linked theory and methods. Goffman appears particularly receptive to Chicago-style ethnography and his early works (*The Presentation of Self in Everyday Life, Asylums, and Stigma*) exhibit much of this flavor. His later works retain these sympathies, but here Goffman displays a more marked tendency to rely on extracts culled from the media rather than (the much more demanding) ethnographic inquiry. As well, while much of his later work elaborates on the themes he introduced in *The Presentation of Self in Everyday Life* and *Asylums* (which are also his two most extended ethnographic ventures), he appears concerned about clothing these notions in the avant-garde sociology of the time.[12]

Although, as will be indicated shortly, some of Goffman's work is readily incorporated into what may be termed "labeling theory," the dramaturgical frame that Goffman popularized is also very well represented in the works of Orrin Klapp (1962, 1964, 1971), and Stanford Lyman and Marvin Scott (1970). Goffman's dramaturgical viewpoint also provided considerable intellectual impetus for many subsequent ethnographic inquiries.

Despite Goffman's originality and prominence within the social sciences, the dramaturgical frame he presents suffers from its inattentiveness to the ways in which *the task or accomplishment aspects of action* are conducted on a day-to-day, moment-to-moment basis. Goffman provides much rich insight into the ways in which people present and sustain images of self at both a personal and an organizational level, and these notions are very important in helping us to more completely understand the contexts in which human group life is accomplished. However, once one moves beyond a consideration of the ways in which impression management ("looking good") is achieved in interpersonal contexts, Goffman's work is of limited value in appreciating how human activity is constituted in practice.[13]

To understand how one manages or performs tasks, builds relationships, acquires perspectives, and the like, one must turn more squarely to the symbolic interaction of Herbert Blumer and studies that have been developed in Chicago-style ethnography. Indeed, as Goffman became more removed from the ethnographic contexts in which his earlier work was developed, his writings become increasingly less valuable for understanding the ways in which human group life is assembled on an interpretive, interactive level.

Labeling Theory

One of the most crucial steps in the process of building a stable pattern of deviant behavior is likely to be the experience of being caught and publicly labeled as a deviant. . . . (B)eing caught and branded as a deviant has important consequences for one's further social participation and self image. The most important consequence is a drastic change in the individual's public identity. (Becker, 1963:32)

The process of making the criminal, therefore, is a process of tagging, defining, identifying, segregating, describing, emphasizing, making conscious and self-conscious; it becomes a way of stimulating, suggesting, emphasizing the very traits that are complained of. (Tannenbaum, 1938:20)

While labeling (labelling) theory was developed primarily around the social construction of deviance, it very much builds on symbolic interaction and the dramaturgical frame. Viewing deviance as a community phenomenon,[14] those taking this (essentially interactionist) approach have focused on the processes by which people: (a) establish definitions of phenomena as "deviant;" (b) become identified as "deviants;" (c) become involved in, sustain, and become disinvolved from "deviant" activities; (d) develop and maintain subcultures; and (e) attempt to regulate deviance both informally and (formally) through control agencies. Although the term *labeling theory* has been cast largely in reference to deviance, it should be noted that these processes of definition, identification, involvement, group alignments, and social regulation are basic to all social groups as envisioned from an interactionist perspective.

One can trace aspects of labeling theory to the works of Shaw (1930), Cressey (1932) and Tannenbaum (1938), but it was Edwin Lemert (1951, 1967) and Howard Becker (1963) who became most prominently identified with this tradition. While Lemert views himself primarily as a "deviance theorist" and has only marginally aligned himself with symbolic interaction, the Chicago-trained Howard Becker much more clearly assumes an interactionist viewpoint. Both scholars (see Lemert, 1951:23–24) encourage a more generic appreciation of the implications of the identification process for people's participation in deviance and other settings. Others who significantly contributed to the development of labeling theory include Harold Garfinkel (1956), Erving Goffman (1959, 1961, 1963b), Orrin Klapp (1962, 1964, 1971), and John Lofland (1969).

In developing his material on labeling (and the concept of "societal reactions"), Lemert was essentially concerned with the impact of people's reactions to deviance for the perpetrator's subsequent involvements in deviance. Identifying or labeling a person as a deviant of some sort was especially central to this process, Lemert observed, for this designation selectively focused others' attention and their reactions to that person. Pivotal to Lemert's formulation was a distinction between primary and secondary deviation. Thus, Lemert noted that many instances of "deviance" could go undetected or might be responded to only in more fleeting manners, whereby the perpetrator maintains an essentially acceptable identity in the community (i.e., retains a definition of "normal" despite involvements in "primary deviation"). Lemert was not concerned with accounting for (unknown, overlooked, or audience-tolerated) instances of "primary deviation," which he argued might come about in any number of ways. Instead, his emphasis was on explaining "secondary deviation" or those behaviors that developed as a consequence of people's attempts to control behavior that they defined as troublesome and in need of regulation, modification, or sanction (ergo, the term, "societal reactions"). Lemert, thus, asked what happened when people were subjected to more extensive and persistent *identification* (and *reaction*, including exclusion) as a consequence of imputations of deviance.

Where designations of deviance and related rejections are more extensive, Lemert argues, these societal reactions encourage "secondary deviation." By sharpening and emphasizing definitions of the alleged perpetrators as "deviants" and recasting their options, control agents or other "upstanding citizens" may promote the stabilization or intensification of the very behaviors that had been seen as troublesome in that setting.[15] When people find themselves stigmatized and excluded from more conventional associations and opportunities, they may find themselves drawn more fully into deviant life-styles (identities, perspectives, activities, relationships), even when they do not so desire; or conversely, they might encounter difficulties exiting from deviant involvements even when they might very much intend to leave this role behind:

> *Secondary deviation refers to a special class of socially defined responses which people make to problems created by the societal reaction to their deviance. (Lemert, 1967:40)*

> *When a person begins to employ his deviant behavior or a role based upon it as a means of defense, attack, or adjustment to the overt and covert problems*

created by the consequent societal reaction to him, his deviation is secondary. (Lemert, 1951:76)

Reflecting notions of an intersubjective or community-based self in process, a great deal of Lemert's work on labeling theory resonates with the interactionist tradition. However, whereas Lemert was primarily concerned with the impact of labeling on people's subsequent involvements in deviance, those more squarely in interactionist tradition (e.g., Becker, 1963; Lofland, 1969; Rubington and Weinberg, 1987) also wanted to consider people's initial involvements in deviance as well as the ways in which the naming process took place. Further, while Lemert is somewhat appreciative of the significance of deviant subcultures for people's subsequent involvements, he stresses the exclusionary nature of societal reactions (via formal and informal control agents). In contrast, the interactionists are much more attentive to the roles that people already involved in deviant subcultures play in the acceptance and recruitment of newcomers as well as the stabilization of people's involvements in particular settings.

Both Edwin Lemert (1951) and the interactionists (to an even more pronounced degree) are concerned with the ways in which deviance is defined by people within particular communities and the ways in which they attempt to enforce these notions of propriety. Particularly noteworthy in this regard are Howard Becker's (1963) notion of "moral entrepreneurs" and Herbert Blumer's (1971) statement, "Social Problems as Collective Behavior."

In discussing *moral entrepreneurs*, Becker posits that definitions of deviance reflect human enterprise as opposed to inherent qualities of an act or actor under consideration. He distinguishes "rule creators" from "rule enforcers" to emphasize the different, but sometimes overlapping, roles that people may assume in attempts to regulate morality in a community context. Becker encourages researchers to examine both the processes by which laws and other rules become established in this or that setting and the ways in which control agents deal with those suspected of violating these rules.

Adding to this thrust, Blumer not only challenges earlier views of social problems as objective conditions, but offers an especially viable model for examining the processes by which people collectively define and deal with "social problems." Thus, he encourages more focused attention on the processes by which situations are *initially defined* as "social problems," and how these definitions *become legitimated* (or "objectified"), as well as the ways in which people attempt to *mobilize others for action, develop official plans and implement the programs* their plans imply. At every point, Blumer draws our attention to matters of ambiguity, influence, and resistance. Together with other scholars working in similar veins,[16] Becker and (especially) Blumer centrally depict the problematic, negotiable, and emergent nature of deviance definitions and control on a broader basis.

Another concept that became prominent through labeling theory is that of *career contingencies*. Although Howard Becker was not the first interactionist to use the term "career" to refer to the course of people's involvements in particular settings over time (see Shaw, 1930, 1931; Cressey, 1932), Becker (1963) emphasized the importance of (a) examining people's involvements in deviance in processual terms and (b) attending to the contingencies or considerations people take into account as they work their way through situations over time. While Becker (1963) focused primarily on the career contingencies of marihuana users and jazz musicians, he and others working in this tradition directed our attention to the ways in which people become initially involved in any situation, when they are more likely to continue, how they become disinvolved from those settings, and when and how they might become reinvolved in earlier pursuits.[17]

As well, since people's careers as deviants typically take place within the context of relationships with a group or subcommunity of others, the interactionists working in this tradition have emphasized the centrality of *subcultures* for understanding people's initial involvements and continued participation in deviance. Indeed, these scholars indicated that since deviance is very much a community phenomenon, most deviance cannot be explained by virtue of individual characteristics or properties. Becker's studies of jazz musicians and drug users have become especially well known in this regard, but early statements attesting to the importance of subcultural features of deviance include Shaw's (1930) discussion of delinquency, Cressey's (1932) analysis of the taxi-dance hall, and Sutherland's (1937) portrayal of the professional thief.

The term *subculture* signifies a way of life of a group of people. Denoting communities within communities, subcultures are characterized by interaction, continuity, and outsider and insider definitions of distinctiveness. Although individual members may vary greatly in the extensiveness of their participation in particular subcultures, both in the short and long terms, it is useful to envision subcultures with respect to the perspectives (or world views) characterizing their members, the identities people achieve as participants, the activities deemed consequential in that context, the bonds participants develop with one another, and the sorts of commitments the people involved make with respect to the setting at hand. These themes are strikingly prominent in Lofland's (1966) examination of a religious cult, Ray's (1961) analysis of drug users, Lesieur's (1977) account of "compulsive gamblers," Prus and Irini's (1980) study of the hotel community, Fine's (1983) inquiry into shared fantasy games, Adler's (1985) study of drug dealers, Prus and Sharper's (1991) statements on hustlers and magicians, Sanders's (1991) portrayal of tattooing, and Wolf's (1991) account of the outlaw biker subculture.

As Simmons (1969) observes, it is important to recognize the ambiguous, shifting, processual and interactive nature of subcultural involvements. Work in this area attests to the mutuality of deviance involvements. People may seek out subcultures, but they may also be eagerly recruited or screened and rejected by other members of the subculture as all the parties involved face the task of working out their interests with others over a period of time. Thus, while the denigrations, rejections, and exclusions generated by control agents may promote secondary deviation (Lemert, 1951, 1967) by dissuading people from pursuing more conventional options, people's contacts with others involved in deviance, likewise, is most consequential in affording (or denying) them opportunities to entertain these other options. In both respects, we develop a fuller appreciation of *deviance as a community phenomenon*.

The "naming process" or the ways in which people acquire identities and reputations as this or that type of person is also articulated with respect to deviance imputations through the works of Garfinkel (1956), Becker (1963), Goffman (1963b), and Lofland (1969). Importantly, the notions of private typings, public designations, audience assessments, and resistances from targets (and others) discussed with respect to deviance, can be applied to any setting in which people type or label others (see Goffman, 1959; Klapp, 1962, 1964, 1971; Prus, 1975a,b, 1982).

In sum, beyond drawing our attention to the reflective and negotiable nature of community definitions of morality, labeling theory stresses the significance of "social typings" for people's subsequent interaction with others and the ways in which people become involved and sustain involvements in particular forms of deviance. Focusing on the processes by which people define and attribute meanings to situations and other people, these students of deviance have contributed a great many valuable insights to the conceptual notions articulated by Mead and Blumer:

> *Involvement in deviant activities and the emergence and stabilization of deviant careers seems consistent with involvements in other spheres of life. Once one permeates the deviant mystique, it becomes apparent that one does not need one social psychology for the deviants and another for the normals. (Prus and Sharper, 1977:168)*

Phenomenological Sociology

While dramaturgical sociology and labeling theory generated a greater awareness of the interpretive tradition within sociology in the 1960s, another set of scholars were independently making some important contributions along similar lines. Two books, *The Social Construction of Reality* (1966) by Peter Berger and Thomas Luckmann, and *Studies in Ethnomethodology* (1967) by Harold Garfinkel, are especially noteworthy in this respect. However, since both of these volumes rely heavily on the works of a Viennese-trained scholar, Alfred Schutz, it is instructive to consider Schutz's work more generally before discussing these two statements and their implications for the interpretive tradition.

The Philosophical Underpinnings of Everyday Life: Alfred Schutz

> *From the outset, we, the actors on the social scene, experience the world we live in as a world both of nature and of culture, not as a private but as an intersubjective one, that is, as a world common to all of us, either actually given or potentially accessible to everyone; and this involves intercommunication and language. (Schutz, 1962:53)*

Deriving considerable inspiration from Max Weber and (the German phenomenologist) Edmund Husserl, Alfred Schutz (1899–1959) undertook a lifelong intellectual agenda (Schutz, 1932, 1962, 1964; Schutz and Luckmann, 1967) of depicting the unique subject matter of the social sciences. Schutz's primary objective was one of detailing the philosophical underpinnings of an interpretive social science, but his work has great significance for the social sciences more generally. Schutz's abilities to incorporate central features of the works of the American pragmatists (especially William James, Charles Horton Cooley, and George Herbert Mead) into his own formulations (Schutz, 1962;1966) has also meant that his work is very much in accord with the interactionist tradition.

In articulating the intersubjective essence of human group life, Schutz cogently depicts the central features of "multiple realities" or worldviews, collective and personal foundations and stocks of knowledge, "common-sense and scientific interpretations," "rationality," and the nature of human conduct. Schutz is primarily concerned with the ways in which people develop shared understandings ("objectifications") of reality and the manners in which people make sense (via "typifications" or categorizations) of the situations they encounter on a day-to-day basis, as well as the ways in which people relate to and develop understandings of each other. Although some of these notions are developed further in Berger and Luckmann (1966), a careful reading of

Schutz's work is merited on the part of anyone interested in the study of human group life.

Reality Construction Theory: Peter Berger and Thomas Luckmann

> *(L)anguage is capable of "making present" a variety of objects that are spatially, temporally and socially absent from the "here and now."... Put simply, through language an entire world can be actualized at any moment. This transcending and integrating power of language is retained even when I am not actually conversing with another. Through linguistic objectification, even when "talking to myself" in solitary thought, an entire world can be appresented to be at any moment (39)... Language is capable not only of constructing symbols that are highly abstracted from everyday experience, but also of "bringing back" these symbols and appresenting them as objectively real elements of everyday life. In this manner, symbolism and symbolic language become essential constituents of the reality of everyday life and the commonsense apprehensions of this reality. (Berger and Luckmann, 1966:39–40)*

> *What remains sociologically essential is the recognition that all symbolic universes and all legitimations are human products; their existence has its base in the lives of concrete individuals, and has no empirical status apart from these lives. (Berger and Luckmann, 1966:128)*

Building centrally on Schutz's formulations, Berger and Luckmann (1966) attracted considerable attention within the sociological community by providing a statement on *the sociology of knowledge*, which was not only extremely well articulated, but which also avoided many of the pitfalls that characterized earlier efforts in this direction.[18] Presenting a theory in which scientific discourse is rooted in the common-sense practices of everyday life, Berger and Luckmann emphasized the intersubjective nature of knowledge and the relevance of the social construction of knowledge for *all* life-worlds. "Knowledge," Berger and Luckmann contend, is a socially constructed phenomenon. From this viewpoint, knowledge is not only a social, historically rooted product, but is also an ongoing social process. As emergent community accomplishments, versions of "reality" reflect the collective interpretations of the world by the people who constitute that community. "Objectivity," thus, is not innate to any state or condition of the world, but reflects the intersubjective consensus attained within particular community contexts with respect to this or that aspect of the life-worlds to which particular sets of people attend. Representing a historical-collective enterprise produced by a community of people interacting with one another, knowledge becomes more firmly entrenched as "objective reality" as people develop, act upon, and transmit these versions of knowing to others. Thus, Berger and Luckmann posit that everything that passes as "knowledge" (from science to art, as well as any "common-sense" practices) is thoroughly and fundamentally a product of social interchange.

The basic ideas in Berger and Luckmann's volume do not appear exceptional when posed against the interpretive frames of Wilhelm Dilthey, George Herbert Mead, Herbert Blumer, or Alfred Schutz, but Berger and Luckmann more explicitly illustrated the centrality (inevitability) of the interpretive paradigm for all forms of knowing and they cast Schutz's work in a style that was much more immediately accessible to the general social science community. Berger and Luckmann had generated a remarkably potent conceptual base that not only enables scholars to transcend "macro" and "micro" issues in sociology, but which, in laying out the foundations for human knowledge about the world, represents a way of reconceptualizing and synthesizing the social sciences more generally. However, like Schutz, Berger and Luckmann failed to provide a methodology that would allow one to investigate the ways in which reality was constructed. While describing themselves as "nonpositivists," Berger and Luckmann conclude on a methodologically vague (but seemingly diplomatic) note. It is not apparent that they are familiar with much of Blumer's work or Chicago-style interaction more generally. Some of the insights that Schutz and Berger and Luckmann generated have been incorporated into ethnographic research by those working within the interactionist tradition, but the profound intersubjective essence of their work has been largely overlooked by scholars in the social sciences.[19]

Ethnomethodology: Harold Garfinkel

Some of Schutz's concepts also appear in *Studies in Ethnomethodology* (1967) by Harold Garfinkel,[20] but Garfinkel took Schutz's work in some very different directions than did Berger and Luckmann. While Berger and Luckmann focused on knowledge as a general problem for sociological analysis, Garfinkel emphasized the interpersonal and experiential nature of Schutz's work. Garfinkel's writings are much more disjointed and obscure than those of Schutz or Berger and Luckmann, but Garfinkel attained considerable prominence by pursuing a variety of methods in the course of expounding upon some of Schutz's concepts.

Ethnomethodology might be defined as the study of the ways in which people make sense of their situations and go about accomplishing their tasks at hand.

Like Schutz, Garfinkel accepts the notion of multiple realities and the inter-subjective nature of human group life. One of Garfinkel's pivotal concepts is "indexicality." Although Garfinkel does not make the linkage explicit, indexicality is very much a restatement of the concept of *verstehen* or interpretive under-standing. Referring to the notion that one may only be able to achieve a more viable understanding of the other to the extent one has a fuller appreciation of both the background circumstances of the other and of the present circum-stances and interests of the other, indexicality is seen as a major feature (limiting and facilitating) of human communication.

Concerned with the ways in which human action is accomplished, Garfinkel sought to find ways of studying the processes by which people managed to do everyday life. His methods range from the creation of breeches, disruptions, and inversions of normal events and practices (to see how people react and adjust); to the analysis of conversations (to see how people use language in practice); to the compilation of extended case-histories (to see how people make sense of and adjust to particular circumstances); to detailed examinations of the ways in which activities are assembled in practice.[21]

One of the most productive lines of ethnomethodological inquiry involves attempts to examine the manners in which activities are accomplished on a "here and now" basis. Through participant-observation, open-ended interviews, and observation, some ethnomethodologists have embarked on research that fairly closely resembles Chicago-style ethnography. It is not apparent that Garfinkel or many of the ethnomethodologists are especially familiar with the writings of Mead and Blumer, or with the ethnographic tradition of the Chicago school, but many aspects of ethnomethodology are compatible with, and have been incorporated into, symbolic interactionism.

While the collective works of Schutz, Berger and Luckmann, and Garfinkel have not altered the basic features of symbolic interaction, their work has served to enrich the perspective in a number of ways. Thus, Schutz more fully details the philosophical underpinnings of the interpretive tradition than does Mead. Similarly, Schutz, Berger and Luckmann, and Garfinkel introduced concepts, such as "multiple realities," "taken for granted realities," "objectifications," "typifications," and other "social constructionist" terminology that has helped those working within the interactionist tradition better express and appreciate features of the everyday world of human lived experience. This work has also broadened the contextual applications of the interpretive tradition to human group life. Thus, for example, Schutz's (1964) consideration of "rationality" as intersubjective accomplishment presents a most instructive foil to Weber's positivist (rational-economic) view of rationality. Likewise, Schutz's (1962) statement on "common sense and scientific thinking" may be seen as having laid the important foundations for both the sociology of knowledge (via Berger and Luckmann, 1966) and for the "new sociology of science" (through Garfinkel, 1967).

Structuration Theory

Structuration, *as the reproduction of practices, refers abstractly to the dynamic process whereby structures come into being. By the* duality of structure *I mean that social structures are both constituted by human agency, and yet are the very medium of this constitution.... The proper locus for the study of reproduction is in the* immediate process of the constituting of interaction. *Giddens (1976:121–122)*

While Anthony Giddens (1976; 1979; 1981; 1982; 1984; 1987) has established himself as a critic of sociology (particularly functionalism, evolutionism, Marxism, positivism, and structuralism and poststructuralism, and to lesser extents phenomenology, symbolic interactionism, and ethnomethodology), this British sociologist has simultaneously been a synthesizer of "macro" and "micro" sociology as well as a noteworthy proponent of the hermeneutic tradition.

Assuming the style of a "classical theorist," Giddens's work encompasses a wide range of topics and multiple levels of analysis, not all of which (compared to Berger and Luckmann, 1966; Blumer, 1969) is systematically or coherently managed. At the same time, however, *structuration*, which draws attention to the ongoing processual constitution and reconstitution of human practices and arrangements, emerges as the essential analytical feature in both his critiques of other viewpoints (e.g., positivism–Giddens, 1974, 1976; Marxism–Giddens, 1981; structuralism and poststructuralism–Giddens, 1987) and in the development of his own notions of the constitution of society (1984). At the base is Gidden's acknowledgement of Dilthey's hermeneutic stance: that human group life denotes an interpretive, formulative process that has its essence in the linguistic sharedness of the community. At the same time, Giddens has maintained an appeal among the less hermeneutically oriented scholars as a consequence of both his emphasis on "structure" and his tendency to embark on grand theory.

However, rather than view structures as causing human behavior, Giddens envisions people as developing certain practices (structures) for the practical accomplishment of this or that concern. Like Schutz (1962, 1964) and Berger and Luckmann (1966), Giddens is concerned with the processes by which human viewpoints and practices become "objectified" or more thoroughly embedded in the course of human group life. Thus, Giddens emphasizes both the accomplishment of structure by situated, minded actors and the dependence of structure on the ongoing human formulation of action. Once practices become institutionalized in particular communities, people employ these frameworks in formulating their activities. However, Giddens stresses, these arrangements more or less continuously become reconstituted (through enhancement, refinement, reformulation, rejection, and replacement) in a more immediate as well as a more enduring manner as people pursue their activities on a situated, day-to-day basis.

Sociology, according to Giddens, is concerned with the study of the life-worlds that are produced by active, reflective beings, who, as skilled interactants, generate, endorse, stabilize, employ, and reconstitute certain practices and arrangements. The "structures" so produced denote (spacial and historical) contexts that simultaneously represent practical limitations (e.g., rules, practices, resources) of sorts for immediate human behavior as well as the enabling foundations on which subsequent human conduct may be built.

The task facing social scientists involves an appreciation of "the double hermeneutic" (Giddens, 1976; 1984); the recognition that social scientists (as minded, interpreting, acting entities) are analyzing other minded, interpreting, acting entities. Like Cooley, Blumer, and the interactionists more generally, Giddens contends that it is essential that researchers immerse themselves in the life-world of the other in order to develop a stronger (intersubjective) awareness of the other, while at the same time recognizing that one's task as a social scientist requires that one also be able to situate this material within the (ongoing, reconstitutionable) conceptual frame of the academic community (Giddens, 1984:285–286):

> *In sum, the primary tasks of sociological analysis are the following: (1) The hermeneutic explication and mediation of divergent forms of life within descriptive metalanguages of social science; (2) Explication of the production and reproduction of society as the accomplished outcome of human agency. (Giddens, 1976:162)*

Readers more familiar with Dilthey, Mead, Schutz, Berger and Luckmann, and Blumer will find much in Giddens that resonates with the theoretical positions of these scholars. Further, while Giddens has criticized Schutz as being too subjective and the interactionists for not attending more fully to structural (and macro issues), these criticisms are not well founded. A closer examination of Schutz (1962, 1964) reveals not only that Schutz's phenomenological sociology is centrally rooted in the intersubjective other, but that Schutz more explicitly and substantially deals with a number of key aspects of the "structuration" process to which Giddens refers than does Giddens himself (as likewise, do Berger and Luckmann, 1966). Similarly, while Giddens endorses ethnographic work in a general sense, there is little direct evidence that he is aware of the value that Chicago-style ethnography has for depicting "structuration" in practice, for envisioning the ways in which people go about accomplishing everyday life in interactive, situated, processual terms. Indeed, had Giddens focused on Herbert Blumer and Chicago-style ethnography (see chapter 4) as opposed to Erving Goffman, Giddens would have found substantial evidence that the interactionists have been concerned with macro-issues as well as with a great deal of what he encompasses in the notion of "structuration." Like Giddens, the interactionists have started with a hermeneutic base but, much more centrally than Giddens, have been concerned about building a solid, intersubjective foundation by examining human lived experience on a firsthand basis. Thus, their work has represented an explicit attempt to generate a theory of human group life "from the ground up," rather than "from the top down," as has typically been done in classical theory. Giddens' statements also have been rather vague with respect to methodological practice, as if he were still trying to bridge broader interpretivist-positivist issues in the field, but in some still indistinct manner. Both Blumer's work on the methodological foundations of the social sciences and Chicago-style ethnography represent vital resources on which Giddens has yet to draw.

In certain respects, Giddens's work is reminiscent of Weber's (chapter 2) attempted structuralist-interpretive synthesis, but Giddens has more steadfastly maintained an interpretive stance, one which he applies to social scientists as well as their subject matters. Still, Giddens's work departs from the hermeneutical tradition in some other respects. First, seemingly in attending to the "why?" vs. "how?" question, Giddens incorporates a set of unconscious motivations into his model. Following Kai Erikson, Giddens (1984) posits that anxiety is inherently discomforting to the human being and thus generates an unconscious motive to embark on turns to security, trust, and predictability. Notions of unconscious motivations are extended somewhat further, into claims that certain underlying structures may (unconsciously) shape people's behaviors in ways beyond that which they find consciously meaningful. While the interpretivists (e.g., Mead, Blumer, Schutz, and Berger and Luckmann) have been cognizant of people's preexisting (community-based) stocks of knowledge and their tendencies to "take things for granted," they have concentrated on the ways in which people attend to situations in more direct, actor-meaningful senses. Giddens has been more speculative in other ways as well. In the style of many classical theorists, Giddens has embarked on some rather sweeping statements regarding the human condition. Somewhat in this same regard, Giddens appears inclined, at times, to fashion himself as a "social critic." In both instances, he tends to slip into looser (objectivist and) structuralist (vs. structurationist) stances. Like Goffman, Giddens's hermeneutically informed work has intrigued many in the sociological community, but to date it has been insufficiently rigorous at both a theoretical and methodological level to generate a viable base on which to develop an intersubjective social science.

The New (Constructionist) Sociology of Science

Sociologists became introduced to the "sociology of science" largely through the efforts of Robert Merton (1957, 1973), but the (new) sociology of science took some different and very important directions, deriving particular inspiration from Thomas Kuhn (1962) and Harold Garfinkel (1967).[22]

Although Merton encouraged sociologists to view science as a community endeavor, his work maintained a strong functionalist cast. He viewed science as another "institution" in society and as such was interested in the ways in which science impacted upon and was affected by other institutions (e.g., religious, political, economic) in society. Merton recognized that science entailed communication, reward systems, and properties (knowledge as property), as well as some struggles for legitimacy, but he felt that scientific knowledge would be generated by adherence to (what he envisioned as) the norms of the scientific community: openness, skepticism, rigorous training, rationality. Merton viewed science as a progressive, systematic accumulation of theory and facts through the practices of scientists.

Interestingly, Merton (1957:472, 480) is critical of Durkheim for not adapting a relativist viewpoint, but it is not apparent that Merton fully accepts a relativist or social constructionist perspective himself. Although Merton argues that scientific pursuits and practices reflect the "social structures" (cultural historical contexts and normative frameworks) within which people operate, his analysis does not go very far in depicting *how* science is produced or challenged. Merton (1957:537) states that "changes in institutional structures may curtail, modify, or possibly prevent the pursuit of science." However, he tends to homogenize or modalize both social structure and human behavior in his analyses with respect to cultural-historical frames and scientific activity.[23] That is, while Merton uses some specific cases of scientific inquiry to illustrate aspects of his analysis, his approach maintains a level of generality that fails to appreciate the *human enterprise* (reflectivity and interaction) involved in the ongoing production (or demise) of scientific endeavors.[24]

Thomas Kuhn, who developed an interest in the history of science while studying physics, emerges as a central figure in the new sociology of science. Although he does not appear familiar with Dilthey, Mead, or Blumer, or with Schutz, Berger and Luckmann, or Garfinkel, Kuhn rather dramatically drew the attention of the academic community to the relativistic and negotiable aspects of science. Envisioning science as a social process characterized by ambiguity, multiple perspectives, human initiatives and resourcefulness, and ongoing sets of interchanges, Kuhn's portrayal of the scientific community in action is highly consistent with the images of social life generated by those working in the interpretive tradition. Science, thus, represents a cultural-political arena involving competing perspectives and interests, influences and resistances.[25]

Kuhn contends that whenever a particular viewpoint or paradigm becomes established or widely accepted in a scientific community, it will become the focus of scientific enterprise or the frame around which research is proposed, conducted, and evaluated. However, when new paradigms are introduced (typically as solutions to problems that existing paradigms were unable to resolve), these alternative viewpoints generally pose threats to those who have organized their routines around the earlier paradigms and the new paradigms may be subject to much (potentially intense) resistance as a result. Paradigm revolutions are not simply matters of novelty or innovation. Indeed, considerable novelty may be readily incorporated into an existing paradigm, and innovations may be sought intensively. However, more sweeping challenges (at the level of basic assumptions) to particular realms of knowledge are more difficult for the practitioners to reconcile. Thus, science is envisioned as another negotiable realm of human enterprise; as a sociopolitical battlefield of sorts involving potentially conflicting perspectives, interest groups, and the like.

Most scientific inquiry involves "normal science" (research that is conducted within a particular paradigm that is considered legitimate at the time), but considerable upheaval may result by the introduction of new paradigms. Although their acceptance is problematic, new or alternative paradigms threaten to throw existing "normal science" into states of disarray or obscurity. Some paradigm struggles have become very well known, such as those pertaining to the Copernican, Newtonian, Darwinian, or Einsteinian revolutions in science. But other, lesser known conceptual and methodological paradigms have very significantly challenged (sometimes successfully) particular subsections of the larger scientific communities. Thus, science is no longer envisioned as a natural, logical cumulative process. Science is seen as a community product and process, which involves an ongoing set of conflicts and negotiations, punctuated by extended but uneven periods of "normal science" (wherein objectivity seems apparent or more readily taken for granted).

Given other developments in the interpretive tradition in the 1960s (Schutz, Berger and Luckmann, Garfinkel), Kuhn's statement appeared at a most opportune time. Since the 1960s historians, philosophers, and sociologists have become increasingly interested in this realm of human enterprise, viewing it as vital to an understanding of knowledge in society. Still, many sociologists and other social scientists have only the most fleeting of familiarities with the new sociology of science.

Building most centrally on the writings of Thomas Kuhn (1962) and Harold Garfinkel (1967), the sociologists most active in developing the new (or post-Mertonian) sociology of science include Barnes (1974), Mulkay (1979), Brannigan (1981), Barnes and Edge (1982), Knorr-Cetina (1981, 1983), Collins and Pinch (1982), Latour (1987), Pickering (1990, 1992, 1993, 1994), and Pinch and Collins (1994). This literature is fundamentally consistent with the tenets of Chicago-style symbolic interaction (Blumer, 1969) and the social constructionism of Schutz (1962, 1964) and Berger and Luckmann (1966), but those working in the sociology of science have not been particularly attentive to the value of these materials. Focusing on the ways in which people make sense of the world, including the taken-for-granted, problematic, and negotiable aspects of human interchange, Garfinkel's work on ethnomethodology (particularly his emphasis on activity as practical accomplishment) has lent itself to some investigations of the ways in which people "do" science. Although researchers who embarked on work in this area could have more easily and productively adopted Chicago-style ethnography as a base, it is not apparent that they were especially familiar with this tradition. Further, despite the exceptionally rich research sites for inquiry that the "physical sciences" represent for Chicago-style interactionism, only recently have some interactionists become more explicitly involved in the study of science as intersubjective accomplishment (see Star, 1989; Clarke and Gerson, 1990; Clarke and Fujimura, 1992; Dawson and Campbell, 1994).

Scholars working in the new sociology of science readily accept (and extend) the enterprise that Merton associates with science. Likewise, they tend to acknowledge the accomplishments that may be achieved by a community of scholars focusing on, investigating, dissecting, assessing, and accumulating information about some phenomenon. However, Kuhn and others working in this tradition are much more attentive to the relativistic and *intersubjective* nature of scientific inquiry than those working in a Mertonian tradition. Those in the new sociology of science are much more attuned to the problematic, reflective, and negotiated features of the human enterprise that underlie the conceptions, methodological practices, and legitimacy of any "scientific" pursuit.

Instead of envisioning an invariant, objective world to be discovered by scientific enterprise, the new sociology of science approach posits that people may assume any variety of orientations toward the world out there, but that each viewpoint is subject to (and may be the focus of a struggle for) intersubjective acceptance. As well, each viewpoint implies a certain type of methodology which, in turn, tends to define not only the nature of reality to be encountered, but also notions of what constitutes significant resistances in the pursuit of this or that image of science. Further, while particular notions of science may become established in any number of ways, scholars who have been organizing their lives (routines and prestige, funding and publication, images and persona) around particular notions of science are apt to be more reluctant to entertain conceptions of science that they envision to interfere with aspects of their current routines. Thus, the study of the processes of influence and resistance becomes central in this realm of human enterprise as well.

The constructionist sociology of science views *science as both a social product and a social process*. If one adopts this viewpoint, the term "science" might be applied to any set of sustained, intensified inquiries into some realm of human awareness. This is not to imply that all realms of "scientific inquiry" are equally valid or productive, for indeed that claim presupposes a fixed reference point. Rather, notions of "science" are judged by reference to particular cultural contexts. Scientific wisdom, thus, is defined by the members of the particular communities in which these pursuits are noted and assessed relative to the bodies of knowledge prevailing at that point in time. Thus, conceptions of "science" will differ from community to community and within communities over time. While existing definitions of science may be used to legitimate or objectify other viewpoints that members of the community wish to establish with respect to others, notions of science are themselves subject to ongoing legitimation or objectification processes within those same communities.

That is, matters of what constitutes "science," how "scientific inquiry" is conducted, and what is recognized as significant information or "scientific fact and evidence" reflect the versions of knowledge that prevail in particular time-cultural contexts. This is not to deny the accomplishments that people have made using particular perspectives and invoking corresponding modes of inquiry and analyses. However, by examining the ways in which "scientific enterprise" takes its shape, the new sociology of science illustrates the centrality of multiple realities (or a plurality of diverse perspectives, including multiple and possibly conflicting views of science), human reflectivity, and the intersubjective nature of *all* forms of knowing.

While Kuhn and other scholars working in the history of science have been focusing on struggles around the intellectual and technical developments in the physical sciences in the past, the interpretive sociologists studying science have been investigating the ways in which "science is accomplished in the here and now." In both cases, the materials they have generated attest to the problematic, reflective, negotiable nature of scientific enterprise. Thus, we have become much more cognizant of the fundamentally socially constituted nature of scientific enterprise. Although researchers and theorists in the natural sciences deal with phenomena that lack the interpretive, interactive essences of human beings, all "scientists" are human beings and, consequently, cannot be understood apart from the [intersubjective] communities in which they themselves operate.

Like developments in dramaturgical analysis, labeling theory, phenomenological sociology, and structuration theory, much of the work in the new sociology of science is readily compatible with the basic features of Chicago-style (Mead, Blumer) symbolic interaction. Taken together, these realms of scholarly pursuit emphasize the necessity of attending to the reflective, intersubjective essence of human lived experience and of utilizing a methodology that focuses on the ways in which people go about (socially) constructing their behaviors (and life-styles) on a day-to-day basis. There are differences in emphasis among scholars working with these variations of the interpretive tradition, but an appreciation of their commonalities and conceptual contributions provides a most valuable framework for approaching ethnographic research; for it is here that social scientists can most directly examine the ways in which people manage their life-worlds in conjunction with others in the "here and now" of human existence.

As readers approach the next chapter, "The Ethnographic Research Tradition," more of the links between theory and research in the study of human lived experience will become apparent, as will the contributions of yet others who have helped shape an intersubjective social science.

NOTES

1. Some might also be inclined to include postmodernism (poststructuralism, deconstructionism) in their conceptions of the interpretive tradition, but the two approaches (postmodernist and interpretivist), as indicated in

chapters 7 and 8 in this volume, require much more conceptual elaboration and disentanglement than is appropriate at this point.

2. Beyond reading Blumer's (most impressive) dissertation, readers may also appreciate Hammersley's (1989:137–146) condensed discussion of Blumer's thesis. While Hammersley (1989:206) remains wedded to the hypothetical-deductive model of science and this obscures his assessments of naturalistic inquiry, pages 113–154 are especially valuable.

3. Like Mead, Cooley, and others working in the pragmatist tradition, Blumer's documentation is less precise than one might have hoped. But Anselm Strauss and Roy Turner, who attended the University of Chicago and the University of California–Berkeley, respectively, both indicated (in personal communications) that Blumer was familiar with some of Dilthey's work (presumably in German). Perhaps most telling was Roy Turner's observation that when he was preparing for his Ph.D. theory comprehensive exam, Blumer asked if he had read Dilthey. Roy said that he hadn't. Blumer then asked about Rickert. No, Roy hadn't read Rickert either. "Well," Blumer retorted, "What are they teaching in theory these days!"

4. Readers should refer to Blumer (1969: 1–60, especially 50–60) for a more sustained, albeit more general, critique of the ways in which human group life is misconstrued in conventional social science.

5. As well, because of the recent attention given to "postmodernism" (post-structuralism, deconstructionism), some consideration (chapters 7 and 8) is given to this viewpoint, which is sometimes alleged to fall within the broader interpretive frame.

6. Only some of these attacks appeared in print (as with the McPhail and Rexroat [1979, 1980] interchange with Blumer [1980]), but were and continue to be evident in classroom and conference settings.

7. The biggest differences between the two schools appear to be methodological; conceptually, there is much more affinity. Thus, interestingly, and somewhat ironically, one of Manford Kuhn's most significant contributions to the discipline is represented by his (1954) critique of the Kinsey studies of sexuality. Here, Kuhn develops a consequential statement on gender and sexuality that is clearly interactionist in a Meadian (and Blumerian) sense.

In another rather ironic twist, Carl Couch (1968) presents an important critique of some of Blumer's earlier writings on collective behavior. Blumer's early work in this area was much more influenced by his contact with Thomas and Park than Mead, and these writings are not particularly consistent with his later statements on symbolic interaction. Couch's criticisms, interestingly, are more typical of Blumer's fundamental position.

8. Maines (1986) provides another overview of the Iowa school and his sense of its direction over the years.

9. For another account of the contemporary Iowa and (traditional, more enduring) Chicago styles of scholarship, see Buban (1986). While Molseed (1994) has continued to proclaim the viability of video recordings as sources of data (in the absence of participant-generated interpretation of the events under scrutiny), some other Iowa scholars who worked closely with Carl Couch (e.g., Stan Saxton, Danny Miller, and Mike Katovich) have become more attentive to interpretive concerns and Chicago-style ethnography.

10. For other statements that discuss Goffman's work with respect to symbolic interaction, see Blumer (1972); Laurer and Handel (1977); Meltzer, Petras, and Reynolds (1978); and Reynolds (1993).

11. One may also note some affinities of Goffman's work and Durkheim's notions of community life and ritual propriety. This seems largely attributable to Goffman's exposure to the works of the (functionalist) anthropologist, A. R. Radcliff-Brown (1958).

12. For other interpretations of Goffman's work, readers are referred to Ditton (1980) and especially the writings of Lofland, Manning, and Brook and Taylor, therein; and Drew and Wooton, particularly the statements by Drew and Wooton, Kendon, Collins, Williams, and Giddens. As well, Lofland's (1984) commentary of Goffman is highly recommended.

13. The notion of the "cloak of competence" is especially pertinent here, as are the works of Edgerton (1967) and Haas and Shaffir (1987). Blumer's (1972) commentary on Goffman's (1971) book, *Relations in Public*, is also relevant in this sense.

14. The notion of deviance as a community phenomenon is evident to some extent in most ethnographic depictions of subcultural practices. However, it may be most striking in Anderson (1923), Cressey (1932), Lofland (1966), Wiseman (1970), Prus and Irini (1980), and Evans and Falk (1986), since these studies establish the interlinkages of various subcultures within the broader community in ways that many other ethnographies do not.

15. Although Lemert does not use the term "secondary deviation" in his (1962) analysis of "paranoia and the dynamics of exclusion," this remains one of the very best illustrations of both labeling theory and the dynamics of human interchange.

16. See Cressey (1932), Sutherland (1950), Gusfield (1955, 1963), and Lindesmith (1959) for some other instances of morality campaigns. Readers interested in the social construction of social problems may also wish to examine Gusfield (1981, 1984, 1989) and Best (1989, 1990).

17. For an elaboration of the "career contingencies" concept and the processes (initial involvements, continuities, disinvolvements and reinvolvements) subsumed by this notion, see chapter 5.

18. Merton's (1957:439–502) discussion indicates some of the limitations of the previous variants of sociology of knowledge derived from Marx, Durkheim, Scheler, Mannheim, and Sorokin. To achieve conceptual integrity, a sociology of knowledge has to be able to deal with both the concept of multiple realities (i.e., the relativism of knowledge) and the objectification (of knowledge) process. By building on Schutz's work, Berger and Luckmann were able to deal with these issues by emphasizing the intersubjective (i.e., interactive, reflective, symbolic) nature of human community life.

19. Berger and Luckmann's work also appears instrumental in fostering a paradigm shift of sorts in psychology, in large part attributable to the scholarship of Kenneth Gergen (1982, 1985).

20. Readers may also wish to see Denzin (1969), Meltzer, Petras and Reynolds (1978), and Reynolds (1993) for other statements that locate Garfinkel's work within the context of symbolic interaction.

21. Clearly, I have "glossed over" Garfinkel's conceptual concerns and methodological practices. For a fuller appreciation of these, see Mehan and Wood (1975). For a particularly succinct formulation of ethnomethodology and its linkages to phenomenological sociology, readers are referred to Zimmerman (1978).

22. The term, "sociology of science" may seem odd, given Kuhn's interest in the "history of science," but Kuhn and several others working in the history of science very much view science as a social product and a social process; an instance of human lived experience.

23. Rather ironically, Merton (1957:445) accuses Weber of this same tendency. Although Merton is more relativistic in his overall approach than was Weber, their tendencies to cling to positivist (causal, structuralist) images of community life prevented them from more fully acknowledging a social constructionist viewpoint.

24. For work reflecting a Mertonian sociology of science, see Cole and Cole (1973), Zuckerman (1988), and Cole (1992).

25. The core ideas with which Kuhn works had been developed in a much-neglected volume by the German scholar Ludwig Fleck (1935). Although direct linkages of influence are not apparent, Fleck's work is quite consistent with the general thrust of intersubjectivity and knowledge of which Wilhelm Dilthey spoke.

4

THE ETHNOGRAPHIC RESEARCH TRADITION

Encountering the Other

Ethnographic research (also "field research," "naturalistic inquiry," "qualitative research," "interactionist research," "Chicago school research," and "participant observation") refers to *the study of the way of life of a group of people.*[1] Although one may find some descriptions of people's life-styles in a variety of documents, including journalistic accounts, autobiographies, diaries, letters, and the like, contemporary ethnography relies primarily on the methods of observation, participant-observation, and open-ended interviews. As well, ethnographers assume the task of achieving intersubjective understandings of the people participating in the settings under consideration. Ethnographic inquiry requires that researchers pursue and present the viewpoints of those with whom they have contact. Thus, ethnographers strive for intimate familiarity with the lived experiences of those they study and they attempt to convey as fully as possible the viewpoints and practices of these people to others.

Whereas the images that most laypeople have of ethnographers likely involves anthropologists heading off to exotic lands to study "the natives" there, naturalistic inquiry is by no means limited to anthropological ventures. Ethnographic research also took early root in the Chicago school of sociology and has been most systematically developed as an interpretive tradition by the symbolic interactionists.

To put ethnographic research in perspective, it is important to first consider some of the historical and anthropological dimensions of field research and related attempts to depict people's life-styles. Following an overview of the historical and anthropological roots of ethnographic research, this chapter focuses on the development of ethnographic research in sociology at the University of Chicago and the roles that those central to this tradition played in its development. Hopefully, this background material will in enable students to appreciate the context in which this community of scholars toiled in their attempts to come to terms with the study of human lived experience.

Historical and Anthropological Dimensions
of Ethnographic Research

In providing a historical overview of the development of ethnographic research, Rosalie Wax (1971:21–41) indicates that the descriptive reporting of cultural life-styles (particularly those people encountered in travels to foreign settings) is almost as old as recorded history.[2] Thus, early impressions of observers of foreign cultures are provided by travellers among the Greeks (fifth century B.C.), the Romans (first century A.D.), and the Chinese (fifth century A.D.). Records also exist of the accounts of Catholic missionaries as well as of other European travellers and traders (including Marco Polo), dating back to the thirteenth century.

Vidich and Lyman (1994) observe that a certain amount of interest in developing an understanding of the life-worlds of the other was fostered from the fifteenth century onward through European contacts with other societies. These included curiosities about tracing the development of the human species, attempts on the part of missionaries to establish converts among "native" populations,[3] and concerns about more effectively implementing the colonization process. These interests appear somewhat haphazard, however, and did not develop into a sustained tradition of any sort.[4]

A noteworthy precursor to ethnographic inquiry was developed in nineteenth century ethnology. Although "ethnology" and "ethnography" are sometimes used interchangeably, the term ethnology is the broader concept (Radcliffe-Brown, 1958:133–135). Ethnology encompasses both the prehistorical and contemporary study of ethnic classifications, language, and living conditions of peoples. Whereas ethnographers concentrate on developing accounts of people's lived experiences derived through interaction with their contemporaries, ethnologists have grounded their work in prehistoric archaeology and images of prehistoric cultures as well as physical anthropology, linguistics, folklore and any other themes thought pertinent to the evolution of people and their cultures.[5] However, despite a pronounced interest in foreign cultures on the part of some nineteenth-century anthropologists (ethnologists), these scholars contributed little to the development of ethnographic inquiry.[6]

Typically, the ethnologists of the nineteenth century studied the accounts of missionaries and other travellers and built their careers around the analysis of these materials. Still, some of these ethnologists assumed a more active role in pursuing information by using contacts with people living in the field as a means of learning more about these cultures (see Evans-Pritchard, 1951:70–73; Urry, 1984:36–40). Thus, ethnologists might send lists of questions in their correspondence with "friends in the field," asking them to comment on these matters from their knowledge of the natives. Indeed, this practice became so institutionalized that some sets of questions were published in *Notes and Queries on Anthropology* (1874).[7] While many of the accounts so gathered were of minimal worth because of communication and comprehension problems, some of these materials are considered quite valuable. These statements were also extremely important for indicating the richness and depth of what had been earlier viewed (and dismissed) as "primitive culture" or "savage life." However, the idea of ethnologists, themselves, actually venturing directly into the field seemed almost unfathomable at the time:

> *It is indeed surprising that, with the exception of Morgan's [1851] study of the Iroquois, not a single anthropologist conducted field studies till the end of the nineteenth century. It is even more remarkable that it does not seem to have occurred to them that a writer on anthropological topics might at least have a look, if only a glimpse, at one or two specimens of what he spent his life writing about. (Evans-Pritchard, 1951:71–72)*

While it is difficult to say just who was the first person to conduct an ethnographic field study, Lewis Henry Morgan (1818–1881) is generally credited (as Evans-Pritchard claims above) with this distinction.[8] Some other accounts of American Indian life (either through the Bureau of Indian Affairs or in conjunction with the Smithsonian Institute) which were generated prior to or about the same era as Morgan's works (see Schoolcraft, 1851; Bieder, 1986; Vidich and Lyman, 1994), but Morgan's efforts were more clearly ethnographic in their thrust.

A lawyer by trade, Morgan and some of his academically inclined western New York associates established the "Grand Order of the Iroquois," a fraternal organization that was concerned about improving the image of American Indians by generating a greater awareness of their customs and character. While members of the group visited local reservations in the area and jointly sustained their enthusiasm for this venture within the order, Morgan emerged as the most dedicated "amateur" in the group and pursued this objective rather extensively. In developing the material on the Iroquois, Morgan was centrally assisted by

Ely Parker (an English-educated Iroquois) who served as an interpreter, observer, informant, and general resource person. Morgan's work was characterized by strong interests in lineage linkages of American Indians with other peoples, and property rights within tribal customs; but his descriptions were considerably more encompassing than this. Although his theories of evolutionary culture have been largely discounted, Morgan travelled fairly extensively in the Midwest and produced some valuable journal materials pertaining to Indian customs (see Morgan, 1959).

Insofar as he was instrumental in establishing a more sustained tradition of scholarship around ethnographic inquiry than was true of most of his predecessors, Franz Boas (1858–1942) is often considered the founder of modern (cultural) anthropology (Herkovitz, 1953; Stocking, 1974). Trained as a physicist and geographer, Boas began his field work with the Eskimo of Baffin Island during some geographical expeditions in the 1880s, but ended up focusing on their life-styles and cultural traditions (folklore). Best known for his work on North American Indians, Boas argued for the necessity of developing texts of native experiences and interpreting their practices within the cultural contexts in which they were situated. Consistent with those working in "folk psychology" (Wundt, 1916; Lindgren, 1939), Boas seems particularly attentive to folklore and native texts; but his work spanned a wide range of fields in anthropology.

While attentive to some aspects of the interpretive paradigm, Boas lacked a well-developed appreciation of the intersubjective nature of human behavior (e.g., consider Mead's statement on the interlinkages of mind, self, and society) and appears to have been at something of a conceptual loss regarding the ways in which to approach the data he and others collected. As well, most of the inquiries conducted by Boas and his students (perhaps the most notable of whom included Ruth Benedict, Robert Lowie, A. L. Kroeber, and Margaret Mead) were rather fleeting, as they attempted to record accounts derived from native informants in very short time spans. They relied extensively on the interpreters they located in each setting and spent very little time learning the local languages or participating in the life-styles of those being studied. It is important to note, as well, that these researchers provided little in the way of methodological instruction for those who would follow:

Only a few of the American ethnographers who were students of Boas or worked in Boas's tradition have told us anything about how they did their fieldwork. Robert H. Lowie (1959) completed an interesting autobiography shortly before his death. His account of his difficult and not very successful first field experience (pp. 4–14) helps us appreciate why he and his fellow students, anxious to be recognized as professionals, were not eager to publish blow-by-blow accounts of their experiences. (Wax, 1971:34)

Kroeber and Lowie never said anything about their own fieldwork in the classes or the seminars I attended from 1939 to 1942. (Wax, 1971:35)

Although Boas and his associates appear to have given much more attention to the study of folklore and linguistics than to the details of field research methodology, the style of inquiry they initiated dominated American anthropology (both conceptually and methodologically) until the 1930s when anthropology became more mixed with the British functionalist tradition represented by A. R. Radcliffe-Brown and Bronislaw Malinowski.[9]

Some other early field investigations were initiated in the late 1890s and early 1900s by the British anthropologists (most notably A. R. Radcliffe-Brown). However, as Wax (1971) observes, their funds for such work were meagre and their trips were conducted in haste. Thus, little time was spent observing the groups being studied, communicating with the people, or participating in their routines on a day-to-day basis. In contrast to the cultural-interpretive frame assumed by Boas, these British anthropologists were very much influenced by the positivist, structural-functionalist, and evolutionary theories of Montesquieu, Saint-Simon, Comte, Durkheim, and Spencer (see Evans-Pritchard, 1951:21–42). They envisioned society in terms of a biological or organic analogy, and were concerned with structural differentiation, system interdependency, and organic evolution. Focusing on the ways in which community life contributed to the maintenance of the functioning or structure of the society being considered, they were not especially concerned about grounding their inquiries within the human lived experiences of peoples in this or that cultural context, but rather concentrated on the organic functioning of societies.

Working with a version of the functionalist paradigm, Bronislaw Malinowski (1884–1942) emerges as an extremely consequential figure in the development and popularization of ethnographic inquiry. In a series of three trips to the Trobriand Islands between 1914 and 1918, the British-trained Malinowski (1922) established himself as the first anthropologist ethnographer to maintain any sort of sustained contact with the population being studied. Malinowski's own participant-observer involvements in this setting seem to have been rather uneven at best and his interviewing appears to have been minimal,[10] but he was especially successful in encouraging other anthropologists to embark on more prolonged excursions into distant communities.

To his credit, Malinowski (1922) introduces his discussion of "native enterprise and adventure in the Archilogica of Melanesian New Guina" with a consideration of fieldwork methodology. This statement does not adequately depict the actualities of Malinowski's own experiences, but it provides valuable insight on how one might go about conducting ethnographic research. Perhaps more consequential, however, is Malinowski's discussion of the final goal of ethnographic research. After encouraging anthropologists in the field to focus on: (a) the organization of the tribe and the anatomy of its culture, (b) the practices that make up the round of everyday life, and (c) the folklore and other indications of native mentality, Malinowski (1922:25) concludes:

> *These three lines of approach lead to the final goal, of which an Ethnographer should never lose sight. This goal is, briefly, to grasp the native's point of view, his relation to life, to realise his vision of his world. We have to study man, and we must study what concerns him most intimately, that is, the hold which life has on him. . . . To study the institutions, customs, and codes or to study the behaviour and mentality without the subjective desire of feeling by what these people live, of realising the substance of their happiness—is, in my opinion, to miss the greatest reward which we can hope to obtain from the study of man.*

Although the ventures of these early researchers (e.g. Boas, Radcliffe-Brown, Malinowski) were crucial in establishing an ethnographic tradition in anthropology, neither they nor those who immediately followed their examples contributed much in the way of a methodological legacy:

> *Only a few of these highly trained and experienced fieldworkers have told us anything about their experiences or methods. Among these the most notable are the writings of Evans-Pritchard, who in 1940 published a brief but brilliant description of the difficulties he experienced doing fieldwork among the Nuer of Africa in the 1930s. (Wax, 1971:37)*

Discussions of methodological issues in anthropology have been complicated not only by the mystique (fascinations) associated with foreign cultures, but also by the very mixed approaches (e.g., structural-functionalism, folklore pursuits, cultural analysis, cultural configuration, Freudian analysis, exchange theory, linguistic analysis, and physical [characteristics, lineages] anthropology) these researchers have adopted. Thus, the most significant methodological contribution of these early ethnographers may have been that of generating enthusiasm for ethnographic ventures into other societies.

Anthropologist ethnographers have made important contributions to research methodology; yet despite the extensive amount of fieldwork conducted by anthropologists in the first half of the twentieth century, it is only since the 1940s (see Richards, 1939; Kluckhohn 1940; Bennett, 1948; Paul, 1953; Henry and Sablerwal, 1969; Freilich, 1970; Ellen, 1984) that one begins to find fuller discussions of fieldwork methodology and the practical and conceptual problems encountered while doing ethnographic inquiry.

Edgerton and Langness (1974:2–5) identify three principles that lie at the heart of contemporary anthropological ethnographic inquiry. The first of these is an emphasis on "participant observation" methodology, reflecting the concern that ethnographers live intimately in the societies selected for study (i.e., share in the day-to-day activities of those people in a manner akin to the participants in that setting). Secondly, there is the recognition that the culture being examined should be considered from the viewpoint of those (people) whose life-styles are being studied. The third dictum is that of holism: that human conduct be contextualized by reference to the setting in which it naturally occurs. Mindful of this point, Edgerton and Langness also make explicit the view that anthropologists should behave in manners such that their own presence has as little influence as possible on the behaviors of those being studied. While individual anthropologists are apt to have somewhat diverse regard for these and other notions of ethnographic inquiry, the concerns expressed by Edgerton and Langness reflect many of the more common perceptions that anthropologists hold with respect to field research.

Paul (1953),[11] Wax (1971), Edgerton and Langness (1974) and Ellen (1984), amongst others, provide valuable statements on how one might go about doing field research in other cultural contexts. What is most striking in these statements, however, is a much fuller appreciation of the difficulties anthropologists are apt to encounter at all stages in the research process (entering the field; communicating with the people; developing comprehension of local perspectives and practices; developing concepts; collecting data; exiting; writing up the analysis, etc.) as a consequence of working in other cultural contexts. Thus, we become more aware of the ways in which matters of interpretation become problematic at *every* point in the research process.

Given the wide range of viewpoints characterizing ethnographic research within the anthropological community, it is not at all apparent how far anthropologists as a group will pursue an interpretive theory of human group life (along the lines of George Herbert Mead and Herbert Blumer, for instance) but they appear to be moving in this direction.[12] At present, however, relatively little of the vast array of anthropological field research focuses directly on social process and human lived experience. As a consequence, it is much more difficult than outsiders may suspect to find material on other societies which is directly comparable to the analysis of human lived experience developed in sociological field research in western societies.

Although cross-cultural comparisons are often touted as highly desirable among scholars in the anthropological community, these comparisons presume that compatible materials are available for the aspects of group life being considered. Anthropologists often work with rather idiosyncratic conceptual notions that do not readily lend themselves to comparisons on a culture to culture basis, and they have made many fewer comparisons of social processes between "foreign cultures" and their own societies than one might expect. This is not to deny the considerable enterprise that has gone into developing the Human Relations Area Files (or the earlier Yale Human Relations Files) that have had the explicit intention of facilitating cross-cultural comparisons. However, the codes employed are largely structural-functionalist and psycho-analytic in nature and are intended to encourage statistical comparisons. There is relatively little appreciation of an interpretive, interactive emphasis on process in this compilation. Viewed in this manner, one might observe that the anthropological community has not developed a set of concepts conducive to the study and comparison of social processes. James Spradley (1979) and Victor Turner (1985) appear to have been moving in this direction, but a great deal of conceptual and ethnographic work remains before this can become a viable option.

The tasks of being accepted (initially and over time) and learning the local language and practices of the (foreign to the researcher) community being studied can be extremely demanding undertakings. There are so many substantive facets of any society (e.g., work, religion, family, deviance, education, recreation) to which researchers could attend that ventures into any society tend to be somewhat overwhelming in this respect as well. Thus, there is a tendency, even where undesired by the researcher, toward expressions of "cultural exclusivity," whereby accounts of practices in the setting are deemed so unique and holistic as to preclude comparisons. This is further reflected in the tendency on the part of researchers to become experts in regional settings (e.g., Oceania, Arctic, American plains Indians), thereby focusing in an extended manner on the life-styles of particular peoples without giving much consideration to parallel social processes in other settings.[13]

Perhaps no less fundamentally, ethnographers in anthropology have not been explicitly encouraged to envision group life as ongoing accomplishment. Thus, lacking a set of more explicit, process-oriented concepts of the sort developed in symbolic interaction, anthropologists have not been making sustained inquiries or developing data more precisely in processual terms. As well, anthropological field researchers are generally not very familiar with (inter-actionist) ethnographic research conducted in their home societies. Overall they have tended to ignore this material; yet it is in this literature that the most precise, processually oriented ethnographic research and conceptual development has taken place. As a result, and despite the immense and sometimes life-risking efforts anthropologists have put into ethnographic research in foreign cultures, one learns relatively little about the ways in which human group life is accom-plished by those in other settings on a day-to-day basis. And we have even less material with which to work in developing precise, more extended com-parisons.

At present, anthropological inquiry seems beset by a number of obstacles. As indicated already, the field is very mixed both conceptually and metho-dologically. Field research has tended to be both rather idiosyncratic and regionally focused. Although some anthropological field work could be synthesized with symbolic interaction, anthropological ethnographers generally have not achieved (or adopted) an intersubjective theory of the sort developed by Herbert Blumer and the interactionists. Typically, as well, the anthropologists have not been attentive to a processually informed methodological and con-ceptual approach. As a result, much of the earlier anthropological work has not been as viable as it might have been, and unless subsequent work is more attentive to the intersubjective features of human lived experience, it too will be weakened.

A second but related challenge facing anthropological ethnographers pertains to the adequacy of their "representations of the other." The issue, of course, is far from new. Indeed, there have been long-standing internal criticisms and debates regarding the integrity of earlier anthropological ventures and practices (e.g., consider Radin's [1933] criticisms of Frans Boas, Margaret Mead, and others). However, the mixed and erratic agendas, conceptual orientations, metho-dological practices, and presentational styles characterizing the anthropological literature have made it vulnerable to "postmodernist criticisms" (e.g., Clifford, 1983; Clifford and Marcus, 1986).[14] Lacking a more coherent, intersubjectively informed theoretical and methodological position, some anthropologists have been quick to question the viability of the ethnographic venture, wondering if researchers have anything worthwhile to convey to their readers concerning their contact with the ethnographic other. While the postmodernist critique may well give anthropologists cause to reflect on their epistemological foun-dations and fieldwork practices, it is hoped that the anthropologists will not return to the styles of the nineteenth century ethnologists who seemed generally willing to conjecture about the other while having minimal or no actual contact with those of whom they spoke. Indeed, this very criticism may well be launched against the postmodernists who also engage in extended "learned discourse" about the other despite minimal contact with the other. In contrast to both the postmodernists and the nineteenth century ethnologists, contemporary anthropologists need to make a case for the necessity of establishing "privilege of presence." At the same time, they will need to make more concerted (conceptually and methodologically informed) efforts to establish intersubjectivity with the other in open and sustained manners with fewer political agendas.

A third major problem exists for the anthropologist ethnographer. Through the forays of earlier anthropologists and other venturers (missionaries, colonists, traders, travellers) into other societies, it has become almost impossible to find cultural groupings who have not been exposed to influences of western nations. This means that unless anthropologists wish to spend their time attempting to reconstruct earlier anthropological accounts with "less tainted" populations, they will have to reorient their emphasis to variants of contemporary, "westernized" experiences and people's encounters and adjustments to cultural spillovers (including such things as urban life-styles, industrialization, assimilation processes, or even styles of cultural preservation and tourism endeavors). The greater worldwide trend toward language standardizations and multinational trade may make the anthropologists' task less demanding in some respects, but the new role of anthropological ethnographer would seem to call for someone who is able to more or less continuously appreciate the multiple (and shifting) realities to which those they study may attend while going about their routines. Should subsequent anthropological efforts more closely approximate those of the interactionist ethnographer, the willingness (and resourcefulness) of anthropological ethnographers to venture into more distant and diverse settings could add particularly vital lines of insight and conceptual refinement to the existing interactionist literature. These inquiries are apt to be especially valuable when they are more explicitly attentive to the interactionist literature and generic social processes of the type discussed in chapter 5.

Although many anthropological ethnographers seem likely to continue working in the more eclectic styles characterizing earlier fieldwork, we may also see more blending of anthropological and sociological inquiry. Whether these blendings will reflect interactionist notions or other analytical themes, of course, remains in question and may very much reflect the fads sweeping the social sciences more generally. It seems unlikely, however, that these ventures will achieve much long-term viability unless appreciations of intersubjectivity are built into every single phase of inquiry.

ETHNOGRAPHY AS A SOCIOLOGICAL VENTURE:
FIELD RESEARCH AT THE UNIVERSITY OF CHICAGO

Although it is often assumed that ethnographers in sociology expropriated the practices developed by anthropologists (perhaps as a consequence of the greater attention given to portrayals of exotic, foreign cultures in the mass media), the two traditions appear to have developed somewhat independently.[15] They are intertwined in some very important respects, to be sure, and W. I. Thomas who helped develop Chicago ethnography was highly cognizant of the field of ethnology and derived some initial inspiration from the work of Franz Boas in particular. As well, by being attentive to the cross-cultural forays of the anthropologists over the years, some sociologists have developed considerably sharper appreciations of human lived experience in western society. Likewise, some of the cross-cultural probes of the anthropologists have provided invaluable foundations for both legitimating the interpretive position assumed by sociologist ethnographers and challenging positivist versions of human behavior. Thus, for instance, anthropological notions of "cultural relativity" are consistent with the interpretive tradition (especially Mead and Blumer), which argues that objects do not have inherent meanings, that objects take on meanings as people act towards these objects, and that these meanings are products of ongoing human interaction. At the same time, however, it is important to recognize that ethnographic research in anthropology developed concurrently with that in sociology; the ethnographic tradition in sociology took root at a time in which very little ethnographic research had been conducted in anthropology and it developed in quite a different manner.

Since ethnographic research in sociology was very much a product of the scholars at the University of Chicago,[16] some consideration will be given to the sociology department as it was constituted in the early years of its existence (1892–1925) and to the faculty who were present at that time. Especially consequential here are the roles that Albion Small, W. I. Thomas, Robert Park, Ernest Burgess, and Ellsworth Faris played in fostering the ethnographic tradition on which Herbert Blumer, Everett Hughes, and others would build.

Early Chicago sociology consisted of a series of intellectual crosscurrents, which ranged from theories of instincts and moral reform, to evolutionary theory and organic functionalist models, to ecological arrangements and city mapping, to the sociology of Georg Simmel and the social psychology of George Herbert Mead. Methodologically, Chicago sociology was also almost as multifaceted as the discipline itself. While George Herbert Mead (philosophy), Ellsworth Faris, and Herbert Blumer maintained a fairly sharp and consistent focus on the social essence of human group life, the other significant figures in the development of Chicago-style ethnography were more diffuse (eclectic) in their modes of analysis. Chicago sociology also assumed an outreaching dimension, such that the city itself was envisioned as a major realm of investigation. Still, no one seems to have anticipated that ethnographic/interactionist research would become established as a major theme in the discipline and become the vital legacy of the Chicago school of sociology.

Albion Small: Organizer and Facilitator

As both the chair of the department of sociology (1892–1925) during its formative stages and as the founder (in 1895) and the chief editor for thirty years of the *American Journal of Sociology*, Albion Small (1854–1926) was in a position to wield considerable influence over the direction of American sociology. However, while he encouraged the pursuit of sociology as an empirical and process-oriented science, Small's major contributions largely reflect his role as an organizer and facilitator rather than a theorist or researcher of note.

Influenced by his earlier contact with Georg Simmel in Germany, Small defined the subject matter of sociology as "the process of human association." Still, Small also envisioned sociology as providing both a synthesis of the social sciences and the means of pursuing the improvement of society through greater social control. Small was instrumental in introducing the works of Simmel and other German social theorists to American sociology, as well as in hiring a number of people who would subsequently forge new directions for the field, but his own work was very eclectic and characterized by themes of social reform to be pursued through education. Despite his lack of conceptual or substantive contribution to the field, Small helped build (and sustain) the stage on which the Chicago school of sociology was to flourish (see Faris, 1967; Matthews, 1977; Christakes, 1978; Bulmer, 1984; Kurtz, 1984).

William Isaac Thomas (and Florian Znaniecki): The Polish Peasant

By 1896, the sociology department at Chicago had four members: Albion Small, Charles Henderson, George E. Vincent, and W. I. Thomas. Like Small, these scholars tended to be rather diffuse in their conceptual approaches to the field, but all were interested in improving social conditions through sociological inquiry. Henderson, who also served as university chaplin and was very much concerned with social reform and city life, died in 1915, leaving little in the way of a sociological legacy. The same was true for Vincent, who moved into senior management at the University of Minnesota in 1911 after having gravitated toward administration for a number of years at Chicago. Although it would be highly inaccurate to describe Thomas's approach as either integrated or systematic, W. I. Thomas (1863–1947) was to become a sociologist of considerable influence.[17]

Thomas had studied with Albion Small and Charles Henderson prior to pursuing graduate studies in Germany, where he had some exposure to "folk psychology" (Thomas, 1896) and the sociology of Georg Simmel.[18] Thomas also read extensively in the field of ethnology and was particularly attentive to the early works of Frans Boas and his associates. At Chicago, Thomas regularly taught the two anthropology courses that might be best defined as cultural anthropology. A scholar of wide-ranging interests, Thomas spent a considerable amount of time pursuing notions of human motivation and race psychology. However, it was his work on the Polish peasant, a project he began in 1908, that most singularly established his reputation as a scholar.

The Polish Peasant in Europe and America (1918, 1920) was a five-volume work, assembled by W. I. Thomas and Florian Znaniecki. They built their analysis of the social and personal disorganization associated with immigration primarily around letters, diaries, and other documents. The study was inspired, as Thomas recalls, in the following manner:

> *I may be oversimplifying, but I trace the origin of my interest in the document to a long letter picked up on a rainy day in the alley behind my house, a letter from a girl who was taking a training course in a hospital, to her father concerning family relationships and discords. It occurred to me at the time that one could learn a great deal if one had a great many letters of this kind. (Thomas in Baker, 1973:250)*

Organized around Thomas's preconceptions of the importance of values and attitudes for behavior, the study was not well conceptualized, conducted, or presented.[19] Nor is it at all clear that this massive document-based analysis would have been very worthwhile had Znaniecki (who Thomas hired to assist him) not been Polish and able to contextualize these materials accordingly (see Blumer's 1939 critique [and Thomas and Znaniecki's reply, enclosed therein]).[20]

Still, the study was groundbreaking and very important in other respects. The documents (and the one extended case-study Thomas and Znaniecki presented) needed to be interpreted within the context in which they had been developed to be sure, but at the same time, they provided much more insight into the human lived experience surrounding immigration than that which had been gained in any quantitative investigation in the area. Consequently, and despite its weaknesses, this study helped define Chicago as a center for a new kind of research. The study was cast in terms of attitudes and values, and focused on personal and social disorganization rather than activity and relationships, but the documents and case study presented contained some highly compelling accounts of people's lived experiences. Thus, while Thomas and Znaniecki's conceptual messages were not well formulated, the materials they collected not only suggested the socially constructed or interactive and interpreted nature of human group life, but also encouraged further investigation along these lines.

Although Thomas left Chicago in 1918, the tradition he helped establish was to flourish, in larger part through the efforts of scholars Thomas had influenced; most centrally Robert Park and Ernest Burgess. Before considering the impact of Park and Burgess, however, it is important to recognize the contributions of George Herbert Mead (philosophy) and one of his early students, Ellsworth Faris.

George Herbert Mead: Symbolic Significances of the Human Group

Although located in the philosophy department, George Herbert Mead (1863–1931) provided much more conceptual clarity to the study of human group life for sociology students than any of the early Chicago sociologists. *Mind, Self and Society* was published posthumously in 1934, but many of the ideas presented there were developed much earlier (see Mead, 1904, 1906, 1909, 1910; Faris, 1937b). Not all sociology students took Mead's courses and not all of those who did would appreciate them. Still, Mead's theoretical frame was not only most compatible with the ethnographic tradition that was to develop at Chicago, but it provided (as Herbert Blumer would later emphasize) much of the conceptual foundation necessary for the study of human lived experience.

Far from reflecting a "subjectivist" or "psychological reductionist" approach, Mead's social psychology was fundamentally and thoroughly *intersubjective* in its essence. As Faris (1936) observes, *Mind, Self and Society* should have been entitled *Society, Mind and Self*, for Mead argued that one had to start with the recognition of society: that the mind and the self developed through interaction with the generalized other. Mead also insisted on a theory of society that recognized the human capacities for self-reflectivity, human agency, and linguistic interchange. For Mead, society was not an abstracted structure, but existed only when people interacted with one another in ways in which they found intersubjectively meaningful.

Beyond Mead's own contributions to the study of group life, two of his students also played vital roles in conveying and extending his notions of social behavior to others at Chicago and elsewhere. While Herbert Blumer (discussed later) was to play an exceedingly central role in the subsequent development of Mead's ideas (under the rubric of "symbolic interaction"), we should also recognize the contributions of Ellsworth Faris, another of Mead's students within the context of early Chicago sociology.

Ellsworth Faris: Ethnographer in the Shadows

Ellsworth Faris (1874–1953), who obtained his doctorate from Chicago in 1914, returned to Chicago in 1918 to fill the vacancy left by Thomas's departure. Faris's contributions were largely overshadowed by those of his higher profile colleagues (earlier by Park and Burgess, and later by Blumer). Still, a close reading of the literature indicates that Faris was a productive scholar and an influential instructor in his own right.

Although Faris published fairly extensively (as indicated by the collection of articles he assembled for his 1937a volume), some of his best work on activity may have been available only through his lectures (see Blumer, 1928:179–202). Nevertheless, Faris's (1937a:61–72) critiques of instinct theories were instrumental in helping free sociology from a set of motivational shackles that had earlier restricted the sociological potential of Small, Thomas, and others. As well, Faris's (1937a:262–288) criticisms of Spencer and Freud, using ethnographic data Faris had gathered during his residence of several years among the tribes of the Upper Congo River, likely deterred some scholars from being influenced by these theorists. As Blumer (1928:179–218) indicates, Faris, even more than Mead, was concerned about elaborating on "the social act." Faris encountered conceptual difficulties by attempting to incorporate into his analysis a great many of the psychological concepts that were popular at the time, but his attention to *social process* was to prove highly beneficial to those (including Blumer) who studied with him. Faris also taught a social psychology course viewed as an introduction to the more advanced course offered by George Herbert Mead[21] and was a valuable resource person for the ethnographic research tradition that was just emerging at Chicago.[22]

Robert Ezra Park and Ernest Burgess: Exploring the City

Prior to his departure from Chicago in 1918, W. I. Thomas established a strong friendship with Robert Park (1864–1944) and encouraged Park to join the department at Chicago in 1913.[23] Park had worked as a newspaper reporter before pursuing graduate studies in Germany. On his return, Park spent some time working as a public relations person and ghostwriter for Booker Washington, a then-prominent Negro (the term African-American was not in use at that time) spokesperson of Tuskegee Institute (see Matthews, 1977:61–84), when he and Thomas met. Like Thomas, Park had obtained some exposure to sociology through Georg Simmel, but his subsequent approach to the field seems to have been influenced more by his contacts with Thomas than his studies with Simmel.[24]

Park's major areas of interest were in the realms of collective behavior, race relations, and urban life. However, a great deal of his work at Chicago was intertwined with that of his junior officemate, Ernest Burgess.

Ernest Burgess (1886–1966) received his doctorate from Chicago in 1913 and joined the department in 1916. For many years Burgess worked closely with, and in the shadows of, the more senior Robert Park. Burgess seems endlessly interested in all inquiries into city life and attempted to blend both quantitative and qualitative research. As well, Burgess was involved in organizational activities and in facilitating the works of others, but his own work is not well defined theoretically. In this regard, Burgess seems to reflect the prevailing currents of the times and the people with whom he had contact along the way.

An important part of Park and Burgess's early acclaim derived from their 1921 text-reader, *Introduction to the Science of Sociology*. This was a massive volume, consisting of statements extracted from the writings of almost everyone thought to be a "sociologist" at the time. Although it was viewed as a major publication in the field (Faris, 1967:37–50) and has served as the model for other introductory texts, this volume provided little in the way of coherent direction for sociology.[25] Thus, despite this volume's popularity, Park and Burgess's more consequential conceptual contributions revolved around the work that their students conducted on the city of Chicago.

Reflecting the general mandate (adopted in 1902) for graduate studies in sociology to envision the city as a sociological laboratory (Kurtz, 1984:60), Park and Burgess strongly encouraged their students to gather all manner of data on aspects of the city and city life. Much of this work had a mapping or ecological flavor (attending to population patterns, living arrangements, migration patterns, and the like), but some of these studies involved more focused investigations of human lived experiences.

As a team, Park and Burgess seemed largely unconcerned about whether the inquiries conducted by their students were qualitative or quantitative, so long as they involved data of some sort on urban life.[26] Overall, however, it was Park, building on his earlier experiences as a newspaper reporter, who seemed especially committed to first hand field observations and inquiries:

> *You have been told to go grubbing in the library, thereby accumulating a mass of notes and liberal coating of grime. You have been told to choose problems wherever you can find musty stacks of routine records based on trivial schedules prepared by tired bureaucrats and filled out by reluctant applicants for aid or fussy do-gooders or indifferent clerks. This is called "getting your hands dirty in real research." Those who counsel you are wise and honorable; the reasons they offer are of great value. But one more thing is needful; first hand observation. Go and sit in the lounges of the luxury hotels and on the doorsteps of the flophouses; sit on the Gold Coast settees and the slum shakedowns; sit in the orchestra hall and in the Star and Garter burlesque. In short, gentlemen, go get the seat of your pants dirty in real research. (An unpublished 1920s quote from Robert Park, recorded by Howard Becker, in McKinney, 1966:71)*

Despite their enthusiasm for fieldwork, neither Park nor Burgess ventured upon much firsthand field research. Indeed, while Park and Burgess and others, such as Faris and Mead provided an environment in which ethnographic work was to flourish, it was their students who would embark on the major ground-breaking studies of city life. Indeed, much more effectively than Thomas and Znaniecki's, *The Polish Peasant in Europe and America*; Park, Miller and Thomas's sequel (1921), *Old World Traits Transplanted*; or Thomas's (1923) *The Unadjusted Girl*, the work of these students would establish an ethnographic tradition in Chicago and in sociology more generally.

Student Ethnographies: Learning by Doing

The most powerful of the early Chicago student ethnographies were *The Hobo* (1923) conducted by Nels Anderson, *The Jack-Roller* (1930) by Clifford Shaw, *The Old Love and the New* (1930) by Willard Waller, *The Taxi-Dance Hall* (1932) by Paul Cressey, *Movies and Conduct* (1933) by Herbert Blumer, *Movies, Delinquency and Crime* (1933) by Herbert Blumer and Philip Hauser, and *The Professional Thief* (1937) by Edwin Sutherland. Although they lacked the ethnographic depth and generated less compelling insights than the works just cited, other published monographs included Frederick Thrasher's (1927) *The Gang*, E. T. Hiller's (1928) *The Strike*, Ruth Shonle Cavan's (1928) *Suicide*,[27] Frances Donovan's (1920) *The Woman Who Waits* and (1929) *The Saleslady*, Louis Wirth's (1928) *The Ghetto*, Harvey Zorbaugh's (1929) *The Gold Coast and the Slum*, and Norman Hayner's (1936) *Hotel Life*.

Since research papers were required in most of the courses Park and Burgess taught, the ethnographies represented by the monographs listed here are not as unique as they might seem. However, these publications created a sharpened awareness of ethnographic research and its potential. The following brief descriptions of some of these works provide a greater sense of the ways in which the ethnographic tradition emerged. Still, readers are strongly cautioned that summary statements of the sort offered here cannot portray the rich and valuable contributions entailed in ethnographic inquiry. There is simply no substitute for reading these valuable and fascinating ethnographic statements in their full, original text.

Nels Anderson

Although Anderson (1961:xiii) indicated that field research was already in vogue at Chicago at the time he undertook the study of homeless people (migrant workers, tramps, bums), the publication of *The Hobo* (1923) was extremely consequential in establishing the ethnographic tradition in the literature. Anderson notes that he was given little direction, beyond Park's encouragement to, "Write down only what you see, hear and know like a newspaper reporter" (Anderson, 1961:xii). However, Anderson had been a hobo for a number of years and *The Hobo* reflects his own experiences as well as observations and interviews with those he encountered in the field.

The Hobo is a study of the lived experiences of homeless men, but it is also a study of urban life. We learn not only about the careers of hobos, but also of the businesses (restaurants, bars, stores, pawnshops), the control agencies, and the social welfare agencies located in these settings, and the ways in which the lives of the people involved in these settings intersected with those of the hobos.

Working with only a minimal sociological background, Anderson produced one of the most compelling ethnographic accounts in the history of the discipline. Perhaps, Anderson's study benefitted from the general problem of "killing time" that characterized the hobo:

> *"Killing time" is a problem with the homeless man. . . . For the vast majority, there is no pastime save the passing show of the crowded thoroughfare. . . .*

> *The homeless man, as he meanders along the street, is looking for something to break the monotony. He will stand on the curb for hours, watching people pass. He notices every conspicuous person and follows with interest, perhaps sometimes with envy the wavering movements of every passing drunk. If a policeman stops anyone on the street, he also stops and listens in. If he notices a man running down the alley, his curiosity is aroused. Wherever he sees a group gathered, he lingers. He will stop and listen if two men are arguing. He will spend hours sitting on the curb talking to a congenial companion. (Anderson, 1923:215)*

While it is not apparent that Anderson could have produced a study of this calibre in a setting in which he lacked this level of familiarity, it was also a sign of how much sociologists had to learn of the world "out there":

> *Even after the publication of* The Hobo, *when I was permitted to take the oral examination for my Master's degree [1925], I was not able to answer most of the questions put to me. Apparently some of my answers must have amused the professors. When I was called back into the room for the verdict, Professor Albion W. Small pointed out to the street, "You know your sociology out there better than we do, but you don't know it in here. We have decided to take a chance and approve you for your Master's degree." (Anderson, 1961:xii)*

It is difficult to say how much other Chicago students benefitted from Anderson's study of *The Hobo*. It may have been the case that many other students saw his inquiry as substantively far removed from their own investigations. However, insofar as human group life consists of people coming together and working out their dilemmas and interests with others, it is difficult to read this volume and not achieve some appreciation of human relations more generally. While it may seem ironic that someone schooled much more in hobohemia than formal sociology should make such an important contribution to the discipline, one of the lessons of ethnographic research is that sociologists and other social scientists can (and must) learn from "the people out there" if they are to develop anything approximating a genuine social science.

Frances Donovan

Although her ties to the department seem somewhat tenuous, Frances Donovan contributed three early ethnographic statements to Chicago sociology: *The Woman Who Waits* (1920), *The Saleslady* (1929), *The Schoolma'am* (1939).[28] These volumes lack the strong conceptual framing developed by Anderson and others, but they very much reflect Donovan's participant-observer roles. Thus, Donovan provides some of the best documentary material available in this era on aspects of the service industry, including waitressing, saleswork, and teaching. More generally, these books represent valuable, early contributions to the "sociology of work."

Clifford Shaw

He never finished his doctorate at the University of Chicago, but in publishing *The Jack-Roller* (1930), *The Natural History of a Delinquent Career* (Shaw and Moore, 1931), and *Brothers in Crime* (Shaw, McKay, and McDonald, 1938), Clifford Shaw made monumental contributions to the study of crime and delinquency.[29] In a consequential break from earlier (and most later) investigations of criminality, which try to account for troublesome behavior in vague generalities or "factors," Shaw provided vital insight into the experiences, dilemmas, practices, and affiliations of youthful offenders. By gathering case histories and accounts of the ongoing practices of juveniles, Shaw was able to make a profound contribution to both the criminological and ethnographic literatures. In the classic, *The Jack-Roller*, Shaw and his teenage informant, Stanley, combine to produce an exceptionally insightful statement on the social essences and career contingencies pertaining to people's involvements in teenage crime. A study of social process, *The Jack-Roller* depicts the day-to-day situations that "street kids" encounter and portrays the reflectivity, enterprise, and interaction involved in the production of delinquency. Although *The Jack-Roller* needs to be viewed within the social context in which it was written, there is no better account of teenage criminality available.[30]

Willard Waller

Another important study published in this tradition was Willard Waller's (1930) *The Old Love and the New*, which deals with people's subsequent adjustment to divorce and widowhood. While Waller obtained his doctorate from Pennsylvania State University, he received his MA from the University of Chicago and the impact of Waller's earlier education is most apparent. Not only is *The Old Love and the New* dedicated to Ellsworth Faris (with acknowledgements to Robert Park and Ernest Burgess), but this book is also developed within the ethnographic tradition represented at Chicago. Building on interviews with divorced and widowed people, *The Old Love and the New* provides much valuable insight into interpersonal relations of an intimate nature as Waller attends to the ambiguities, complexities, and dynamics of people's love lives and the commitments, complexities and frustrations their situations entail. While Waller incorporated some (minor) psychoanalytic themes into his analysis, he nonetheless provided one of the earliest methodological statements on ethnographic research (Waller, 1930:314–331).

Paul Cressey

Paul G. Cressey's (1932), *The Taxi-Dance Hall* represents another early ethnographic study of major consequence. Although taxi-dance halls (settings in which male patrons would dance with the woman of their choice for a "dime a dance") are very much recreational facilities of the past, Cressey's study has exceedingly profound implications for understanding the social organization (and control) of commercialized intimacy (see Prus and Irini, 1980). In developing this study, Cressey undertook three tasks. First, he wanted to depict the social world of the taxi-dance hall as experienced by the owner-managers, the workers they employed, and the patrons who spent money in these settings. Second, he sought to develop a natural history of the taxi-dance hall as an institution. Third, he wanted to consider the attempts by moral agents in the community to control this realm of human behavior and the reactions of those whose lives they attempted to control. When Cressey encountered difficulty getting the owners and managers of taxi-dance halls to cooperate with him in this study, Cressey and his student associates assumed roles as covert participant-observers in these settings. Operating in the capacity of "undercover investigators,"[31] Cressey and his associates not only amassed some very valuable materials on the careers of the people (owners, workers, patrons) involved in the subculture of the taxi-dance hall, but they also provided some of the very best material available on the dynamics (reform and resistance) of control in community life.

Edwin Sutherland

By working with an established thief (Chic Conwell), Edwin Sutherland Produced *The Professional Thief* (1937), one of the most important books ever written in the field of criminology. Working somewhat in the style of Shaw and *The Jack-Roller* and depicting the social world, life-styles, and practices of the professional thieves, Sutherland not only drew scholars' attention to the centrality of the thief subculture (perspectives, identities, relationships, and activities) in accounting for people's involvements in criminality but also provided a striking challenge to those who argued that criminality was inborn or reflected a lack of personal competence and social skills. *The Professional Thief*, along with the "theory of differential association" (Sutherland, 1939) that it inspired, were to have a major impact on sociological conceptions of criminality. Indeed, Sutherland argued, criminality was learned, like any other human behavior, and had to be understood with respect to the interactive contexts in which people found themselves.[32]

CHICAGO SOCIOLOGY IN TRANSITION

When Robert Park retired in 1933, the Chicago school lost some of its impetus for ethnographic research (also see Cavan, 1983). Ernest Burgess, who figured so centrally as Park's co-worker in fostering the ethnographic tradition, did not retire until 1951, but Burgess became much more involved in quantitative sociology and the general atmosphere in the department changed considerably. Ellsworth Faris, who retired in 1939, had earlier assumed the responsibility of chairing the department as well as occupying more demanding positions in professional sociological associations. Thus, he also drifted away from an active role in ethnographic research. It is in the context of these circumstances that Everett Hughes and Herbert Blumer (two students who graduated from Chicago in 1928) became so central in providing continuity of this tradition. Unlike Park and Burgess, who often worked much more as a team, though, Blumer and Hughes worked quite independently.

Herbert Blumer began teaching at the University of Chicago as he finished his dissertation (1928) and remained there until his departure in 1952 for the University of California, Berkeley. Everett Hughes graduated in the same year but went to McGill (Montreal) to teach for a decade before returning to Chicago in 1938 (and remaining there until 1961). Although both Blumer and Hughes reflect the broader intellectual setting in which they were trained, Blumer worked primarily in the tradition of George Herbert Mead, whereas Hughes was most centrally influenced by Robert Park. They shared mutual interests in ethnographic research and Meadian social psychology. However, while Blumer was much more concerned with addressing and clarifying issues pertaining to theory, research, and methods, Hughes was much more eclectic and attempted to incorporate whatever approaches struck him as promising at the time.[33] Blumer, thus, is the much more persistent and consistent advocate of a theoretical viewpoint conducive to ethnographic inquiry. Hughes displays strong affinities for ethnographic research of an interactionist nature, but he also seems concerned with developing a synthesis of ecological, functionalist and interactionist notions in much of his work (see Helmes-Hayes, forthcoming). In contrast to Herbert Blumer, Everett Hughes gave little attention to issues of epistemology or the interrelatedness of theory and research and was minimally concerned about the diverse sets of assumptions he made in moving across conceptual schemes. It was Blumer who provided the conceptual frame around which most of the ethnographic studies at Chicago in this era were built, but Hughes was very supportive of students doing ethnographic research, particularly in the areas in which he had strong substantive interests (e.g., occupations, professions, ethnic relations).

Everett Hughes: Sociologist at Work

(F)ield work is not merely one among several methods of social study but is paramount. It is, more than other methods of study, itself a practice, consciously undertaken, in sociology itself—in the perceiving and predicting of social roles, both one's own and those of others. It consists of exchanges of gestures, to use the terms of George Herbert Mead. (Hughes, 1961:vi)

The outstanding peculiarity of this method is that the observer, in greater or less degree, is caught up in the very web of social interaction which he observes, analyses and reports. (Hughes, 1961:xiv)

This has a peculiar corollary. The problem of learning to be a field observer is like the problem of learning to live in society. (Hughes, 1961:xv)

When Everett Cherrington Hughes (1897–1981) returned to the University of Chicago as an instructor in 1938, he assumed a role very much akin to that which Park had held. Hughes also shared many of Park's substantive interests. Like Park, Hughes worked with theoretically mixed conceptions of community life. Hughes's primary interests were in the sociology of work (especially occupations and professions) and race and ethnic relations, but his approaches to these fields were almost as eclectic as the literature he encountered.[34] As with Park, only some of Hughes's students were strongly ethnographic in their research inquiries, but Hughes nonetheless fostered these interests.

While Hughes's list of publications is quite striking, a great many of his writings are also Park-like: short, almost journalistic in nature. Hughes addresses an issue, writes clearly, and introduces some interesting points and illustrations, but he seldom develops his concepts very fully. For instance, Hughes was concerned with the ways in which institutions (especially work and the economy) take their shapes, particularly from the viewpoints of those participating in the settings under consideration, but his work is far from systematic, even here.

Thus, while Hughes introduces important notions such as, "Good People and Dirty Work" (Hughes, 1971, I:87–97), "Mistakes at Work" (Hughes, 1971, II:316–325), and "The Humble and The Proud: The Comparative Study of Occupations" (Hughes, 1971, II:417–430), these and other conceptural themes are never integrated or cast into a very coherent interactionist sociology of group life. Instead, it is as though Hughes hoped that somehow his work, and that of his students, would eventually coalesce into a participant (viewpoint) informed science of institutional life.

Although Hughes was involved in the development of two major ethnographies, *Boys in White* (Becker, Hughes, Geer, and Strauss, 1961) and *Making the Grade* (Becker, Hughes, and Geer, 1968), Hughes defined his own role largely as one of an entrepreneur ("front man") in both instances (1971, II:417). Thus, while Hughes did some field research in both cases, he never conducted a major ethnographic study.[35] Still, Hughes's interest in substantive areas, particularly the world of work, was central in attracting and stimulating a great many research projects by his students and many of these had a clear ethnographic thrust. Some noteworthy ventures include the study of jazz musicians (Howard Becker), factory workers (Donald Roy), physicians (Oswald Hall), funeral directors (Robert Habenstein), junk dealers (Jack Ralph), janitors (Raymond Gold), and cab drivers (Fred Davis).

Like Park as well, Hughes provided little written material on field research. His fullest statement on ethnographic research is developed in his introduction (v–xv) to Junker's (1961) book of field research, and Hughes's material is as much a commentary on the Department of Sociology at the University of Chicago as a statement on ethnographic inquiry.

It may well have been as an advisor in the area of work and occupations that Hughes was strongest conceptually. For it was here that Hughes clearly pressed his students not only for in-depth examinations of particular occupations and work settings, but also for the pursuit of conceptual themes common across occupational settings. Some of these themes he put in an "*Outline for Sociological Study of an Occupation*," which Hughes (1971, II:419) indicates was used as an organizational scheme by a whole generation of students. It is difficult to tell just how much inspiration any particular student derived from Hughes's outline or other inputs. Still, there is little doubt that some of the most valuable and exciting ethnographic works on the sociology of work were developed through student contact with Everett Hughes. And, perhaps, through his emphasis on developing comparisons or using the generic features of settings, Hughes provided one of his more important ethnographic legacies:

Everett taught me to think comparatively, to look for hidden similarities, for variations on basic sociological themes, in the welter of concrete data. We generally think of comparative research carried on in more than one society, but Everett's meaning was more flexible and more rewarding. He taught us to compare parts of our own society with one another, to compare one time with another, to see the small differences between closely related phenomena that had great theoretical import. (Becker, in Becker, Geer, Reisman, and Weiss 1968:272)

Herbert Blumer: Providing the Conceptual Base

Now about the situation back in Chicago in that period. What impressed me the most was the fact that under the tutelage of Park—reflecting, let us say, the continuing tradition of Thomas—there was major emphasis placed upon what seems to me to be absolutely in order at the present time. And that is, the need of actually getting out and observing life as it is going on if one proposes to undertake studies of it or advance any theoretical analysis of it. . . . And more and more over the years, as I have had occasion to reflect on what is going on in sociology, the more convinced I have become of the inescapable need, and consequently the very impressive merit, that attaches to that type of approach. . . . (T)he premise that underlay the work of Park and Thomas, with their recognition that there are people, wherever you find them constituting any group—a small group or a huge society or an institution or what not—there are people who are engaged in living, in having to cope with situations that arise in their experience, organizing their behavior and their conduct in the light of those situations which they encounter, coming to develop all kinds of collective arrangements which are collective affairs. And this, it seems to me, is the thing that normally marks the position of the so-called "Chicago School." (Blumer, in Lofland, 1980:261)

While Everett Hughes encouraged Chicago students to pursue research in a variety of substantive settings, it was Herbert Blumer who provided the theoretical foundations for ethnographic inquiry not only for students at Chicago but for scholars more generally.

Perhaps because he is so well known for his theoretical work, Blumer's own ethnographic contributions have been largely overlooked. Blumer never published a participant-observer study per se, but his work on the movies (Blumer, 1933; Blumer and Hauser, 1933) was largely ethnographic in nature, and made extensive use of interview materials and written accounts that people had provided regarding their experiences with this medium.

Movies and Conduct by Herbert Blumer and *Movies, Delinquency and Crime* by Herbert Blumer and Philip Hauser focus on the ways in which people (especially adolescents and children) deal with the images of life they encounter in the media.[36] *Movies and Conduct* examines a number of socialization issues to which viewers might attend. Included here are considerations of the impersonation and imitation of movie characters and their practices, daydreaming and fantasy, emotional stimulation (fear, sorrow, romance, sexuality, thrills, and excitement), and other schemes of life (e.g., stereotypes, parental relations, aspirations). *Movies, Delinquency and Crime* more narrowly addresses the direct and indirect influences that viewers of movies associated with their participation (or reluctances thereof) in delinquency and crime.

In both instances, movies are seen as socially contrived sets of messages that entail ongoing interpretation and adjustment. Insofar as movies are seen to provide images of others dealing with situations of relevance to the viewers, opportunities for socialization into adolescent (e.g., dress-styles, sexuality) and criminal (e.g., techniques, life-styles) roles, this medium becomes consequential. While some questionnaire data are used to provide percentages of participation rates in these two studies, the analyses are very centrally developed around written accounts or interview materials regarding people's experiences with the movies and the images they derived therein. Both volumes extensively use extracts from these sources to portray the interpretive, interactive, and adjustive aspects of encounters with the mass media.

Blumer never developed an ethnographic statement on industrialization or labor-management relations, but his writings in this area (Blumer, 1947, 1948, 1958, 1960, 1990) reflect the stock of knowledge he had acquired as a consultant and labor arbitrator (Wiseman, 1987:244) and clearly benefit from these contacts.

It also appears that Blumer was diverted, by other pursuits, from completing an ethnographic study of the underlife:

> *I spent an afternoon talking with Herbert Blumer at his office in 1982. It was most interesting! Herbert Blumer was eighty-two years old at the time, and was experiencing deteriorating health, but mentally he was still very quick and coherent. We talked about theory and methods in ethnographic research, about the Chicago school and people such as Ed Sutherland and Erving Goffman, and Blumer gave me my own lecture on symbolic interaction. . . . As we talked, I was struck by his apparent comfort and familiarity with the life-styles and activities of the people depicted in* Road Hustler *(Prus and Sharper) and* Hookers, Rounders, and Desk Clerks *(Prus and Irini). Amongst other things, he mentioned that*

*he had spent many Saturday afternoons talking with people in the waiting room
of his friend, Dr. Reitman (who had been instrumental in facilitating Nels
Anderson's study, The Hobo). Many of Reitman's clients lived on the margins
of society or were underworld characters of sorts. Blumer, it seemed, had spent
a great many hours listening to these people discuss their life-situations. It was
Blumer, as well, who had introduced Broadway Jones (Chic Conwell) to Ed
Sutherland. Evidently, Blumer had anticipated doing some work in this area
but the research never materialized, perhaps as a consequence of being distracted
by other pursuits.* [37] *(notes)*

Having discussed Blumer's approach to the study of human behavior and
his devastating critiques of mainstream social science in chapter 3, it may be
best to concentrate on the implications of these notions for ethnographic research.
Three themes might be emphasized here. The first concern pertains to respecting
the essence of the subject matter one studies (i.e., the nature of human behavior
in the case of the social sciences). The second theme deals with the necessity
of achieving intimate familiarity with one's subject matter. The third concern
revolves around the necessity of developing generic or transsituational concepts.
These notions (also see chapter 8) are central to Blumer's emphasis on the
paramount reality of the social world and the importance he places on developing
a careful, sustained, and intimately informed understanding of human group life.

Respecting the Nature of Human Group Life

The first and most basic starting point for Herbert Blumer's notions of
ethnographic inquiry pertains to the necessity of attending to the natural features
of human association. Like Mead (and especially Dilthey), Blumer was concerned
that any methodology by which we would attempt to study human group life
be centrally cognizant of those aspects of human interchange.

While Blumer recognizes that all objects (human, animal, inanimate, images;
anything of one's awareness) are subject to interpretation and reinterpretation
through human interaction, he emphasizes that *the study of human group life
generates some unique problems for researchers.* The study of social life involves
the study of active, interpreting, interacting agents. Since humans realize their
essence through ongoing, reflective interaction with others, people can not be
understood by reference to their individual properties. Thus, Blumer (1928)
observed that not only were the methods employed by those in the physical
sciences inappropriate for comprehending human group life, but it was not
apparent that the study of human behavior could be considered scientific by
the standards of the physical sciences. Blumer stopped just short of positing

that the study of human behavior would require a reconceptualization of the nature of science, but this seems the inevitable conclusion.

Writing prior to the new sociology of science (see Kuhn, 1962; Knorr-Cetina, 1981; Latour, 1987), Blumer had underestimated the extent to which the physical sciences are social essences (i.e., social products and social processes). Thus, his writings convey a somewhat unwarranted regard for the objectivity of the physical sciences. However, his mistake was only in failing to appreciate the closer approximation of the physical sciences (by virtue of the human researchers and social communities involved) to his views of the human sciences, rather than the self-destructive error that most positivist social scientists make in attempting to force the social sciences to become more like their (unfounded) nineteenth-century images of the physical sciences.

As such, Blumer's notions of an interpretive social sciences not only remain exceedingly vital for the social sciences, but are also much more consequential for understanding practices within physical sciences than he anticipated. Simply expressed, it means that science can be studied in the same ways we might study any other realm of human behavior, as an instance of "symbolic interaction."[38]

Achieving Intimate Familiarity

Although Blumer (1928) was skeptical that the social sciences could ever achieve the conceptual and methodological rigor that he associated with the physical sciences, he recognized that it was much more important that one respect the nature of the phenomenon being studied than to pursue methods (however rigorous these might seem) that would violate the very essence of the phenomenon being studied. Thus, while Blumer clearly had reservations (especially concerns pertaining to researcher variability, respondent openness, and problems of comparisons) about sympathetic introspection (Cooley's term for ethnography) as a mode of scientific research, he also envisioned ethnographic inquiry as the *only* way one could achieve intimate familiarity with human group life as it is actually accomplished:

> *No one can catch the process merely by inferring its nature from the overt action which is its product. To catch the process, the student must take the role of the acting unit whose behavior he is studying. Since the interpretation is being made by the acting unit in terms of objects designated and appraised, meanings acquired, and decisions made, the process has to be seen from the standpoint of the acting unit. It is the recognition of this fact that makes the research work of such scholars as R. E. Park and W. I. Thomas so notable. To try to catch the interpretive*

process by remaining aloof as a so-called "objective" observer and refusing to take the role of the acting unit is to risk the worst kind of subjectivism—the objective observer is likely to fill in the process of interpretation with his own surmises in place of catching the process as it occurs in the experience of the acting unit which uses it. (Blumer, 1962:188)

Developing Concepts

To speak of a science without concepts suggests all sorts of analogies—a carver without tools, a railroad without tracks, a mammal without bones, a love story without love. A science without concepts would be a fantastic creation. (Blumer, 1931:515)

The third major concern Blumer expresses with respect to inquiry into human behavior is that researchers develop concepts that (a) are sensitive to the phenomenon being studied and (b) foster comparisons and contrasts (i.e., generate conceptual refinements). Thus, he encourages a constant receptivity and openness on the part of researchers to continually adjust their preconceptions to the images of the phenomenon that they encounter in the course of conducting their inquiry. While Blumer emphasizes the necessity of developing concepts that are attentive to individual instances of the features of human behavior under consideration, he also stresses the desirability of conducting research that lends itself to comparisons. However, he is fundamentally concerned that any comparisons being made utilize concepts that are attentive to the lived features of human group life. Readers will realize that this emphasis lies at the root of much of Blumer's criticisms of quantitative analysis. Since the value of any "counting" is fundamentally and ultimately contingent on the viability of the categories with which one works, the ensuing analysis can be no better than the ways in which variables are conceptualized and operationalized. Unfortunately, since very few quantitative studies are attentive to the interpretive, interactive nature of human group life, they can offer little to an understanding of the ways in which human lived experience is constituted.

As well, and in contrast to those who would argue for the necessity of remaining at the level of the individual (idiographic) instance; that each instance can only be appreciated in respect to itself, Blumer observes:

(T)he drawing of abstractions, the formulations of universals, does not annihilate the unique in the sense of transforming its rich individual content into less meaningful general content; rather, the universal is complementary to the

individual; instead of subtracting from the individual, it adds to the individual. (Blumer, 1928:349)

Blumer uses the term *sensitizing concepts* to refer to these tentative, analytical notions. Sensitizing concepts suggest subsequent lines of inquiry and assessment, but in each case the researcher has the obligation of making the concepts match up with the circumstances at hand rather than making the data fit the concepts. It is here, too, that Blumer envisions the potential of "generic social processes" (see chapter 5) for providing a framework that would allow researchers to compare inquiries and assess the viability of these concepts on an ongoing basis.

Carrying On the Tradition

The ethnographic tradition, begun at the University of Chicago, has proliferated considerably over the years. To a large extent, this can be attributed to the students of Herbert Blumer and Everett Hughes and those who studied with them. Thus, for instance, among the Chicago-trained scholars (Hughes's and Blumer's students), ethnographic research has been promoted by researchers such as Howard Becker, Anselm Strauss, Alfred Lindesmith, Gregory Stone, and Donald Roy. Noteworthy proponents of the ethnographic tradition graduating from Berkeley (Blumer's students) include people such as Jacqueline Wiseman, John Lofland, Lyn Lofland, and John Irwin. The interactionist tradition has continued to build on the materials published by these people and their students, but over the past few decades it has been buttressed by the contributions of a much wider community of scholars, many of whom have had little or no first-hand contact with these scholars.

The ethnographic tradition has also been greatly strengthened by the development of three journals oriented toward ethnographic research: *Journal of Contemporary Ethnography* (formerly *Urban Life*), *Symbolic Interaction*, and *Qualitative Sociology*. While some ethnographic research continues to be published in other "general" or "mainstream" journals, these journals represent major forums for field research. As such, these journals denote exceedingly vital arenas for the development and continuity of the ethnographic tradition. As well, the development of a scholarly association, *The Society for the Study of Symbolic Interaction*, has been of major consequence in providing settings (conferences) in which scholars involved in this style of research meet and share materials they have developed and the research problems they have encountered.

The interpretive tradition waned somewhat between the 1940s and early '60s, under the aura of scientism and the "hyped-up" promises associated with quantitative analysis in sociology. It was here, largely through the efforts of Herbert Blumer and his insistence that social scientists attend to human lived experiences and of Everett Hughes and his interest in the sociology of work, that the tradition survived and maintained its vitality. Somewhat related viewpoints emerged in the 1960s, most notably through the works of Erving Goffman (dramaturgical analysis), Harold Garfinkel (ethnomethodology), Peter Berger and Thomas Luckmann (the social construction of reality), and Thomas Kuhn (history of science). These scholars, along with Howard Becker, Anselm Strauss, Gregory Stone, John Lofland, and others who persisted in doing ethnographic research during an era in which quantitative analysis clearly dominated sociological thinking and practice, played major roles in once again redirecting attention to the necessity of studying human lived experience.[39] We have also seen, in recent years, a resurgence of attention directed toward hermeneutics and the works of Wilhelm Dilthey and others of this genre (see Mueller-Vollmer, 1989). However, despite the important contributions of these writings, no more viable approach to the study of human lived experiences can be attained than through the Chicago-style ethnographies discussed herein. Indeed, while far from perfect, interactionist ethnography represents the approach that affords social scientists the greatest opportunity for developing a more fully intersubjective approach—a social science that is genuinely grounded in human lived experience and in the social production of action.

At the same time, it might be useful to briefly mention some of the obstacles that make it difficult for scholars to maintain this focus. First, interactionist ethnography is a very time-consuming, labor intensive undertaking, which requires extensive patience, perseverance, and an ability to handle a great deal of ambiguity, as well as the willingness and ability to venture into the life-worlds of the other (the researcher as student-apprentice). It is so demanding, in fact, that few people do more than one ethnographic study in their lifetime. Likewise, although ethnographic studies are likely to be the most compelling and groundbreaking forms of research that graduate students may conduct, many are reluctant to venture into these more ambiguous, open-ended inquiries when they can do something "quick and dirty" with quantitative data. Secondly, this style of research does not lend itself to the sorts of simplified versions of reality and quick fixes typically sought by government agencies and other control agencies or interest groups prepared to fund research. This means that ethnographers typically work with very limited resources and are seldom in a position to obtain the "big dollar, high prestige grants" that quantitative researchers can pursue by promising to generate quick results for eager (but poorly informed) bureaucrats.

Third, in contrast to quantitative research, which can be readily packaged and presented in highly distilled manners, ethnographic research assumes an expansive quality. Not only is ethnographic material much more difficult to manage and analyze, but it is also much more difficult to condense and prepare in forms that lend themselves to a page length that journal editors and book publishers most commonly desire.

Fourth, ethnographic research is people work. It assumes that researchers will not only be willing to put their own identities on the line and subjugate their viewpoints to those of the other, but that they will be able to approach, access, and maintain viable working contacts with the host of other people that they might encounter in the process of conducting the research.[40] As well, since outsiders may have a variety of concerns regarding either the (dis)respectability of some people or practices being studied or the ethics of aspects of inquiry, ethnographers commonly also have to contend with a variety of moral entrepreneurs and the obstacles they pose.

All of these considerations mitigate against the ethnographic enterprise. It is much easier and less risky, on numerous fronts, to sit in one's office and reflect in seemingly learned manners about this or that aspect of the human condition, or to send out questionnaires or run people (increasingly as "paid workers") through experiments of some sort. Fortunately, some scholars have remained genuinely curious about the other and have been sufficiently determined to pursue some sort of sustained, firsthand contact with the other. Hopefully, and despite the many obstacles that field research entails, a conviction about establishing intersubjectivity with the other will persist because it is only in developing intimate familiarity with our human subject matter that we may make any claims to being a genuine social science.

Chapter 5 introduces another obstacle facing those seriously pursuing an intersubjective social science, the task of developing a body of concepts that is attentive to ongoing ethnographic inquiry.

NOTES

1. The term, "ethnography" is derived from the Greek expression "ethnos" (peoples; ethnic cultures). Ethnology is the study of peoples; ethnography refers to descriptive accounts of people's life-styles.

2. For two early historical accounts of the development of ethnographic or cultural anthropology, see Haddon (1934) and Lowie (1937). Also see Boas's (1904) statement in Stocking (1974). Albeit highly abbreviated, readers may find Garbarino's work (1983) helpful in tracing the development of sociocultural theory (and research) in anthropology.

3. See Bowden (1981) for a historical account of Christian missionary contacts (and cultural conflicts) with North American Indians.

4. As Wax (1971) notes, some depictions of the living conditions of peasant life-styles, prison life, and prostitution can be found in the eighteenth century writings of Arthur Young and John Howard of England, and Alexandre Parent-Duchatelet of France, respectively. Still other descriptive materials were developed in the course of studies of the poor by the British reformers Charles Booth, Beatrice Potter (Webb), and Sydney Webb in the 1880s–1920s. Although other scholars may have derived inspiration from some of these earlier works, no subsequent ethnographic tradition seems to have emerged as a consequence of these endeavors.

5. This form of ethnology was prominent among British, American, and German anthropologists. One important branch or version of ethnology was that of "folk psychology," which developed in Germany in the later 1800s (Wundt, 1916). See Lindgren (1939) for a fuller statement on the collection and analysis of folklore.

6. Radin (1933: 61–86) provides an instructive discussion of early studies on the parts of Dutch, Russian, and Danish ethnologists. In the absence of translations, however, this material largely has been neglected by English-speaking scholars.

7. It should be acknowledged that these ethnological interests were highly diffuse and nonsystematic. Indeed, they only marginally focused on the lived experiences of the peoples being studied.

8. See Lewis Henry Morgan (1851) *The League of the Ho-de-no-sau-nee or Iroquois*. For accounts of the works of Lewis Henry Morgan and other early ethnologists (1820–1880) specializing in North American Indians, see Bieder (1986). Other early sustained ethnographic accounts of American Indian life can be found in the writings of James Mooney (1965 [1896]) and Frank Hamilton Cushing (1979).

9. Indeed, as with sociology, anthropology became increasingly structural-functionalist in its cast in the 1930s–1970s, and only more recently have some field researchers in anthropology returned to more interpretive (hermeneutic) modes of analyses. It was popular, in the 1930s–1970s to view structural functionalism as "scientific." This was used as a lever by

those promoting this paradigm to establish a greater prominence for this orientation than that presumably obtainable through Boas's historical approach (see Stocking, 1974:18). Herskovitz (1953) and Stocking (1974) provide valuable overviews of Boas's approaches and contributions to field research. Readers may also wish to consult Stocking (1979), Garbarino (1983) and Ebihara (1985) for other materials that deal with some of these transitions in emphasis.

10.   Although released only much later, Malinowski's (1967) diary provides a fuller indication of the difficulties, frustrations, and distancing that characterize his work. See Young (1979) for an overview of Malinowski's research and extensive writings on the Trobriand Islanders.

11.   Paul's (1953) statement is a very thoughtful and succinct review of matters pertaining to field research practices and the practical difficulties researchers have had in their attempts to access and maintain viable working presences within unfamiliar communities. Experienced ethnographers would especially appreciate this paper.

12.   Among anthropologists, Victor Turner (1985, 1986) most notably has been championing an interpretive, processual anthropology, one rooted in the works of Wilhelm Dilthey. Also consequential in this regard is Moore's (1975) statement on social process. Elvi Whittaker's (1994) paper draws out in a very valuable manner the contributions that the conceptual frame developed by Herbert Blumer could make to contemporary anthropological work. Although the theoretical position of symbolic interaction is not well articulated in his volume, James Spradley's (1979) otherwise excellent statement on ethnographic inquiry is also informed by Blumerian assumptions.

13.   These points were driven home very clearly in a conference, "Deviance in a Cross-cultural Context," held at the University of Waterloo in 1984. The conference was organized by two anthropologists and two sociologists (symbolic interactionists) and involved presentations from over forty ethnographers working within these disciplines. Although interactionists examining deviance may have difficulties drawing comparisons between studies of two or more contexts (conducted by different researchers) in western society, these difficulties are acutely frustrated when one searches for comparable data across cross-cultural contexts. Not only are the interactionist concepts of deviance much more precisely defined than are those with which anthropologists work, but the modes of inquiry utilized by the interactionists are much more focused and consistent than those characterizing probes on the part of anthropologists. Similar problems

may very well exist with respect to other processual comparisons one might attempt to draw in other substantive areas (e.g., religion, marketplace exchanges) on a cross-cultural basis.

Although only minimal attention is given to social processes as envisioned here, those interested in the comparison problem in anthropology more generally may wish to examine the collection of papers on this topic edited by Holy (1987).

14. For more extended considerations of postmodernist issues and critiques as these pertain to ethnography in anthropology and sociology, see chapters 7 and 8.

15. The linkages are not at all well documented, but it seems that a fuller appreciation of ethnographic inquiry also reflects social worker involvements in "case studies." Denoting essential manners of tapping into people's lived experiences, case studies (individuals and relationships) in social work appear to have been well established before ethnographic research in sociology was begun. Thus, judging by Richmond's (1917) preface, case studies were very much the stock in trade of social workers by the turn of the century. Although he was not affiliated with or attentive to the Chicago school, the sociologist F. Stuart Chapin (1920), in his (first sociological) text on social research, built explicitly on the case study approach as articulated by Mary Richmond. At the same time, however, scholars in social work (Bosanquet, 1898; Richmond, 1917), appear to have been familiar with some of the works of William James and Charles H. Cooley. In a more general sense, it is also worth noting that not only did many early sociologists have strong interests in the ministry (including Small, Henderson, Thomas, and [Ellsworth] Faris at Chicago) and social welfare, but that much research in sociology arose in response to (and was justified by) desires to find more effective ways of dealing with social problems.

16. Two early exceptions of note are the Lynd and Lynd's (1929) *Middletown* and Whyte's (1943) *Streetcorner Society*. As Vidich and Lyman (1994) note, the Lynds worked with an anthropologist in developing the first (1929) study of Middletown. Later, they developed Soviet sympathies and their (1937) *Middletown in Transition* represented a base around which they encouraged Marxist-oriented community studies at Columbia University. Although quite different in its thrust, Whyte's study also lacks the conceptual (constructionist) orientation of Chicago-style ethnography. As indicated in the [1955] methodological appendix, Whyte had some later contact with Everett Hughes and Buford Junker. However, Whyte indicates

that his methodological practices and conceptual scheme were influenced by Lloyd Warner (1941, with Paul Lunt) and his associates. While Whyte was cognizant of some social anthropology, even later (1955) he seems quite unaware or inattentive of the interactionist ethnographic literature.

17. See Janowitz (editor) in Thomas (1966) and Baker (1973) for valuable biographical materials on W. I. Thomas.

18. As Thomas (Blumer, 1939:103) indicates, he was also influenced by the works of the functionalist Herbert Spencer during his studies in Germany. This pull, between the functionalist emphasis of Spencer and the processual orientation of Simmel, would appear to account, in part, for the lack of conceptual coherence in Thomas's work.

19. However, the study was exceedingly well funded! In 1908, Miss Culver of the Hull House in Chicago agreed to support Thomas in a vaguely conceptualized study along these lines to the amount of $50,000 (Thomas, in Blumer, 1939:103).

20. Blumer (1939:3) also provides a listing of some other reviews of *The Polish Peasant in Europe and America.*

21. Interestingly, it was Blumer rather than the more senior Faris who assumed Mead's more advanced social psychology course when Mead became ill. Faris (1937b) clearly appreciates Blumer's competence to do so and comments on this as an entirely appropriate measure.

22. Although Blumer studied with Mead, it was the sociologist Ellsworth Faris who was Blumer's (1928) dissertation advisor. According to Everett Hughes (Lofland, 1980:257), Faris also figured prominently in Hughes's education. I mention this because Blumer and Hughes were to play major roles in the subsequent development of Chicago sociology.

23. For more extended discussions of the impact of Robert Park on Chicago sociology, see Faris (1967), Baker (1973), Bulmer (1984), and especially Matthews (1977).

24. It is often observed that Robert Redfield, Park's son-in-law, became a prominent figure in the anthropology department at Chicago and that this represented another link between the two disciplines. However, there is little evidence that Redfield was much informed by Chicago interactionism or played a significant role in shaping interactionist ethnography.

25. Whatever coherency this volume achieves is largely attributable to its sixty-page introduction (written by Park). Interestingly, though, this statement is rooted rather clearly in aspects of the processual features of the sociologies of Auguste Comte, Herbert Spencer and Emile Durkheim, rather than in the works of Simmel, Cooley, or Mead.

26. In a methods text developed to serve as a classroom companion for the Park and Burgess text, Palmer (1928) provides us with a good sense of methods in vogue at the Department of Sociology at the University of Chicago at the time.

27. Although her conceptual emphases were considerably more mixed than that of some other Chicago students, Ruth Shonle Cavan also drew attention to ethnographic research in her study, *Suicide* (1928). Cavan followed Durkheim's quantitative, functionalist (1897) analysis of suicide to some extent, but supplemented this fairly extensively with case studies derived from documents (e.g., letters and diaries) left by the deceased and from contacts with friends and relatives. Cavan (1983), who also taught at the University of Chicago for a number of years, provides another interesting, albeit brief, account of early Chicago sociology.

28. Although Donovan (1920, 1929) very clearly assumes the role of participant observer, her linkages to Chicago sociology may be described as "soft." A third book by Donovan (1939), *The School Ma'am*, while reflecting nineteen years of teaching experience, is much more modalistic (she provides sweeping generalizations) and prescriptive in its presentation. Donovan provides little indication of sociological concepts or generic (transsituational) insights as she (1920, 1929, 1938) moves from one context to another. In this respect, while her two earlier volumes are more attentive to the actualities of people's experiences as waitresses and salesladies, her statement on teaching seems more typical of a genre of journalistic accounts reflecting the insights authors wish to share with others. Dorothy Dix's (1939) classic, *How to Win and Hold a Husband*, which builds on her experiences as a confidante of sorts, provides somewhat similar insights on people's heterosexual relations, and is likewise cast in a somewhat prescriptive mode.

29. The term jack-roller refers most specifically to someone who steals from intoxicated persons, but also denotes people apt to be involved in a variety of forms of street-related theft, "whatever one can scuff up," so to speak.

30. Although Snodgrass only partially captures the ethnographic sensitivity of Clifford Shaw, readers may be interested in Snodgrass and the Jack-Roller (1982) and Snodgrass (1983). This is a fifty-year follow-up of the career of "the jack-roller" who appears in Shaw's (1930) volume.

31. In addition to the very valuable statement represented by *The Taxi-Dance Hall*, readers may also wish to read Cressey's (1983) early statement on field research and Dubin's (1983) discussion of the roles of those attempting to assist Cressey in his research.

32. For an updated overview of major ethnographic research on hustlers and thieves as well as a sequel to Sutherland's, *The Professional Thief*, see Prus and Sharper (1991). See Vold (1951) for a fuller appreciation of Sutherland's career and contributions to the criminological literature.

33. Although Hughes seems perpetually concerned that sociological research represent the viewpoints of the people being studied, and often encourages a comparative theme across substantive settings, he (1971:vi) uses the term *free association* to refer to his (rather situated) sociological meanderings.

34. While this discussion is very much focused on the ethnographic research tradition, it should be noted that Everett Hughes's writings and interests extended into a variety of other areas as well. Thus, for instance, his *French Canada in Transition* (1943) is considered a classic in ethnic relations. His contributions to social stratification are also deemed noteworthy by scholars working in that area (Helmes-Hayes, forthcoming). Also see Helmes-Hayes for an extended bibliography of Hughes's work.

35. Hughes's own closest approximation to an ethnographic study is his volume, *French Canada in Transition* (1943).

36. Published as part of the Payne Fund Studies of Motion Pictures and Youth, these very insightful volumes have been largely overlooked by scholars in the ethnographic/interactionist traditions as well as those interested in socialization processes and the media more generally.

37. See Lofland (1980) for a fuller statement from Blumer along these lines.

38. Symbolic interaction in no way denies the accomplishments of the physical sciences or the intense enterprise that many scientific productions entail. However, it does focus our attention on the socially constituted and objectified nature of all knowledge (including that defined as "science").

39. Noteworthy, too, in more recent years (1980s), is the devastating set of critiques launched against positivism (causation, objectification, quantification) across the social sciences, along with a partial recognition from within the positivist tradition of the lack of substance in the positivist endeavor (see Prus, 1990, 1992b).

40. Interactionist ethnographers have also been critical of their own practices. For discussions of researcher roles, pitfalls, and dilemmas, see Adler and Adler (1987), Fine (1993), and Mitchell (1993).

5

GENERIC SOCIAL PROCESSES

Transcontextualizing Ethnographic Inquiry

It does not seem extreme to say that those brilliant social philosophers who have developed the sociology of conflict might have found adequate material for their discussions without having left their own classrooms. Nearly all the classic concepts apply to life in the school room, war, feuds, litigation, conflict of ideals, victory, conciliation, compromise, conversion, accommodation, and assimilation. (Waller, 1932:351)

Examining the ways in which people accomplish their activities on a day-to-day basis, ethnographic research provides an exceptionally rich and viable means of uncovering insights into people's lived experience.[1] Moreover, since it attends to the interpretive and interactive dimensions or the intersubjective features of human group life, ethnographic research is essential if one hopes to achieve "intimate familiarity" (Blumer, 1969) with ongoing community life. Hence, it is extremely useful and instructive in many ways to accumulate ethnographic studies that carefully describe the perspectives, practices, dilemmas and interchanges of people in this and that setting. Indeed, there is no better way of achieving a working understanding of substantive settings than through sustained ethnographic inquiry. Still, we also may use this rich, textured data as a base for formulating concepts that transcend the particular settings in which the data was gathered.

To the extent that we are able to delineate concepts which have transsituational or cross-contextual relevance, we may not only be able to tie together a great deal of research that would otherwise remain disconnected or scattered across a range of substantive contexts, but we may also be able to produce a body of concepts that could be used as a resource in subsequent ethnographic

141

research. These inquiries, in turn, could be used as a basis for further assessing, refining, and (if necessary) rejecting concepts pertaining to the study of human group life.[2]

This emphasis on transcontextual processes also encourages scholarly exchange and conceptual cross-fertilization. By attending to concepts which are applicable to a wide variety of contexts, researchers working in very different substantive settings (e.g., ballet, outlaw bikers, religion, schools) may not only benefit from the research undertaken in other settings, but they will likely find that they have a much broader community of scholars with which to discuss all aspects of their work than would otherwise have been the case.[3]

Further, as Blumer (1928:349) observes, concepts (such as generic social processes) do *not* destroy the unique or idiographic features of particular instances of human lived experience. Instead, they provide the vital medium through which similarities and differences may be more fully recognized, investigated, and appreciated on a case-by-case basis. Thus, the emphasis on generic social processes in no way minimizes or is intended as an alternative to ethnographic research. To the contrary, for students of human behavior this conceptual thrust represents an essential means of enhancing the potential value of each instance of ethnographic inquiry.

For our purposes, the term *generic social processes* refers to the transsituational elements of interaction—to the abstracted, transcontextual formulations of social behavior. Denoting parallel sequences of activity across diverse contexts, generic social processes highlight the emergent, interpretive features of association. They focus our attention on the activities involved in the "doing" or accomplishing of human group life.

GENERIC SOCIAL PROCESSES AND THE STUDY OF HUMAN GROUP LIFE

This emphasis on "generic social processes" can be traced to Georg Simmel, who in his analysis of "sociation" argued for a clear distinction between form and content. For Simmel, "form" was the subject matter of primary consequence; "content" provided the necessary but inevitably promiscuous background. Thus, rather than attending to the "cultural content" of events and people's experiences in settings, Simmel (1950; 1955; 1978) directed our attention to the dimensions of association. For Simmel, these included group alignments and relationships (e.g., triads, conflict, competition, coalitions), identities and disclosures (e.g., strangers, secrets, deceptions), activities (e.g., games, contests, conversations), and evaluations and commitments (e.g., price, value, exchanges). One also finds concepts that are transsituational in the works of other sociologists (e.g., Durkheim, Marx, Weber),[4] but only some sociologists explicitly attend to community life as a reflective, actively constituted phenomenon. Thus, of the more commonly recognized founders of the discipline, it is Simmel who most clearly generates concepts that either depict social processes or facilitate the delineation of social processes.

While all paradigms deal in abstractions, our concern is primarily with concepts that embody an *interpretive process*. The emphasis is on what Blumer (1969) calls the "active forging of social structure." Rather than viewing people as the (depersonalized) agents through which "external" or "internal" forces ("factors") exert their impact on group life,[5] we assume a conceptual approach that envisions group life as an ongoing series of constructions shaped by active, living, thinking beings.

Generic social processes do not exist to the exclusion of other sociological concepts.[6] Indeed, many other sociological concepts may sensitize us to particular processes. But unless we concentrate on *social* processes, we will not be able to achieve a theory of action that is grounded in the experiences of human beings.

This emphasis on process should not be taken to imply that content (or context) is not important. For a great many purposes, content and process are inseparable. And, as ethnographers, we face a central task of maximizing contextual depth in our inquiries. However, we have a choice of continually piling up isolated accounts of community life or striving for a theory of action that builds on these rich and contextually diversified inquiries. The latter routing, as Zerubavel (1981) notes, requires that ethnographers commit themselves to making more focused observations while pursuing ethnographic detail more generally.

The Chicago Influence

Georg Simmel (1950) might be considered the founder of generic (especially processual) sociology (via the study of the "forms of association"), but his message has not had the direct impact on the discipline that one might have anticipated. In part, this seems attributable to Simmel's wide breadth of topics and his tendency to generate seemingly definitive statements on matters he undertook to analyze.[7] As well, a sociology founded on "forms" (or generic concepts) lacks much of the immediate appeal that more substantively focused ("hot topics") writings hold for most consuming audiences. But, perhaps no less importantly, Simmel provided little indication of a methodology appropriate to an exploration of the forms of association.[8] Although the linkage to Simmel appears somewhat nebulous and even inadvertent at times, a methodology and a theory largely consistent with Simmel's formulations was subsequently to develop at the University of Chicago (see chapters 2–4 in this volume).

In the early 1900s, Chicago sociology pretty much covered the waterfront of what was vaguely defined as sociology, but there was a strong underlying appreciation of generic interactional sociology. Simmel's influence appears to have been fostered most directly by Albion Small, W. I. Thomas and Robert Park,[9] but other key figures in "Chicago interactionism" (e.g., Mead, Blumer) also evidence a strong intellectual affinity with Simmel. In analyzing a variety of realms of group life, these and other Chicago sociologists generated many valuable insights on concepts involving phenomena such as selves and identities, natural histories and careers of involvements, and assimilation, marginality, and conflict. There was much unevenness, reflecting a considerable diversity of input, emphasis, and anticipation, but it was a strikingly productive milieu with respect to ethnographic research and a process-oriented sociology.

While a number of people (e.g., Thomas and Znaniecki, Shaw, and Burgess) played important roles in the development of fieldwork at the University of Chicago,[10] Robert Park and Everett Hughes seem particularly instrumental in promoting ethnographic inquiry as a means of achieving "intimate familiarity" with the life-worlds that sociologists sought to study. As much as any, Park and Hughes were effective in "making fieldwork come alive," both through their own work and in that which they encouraged others. They were receptive to the derivation of "common themes" and "contingencies," but their analytical comparisons were of a softer variety. They utilized many of Simmel's concepts, but they were much less "formalistic" than was Simmel.

If the development of a generic processual sociology had relied centrally on the influence of Park and Hughes, it would have been much more vaguely formulated in thrust. However, the University of Chicago was also the home base of George Herbert Mead and Herbert Blumer. Mead (1934), like Simmel, thought generically. Nevertheless, his "sociology" (philosophy of social behavior) assumed a much more holistic quality than did that of Simmel. Mead's contribution to sociology was the elaboration of a fundamentally *intersubjective* conception of "mind, self, and society." This was the message that Blumer was to champion.

While Mead forged the fundamental shape of interactionist theory, it is Blumer who refined symbolic interactionism and who put it into a more distinctively sociological cast. It is Blumer, also, who fought for the existence of an intersubjective sociology in a discipline largely characterized by concerns with cause and effect on the one hand, and by reform measures of various sorts on the other.

Like Simmel, Mead seems minimally concerned about providing guidelines for an empirical assessment and exploration of the conceptual scheme that was to later become known as symbolic interaction. Blumer, however, took a strikingly different stand. Blumer insisted on empirical exploration and assessments of concepts. He did not instruct much by direct example, nor did he generate guidebooks. However, he very cogently provided (a) a rationale for the inseparability of theory and research; (b) conceptual guidelines for doing interpretive sociology; and (c) wellfounded critiques of the methods of social science that violate the central features of group life as an emergent, intersubjective phenomena. Working in an environment rich in ethnographic tradition (e.g., Park, Hughes, Shaw), Blumer emerges as the key figure in the development of a generic, process-oriented sociology. And, it is very much on the foundations provided by Herbert Blumer that more specific formulations of generic social processes have been developed.

Other Statements on Generic Social Processes

Despite a seemingly widespread acceptance of the desirability of a generic, process-oriented sociology (via Simmel, Mead, Blumer) on the part of interactionists and other interpretive sociologists (e.g., Schutz, 1962, 1964; Berger and Luckmann, 1966; Garfinkel, 1967), one encounters only a few more sustained attempts to pursue generic conceptualizations in the literature. These are found in the writings of Miyamato (1959), Glaser and Strauss (1967), Strauss (1970), Lofland (1970, 1976), Lester and Hadden (1980), Bigus, Hadden and Glaser (1982), and Couch (1984).

Frank Miyamato (1959) draws our attention to the "social act" as a primary, but much neglected, generic feature of group life. In particular he wishes to emphasize the temporal or processual dimensions of acts as elements for study. Thus, he stresses the fundamental interlinkages of acts and argues for their value in understanding events and organizations (networks of social acts). Although noting that typologies of acts have resulted in largely sterile endeavors, Miyamato found himself unable to offer clear directions that researchers might pursue in studing social action.

Grappling with the problem of closing "the devastating gap between speculative theory and descriptive empiricism," Glaser and Strauss (1967) and Strauss (1970) are much more precise in their proposals. Focusing on "the discovery of grounded theory," they make a very clear case for developing a cumulative awareness of the viability and dimensions of particular concepts. This is to be done by more systematically exploring conceptual variants in a plurality of settings. Pointing out the dangers of deriving formal theory from a single substantive area (80–82) as well as the shortcomings of developing theory in the absence of substantive applications (90–92), Glaser and Strauss (1967: 79–99) propose the development of "formal theory," which is based on conceptual comparisons across substantive contexts. Eschewing the researcher-theorist dichotomy, they encourage sociologists to make concerted appraisals of concepts across settings that seem both dissimilar and similar relative to the essence of particular concepts:

> *If we do not practice such modes of extending grounded theories, then we relegate them, as now, mainly to the status of respected little islands of knowledge.* . . . *Sociologists continue to develop both speculative theory and general theoretical frameworks without recognizing the great differences between these formulations and theory which is grounded in data. (Strauss, 1970:53)*

Echoing Glaser and Strauss's (1967) concerns with grounded theory, Lofland (1970) encourages greater concern with generic analysis on the part of inter-actionists. Attempting to focus the efforts of his colleagues in this article, Lofland outlines the central tasks this involves:

> *By actually following through I mean more specifically that the investigator goes to the time and trouble (1) to assemble self-consciously all his materials on how a given phenomenologically problematic topic is dealt with by the persons under study, (2) to tease out the variations among his assembled range of instance of strategies, (3) to classify them into an articulate set of what appears to him to be generic or phenomenological types of strategies, and (4) to present them to the reader in some orderly and preferably named and numbered manner. (Lofland, 1970:42)*

> *Moreover, given the virtual lack of codified concepts to draw upon, strategic analysis requires from the analyst considerable effort at creative discernment. It requires that he pour over his materials with great intensity, very much on the model of the procedure outlined by Glaser and Strauss. (Lofland, 1970:44)*

In a later statement, Lofland (1976:31–33) adds:

> *To conceive a situation generically is to discriminate and bring forward social aspects that possess more generalized, more common, more universal relevance.* . . .

To scrutinize a situation generically is to seek out its abstract, transcendent, formal, analytic aspects. (Lofland, 1976:31)

Although he organized his subsequent analysis of generic processes around a typology of interactional scales or sizes (e.g., encounters, roles, groups, organizations) of human association rather than the dimensions (e.g., acquiring perspectives, developing relationships) of association, Lofland (1976) attempted to formulate a set of generic social processes around these (size, purpose) group themes. While Lofland's book differs somewhat in its focus from the present statement, his work is highly recommended both for elucidating aspects of generic social processes and for its attentiveness to the literature. Indeed, it provides a very valuable context within which to more fully appreciate the present statement. Unfortunately, Lofland's very instructive volume has not received the (considerable) attention that it merits with respect to ethnographic inquiry.[11]

Also building on Glaser and Strauss's (1967) work, Lester and Hadden (1980) most directly address the desirability of developing grounded theory within ethnomethodological research; however, their message is relevant to interpretive sociology more generally. In particular, they note the tendency for researchers concerned with thorough analyses in substantive settings to become diverted from possible comparisons along transsituational lines. Clearly, they do not intend to curtail ethnographic inquiry, but wish to promote the development of theory grounded in a plurality of ethnographic contexts.[12]

These themes are similarly pursued by Bigus, Hadden, and Glaser (1982). Using the term *basic social processes* synonymously with *generic processes*, they draw even more explicit attention to the desirability of focusing on "activity" (vs. substance) as the central feature fostering cross-contextual comparisons and the development of grounded theory.

In a move that was to bring the Iowa School much closer to the processual orientation that had long characterized the Chicago school of interactionism, Carl Couch reiterates much of Blumer's (1969) basic message:

(T)he problems have been (1) a failure to formulate studies that allow for an assessment of the utility of central concepts on the basis of sustained and systematic examination of empirical phenomena, (2) a failure to focus on social processes and social relationships, and (3) a failure to develop methodological procedures that produce data that can be researched and shared. (Couch, 1984:2)

Noting that "social life is manifested in process," Couch proposes that we focus on the forming of social structures. Although this clearly speaks to the essence of symbolic interaction, the solution he proposes is that we study the structuring of interaction by analyzing videotaped interpersonal communications. In contrast to the ethnographic perspective posited by Blumer and the preceding scholars which emphasizes the necessity of working with interactionally derived data, Couch attempts to study the formation of generic processes by relying on researcher interpretations of observational recordings.[13]

Taken together, these scholars direct our attention to the desirability of developing a generic sociology focused on the "social production of action." Each alerts us to the value of a process-oriented sociology, one that considers the *how* (rather than the why) of group life. Further, with the possible exception of Couch (1984), each has indicated the necessity of grounding these notions in the ongoing experiences of people *doing* group life.

ACHIEVING ETHNOGRAPHIC TRANSCONTEXTUALITY

Generic social processes address the emerging, sequencing, unfolding, ongoing features of group life. They deal with the shaping, the forging, the forming, the constructing, the implementing, the ad hocing, the building up, of human interaction. As Blumer (1969) notes, process encompasses the interpreting, planning, anticipating, doing, experiencing, assessing, and readjusting features of action.

Viewed thusly, process does not deny planning or the development of routine practices and recipes for action. Neither does it ignore the temporal (historical) or the organizational (relational) linkages of action. Rather, it locates activity squarely in these contexts. Process incorporates the perspectives of the participants, as well as people's capacities for reflectivity, their abilities to influence one another, and their tendencies to develop and act upon particularistic relations with others. This notion of process also encompasses the problematic and uncertain features of group life, the dilemmas people experience, and their attempts to come to terms with these.

A key to transcontextual conceptualization, the notion of process needs to be cast in more precise terms. It is in this respect that the acknowledgement of a "career" or "natural history" of some phenomenon is so valuable. The concept of career or natural history includes four subprocesses: (1) initial emergence, (2) continuity (and intensification), (3) discontinuity (and dissipation), and (4) possible reemergence. Each of these processes is worthy of attention on its own, but taken together they provide a more holistic approach to the "life spans" of particular phenomena. Used in this manner, the concept of a career far transcends the occupational context and provides us with a means of tapping into the ongoing substance of everyday life.

Working from this framework, one may focus, for example, on careers of identities, careers of activities (events, negotiations), careers of relationships, careers of social movements and organizations, and careers of role participation. In each case, one would attend to the emergence of some phenomenon, the continuity and possible intensification of this occurrence, its eventual dissipation, and possible subsequent reemergence. Approached in this manner, one could examine the contingencies affecting occurrences involving solitary actors as well as those which entail more overt interaction (e.g., encounters, exchanges, relationships, subcultures). By focusing on the processes involved in the careers or natural histories of social phenomena, researchers working in substantively diverse settings may draw important comparisons across contexts by attending to one another's work.

As one of but a great many efforts that must go in this direction if we are to achieve and sustain a generic sociology, the following listing is offered as a heuristic device for envisioning process in a more concerted fashion. This listing is necessarily tentative, but provides an umbrella for encompassing a great many of the concepts the interactionists and other interpretive sociologists have developed over the years.

The processes following not only signify key elements of people's involvements in situations, but also define the essence of community life. These processes are interdependent and need to be viewed holistically if we are to develop a fuller appreciation of each. Nevertheless, each process encompasses several (sub)processes within, and on these levels each is amenable to empirical inquiry. While most of these processes are strikingly evident at an interpersonal level, some of these processes take into account larger scale human enterprise, such as organizational interchanges, fashions, crusades, social movements, and collective behavior. Viewed thusly, these notions allow analysts to maintain a rather consistent interactionist approach across wide ranges of human interchange.

Insofar as the listings following are fairly detailed, it may be useful to provide readers with an overview of the major processes and subprocesses encompassed by this statement.

1. *Acquiring Perspectives*
2. *Achieving Identity*
3. *Being Involved*
    Getting started

    Sustaining and intensifying involvements
    Becoming disinvolved
    Becoming reinvolved
4. *Doing Activity*
    Performing activities
    Influencing others
    Making commitments
5. *Experiencing Relationships*
6. *Forming and Coordinating Associations*
    Establishing associations
    Objectifying associations
    Encountering outsiders

The following statements outline these processes and provide more detailed listings of the subprocesses they entail. To better illustrate or help readers appreciate the generic processes being discussed, I've pulled extracts from some of my own ethnographic research. One set of materials comes from a study of card and dice hustlers (1977), which in the expanded version (Prus and Sharper, 1991) also includes an interrelated study of magicians (two sets of practitioners whose routines are steeped in image work and deception). The other extracts are drawn from a study of marketing and sales activities (Prus, 1989a,b). I've used just a single extract on each occasion, from one of the two sources. These extracts cannot be expected to convey the full range of the subprocesses entailed in any of the generic social processes under consideration, but may foster a fuller understanding of the transsituational nature of these processes.

Acquiring Perspectives

I don't know where salesman became such a dirty word, but you look at the courses people are offering and they will use just about every other word than salesman. . . . I just don't see it, because you can have all the geniuses in the world inventing products and all the skilled manufacturing going on, but if you don't have a salesman moving that item, everything else ceases to be. I don't know if we are actually teaching people to look down on sales on a blackboard or just teaching us that attitude in more casual ways. But I know that there are very few salespeople who would want their children to go into sales and even probably fewer people overall who would be proud of their children if they were successful in the world of sales. They would rather have them doctors, lawyers, and teachers and university professors and such. And in sales, you can be very successful, living a good life-style and doing an interesting job and yet they are looked down on. When you think about sales, it's so basic in terms of all areas of life and it just seems true for all different societies and throughout history. (furniture) [Prus, 1989b:102]

Representing interpretive frameworks or viewpoints (also worldviews, paradigms, versions of reality) for making sense of the world, perspectives provide the substantive content for association. Definitions of "fads" and "fashions" are encompassed in the concept of perspective as are traditions, notions of rationality, and political and religious beliefs, as well as language and other symbols. Perspectives also encompass people's definitions of rules, norms, prevailing practices, lines of authority, consensual understandings, and other "rules of thumb" people develop to provide guidance of a generalized nature.[14] Aimed at versions of the "generalized other" (Mead, 1934), these "organizational principles" are seen to transcend particular actors and situations. And, as they are envisioned to receive more extensive consensual validation by members of the (sub)communities in question, perspectives take on a heightened aura of "objectivity" (Schutz, 1971).

Although people may attend to things in quite varied manners, they evidently have no choice over the perspectives to which they are first exposed. Thus, while their early understandings are apt to be quite uneven and precarious, people seem likely to take these initial viewpoints for granted until they define these as ineffective in dealing with their circumstances or find these directly challenged by people promoting alternative viewpoints. It is apparent, however, that perspectives are contingent on continued affirmations for their existence and impact. They are subject to ongoing interpretation and assume cooperation and other enterprising activity on the part of those exposed to these particular "notions of reality." By delineating the subprocesses entailed in "acquiring perspectives" along the lines following, researchers may be better able to examine the ways in which people contend with the cultural content they encounter:

* *Encountering perspectives (definitions of reality) from others*
* *Assessing (new, incoming) perspectives and resisting unwanted viewpoints*
* *Developing images of objects (including images of other people and oneself)*
* *Learning (cultural) patterns of objects (e.g., rules of thumb, norms, fashion)*
* *Defining situations (i.e., applying perspectives to the "cases at hand")*
* *Dealing with ambiguity (lapses and limitations in existing explanations)*
* *Resolving contradictions (dilemmas within and across paradigms)*
* *Extending or improvising on existing perspectives*

* *Promoting (and defending) perspectives to others*
* *Rejecting formerly held viewpoints*
* *Adopting new viewpoints*[15]

Achieving Identity

> *I like to hang out with creative magicians. I don't like to hang out with guys who do box tricks. I like to hang out with people who are knowledgeable about magic, who have dedication and enthusiasm, upbeat. . . . I don't change my standards for judging people when it comes to magicians. The only exceptions I make is that there are some incredibly talented magicians who are incredible jerks, so you have to appreciate just their art and forget about the rest. . . . The people I hang around, in magic, it's called, "the underground.". . . There's a loose knit community of people, people who take magic seriously. . . . They give a lot of thought to magic. . . . They create magic, they talk about it. They write about it, read it. They study it, exchange ideas. They get together at these conventions and perform it for each other. They're very much on top of what's happening in magic. . . It's very, very different from a magic club, belonging to a magic club. I used to belong to some magic clubs, but I don't belong any more. (magician)*
> *[Prus and Sharper, 1991:275]*

"Identity work" is contingent on people's capacity for "self reflectivity;" it requires that one begin to take oneself into account in developing lines of action or that one become "an object unto oneself." Reflecting the perspectives one has on the world, people's identities or self-other definitions are not only situated within those realities, but also are influenced by the ongoing shifts in perspectives that people normally undergo over time and across situations. However, in contrast to the more generalized quality of perspectives, identities have a more immediate and personalized ("you and I") focus. Additionally, to the extent people associate identities with the treatment they receive, they tend to be concerned about maintaining acceptable images (especially avoiding disrespectability).[16]

As products of interaction, people's identities are also fundamentally linked to the identities of their associates. Consequently, identity work reflects ongoing assessments and negotiations as the parties involved jointly endeavor to work out self and other definitions. The processes entailed here include:

* *Encountering definitions of self from others*
* *Attributing qualities to self (self definitions)*

* *Comparing incoming and self-assigned definitions of self*
* *Resisting unwanted identity imputations*
* *Selectively conveying information about self to others*
* *Gleaning information about others*
* *Assigning identities to others*
* *Promoting specific definitions of others*
* *Encountering resistance from others*
* *Reassessing identities imputed to others*[17]

Being Involved

> *Most people in business would like their own store, company, whatever. But most don't have the money and like me, they're too chicken to risk what they do have. . . . And, if you move up in the organization and the pay starts to get pretty good, then there's even more incentive to stay with the company your with. (men's clothing) [Prus, 1989b:81]*

"Being involved" denotes the sequencing of people's participation in settings. Emphasizing the "how" (vs. why) of involvements, consideration is given to the histories or ("careers") of people's participation in particular situations (Becker, 1963; Prus, 1984). While focusing on one involvement at a time, each involvement is best envisioned against a backdrop of multiple, shifting, and potentially incompatible involvements in other settings. The processes prominent here are: (*a*) initial involvements, (*b*) continuities, (*c*) disinvolvements, and (*d*) reinvolvements.[18]

Getting Started (Initial Involvements)

> *With the crafts, it's not unusual to see other members of the family getting involved. It's usually the wife to get involved first, and then the husband or the children get dragged into it. It works the other way too, but it often becomes a family thing. (crafts) [Prus, 1989b:78]*

Although any of the following routings (seekership, recruitment, closure) may dominate people's involvements in particular settings, involvements often reflect combinations of these elements.[19] While not pivotal in all cases, any reservations people have may mitigate against particular involvements.

* *Engaging in "seekership" (pursuing self-attributed interests)*
* *Being recruited (others attempt to foster interest, encourage participation)*

* *Experiencing "closure" (perceiving pressing obligations, limited choices)*
* *Managing reservations (overcoming doubts, stigma, risks)*[20]

Sustaining and Intensifying Involvements (Continuities)

> *I enjoy the comaraderie that exists between the other retailers, say at the sales club, because there are people there that you feel that you have something in common with. Unfortunately, we've found that being in business for yourself, it has almost alienated ourselves from the circle of friends that we had before. A large part of it, is that when you start out, you are almost consumed by the petty, and not so petty, day to day concerns of doing business. It's very hard to carry on even a casual relationship with people who have regular jobs and have a separate social life. Now, maybe it's that we're not relaxed enough, but we find that it's always on our minds. (appliances) [Prus, 1989b:83–84]*

Once people have become involved in particular situations, we ask when they are likely to continue (and intensify) their participation in those settings. People's involvements in situations can vary immensely along the following dimensions:[21]

* *Internalizing perspectives (viewpoints consistent with particular involvements)*
* *Achieving identity (self and other definitions consistent with particular involvements)*
* *Accomplishing activities (competence and composure in the focal setting)*
* *Making commitments (making investments, developing dependencies)*
* *Developing relationships (experiencing positive bonds with others in the setting)*
* *Foregoing alternative involvements (neglecting options, "bridge-burning")*

Becoming Disinvolved

> *It's tough to get out of the business. First, where else can a guy like this make this kind of money, say without gettting into other kinds of crime.... So the money thing is probably the biggest single thing.... But say a guy wants to go straight and maybe he's willing to take a cut in pay, here's another problem. How is he going to get this legitimate job? Who's going to hire him? What training does he have? Telling an employee that you're an experienced crap hustler won't go over too well. What does he say he's been doing all those years? Or maybe he can't get references or get bonded or maybe he's getting up in age. A lot of hustlers at different times stop and think, "What kind of job could I get?" (hustler) [Prus and Sharper, 1991:131]*

Insofar as it is unlikely that people would be uniformly highly involved in all dimensions of the situation at hand, we may see continuity and discontinuity as closely intertwined. Indeed, not only are people's involvements in many situations apt to be partial with respect to one or more of these dimensions, but we would also expect that people could question the viability of their involvements along any of these dimensions at any point in time. The following suggests some basis on which disinvolvement is more likely, but it should not be assumed that dissatisfaction on any one dimension would necessitate disinvolvement (i.e., consider the problems of simultaneous disentanglement on all of these dimensions). The (perceived) availability of feasible options seems central, as do the other elements defining one's participation in a more complete sense:

* *Questioning viability of perspectives (facing obstacles, dilemmas)*
* *Reassessing identity (consistent with desired images?)*
* *Finding activities troublesome (boring, unpleasant, cumbersome)*
* *Being freed-up from existing commitments (free to "relocate")*
* *Severing relationships (conflict, animosity, exclusion)*
* *Encountering opportunities for alternative involvements*[22]

Becoming Reinvolved

> *We do a lot of [trade] shows. Some we have stopped doing altogether because we didn't feel we were getting sufficient response. Some you can tell are good, because you get a lot of orders on the spot. Those are the ones we wouldn't want to pass up. But others don't do that much for you. And it's the old thing of, "Where do you want to put your money?"... Over time, you sort them out, the good shows and the not so good shows. But a lot are iffy too. You don't really know which way to go. Or with some, you know they would be better if you had a better location at the show. So that's something else, the position at these shows. If you can swing a better spot for the next time, that might be the deciding thing in your return. There really are good locations and deadly locations. (manufacture-industrial) [Prus, 1989b:300]*

Should people's subsequent involvements be found unsatisfactory (vis-à-vis perspectives, identities, activities, commitments, relationships), then reinvolvement in an earlier situation appears more likely. This seems more common as people begin:[23]

* *Defining opportunities for reinvolvements in former situations as more feasible than current pursuits*
* *Noting greater changes to self or situation that would justify reinvolvement*
* *Finding that they have less extensively organized their routines around their present involvements (i.e., disentanglement is more easily accomplished)*

Doing Activity

Buying is critical for the survival of the business and if it doesn't move, then you're in a lot of trouble. This is where fashion buying becomes especially risky, because, "what people say they want" and "what they end up buying" are two different things. So one of the big questions you ask yourself, when you are looking at new merchandise and new lines is the question, "Will it move?" It is also tricky, because what may be popular one week, where your racks get cleaned out of a particular line of merchandise may not be a good item to reorder for the next week. You just don't know where the customers are going to concentrate their buying. (women's clothing) [Prus, 1989b:153]

Although people's activities have important implications for their subsequent viewpoints and identities, activities acquire their meaning or purposiveness relative to both the perspectives from which they are envisioned and the identities of the people involved. Since the preceding discussions of perspectives and identities have already been cast in action (do-ing) terms, our attention turns to three other realms of activity. These include (*a*) performing activities, (*b*) influencing others, and (*c*) making commitments.

Performing Activities

When someone is doing a small show of, say, fifty people, it is very different from working on a large stage. You have far greater levels of intimacy. The performer is much more visible. You can see the guy sweating, or you can see that he has food stuck in his teeth, because often they'll bring you out to perform after the dinner. It can be distracting for the performance, because people look at you. They can study you in great detail,[13] whereas on the stage, you have a lot more distance and they simply wouldn't see these things. (magician) [Prus and Sharper, 1991:225]

[13] *Sharper: This is exactly the case [cheating at poker games]! They can study you. . . . Sitting at a poker game people do study you. . . . These guys (magicians) are saying that you're so close to them, it gets very personal. I notice some people have a lot of trouble with that. We had one fellow who didn't want to talk. He's a good card mechanic, but he wouldn't talk, no discussion. And they'd (other players) kind of wonder, like, "What's he doing here? Where are you from?" So sitting at a poker game people do study you, they do! And, again it relates to, if you make unnatural moves, then the studying gets more intense, so you have to be careful! [Prus and Sharper, 1991:240]*

The "performance of activity" assumes the processes outlined in "getting involved," but highlights the "problematics of accomplishment." It should be noted that no assumption is made about people acting "wisely" or "rationally" in any objective sense. Wisdom and rationality are not only matters of definition, but these notions are also apt to be worked out in process (see Prus, 1989b, especially 139–142). Indeed, while people may try to act in manners that they deem wise, rational, and the like, reality is not theirs alone to determine. Indeed, matters of ambiguity, uncertainty, and resistance on the part of others can make human endeavor particularly problematic. The processes relevant to performance include:

* *Making (preliminary) plans*
* *Getting prepared*
* *Managing stage fright (reservations, if any)*
* *Developing competence (stock of knowledge, tactics, applications)*
* *Coordinating events with others (team members and others)*
* *Dealing with ambiguity, obstacles, resistances, and distractions*
* *Conveying images of competence (displaying ability, composure)*
* *Encountering competition*
* *Making ongoing assessments and adjustments*[24]

Influencing Others

> *When a good salesman gets a hold of him, he spends time with them, and time is an important element. If you spend time with somebody, show them the car, demonstrate the car with them, listen to them, there's an obligation there. Because all the dealers sell for pretty close to the same amount as the others, so more (important) than the money is the time you're spending with the customer, the comaraderie, the trust you establish with the people, the confidence you establish. (auto) [Prus, 1989a:110]*

The influence or persuasion process reflects attempts on the part of people to "gain the cooperation or commitments of others" with respect to both "one to one" and more diversified "group" situations. When dealing with larger groups of people, matters of complexity and ambiguity typically become more noteworthy, as do distractions, challenges, and lowered levels of personal (target) accountability. As well, one's opportunities for role-taking are lessened when one faces the task of "pitching" to more generalized audiences as opposed to interpersonal others. This may involve some additional frustration and result in the creation of some unique group-directed tactics, but otherwise the same basic processes appear to hold for these instances as well. Here, we may consider how people go about:

* *Formulating (preliminary) plans*
* *Role-taking (inferring/uncovering the perspectives of the other)*
* *Promoting interest in one's objectives*
* *Generating trust*
* *Proposing specific lines of action*
* *Encountering resistance*
* *Neutralizing obstacles*
* *Seeking and making concessions*
* *Confirming agreements*
* *Assessing "failures" and recasting plans*[25]

Making Commitments

> *I eventually gained (name's) confidence and I studied with him every week for about five years, four or five hours at a time, just talking about magic. He was showing me things, teaching me his thoughts and principles of his work. There was no consideration that passed, there was no money exchanged. He just did it because he was pleased that someone was that interested in his work, someone whom he thought had the ability to continue the tradition, so to speak. (magician) [Prus and Sharper, 1991:234–235]*

Commitments assume a variety of forms and may include physical investments as well as claims made to oneself or others. Some commitments are clearly desired by the parties making them, but others may be exceedingly tentative or reflect earlier resistance. The processes of "putting one's money down" or "buying into" specific situations can have important consequences for subsequent behavior. To the extent people acknowledge their earlier commitments, these can significantly limit their choices (i.e., closure). Subprocesses of relevance include:

* *Exploring and assessing options*
* *Dealing with (any) earlier commitments*
* *Avoiding commitments ("elusive targets")*
* *Minimizing or diversifying investments ("hedging bets")*
* *Organizing routines around particular activities*
* *Neglecting other options ("closure by default")*[26]

Experiencing Relationships

No trick is ever the same, even for the same magician. You're always performing for different audiences and each person can make different inferences about what's going on. You'll get some who don't understand the concept, they don't know what is going on, and others, say, who are more superstitious or scared because they link magic with the supernatural. You might have some trick, the one with the balls, for instance, where you start out with two balls and give one to one of the spectators, a woman say. Now, however, the second ball vanishes from your hand and reappears in her hand. Is she amazed? Entertained? Frightened? She might just say, "This is silly!", and throw both balls back at you. You never know how people will react to you! (magician) [Prus and Sharper, 1991:245]

Like the elements preceding, relationships may be largely subsumed by the "doing of activities." However, the selectivity and continuity of association entailed by interpersonal "bonding" signifies a vital element in social life. Relationships imply perspectives, identities, activities, and commitments, and these can be powerful elements shaping the associations that people develop with one another. Since they also entail process, relationships have natural histories or careers (initial involvements, continuities, disinvolvements, reinvolvements), but matters of "intimacy and distancing" become especially prominent here as people try to achieve levels of selectivity and continuity with which they feel comfortable. The following processes seem central to considerations of people's relationships with others:

* *Getting prepared for generalized encounters*
* *Defining self as available for association*
* *Defining (specific) others as desirable associates*
* *Making approaches/receiving openings from others*
* *Encountering (and indicating) rejection/acceptance*
* *Assessing self and other for "goodness of fit"*
* *Developing interactional styles (in each relationship)*
* *Managing openness and secrecy*
* *Developing understandings, preferences, loyalty*
* *Managing distractions (and outside commitments)*
* *Juggling (multiple) relationships*
* *Severing relationships (disentanglement)*
* *Renewing relationships*[27]

Forming and Coordinating Associations

> *You promote the mall, the whole mall as an interesting, exciting, fun place to shop. You have an overall advertising budget, and then you go to all the businesses and get them to promote the mall by cooperative advertising in the newspapers, radio, t.v., advertise your "Sidewalk Sales," "Boxing Day Specials," all those sorts of things. (mall) [Prus, 1989b:71]*

The notion of forming or generating associations with others centrally builds on the generic social processes just discussed, but it is also contingent on people recognizing the advantages of encompassing the efforts of others into their objectives. These associations can vary greatly in size, duration, formality, and the like. However, they involve attempts to obtain the cooperation of others with respect to ventures that people are unwilling or unable to pursue on their own. While not all of these ventures will be developed very fully or successfully, three subprocesses seem relevant in a great many cases. These are: establishing associations, objectifying associations, and encountering outsiders.

Establishing Associations

> *As a franchise, we try to be distinctive, and the idea is that as a result, the whole is greater than the parts. It makes you seem more prominent in the public eye. So if you're doing your job, and they're doing their jobs in the other communities, it may look as though we're doing a lot more business than we actually are. And that's precisely what we want to happen, to get a higher profile. It impresses people, and if we can do that, we're likely to get more business.... Most people, I think, feel more comfortable listing with a national company. They feel that if it's bigger, it's better. They feel that a larger company, with a larger image, will do a better job.... In other cases, where they've been happy with your service, they'll contact you again, or tell others about you. We encourage that, but I think that more and more people are going to national companies and I think that that is why the franchise system has been so successful. The smaller companies just can't offer the training or the benefits of the larger organization.... For someone starting out, new, one has to get the name, the recognition, the system, the back up assistance the franchise system offers. It's very difficult for an independent to open up an office and be very successful these days. It can happen, and it will happen, but the odds are against you. There are enough uncertainties in real estate without that! (real estate) [Prus, 1989b:72–73]*

Here, we recognize the task of, and enterprise involved in, incorporating others into a collective entity (i.e., group, venture, team, side, agency, organization, gang, committee, department, office, crew, mob, band, tribe, cult). People involved in more fleeting alignments may circumvent or truncate some of the following processes, but those people involved in longer term ventures seem likely to pursue activities of this sort:

* *Anticipating the value of collective enterprise*
* *Involving others in the venture (recruitment, screening, minimizing reservations)*
* *Justifying the group (developing perspectives, moral viewpoints)*
* *Celebrating the venture (witnessing, recognizing, emphasizing—within the group)*
* *Defining the team (membership criteria, positions, responsibilities)*
* *Establishing communication forums (interpersonal, media)*
* *Pursuing resources for the group*
* *Arranging member assemblies (encounters, practices)*
* *Providing instruction for members (perspectives, techniques)*
* *Monitoring members*
* *Assessing member performances*
* *Motivating and disciplining members*
* *Rejecting and reinstating members*
* *Facing internal upheaval (splintering, factions, challenges from within)*
* *Facing generalized loss of interest*
* *Dealing with dissolution*
* *Attempting to revitalize cooperative ventures*[28]

Objectifying Associations

> *Advertising creates an aura. The advertiser convinces the consumer that you are the best person to go to.... They're your front man! It's kind of a recommendation.... The unfortunate part of it is that as a new person going into business, you're more dependent on advertising than an established business. But, unfortunately, the costs of advertising being what they are, you can't get the kind of advertising you really need. (appliances) [Prus, 1989b:208–209]*

Although the coordinators of some associations may intend that they remain unnoticed within the larger community, on a great many occasions the participants are interested in establishing a prominence for their groups that is more obvious to both members and outsiders within the community. Even those groups who wish to "go undercover" for a variety of reasons may adopt certain practices to make their venture appear "more real" to their members. Those desiring community-wide objectification (Berger and Luckmann, 1966) may be even more outreaching in their efforts. Insider practices such as the following are particularly noteworthy in fostering a group presence in the community:

* *Developing a group identity (name, logo, flag)*
* *Stipulating justifications for existence and operations*
* *Creating identity markers for members (uniforms, appearances, signs)*
* *Defining exclusiveness (selectivity, oaths, codes, jargon)*
* *Establishing a public presence (announcements, advertising, rallies, protests)*
* *Legitimating the group publicly (endorsements, credentials, charters, licences)*
* *Demarcating territories and jurisdictions (buildings, places, locations)*[29]

While everything that insiders do with respect to particular associations may be seen to help establish these (groups) as distinct entities within the community, the objectification process is further intensified when outsiders also engage in "identity-work" pertaining to the groups at hand. The outsiders who become thusly involved may have rather diverse interests (curiousities, fascinations, entertainment, knowledge, fear, condemnation, control, elimination) with respect to the subculture in question, but insofar as they serve to identify, conceptualize, talk about, and act toward particular associations as if they were more unique, prominent, consequential, and the like, these outsiders may be seen to contribute to the overall profile of particular groups within the community. The following outsider practices are relevant here:

* *Defining a set of people as constituting a group or interactive entity within the community*
* *Associating (assigning, acknowledging) specific names (and other identity markers) with the group*
* *Attributing particular properties (qualities and evaluations) to the group*
* *Discussing (talk, rumor, media messages) the group with others in the community*
* *Making more concerted effort (reflecting curiousities and fascinations to condemnations and control concerns) to attend to, or deal with, the group as an entity within the broader community*

Encountering Outsiders

Our "Sales" store had a very different clientele than our store a few blocks down the street, which did not carry the "Sales" items on a regular basis. People who came into the "Sales" store tended to be older, much more picky, harder to sell, they wanted to pay half the price and to get twice the value. They were very rough, more difficult to deal with, a lot more problems with returns than what

*you would get with the same merchandise in our other stores. . . . That type
of person does get drawn into the other stores when you're having a "Sidewalk
Sale," a mall promotion, something like that. . . . The "Sales" shoppers are
messier, rougher. They're a little neater in neater stores, but they're messier than
your general customers. (mixed clothing) [Prus, 1989a:245]*

Once associations are established, members may make contact with a variety
of individuals and groups within the larger community of operation. Outsiders,
variously, may represent: targets (i.e., potential members, supporters, prospects,
clients, customers, patrons, cases, suckers, marks, patients, inmates) for association's enterprises; potential partners for particular cooperative ventures; adversaries (competitors, enemies); or rather ambiguous members of the community
at large. While the association's interests in particular individuals and groups
can be quite wide-ranging, the following matters tend to be of concern more
generally:

* *Representing the association('s interests)*
* *Making contact with outsiders (establishing co-presence, making the scene)*
* *Defining the theatre of operation (places, objectives, strategies)*
* *Identifying outsiders (targets, cooperators, adversaries, witnesses, nobodies)*
* *Pursuing associational objectives through the others (cooperation, influence work)*
* *Confronting outsiders (challenges, competitions, conflicts)*
* *Protecting (sometimes concealing) the association from the outsiders*
* *Readjusting group routines to more effectively deal with the outsiders*[30]

CONCLUSION

*You could be the greatest mechanic [card/dice manipulator] in the world, but
it only counts when you make the moves under pressure, when the money is
on the line and that's good performance and I found that takes staying in there
and doing the work. It's not something that you can just go in and do. It has
to be learned under pressure! And the more pressure that you're under, the easier
the other parties are. Like I've been to parties where I just wouldn't make a
move, I don't know why, but I just wouldn't! (My partner) would be in there,
moving a mile a minute. He'd come out, and he'd get mad at me, "Come on!
Come on!" And then I would go ahead and work. . . .*

*They were also the ones, like (name). Just give him the cubes, and he could
really shake, rattle and roll those dice! Like this guy was terrific! Snap his fingers
and whip the other set against the wall and still have that other set concealed. . . .*

*I remember first watching him and we're going to this party and I thought,
"Gee, I've got no chance to work tonight!" But when we went to this party,
a good party, my boss comes over to me and hands me my tools (dice) and I
thought, "What's going on here?" So we worked that night and I couldn't wait
to ask him as we were going home, when (name) was gone, he had his own
car. And I said, "(Boss), how come you gave me the tools and not (name)? That
guy just makes those things disappear!" He says, "Yeah, but as soon as he gets
in a game he gets the gulps! He won't make a move under pressure!" So you
can be great with your peers and great showing other people, or maybe if you're
with people who have no idea what you're doing at all. But under the money
pressure and the pressure of, "You've got to make the move, now," he couldn't
handle it. He wouldn't make the move. He'd always find a reason. There's ghosts
disguised this way, or it wasn't right. It wasn't the right time. I don't think
the move should be made now. (card and dice hustler) [Prus and Sharper,
1991:298]*

Focusing on the life-worlds of the other, ethnographic research is rooted in
the experiences and activities of people. It attends to their meanings and practices,
their dilemmas and uncertainties, and to their attempts to work out their situations in conjunction with those of others whose lives intersect with their own.
It is an approach oriented toward the intimate understanding of group life and
all of which group life consists.

The notion of a generic processual sociology builds on these concerns
by examining parallel activities across contexts. Whereas ethnographic research
allows us to be very sensitive to each particular context (and the meanings of
each context for the participants therein), the emphasis on process enables us
to maximize conceptual development. By drawing comparisons and contrasts
across settings, we not only arrive at a richer understanding of each setting,
but of similar processes across a wide range of settings. In doing so we have
the opportunity to assess previous findings and to work towards fuller, more
qualified conceptualizations of human association. Indeed, only by being acutely
attentive to the ways in which "people experience and shape their worlds"
and drawing parallels across situations can we hope to achieve a "theory of
action" that reflects group life as it is accomplished.

The generic social processes outlined here are tentative rather than definitive
renderings of the interactionist/ethnographic literature. It is expected that they
will undergo revisions as people attempt to assess and define their viability
across other research sites. This does not, however, diminish the value of generic
social processes for the field of sociology or the social sciences more generally.

Because the generic social processes developed here are viewed as part of an ongoing formulative process that is oriented toward a comprehensive understanding of the ways in which human group life is accomplished, this set of concepts represents a unique and powerful heuristic device. First, this statement builds on an analytical framework that not only maintains remarkable coherence with respect to theory, methods, and research, but also provides the means by which so called "micro" and "macro" sociological issues can be synthesized in a conceptually consistent manner.

Second, attention to generic social processes enables scholars to transcend diverse substantive areas while maintaining highly detailed analyses of particular settings. This clearly fosters conceptual cross-fertilization on the part of scholars working in very different substantive settings. Third, by creating an analytical grid with which to assess and incorporate (in a dynamic manner) research in the field, this and subsequent statements on generic social processes can greatly facilitate conceptual stock taking as scholars become more attentive to the contributions as well as suggest gaps and lapses in the literature. This provides researchers with a series of analytical themes to which they may attend (and assess) in developing their research. Fourth, generic social processes represent pivital communication media through, or forums around, which scholars may discuss their research in more focused and meaningful manners.

Fifth, by focusing on the processual or emergent features of human action and interchange, generic social processes suggest essential ways of reorienting the sociological enterprise around the forms of association that Simmel proposed (in contrast to a functionalist emphasis on institutions). Not only would this foster a great many cross-contextual insights in the discipline, but an emphasis on generic social processes also alerts scholars to the necessity of attending to human lived experiences and the ways in which human group life is accomplished on a day-to-day basis. Finally, insofar as generic social processes enable scholars to readily transcend substantive realms (e.g., politics, marketing, recreation, education, religion, and the like), an emphasis on generic social processes represents a particularly viable, conceptually coherent, and empirically grounded means of generating highly meaningful and sustained interdisciplinary linkages in the social sciences. Indeed, an application of generic social processes (and the underlying interactionist conceptual scheme this implies) suggests that the major differences exist not between scholars in different disciplines, but rather between those who centrally consider the ways in which various aspects of human community life are accomplished, in practice, by thinking, acting, and interacting people, and those who do not.

Viewed in this manner, generic social processes offer a great deal of potential to those seriously interested in pursuing the study of human lived experience, in all its facets. At the same time, however, as Blumer cautions, a great deal of challenge remains for those embarking on this endeavor:

> *I don't think that there is any short-cut way of arriving at the formation of such judgments; it has to be done in the slow and tedious manner of developing a rich and intimate familiarity with the kind of conduct that is being studied and in employing whatever relevant imagination observers may fortunately possess. The improvement in judgment, in observation, and in concept will be in the future, as I suspect it has been in the past, a slow, maturing process. (Blumer, 1940:719)*

NOTES

1. A somewhat related, earlier version of this paper was published in the *Journal of Contemporary Ethnography* 1987 (16):250–293. Likewise, two other variations of this statement on generic social processes recently have been published elsewhere (Prus, 1994a, 1994b). All are somewhat different, but this is the most recent and generally most adequate of all of these statements. While I have done some "tinkering" with the GSPs generally (and have added more bibliographic references), I would particularly draw readers' attention to the section on *forming and coordinating associations* in the present version. This material addresses a very important theme that was underdeveloped in earlier statements. Indeed, it might be observed that this material rather explicitly lays out a means of bridging so-called "macro" and "micro" issues in a consistently interactionist, process-based manner. Although this bridging has been implicitly (and sometimes explicitly) acknowledged by interactionists for decades, the material presented here underscores the reflective enterprise that undergirds "organizational dynamics."

2. Although seemingly unaware of much of the literature on which the present statement is built, a somewhat parallel task has been suggested by Noblit and Hare (1988) under the term, "meta-ethnography." Despite this intriguing term, Noblit and Hare provide little direction concerning the ways in which meta-ethnography might be accomplished. The present statement on generic social processes, then, may be seen as extending their project along more focused, processual dimensions.

3. See Dietz, Prus and Shaffir (1994) for a collection of ethnographic studies that has been organized around the generic social processes examined in this chapter.

4. Although Wilhelm Dilthey (see Makkreel, 1975; Rickman, 1976, 1988; Ermarth, 1978; Plantinga, 1980) is one of the major figures in the development of a hermeneutic social science, and an intellectual precursor to the symbolic interactionism of George Herbert Mead and Herbert George Blumer, textbook writers generally have been tardy in acknowledging Dilthey's role as a central founding figure in the human (social) sciences.

5. Garfinkel's (1967:35–75) depiction of the "cultural dope" (the sociologists' human who acts in certain ways because of prevailing societal conditions) and the "psychological dope" (the psychologists' counterpart) is very apropos here. Albeit with different purposes in mind, Harré and Secord (1972), Gergen (1982) and Carlson (1984) provide somewhat related critiques of psychological social psychology.

6. Clearly, I am not denying the "generic" or abstract applicabilities of other sociological formulations to human group life (e.g., consider Merton's [1957] typology of adaptation to deviance, Parsons's [1951] pattern variables, Sorokin's [1937–1941] conceptualization of cyclical change, or Homan's [1958] exchange theory). Further, while these scholars themselves engage in much interpretive work in their attempts to show how their conceptualizations could apply to a wide range of human settings, their models are *not* grounded in the ongoing, interpretive dynamics of human association. Sociologists may apply these and other constructs to a wide range of human groups, but a great many sociological constructions are not attentive to the intersubjective features of human association and for this reason are not seen to qualify as "generic social processes." Insofar as these conceptualizations are inattentive variously to the (multi) perspectival, reflective, negotiable, relational, and processual features of everyday life, they violate central features of the social essence of human lived experiences.

7. Goffman's works (especially 1959, 1961, 1963a, 1963b, 1971, 1974) come readily to mind in this respect, as well as in Goffman's insatiable quest for generic features of association. Although Goffman's own propensity for fieldwork is vastly overshadowed by his exceptionally rich, penetrating, and engaging analysis, Goffman emerges as an exemplar par excellence of the production of generic concepts through ethnographic research. Much of Goffman's analyses focus on ongoing identity work within the context of situated community morality, and only some of his concepts are

processual in nature. However, the materials Goffman gathered on community life in the Shetland Islands, and on the underlife of the mental hospital, as well as through his continued observations of the drama of everyday life, were vital not only in shaping his own conceptualizations of the social world, but (through his subsequent analyses) also had strikingly profound impact on the social sciences more generally.

8. Zerubavel (1981) explores this issue at greater depth, arguing for the natural affinity of Simmel's work with focused ethnographic inquiry.

9. Levine (1971:xlviii–lviii) provides a very valuable depiction of Simmel's influence on American sociology via Small and Park.

10. As Palmer's (1928) statement testifies, fieldwork was significantly established as a methodology by that time. Park and Burgess (1924:58–59) provide a bibliographic listing of "methods of sociological research" to that date.

11. As a case in point, I observe that I was not as familiar with this volume at the time that I originally prepared this statement as I would have liked to have been in retrospect. The Lofland (1976) volume is a very valuable resource for those embarking on ethnographic inquiry.

12. See Prus (1987) for a brief discussion of some of the obstacles facing people attempting to develop and apply generic social processes in research contexts.

13. In the course of conducting their studies, Couch and his associates (1986a,b), however, have tended to impute meanings to the acts of others rather than inquire into the meanings that participants themselves have for their activities. Thus, while appreciating the potential of any record of human behavior, we should be most concerned that the interpretive processes underlying record construction (and usage, including analysis!) not be subordinated to the pursuit of a "more scientific technique." In referencing recorded statements as a data base, one may be particularly reminded of Blumer's (1939) very insightful appraisal of Thomas and Znaniecki's *The Polish Peasant in Europe and America* (a critique which they acknowledged to be exceedingly well founded). The implication is that we should be extremely cautious of "content analysis" when we lack the interpretive assistance of those doing and/or assembling those "documents." Under these circumstances, the perspectives of those interpreting the data become increasingly central in determining the "meanings" these materials are subsequently purported to have.

14. These "organizational principles" are sometimes envisioned as constituting the essence of "social structure." Organizational guidelines are certainly basic to group life, but the term "social structure" is more accurately

applied to the *processes* that people invoke as they take one another into account in developing the lines of action that taken together constitute group life. Viewed thusly, normative frameworks represent socially constructed processes that provide greater longevity to particular cultural themes (or other shared "understandings").

15. Most ethnographies nicely illustrate themes pertaining to "the acquisition of perspectives" and most almost inevitably address notions of identities, involvements, activities, and relationships as well, for these elements are very much interrelated in subcultural life-styles. Some book-length ethnographies that do a particularly effective job of conveying the ways in which people become exposed to, and familiar with, particular worldviews include: Anderson (1923), Shaw (1930), Blumer (1933), Blumer and Hauser (1933), Sutherland (1937), Becker et al. (1961, 1968), Goffman (1961), Lofland (1966), Scott (1968), Wiseman (1970), Bartell (1971), Prus and Irini (1980), Dietz (1983), Fine (1983), Schneider and Conrad (1983), Kleinman (1984), Evans and Falk (1986), Stebbins (1990), Adler and Adler (1991), Charmaz (1991) and Wolf (1991).

16. Although the development and alteration of collective or group identities generally entail more complex processes of presentation, typification, designation, assessment, resistance, and retypification than do those directed toward single individuals, the themes subsequently listed in the text would appear to apply in rather parallel manners to definitions directed toward collective or singular targets.

17. Ethnographic monographs that are particularly attentive to identity work and self images include: Edgerton (1969), Bartell (1971), Dietz (1983), Schneider and Conrad (1983), Evans and Falk (1986), Haas and Shaffir (1987), Charmaz (1991), Sanders (1991) and Wolf (1991). For reviews of the literature on "identity work" as this pertains to type-casting, public designations, and resisting unwanted imputations, see Prus (1975a, 1975b, 1982). These reviews build centrally on the conceptual work of Goffman (1959, 1963b) and Klapp (1962, 1964, 1971), amongst others.

18. Among the monographs that more explicitly address involvements or career contingencies in ethnographic inquiries are: Shaw (1930), Cressey (1932), Sutherland (1937), Becker et al. (1961), Lofland (1966), Bartell (1971), Ditton (1977), Lesieur (1977), Dietz (1983), Fine (1983), Haas and Shaffir (1987), Prus and Irini (1980), Adler and Adler (1991), Prus and Sharper (1991), Sanders (1991) and Wolf (1991).

19. In a more complete sense, one should also note the existence of "imposed" (e.g., physiological/medical complications) and "inadvertent" (accidental, unwitting) involvements.

20. The matter of initial involvements is given particular attention in Shaw (1930), Cressey (1932), Sutherland (1937), Becker et al. (1961), Lofland (1966), Bartell (1971), Ditton (1977), Lesieur (1977), Fine (1983), Haas and Shaffir (1987), Prus and Irini (1980), Prus and Sharper (1991), Sanders (1991) and Wolf (1991).

21. Since the processes (reflecting perspectives, activity, identity, relationships, and commitments—PAIRC) outlined here are central to understanding people's continuities in particular situations, they also serve to frame the dynamics of ongoing subcultural or community life more generally. Thus, while each of these processes is addressed in greater detail elsewhere in this chapter, it is important to locate these notions with respect to people's individual involvements in particular situations or realms of activity. Researchers may also wish to track people's involvements in specific situations against the background of the multiple and potentially competing involvements in which they may find themselves over time.

    For materials that specifically attend to continuity of role involvements, see Shaw (1930), Cressey (1932), Sutherland (1937), Becker et al. (1961), Becker (1963), Lofland (1966), Bartell (1971), Ditton (1977), Lesieur (1977), Prus and Irini (1980), Fine (1983), Adler (1985), Steffensmeier (1986), Haas and Shaffir (1987), Prus and Sharper (1991), Sanders (1991) and Wolf (1991).

22. See Ebaugh (1988) for a review of the literature on "Becoming an Ex," as well as an instructive attempt to formulate the generic social processes constituting disinvolvement. As with the interconnectedness of continuity and disinvolvement, it is most important to be attentive to the interlinkages of the disinvolvement and reinvolvement processes. The implication is that all of these notions are much more fluid, partial, and ambiguous than commonly supposed.

23. Only a few studies have addressed the reinvolvement process in a substantial manner. See Ray (1961), Wiseman (1970), Lesieur (1977), Prus and Sharper (1977), and Prus and Irini (1980). Taken together, these studies suggest that considerable vacillation (disinvolvement and reinvolvement) may represent commonplace experiences for people involved in, and attempting to disentangle themselves from, many situations.

24. The following book-length monographs provide some of the more focused materials on how people accomplish activities: Anderson (1923), Shaw (1930), Emerson (1969), Bartell (1971), Letkemann (1973), Hargreaves et al. (1975), Ditton (1977), Lesieur (1977), Prus and Irini (1980), Ross (1980), Knorr-Cetina (1981), Dietz (1983), Fine (1983), Mitchell (1983),

Schneider and Conrad (1983), Albas and Albas (1984), Powell (1985), Steffensmeier (1986), Adler and Adler (1991), Charmaz (1991), Prus and Sharper (1991), and Wolf (1991). For detailed illustrations of these particular subprocesses, see Prus (1989b).

25. Notions of persuasion (influence and negotiation processes) are especially evident in the following monographs: Shaw (1930), Sutherland (1937), Festinger (1965), Lofland (1966), Emerson (1969), Wiseman (1970), Bartell (1971), Prus and Irini (1980), Ross (1980), Fine (1983), Latour (1987), Prus (1989a,b) and Prus and Sharper (1991). The subprocesses outlined here are most extensively detailed in an analysis of interpersonal selling activity (Prus, 1989a).

26. For book-length ethnographies that attend more explicitly to the commitment-making process, see Lofland (1966), Bartell (1971), Lesieur (1977), Prus and Irini (1980), Haas and Shaffir (1987), Prus (1989a,b), Prus and Sharper (1991) and Wolf (1991).

27. The development, maintenance, and severance of relationships is given more explicit attention in the following monographs: Shaw (1930), Waller (1930), Hunt (1966), Lofland (1966), Wiseman (1970), Bartell (1971), Lesieur (1977), Prus and Irini (1980), Fine (1983), Adler (1985), Steffensmeier (1986), Vaughan (1986); Prus (1989a), Prus and Sharper (1991) and Wolf (1991). Lemert's (1962) analysis of "paranoia and the dynamics of exclusion" deserves special recognition as one of the best accounts of interpersonal relationships.

28. The following materials ethnographically depict the ways in which people attempt to establish groups or associations of sorts. See: Sutherland's (1937) professional thieves; Karsh et al.'s (1953) union organizers; Rubington's (1968) bottle-gangs; Lofland's (1966) doomsday cult; Prus and Sharper's (1977) road hustlers; Adler's (1985) drug dealers; Prus and Frisby's (1990) party plans; Wolf's (1991) outlaw bikers; and Grill's (1994) political recruitment practices.

29. For instances of "objectification" practices of groups wishing to become known in the community at large, see Goffman (1961), Wiseman (1970), Gusfield (1981, 1989), and Prus (1989a,b). For examples of internal objectification practices among those wishing to remain unnoticed in the larger community, see Sutherland (1937), Prus and Sharper (1977). Still other groups may desire or flirt with a semi-public recognition (e.g., taxi-dance hall operators [Cressey, 1932], drug dealers [Adler, 1985], fences [Steffensmeier, 1986], action bars [Prus and Irini, 1988], outlaw bikers [Wolf, 1991]).

30. Those interested in the ways in which groups (organizations) make contact with and deal with outside parties (e.g., targets, clients, suspects, etc.) may wish to examine: Cressey (1932), Sutherland (1937), Goffman (1961), Emerson (1969), Wiseman (1970), Prus and Sharper (1977), Prus and Irini (1980), Ross (1980), Haas and Shaffir (1987), Prus (1989b), and Wolf (1991).

6

EXPERIENCING EMOTIONALITY

Affectivity as a Generic Social Process

If you get that sale, that contract, there isn't another thing in the world that gives you that same sense of thrill, accomplishment! You have that interrelationship between two people and when you come out on top, there isn't a better feeling in the world than having done that! (manufacture-industrial) [Prus, 1989a:264]

This statement on emotionality is very much an extension of the generic social processes discussed in chapter 5. However, because it deals with a subject matter that has (a) been pursued much less explicitly and systematically in the interactionist literature than have the other generic social processes and (b) has often been relegated to realms of psychology, emotionality as a generic social process merits more focused attention than could be given within the context of the preceding chapter.

In what follows, I will first indicate how emotionality may be approached from an interactionist perspective. The emphasis shifts next to considerations of people learning definitions of emotionality in their particular life-worlds, developing techniques for expressing and controlling emotional experiences, and experiencing emotional episodes and entanglements. Although somewhat abbreviated, this material represents both a set of themes around which existing ethnographic research may be synthesized with respect to people's experiences with emotionality and a conceptual schema which may suggest some lines of inquiry for future ethnographic research.

Recognizing that emotionality, as a generic social process, is pertinent not only to the study of human lived experience more generally, but also to the ethnographic enterprise more specifically, I have also used this chapter as an occasion on which to reflect upon some of the practical dilemmas that ethnographers encounter with respect to managing emotionality in the field. Given the parameters of the larger volume in which this discussion is embedded, it has been necessary to condense this material rather severely. Hopefully, though, these more pointed discussions of matters such as maintaining composure, managing intimacy and distancing, and sustaining enthusiasm, amidst considerations of the primary task of "achieving intersubjective integrity with the ethnographic other," may lend themselves to further reflections on the part of readers.

EMOTIONALITY: INTERACTIONIST DIMENSIONS

Consistent with the basic tenets of an interactionist paradigm, this discussion of emotionality or affectively defined experience begins with *the assumption that expressions of emotions and gestures are not inherently meaningful but rather reflect the social contexts in which people find themselves.* This is not to deny any biological sensations or behavioral practices that people may associate with particular emotional states, but only to posit that *perceptions (delineations) and definitions of states as "emotional" ones entail interpretive processes that are rooted in the (intersubjective) communities in which people find themselves.*

For our purposes, emotional activity encompasses a wide variety of affective experiences ranging from shame or embarrassment to frustration, anger, jealousy, fear, hurt, discouragement, discomfort, despondency, and distancing, to composure, intimacy, happiness, pride, love, enjoyment, fascination, enthusiasm, and excitement. Presumably, as well, although people in different life-worlds may commonly invoke (notice, define, act toward) particular emotional states in certain kinds of settings rather than others, no emotional state is seen as the exclusive or automatic domain of any particular type of setting. The anthropological literature (see LaBarre, 1947; MacAndrew and Edgerton, 1969; Heelas, 1986; Lutz, 1988) suggests that while people in different cultures all display wide ranges of emotional experience, the nature and ways in which "emotions" are defined, experienced, managed, and expressed can vary immensely from one life-world to the next. Since different emotions may be expressed in seemingly similar manners and seemingly similar emotional states can be expressed in quite different manners across societies, this same literature also suggests that an appreciation of cultural relativism or cultural framing is critical to comprehending these experiences.

The interactionists have sometimes been accused of neglecting people's affective experiences (Meltzer, Petras and Reynolds, 1975; Stryker, 1980), but a considerable amount of interactionist ethnography is pertinent to emotionality (although it has seldom been explicitly referenced as such). Thus, for instance, much of the interactionist literature on deviance attends to people's experiences with *stigma, shame, disrespectability, or embarrassment* in some manner (Waller, 1930; Davis, 1961; Goffman, 1963b; Edgerton, 1967; Prus and Irini, 1980; Schneider and Conrad, 1983; Sanders, 1991). As well, consideration has been given to a variety of other affective experiences, including *intimacy and distancing* (Waller, 1930; Cressey, 1932; Bartell, 1971; Prus and Irini, 1980; Vaughan, 1986; Hopper, 1993); *distrust and suspicion* (Lemert, 1962; Adler, 1985); *frustration, anger, and violence* (Prus, 1978; Athens, 1980; Prus and Irini, 1980; Dietz, 1983; Wolf, 1991); *ambiguity, ambivalence, and confusion* (Shaw, 1930; Lofland, 1966; Gubrium, 1975; Fine, 1983; Schneider and Conrad, 1983; Haas and Shaffir, 1987; Charmaz, 1991; Sanders, 1991; Sandellowski et al., 1991; Wolf, 1991; Weger, 1992; Karp, 1993); *stage fright and fear* (Haas, 1977; Bartell, 1971; Prus and Irini, 1980; Mitchell, 1983; Prus, 1989a; Charmaz, 1991; Wolf, 1991); *composure and coolness* (Sutherland, 1937; Finestone, 1957; Goffman, 1959, 1963b; Becker, 1963:79–119; Klapp, 1962, 1964, 1971; Emerson, 1970; Haas, 1972, 1977; Haas and Shaffir, 1987; Prus, 1989a; Prus and Sharper, 1991); *enjoyments, entertainment, and recreational pleasantries* (Cressey, 1932; Blumer, 1933; Blumer and Hauser, 1933; Becker, 1963:41–58; Bartell, 1971; Prus and Irini, 1980; Stebbins, 1990, 1994; Prus and Dawson, 1991; Wolf, 1991); *enthusiasm, devotion, fascination, and excitement* (Blumer, 1933; Blumer and Hauser, 1933; Lofland, 1966; Bartell, 1971; Lesieur, 1977; Fine, 1983; Mitchell, 1983; Prus, 1989a; Adler and Adler, 1991; Prus and Sharper, 1991; Sanders, 1991; Wolf, 1991).

None of the preceding works was intended as a statement on "emotions work" per se, but it is difficult to deny the significance of these materials for understanding the accomplishment of emotional expression (and control) in a variety of contexts. Indeed, interactionist accounts (particularly ethnographic materials) provide invaluable insights into the ways in which "emotional states" are interwoven in the fabric of human lived experience. Still, readers should be aware that the interactionist ethnographic literature on emotional experiences has not been developed in a very explicit or sustained manner and this material should be approached accordingly.

Although they, too, have largely neglected the contributions of interactionist ethnographies to the study of emotions, Shott (1979), Denzin (1984), Lofland (1985), McCarthy (1989), Ellis (1991), Johnson (1991), and Brisset and Snow

(1993) more explicitly have contributed to the development of an interactionist approach to the study of emotional experience.[1]

Of these statements, Denzin (1984) provides by far the most comprehensive discussion and (some claims about knowing the other better than the other knows oneself, aside) one that is very consistent with the position taken here. In particular, Denzin emphasizes that while emotions are experienced by people as "self-body state feelings" of sorts, these experiences are *intersubjectively informed* or are meaningful only within a community context. Emotions are not experienced in any pure, intrinsic, individualistic manner, but rather reflect people's awarenesses of Mead's (1934) "generalized other." Second, emotional experiences are *activities* and should be approached in process terms, as formative processes involving (socially) minded, interacting beings. Not only are notions of emotional experience learned through association with others, but since they are subject to *ongoing definition and interpretation* both on a *self-reflective* and *interactive* basis, instances of emotional experience are *problematic, situational, and temporal* in essence.

While people may only partially be able to control and direct their emotional experiences, this does not differentiate emotional activity from other realms of human involvement and activity, for in the struggle for human existence there is much that people cannot control or direct on either an individual or a collective basis. The inability to entirely direct and control emotional experiences, therefore, does not remove emotional experience from the realm of human enterprise or intersubjective accomplishment. Indeed, and to the contrary, there is much to be gained by approaching the study of emotion in process terms, as a matter of human endeavor and intersubjective accomplishment (and frustration). Denzin's (1984) work is very suggestive in this respect, but more is needed. Although it is necessary to generate firsthand accounts of people's experiences (and activities) with respect to emotionality, an interactionist appreciation of emotionality can be furthered by heightened attentiveness to the social processes that transcend emotional experiences across wide ranges of emotional contexts.

Three processes central to emotion work should be delineated: (1) *learning to define emotional experiences*, (2) *developing techniques for expressing and controlling emotional experiences*, and (3) *experiencing emotional episodes and entanglements*. Clearly, I can do little more than to sketch out a number of subthemes entailed in these processes. However if, these discussions accomplish no more than to sensitize readers to some commonly overlooked, but consequential features of emotionality as lived experience, then their purpose may be well served.

Learning to Define Emotional Experiences

It's very easy to get down. It's like a very emotional roller-coaster. It really is!
I've never encountered anything like it before. . . . It's incredible to watch, when
you've been through it a few times and it feels like it's going to strike again.
And it doesn't have any relation to whether you're working or not. There are
times when you just have difficulty getting up and going to the open houses.
It's easy to lapse into not doing those things. And there are days when you're
just sailing. When you're hot, you're hot! That is how it is. . . . It can be really
slow at times, and then all of a sudden, in a couple of days, you can't believe
how things are working out. And before that, it didn't seem to matter what
you did, you couldn't make a sale. And it's very difficult to keep yourself up.
After a while, you start to realize that you have to go with the flow. But it's
a very emotional roller-coaster kind of existence. . . . It can cause a lot of stress
in a family. I know it has in ours. (real estate) [Prus, 1989a:267]

As with other aspects of human community life, people appear to learn notions of "what it means to be emotional" from contact with other people. Thus, the subprocesses outlined in the earlier section on "acquiring perspectives" seem entirely applicable here. In learning about the cultural moralities and significances of the life-worlds in which they find themselves, people acquire notions of affective human states as well as learn about the sorts of experiences that humans may have with these states. In developing understandings of the generalized other (Mead, 1934) or attaining frames of reference for approaching their daily routines, people learn about modesty, disgrace, fear, happiness, indignation, pride, and the like.

Although people may unwittingly invoke behaviors that others may define as emotional states (as with infants appearing happy, angry, etc.), our emphasis here is on people acquiring capacities for defining situations in emotional terms on their own. The focus is on people (a) developing generalized images and understandings of emotional states as these are viewed in the community at large, (b) learning cultural recipes or "rules of thumb" (how to tell when) to define situations as emotional ones, and (c) applying those cultural understandings and recipes to the specific "cases at hand." This in no way denies the abilities of others to offer, suggest, or attempt to impose their understandings, rules of thumb, or definitions of the situation on the focal actor, but draws attention to the points at which people define themselves as being in emotional states or situations. The key themes here are:

* *Learning cultural perspectives on (and understandings of) emotionality*
* *Learning cultural recipes for defining situations in emotional terms*

* *Invoking or applying cultural emotional recipes in specific situations*
* *Encountering, assessing, and assimilating notions, recipes and situational definitions of emotions from others*[2]

Developing Techniques for Expressing and Controlling Emotional Experiences

Messy shoppers can be a problem, especially if you have merchandise on "Sale." And here I've noticed that you can have the same items, where they're on "Sale" the next day, and you'll find that the customers now treat the items with less respect than they would have the day before. It can be the same rack in the same location in the store, and yet they're much rougher with the merchandise when you put them on 20% or 30% off. . . . And with the staff, it's the same way, I have to get the girls to think that the "Sales" items are just as important, just as valuable to the store as the other merchandise. Just because it's on "Sale" doesn't mean that you can show less respect for the items or the customers who are buying the merchandise. And that's a problem too. Some of the "Sales" customers are more difficult, more demanding. They want to know what's wrong with this and that, "How come it's put on Sale?" "Bet you marked it up to mark it down!" So the "Sales" customers are more frustrating for the staff and after you meet a few difficult customers, and you're busy, getting run off your feet, it is more frustrating. It's more difficult to maintain your composure. (women's clothing) [Prus, 1989a:246]

In addition to acquiring stocks of knowledge and rules of thumb regarding the existence and nature of emotional situations and states, people also learn how to "do emotional activity." As suggested in the earlier discussion of "doing activity" (chapter 5), matters of doing performances, influencing others, and making commitments appear quite consequential in appreciating the nature of emotions work.

At a performance level, people not only learn (sometimes through explicit instruction) how to monitor their own situations and behaviors, but they also learn to express and manage particular emotional themes and states. These notions presume attentiveness to the generalized other, human capacities for self-reflectivity, and more or less ongoing sets of adjustments to situations as these develop. Further, beyond learning ways of monitoring, expressing, and controlling their own emotional states, people generally also learn ways of monitoring, assessing, and influencing (affecting) the emotional states that others around them may experience. The relevant processes would appear to include:

* *Learning to attend to emotional themes in the setting at hand*
* *Learning ways of expressing emotional themes*
* *Learning ways of controlling emotional themes*
* *Coordinating emotional themes with others (team members and others)*
* *Dealing with ambiguity, obstacles, resistances, and distractions*
* *Conveying images of competence (displaying ability, composure)*
* *Encountering competition in defining, expressing, and controlling emotional expressions*
* *Making ongoing assessments of, and adjustments to, one's emotional expressions*
* *Monitoring, assessing, influencing others' emotional practices and experiences*[3]

Experiencing Emotional Episodes and Entanglements

You just give them a couple minutes in the store, and then go over with a smile, "Hello, how are you doing today?. . . Something special you're interested in?. . . Looking for something for a special occasion?" And most times, you get, "I'm just looking." "Just browsing." You get that all day. You hear that in your nightmares! You can see them coming. And then you get the ignorant ones who say nothing. They say nothing. You walk up to them, "Hi, how are you doing? Are you interested in the suits?" Nothing! That's it, that's my level. I'm not going to push, I'll just say, "That's it!" to myself, and I'll walk away. And I'll tell the rest of the staff, "He didn't say a word. And everyone knows, "That's it. If they want help, they've got to come to us, call us over." Because that's really rude!. . . I've seen some of our staff really get mad about that. I've had some that will just come storming back. And what can you really ask them to do? Go back and be nice? She's tried that already. You can try to be congenial, friendly, and it's just like there's a wall, and they're not even listening. It's rude, but you get that a lot, and if that happens two or three times in a day, you're burning! You're ready to kill the next one who does something really stupid or rude. That's horrible! (men's clothing) [Prus, 1989a:188]

While emotional experiences may add elements of interest or drama to a great many situations, those that more explicitly involve interactions with others have the potential to be more dramatic overall. Like other (symbolic) interactions, emotional interchanges may be viewed best in process terms. One cannot predict just how particular encounters will work out despite the postures assumed by one or other parties at the outset, but we do know that human interchange has an emergent quality. Consequently, we may invoke the discussion of "being involved" (chapter 5) and ask about people's initial involvements, continuities and intensifications, discontinuities and dissipations, and reinvolvements in particular emotional states, as we attempt to follow the histories of these episodes.

The notion of initial involvements draws attention to the ways in which people first became caught up or drawn into the episodes at hand. Building on the earlier discussion of "initial involvements," the following processes seem especially pertinent to people's participation in emotional themes:

* *Developing interests in, or fascinations with, particular emotional themes*
* *Being recruited or encouraged to participate in particular emotional themes*
* *Feeling obligated to experience/express/control particular emotional themes*
* *Overcoming reservations about involvement in particular emotional themes*[4]

While people may learn notions of emotional states and ways of applying these notions to the situations in which they find themselves in a general sense, it is important to appreciate that emotions may be experienced on a more solitary (sometimes totally secretive) or isolated basis as well as on a more direct, interactive basis. It might be argued that most, if not all, experiences of emotionality have some solitary or unshared components to them, since people may have difficulty completely and accurately communicating their feelings with others. Likewise, most, if not all, instances of solitary emotion entail some awareness, attentiveness to, or interaction with others (on a specific or generalized basis). Still, it may be instructive to acknowledge the somewhat differing dynamics of more solitary vs. more interactive instances of emotional experiences and expressions.

Solitary Emotional Episodes

What I don't like about sales is all the travel. Because when you are on the road you do get pretty lonely and there is a lot of pressure on you too. You have to eat by yourself, so you have supper and breakfast and lunch, usually by yourself, with no one really to talk to. You might have the odd person you are doing business with, but more likely than not, you're eating by yourself. . . . Then, of course, if you are in a slump, there is more pressure and so that is a problem too. But it can also turn around, so it certainly has its ups and downs. . . . Life on the road is not all that it is made out to be. It's not just a bundle of good times. And if you are into that, you get a bad reputation with the company, so it's a lonely kind of life. You're by yourself and when you're driving around, you especially experience that pressure. . . . And it's also hard to sell if you need the money because then there is more pressure on you. And then when you get a customer, someone who wants to buy your lines, you tend to sell them all that you can. And, as a result, you bury the prospect in your products. And that's not good, because you then kill your future sales, and that person won't be too happy to see you next time. (wholesale-giftware) [Prus, 1989b:272]

Although continuities in particular situations often reflect some mutuality (i.e., acknowledgement, acceptance, or enthusiasm) of interchange on the part of others, people (as self-reflective entities) sometimes will persist with particular emotional themes in the absence of any explicit interaction with, or encouragement from, others. Thus, while affective states such as love, hatred, jealousy, embarrassment, or excitement may reach very intensive states as a result of ongoing interpersonal exchange, people may nonetheless persevere with these or other emotional themes on a more secretive, solitary basis or in the absence of support (inattention; or even with resistances, challenges, and objections) from others. Simply labeling the persistence of solitary emotional themes as "obsessions," "fixations," or instances of people "losing it," when they seem overly involved in particular emotional states, does nothing to explain the situations at hand. It is much more important to attend to the natural histories of such instances. These cases of "encapsulation" or "engrossment" (Cressey, 1953; Lemert, 1962; Lesieur, 1977) are best viewed in developmental terms. The processes relevant to prolonged solitary pursuits include:

* *Developing more intensive fascinations with particular emotional themes[5]*
* *Experiencing more acute obligations to pursue particular emotional themes*
* *Making more extensive commitments to (or becoming reliant on) particular emotional themes*
* *Avoiding, disattending to, or dismissing, communications with others which discourage focal emotional themes*
* *Failing to attend to, or define, alternative emotional themes as viable pursuits[6]*

Interactive Emotional Episodes

We have internal contests, because you have to keep the people excited, motivated. Sometimes these are individual competitions, sometimes team events, where you divide the staff into a couple of teams and introduce some incentives that way. . . . We will also increase commissions on certain cars that are not moving so well otherwise, to get the staff more involved in showing this particular line of automobiles or trucks, whatever, or maybe a night out for the wife and family if you sell one of these. Things like that. . . . Whoever makes the first sale of the day gets a new pair of shoes, any little thing. Not very expensive, but motivational. (auto) [Prus, 1989a:272]

Many instances of emotionality that others associate with specific people (targets) may be casually dismissed (as insignificant, entirely situationally motivated, or commonplace). However, when others in the community consider the emotional states associated with certain people (targets) to be worthy of further attention, these others (agents) may (knowingly and unwittingly) sustain targets' involvements in those emotional themes. Other people may encourage the expression of emotional themes they deem desirable in a number of ways. But, even when they (agents) may specifically attempt to discourage the expression of particular emotional themes, they sometimes promote community-based identities of targets which foster their careers in particular emotional themes by drawing increased attention to the "emotional failings" envisioned to characterize those individuals.[7]

In addition to acquiring identities with respect to other aspects (e.g., work or recreational involvements) of community life, people may also be defined with respect to their involvements in, and styles of expressing, particular emotional themes. Others are sometimes intensely interested in testing and assessing people's reactions (e.g., composure—Lemert, 1962; Haas, 1972, 1977; Prus and Irini, 1980; Haas and Shaffir, 1987; Prus and Sharper, 1991; Wolf, 1991) to certain kinds of situations, but even in more casual contexts people are often categorized by the ways in which they express (and control) their emotions.

The preceding discussion of the subprocesses entailed in "achieving identity" (chapter 5) is especially germane to this realm of typification (also see Garfinkel, 1956; Klapp, 1962, 1964, 1971), as is an appreciation of the significance of labels and reputations for stabilizing particular forms of emotional expression.[8] Thus, while many designations of emotionality may be seen as rather tentative, situated, or fleeting (e.g., a little upset, temporarily depressed, a flash of anger), and some potentially implicating typifications may be resisted quite successfully, other "emotionality tags" may be acknowledged and come to represent central features of the ways in which people perceive themselves as well as the manners in which others view and act toward them over time. Further, while some emotionality labels may be formally administered (e.g., psychiatric designations as paranoid, schizophrenic, neurotic), others may be sustained at more of a "grass roots" level (i.e., consider designations such as "flake," "whacko," "spastic," or somewhat conversely, "cool," "together," "composed").

Mindful of the interactionist literature on "continuities" more generally, we may expect that people's longer term involvements in particular emotional themes are more likely to be sustained when people find themselves:

* *Encountering viewpoints (from others) conducive to particular emotional themes*
* *Attaining identities (self and other definitions) consistent with particular emotional themes*
* *Becoming more adept at utilizing particular emotional themes in dealing with others*
* *Making commitments to (developing strategies, stylistic practices of implementing, reliances on) particular emotional themes in the community of others*
* *Developing relationships (e.g., friendships and animosities) around particular emotional themes*
* *Foregoing alternative emotional themes (neglecting or disattending to other emotional themes)*[9]

In addition to sustaining people's involvements in particular emotional themes over time, one's associates (ergo, "emotional associates," Denzin, 1984) may also intensify or escalate people's sense of emotionality on a "here and now" basis. Some of these interchanges may be relatively isolated events between interactants, but others may reflect earlier or anticipated exchanges to which one or other participants may refer in interpreting, defining, and acting toward the situation at hand.

When the exchanges in question are more isolated, the parties (as interactive strangers) involved may pursue their interests in various manners but seem apt to invoke notions of "the generalized other" (Mead, 1934) in dealing with each other. Since situations become emotional experiences only when they are so defined by one or other parties, the nature and direction of any emotional theme seems rather precarious. Definitions of situations as emotional ones, thus, may very well depend on people's pre-existing interests and on the particular aspects of the other(s) to which they attend. Insofar as the other is seen to offend or exemplify the ideals of some particular emotional theme to which someone attends or invokes, then the encounter takes on the character of a more noteworthy emotional experience. These definitions may be confirmed or recast as the encounter takes place, but people's indignations or enchantments would appear at the outset to very much reflect both their self-defined interests in the situation at hand and their images of the generalized other.

A noteworthy exception involves situations in which people experience *spill-overs* (Prus, 1978), wherein one or more parties carries certain emotional states over from a prior (unrelated) situation into the present context. In these cases, one or more of the interactants have not cleared themselves of earlier "emotional baggage" before entering into the present interchange. Since these people introduce elements into the situation that would not typically be antici-pated with a generalized encounter in that setting, these participants may be seen to encourage more intense (positive and negative) interchanges than might otherwise be the case. People encountering these "emotionally (pre)charged others" may find themselves overwhelmed and even shocked by the intensity with which the interchanges involving these others may proceed, more or less from the onset.

When people have been interacting with one another over a period of time, on either an intermittent or more sustained basis, their immediate (more highly situated) interchanges may be very much affected by any of the preceding elements of their earlier exchanges to which they attend. More enduring involvements may be seen as a stringing together of a series of situated exchanges, often with some set of noteworthy emotional themes. Indeed, although some interchanges may denote one-time, highly situated instances, others may have an episodic history with earlier exchanges contributing to *build-ups* (Prus, 1978) of emotional intensity that may be carried over into these (same) people's subsequent interactions. Some of these build-ups may revolve around certain kinds of activities and particular emotional themes, but other intensifications may come about as the parties involved find themselves reacting more uniformly (negatively or positively) over a range of activities and emotional subthemes.

Pulling these notions together, it appears that the central processes involved in intensifying emotional experiences with others include:

* *Defining the immediate situation more explicitly in emotional terms*
* *Overtly expressing emotional themes in the immediate situation*
* *Carrying emotional themes over from earlier (outside) encounters (spill-overs)*
* *Establishing a mutuality of focus with the other around a particular emotional theme*
* *Developing more uniform modes of viewing and acting toward the other with respect to particular emotional themes*[10]

Like continuities, disinvolvements from emotional episodes may reflect the activities of others as well as the participants' own, more individualided, redefinitions of situations. Generally speaking, as with other involvements, people appear to find it more difficult to sustain emotional states on their own. Thus, many emotional interchanges (and themes) seem apt to dissipate when the interactants fail to endorse or acknowledge one another's expressed interests or affectations. As well, even when people have been extensively caught up in particular emotional themes, they may begin to question aspects of their situations on their own or with some prompting from others. The earlier discussion of disinvolvement suggests that the subprocesses most relevant to an understanding of the emotional disengagement or disentanglement process are:

* *Questioning earlier invoked perspectives (and definitions) regarding particular emotional themes*
* *Finding that the activities entailed in pursuing particular emotional states are difficult to sustain*
* *Disliking the sets of self and other identities associated with particular emotional entanglements*
* *Reassessing the commitments (risks, costs, relative gains) entailed in maintaining particular emotional states or entanglements*
* *Defining alternative emotional states or entanglements as more viable (more desirable, readily accessible, encouraged by others)*[11]

While many emotionally focused interchanges have clearer or more definite endings, others may be subject to considerable vacillation. Whether these occur on a more solitary or interactive basis, they may be characterized by an unlimited number of disinvolvements and reinvolvements as people attempt to come to terms with the diverse sets of perspectives, identities, activities, commitments and relationships that they associate with different emotional themes.

In concluding the first part of this chapter, I am very much reminded of the tentative nature of this discussion. First, although an interactionist analysis of emotionality seems entirely appropriate given the intersubjective essence of this phenomena, I have been able to do little more than make explicit or sketch out some key features of people's emotional experiences. Second, as indicated at the outset, although much (interactionist) ethnographic research is pertinent to the conceptual analysis of emotionality, relatively few of these studies have approached emotionality as the central focus or even a highly sustained or developed subtheme. While I am clearly not proposing that people envision emotionality as the most vital or essential feature of the generic social processes discussed in this volume (a concerted emphasis on activity seems much more fundamental to an appreciation of the human condition), it is hoped that this discussion may prompt researchers to be more attuned to emotionality both as an intersubjective accomplishment and as a consequential subtheme to be pursued in ethnographic inquiries. Third, as with the generic social processes more generally, I am mindful of some different ethnographic research strategies, any of which might be productively applied to the study of emotionality as an interactionist phenomenon. Thus, researchers interested in this subject matter may find themselves deliberating between (a) a concerted focus on some particular emotional experience in either a single substantive field or on a broader, multi-contextual basis; (b) a heavily focused attentiveness to a variety of emotional themes in a single or multi-contextual frame; (c) a concerted emphasis on one or more emotional themes among a smaller set of people [across the contextual frames they experience] over an extended period of time; or (d) an explicit attentiveness to "experiencing emotionality" as but one of several social processes that one might examine in some particular context. Since each of these tactics may offer researchers certain advantages in examining "emotionality as a generic social process," I am reluctant to recommend one of these approaches over others. Perhaps, by making some of the subprocesses entailed in experiencing emotionality more explicit, the material presented here may encourage a variety of ethnographic inquiries along these lines and provide a rudimentary basis on which to make more precise and sustained comparisons (and contrasts) with respect to "experiencing emotionality."

More centrally I would contend that it is only by engaging in sustained, firsthand contact with the ethnographic other that social scientists may be better able to appreciate emotionality as an aspect of the human condition. Still, contact with the ethnographic other poses yet other challenges for the researcher and, when approached more reflectively, sheds further light on the processes and problematics of "experiencing emotionality" in the context of human interchange.

EMOTIONALITY AND THE ETHNOGRAPHER SELF

Maintaining enthusiasm, that's one of the real keys to this business. You can't let any problems or disappointments show or affect you when you're dealing with the next customer. You have to be prepared to spend time with the customer and be pleasant, keep your spirits up. If you don't, you won't be in this business long. It's just that important! (women's clothing) [Prus, 1989a:255]

Not unlike the salesperson just quoted, ethnographers often find themselves trying to maintain dramaturgical discipline (Goffman, 1959) or manage the emotional themes they experience in the midst of the assortment of interchanges, ambiguities, and challenges that characterize field research. Some of these situations may be truly puzzling and represent instances for further ethnographic inquiry, but researchers also inevitably find themselves engaged in various aspects of "emotions work" as they attempt to maintain expressive control (and manage intimacy and distancing) with respect to those they encounter. Mindful of issues of this sort, it may be useful to conclude this chapter by considering emotionality in the field setting and some of the ways in which ethnographers attempt to maintain their central research objective.

Sustaining the Ethnographic Focus

By virtue of their dual roles as social scientists and participants in the life-worlds of others, field researchers are in particularly precarious situations. The primary objective of those doing ethnographic research is to achieve an exceptionally viable level of intersubjective familiarity with the life-worlds of the ethnographic other and to convey images of this world to others (outsiders) in an open, complete, comprehensible, and (scientifically) responsible manner. At the same time, however, field researchers fundamentally and centrally depend on those in the field for their cooperation in this endeavor. This requires that researchers be prepared to enter into relationships with a variety of other people (often strangers) who may or may not be especially fond of one another or particularly receptive to the "newcomer" that the field researcher represents.

When embarking on ethnographic inquiry, researchers enter into complex social worlds and open themselves to interchanges with others in ways that can only be vaguely anticipated at the beginning. As well, in addition to researchers' prevailing commitments to the social science community and the problematics of learning about this (often new) social setting, ethnographers also are expected to manage those aspects of their outside lives (moralities, practices, relationships) which may not correspond with those of the people whom they encounter in the field. These are important considerations. Whether researchers realize it or not, they are more or less continuously "on stage" while in the presence of others in the field. Ethnographers may be there to learn about the others in the setting, but the *people in the field* can observe, learn about, draw inferences, talk about, obstruct, and otherwise adjust to, those attempting to study them. There is no reason to presuppose that those one encounters in the field will automatically share the objectives, or respect the constraints, with which the researchers may be endeavoring to work. People's interests may be compatible in some ways with those of the researcher they encounter, but they may also be entirely at odds with these. For instance, at the outset, some people may define the researcher as a nuisance or even in adversarial terms. The dramaturgical presence (Goffman, 1959) one achieves in the field can be central to the overall success of the ethnographic venture because those embarking on these endeavors typically find themselves caught in a variety of cross-interests and dilemmas.

Ethnographic Research and Generic Social Processes

In discussing emotionality and the ethnographic self, it is important to appreciate that, like others (citizens at large) opening themselves to encounters with other people in the community, field researchers very much experience the generic features of human association in the course of conducting ethnographic inquiry. First, although they needn't accept the viability of the viewpoints of those they encounter as reference points for all matters of personal activity, ethnographers are faced with the task of acquiring perspectives, or at least attaining a good working familiarity with the world views of those they purport to study. Likewise, while researchers may be able to implement other identities when outside the ethnographic context, there will always be the matter of achieving a viable set of working identities with respect to others in the field research setting. Typically, this means projecting and sustaining images of a self that those in the community would find (minimally) tolerable and (more desirably) comfortable and trustworthy. Researchers sometimes experience "stage fright" (Lyman and Scott, 1970) or worry about their abilities to feel comfortable with those they encounter, but the more crucial research concern is one of having the others define and act toward the researcher at hand as a trustworthy, interested person.

Third, like those they encounter, researchers also "do things." Exactly what they do in particular situations may depend significantly on their modes of entry and their abilities (and interests) to accomplish the activities characterizing the life-world they are studying. Minimally, though, field researchers are apt to find themselves adjusting their own research (activities) in ways that accommodate the involvements and practices of others in the setting. Sustained involvements in the field may also result in more extensive investments in the situations at hand than the researchers had anticipated, but field research typically requires adjustments in other realms of researchers' lives as well, as they more fully organize their routines around the research setting.

Further, whereas some relationships developed in the field may be very fleeting, more enduring projects typically result in researchers developing more sustained relationships with particular members of the context under consideration. Given their goal of achieving intimate familiarity with the life-worlds of the other in a more comprehensive sense, researchers may wish to be mindful of the sorts of affiliations that they develop with particular others in the setting. These may significantly affect researchers' abilities to access other people in the setting as well as their opportunities to learn more fully about the life-worlds at hand. Alliances developed in the field can be both productive and costly for the ethnographic enterprise as they may affect people's willingness to associate with, and disclose certain kinds of information to, the researchers at hand. Researchers' outside (home, office) relationships also may represent emotional complications with which the researcher may have to deal. Sometimes these relationships undergo dramatic changes as researchers and these other associates attempt to come to terms with the researchers' involvements in the field.

Researchers also commonly find themselves somewhat involved in the tasks of attempting to negotiate their way through the organizational (formal and otherwise) routines that (ethnographic) others have established, as well as on occasion attempting to establish and coordinate associations (e.g., research teams) of sorts. For those embarked on field research, then, the ethnographic enterprise very much parallels the processes characterizing people's involvement in any other community or subculture within. Cutting across these other processes, the matter of "experiencing emotionality" adds one more element of a trans-contextual nature with which ethnographers in the field have to contend.

Like others who venture into particular arenas and attempt to deal with the people (often strangers) they encounter there, ethnographers may find themselves dealing with considerable ambiguity, uncertainty, and stage fright. Not only do they attempt to learn about and define the parameters of the field, but they must also tentatively envision their own lines of action and contemplate ways of approaching and relating to those in the field. As with other newcomers, the matters of "fitting in" and "establishing trust" with "the locals" can be consequential to researchers' abilities to attain and maintain viability in the setting. While some people in the setting may be welcoming and accepting of the researcher (although not necessarily for any reasons related to the research, itself), researchers may also encounter more overt instances of confusion, resistance, and rejection on the part of others. The situation is compounded somewhat, too, in the sense that the researcher is engaged in the process of trying to comprehend the larger life-world at hand while simultaneously attempting to learn about the particular people being encountered and the ways in which the people in the setting relate to one another. This not only means suspending much of one's own (cultural) interpretive tendencies, but also attempting to learn about the general viewpoints and practices of the ethnographic other amidst any widespread contradictions (in the setting) and the more idiographic exceptions one may encounter in the field.

As with other people in the setting, researchers may encounter deliberate deceptions, trouble, ridicule, upsets, fears, and animosities. Researchers sometimes think that their research mandate should privilege them for, or exempt them from, certain kinds of treatment, but the other people in the setting need not (and should not be expected to) share the researcher's definition of the situation. As well, researchers face the task of managing their own moralities (and any related senses of fair play and justice) in settings not of their own construction. Thus, in addition to the challenges entailed in learning about the life-worlds of the other in a more direct sense, ethnographers face the task of managing their own emotional states (as private experiences) as well as the ways in which they express any emotional themes to others.

Managing and Expressing Emotionality in the Field

The matter of experiencing emotionality in ethnographic inquiry has been the subject of considerable discussion. In practice, researchers have adopted a wide variety of viewpoints on the extent to which, and the ways in which, they might most appropriately handle emotionality in the field (see Adler and Adler, 1987; the collected papers in Shaffir and Stebbins, 1991; Fine, 1993; and Mitchell, 1993). Minimally, it is apparent that field researchers often have difficulties managing their own affective states and some have significantly allowed these to protrude into, and interfere with, the research process. Fortunately, more extensive emotional intrusions clearly do not characterize ethnography across the board. The more consequential "emotional failings" (e.g., disinterest in the views of the ethnographic other, moralism, creative misrepresentation, expressive self-enchantments) apply in some cases (instances and genres of ethnography, such as Marxist and postmodernist efforts) much more than others. Here, many difficulties pertaining to emotionality and the ensuing representation of the other have come about because these scholars have failed to respect the viewpoints of the ethnographic other. For most other ethnographers, problems pertaining to emotional self-expression are much more situated or occasional as opposed to systematic or prototypic.

Still, as social scientists, we have an obligation to encourage and produce ethnographies that are highly attentive to the accomplishment of human activity and are maximally concerned about openly and comprehensively conveying the viewpoints of the other in the entire process of developing ethnographic inquiry. Thus, beyond scrutinizing the ethnographies we encounter as closely as possible for their intersubjective authenticity, *we have a particular obligation to maximize the intersubjective integrity of the works we produce.*

In what follows, I would briefly like to discuss some aspects of "emotional work" or "dramaturgical discipline" as this pertains to the pursuit of the ethnographic enterprise. I have drawn particularly on the lessons I've learned as an ethnographer in the field,[12] but I have also benefitted from countless observations and discussions of the ethnographic research process with academics, students, and people in the community at large, as well as from exposure to the ethnographic literature more generally. Because field research involves the pursuit of intersubjective familiarity in settings that are far beyond our capacities to anticipate (never mind control), ethnography is an especially demanding form of inquiry. Hopefully, this discussion may be helpful, then, in alerting ethnographers (especially newcomers to the field) to some of the pitfalls that could nullify what otherwise might be highly productive pieces of work.

In addressing a number of emotional themes that seem consequential for one's abilities to operate more effectively within the ethnographic context, I assume a self-reflective ethnographer, someone who is attentive to monitoring and adjusting one's emotional themes on both a private and a more public, expressive level. I also assume an ethnographic attentiveness to the emotional themes that others may be experiencing and expressing, as well as a concern about minimizing the extent to which one becomes unduly caught up in the emotional themes that others may express. I do not assume that ethnographers will be uniformly mindful of these matters or that individual ethnographers will be able to sustain a uniform level of dramaturgical discipline in the field. It appears, however, that matters of purposiveness or commitment to the research agenda, composure, tolerance, patience, enthusiasm, congeniality, and an ability to live with ambiguity, as well as an endless curiosity and concern with learning about others are central to an appreciation of both ethnographer emotionality in the field and a reasonably successful research venture.

Because field research is so open-ended, it is most important that researchers *focus centrally on the task of achieving intersubjectivity with the other*, of gaining intimate familiarity with the life-world of the other. One is there to learn about the ethnographic other, and to do so as thoroughly and completely as possible. This implies a commitment to the objective at hand, and a related willingness to suspend some other interests and agendas that one might be otherwise tempted to pursue. This means relentlessly accumulating information about the other, and probing as extensively as possible regarding specific experiences, instances, meanings, variations, hesitations, failures, successes, and adjustments. Since the field invariably denotes a complex social arena, with interwoven sets of *activities*, actors, events, conflicts, friendships and animosities, and the like, researchers may become diverted by all sorts of matters. If this seems to be happening, then renewed attentiveness to the primary objective seems in order. Personally, I have found it most productive to concentrate on people's *activities*, to find out as much as I can about all of the things that they do and the ways that they deal with the situations in which they find themselves. In talking about and explaining their activities, people invariably make reference to perspectives, relationships, identities, emotions, and the like. As an ethnographer I want to be attentive to these things in some detail as well, but the focus on activity has been extremely valuable for maintaining a more consistent emphasis on the pursuit of intersubjectivity, given all the things to which one may attend in any field setting.

Although researchers may be able to learn some things on more covert levels, or even in situations in which the people with whom they are dealing are somewhat distant or reluctant to cooperate, ethnographers are very much dependent on the willingness of those with whom they associate to educate them about their life-worlds. Thus, beyond their own sense of objectives and conceptual foci, researchers find themselves thoroughly embedded in shorter and longer term instances of "people work." This implies a more or less continual set of definitions and redefinitions, and adjustments and readjustments of the researcher to those encountered in the field. Given the complex, ambiguous, and emergent nature of human relations, there is no definitive set of instructions that one can provide to insure success in the field. At the same time, though, researchers appear to fare better overall when they attend more fully and openly to others in the manners following.

First, with the possible exception of some people who may wish to conduct their lives with particular secrecy, most people seem to appreciate the company of those who are *genuinely interested* in them. From a researcher's viewpoint, this would mean taking the time and effort to inquire, experience, situate and contextualize all aspects of the research setting and the ethnographic other in great detail. It would involve attending to the other's definition(s) of the situation over time, including concerns, obstacles, options, ambiguities, excitements, boredoms, disaffections, and hesitations as these develop on a reflective, interactive basis. Taking a genuine interest in the other implies that there is something precious about the experiences of the other and that one intends to develop a fuller appreciation of the lived experience of the other. Ideally, ethnographers would be intensely interested in everything that people do; in which case, these scholars would be able to pursue any and every realm (and case) of human endeavor with great intrigue and care. Not unlike other people, though, researchers often define certain realms or substantive arenas of human life as more (personally) interesting (or conversely, more boring or disenchanting) than others and may have difficulty taking (and indicating) genuine interests in the experiences of everyone encountered. This does pose practical limitations for those in the social sciences. While researchers are sometimes able to minimize the significance of some intrigues and disaffections by working within certain settings, the problem of maintaining genuine interest in every case at hand still remains. Unless researchers are prepared to emphasize the precious nature of everyone's experiences in the context, the project is likely to be less complete and valuable as a result. Consequently, while it may be easier to take an interest in certain people and events encountered in the field than others, it may be important to remind oneself of the significance of taking interest in every instance of the other because of the valued intersubjective essence every other represents.

In working with people, it is also important that researchers try to adopt and sustain a *congenial disposition* throughout their contact with the field. While this is most easily accomplished with a receptive set of others, it may be even more consequential in settings or occasions in which friendliness or openness is less evident. Distancing, rudeness, and other forms of rejection encountered in the field can often be overcome when researchers maintain more pleasant or relaxed orientations with respect to those they meet in the setting. When one fails to maintain a cordial disposition, the losses may be greater than what might first seem; people in the field also monitor you, and they can talk about (and adjust to) you in any way they want.

Maintaining composure is somewhat related to the matter of congeniality, but draws attention to the importance of researchers developing a more tolerant, trustworthy image or reputation in the setting. Composure should not be taken as synonymous with a lack of interest, but rather denotes an element of balanced control over oneself in the field situation. I've found that composure is an invaluable aspect of sustained field research. While researchers often are able to move into other settings afterwards, the people in the research setting often do not have that option. Consequently, they tend to be concerned that those to whom they are disclosing (often vast amounts of personal) information are people who can be trusted to maintain a presence of self within the field more generally. In another sense, too, it is important for researchers to maintain confidences as much as possible within the situation, and on the outside. Researchers may inadvertently and innocently become embroiled in matters beyond their control, but it is most unfortunate when they are the source of their own undoing.

In part, composure also seems related to a stance of *noninterference*, to the adoption of a nondisruptive posture in dealing with those whom one encounters. As a rule of thumb, I will not take anyone into the field with me who I think may have difficulty maintaining composure or who seems apt to become easily indignant over things one might experience. These people can create immense interpersonal difficulties for you. If ever I'm more inclined to take an active role in invoking my own sense of morality or humanism in the field, I find it instructive to recall that these people didn't invite me to study them. And, even if they did, studying them and judging them are two different things. It is particularly unfortunate when ethnographers become so caught up in their own emotional concerns that they become upset with others in the field for "being themselves" and chastise or ridicule those they study at the time (or even later, in back regions).[13] As in our study of the hotel community (Prus and Irini, 1980), my viewpoint is this, "It may not be my way of life, but it's their way and if I can't accept that, it's time for me to find another setting." At times, it may be advantageous to side with this or that subgroup within the research context, but unless this pertains to a specific research issue, it seems that researchers who wish to remain in the situation for longer periods of time will likely fare better when they maintain a nonjudgemental, nonpartisan position. A sense of humor, which accommodates or indicates a tolerance of the other, can be a great asset in the field, particularly should things become a little tense.

Another type of situation with which ethnographers may experience difficulty are those in which one member of the community with whom the researcher has some dealings becomes upset with another member of the community. Although it may be interesting and worthwhile, given certain research agendas, to see how these situations work out over time, the danger is that the ethnographer may become emotionally entangled in (drawn into) a situation that may subsequently jeopardize one's project (and possibly one's well-being). Although each situation is somewhat unique, and things sometimes develop so quickly or in ways that take the ethnographer by surprise, I've found that composure and a sense of humor can be major assets in dissipating disaffections on many occasions.

In general, researchers seem advantaged, too, when they concentrate more on the life situations of the other, and minimize concerns about *establishing self-worth* in the setting. Matters pertaining to pride, personal disaffections, self-importance, and the like, are luxuries that may be very costly for those wishing to permeate the life-world of others in a more comprehensive and intimate manner. There may be times when people in the setting expect researchers to project auras of significance, but for the most part I've found that people very much appreciate contact with someone who is genuinely interested in learning about, as opposed to trying to impress, them. In this regard, I've become more attentive to the importance of explaining things to people, telling them of my own limited knowledge in the area, and asking them if they would like to help me with the project at hand. As well, it should be appreciated that researchers will almost inevitably make some mistakes in the field or say or do things that in one or other ways may offend the sensibilities of the other. Fortunately, in many cases, as with people's relationships more generally, researchers willing to engage in remedial interchanges (Goffman, 1963a) may be able to salvage (through apologies, fuller explanations, even temporary absences to let others "calm down") some situations that have taken negative turns from a research perspective.

In the course of doing and talking about field research, I've also observed that researchers who are able to overcome their own particular *mystique(s)* with the field or about the people they meet are generally advantaged in the quest for attaining intersubjectivity with the other. Insofar as researchers do not know what they may see, hear, or experience next, it seems advisable to be prepared for some uncertainty. People who are unable to dispose of outside moralities in the presence of the ethnographic other are not apt to be as well received, particularly when they begin to moralize, challenge, or otherwise impose outsider viewpoints on the group at hand. In general, people do not expect that others (researchers or anyone else) should closely imitate them or try to think and act "exactly as they do," but they do not want to be threatened by the differences or to experience intolerance of their activities on the part of those (researchers and others) with whom they live, think, and act.

Another area in which "emotionality" sometimes becomes problematic in the field revolves around the issue of *maintaining enthusiasm*.[14] This concern tends to become more acute when researchers are working on a more solitary basis in the field. Ethnographic research is wearying, and entails a more or less continual adjustment to others, not all of whom are receptive to the ethnographic enterprise. Often, too, researchers first approach those who they think will be most accepting of their proposals. Should these ventures be rebuffed, it is easy to become discouraged or for one's sense of stage-fright (Lyman and Scott, 1970) in approaching others to become intensified. Even when one better comes to terms with aspects of resistance and rejection, these experiences can still be disappointing. Field research is an exceptionally demanding (mentally and physically), open-ended mode of inquiry, which often takes one into perplexing realms of ambiguity. It is easy to experience "battle fatigue." As well, since the people one encounters in the field typically have their own agendas, field researchers cannot expect others to maintain the researcher's sense of enthusiasm.

Having worked closely with C. R. D. Sharper (1977; 1991) and Styllianoss Irini (1980), I can readily attest to the value of having a (congenial) partner in the field with respect to maintaining enthusiasm. In fact, neither project would have materialized if not for their assistance throughout. Beyond the ethnographic others and members of one's research team, however, I have found it very helpful to talk about ongoing research projects with many people, including colleagues in my department, scholars encountered at meetings and in other settings, students, and (nonacademic) outsiders who have taken interests in particular studies for one or other reasons. In addition to sharing their stocks of knowledge, raising questions, offering suggestions, and the like, these people have been highly instrumental in fostering the sense of personal vitality that ongoing field research requires. As well, I have sometimes taken people into the field with me. They've usually enjoyed the experience and the people in the field generally have found it interesting to meet and talk with them. In addition to helping me sustain enthusiasm, the ensuing field encounters have sometimes enabled me to gather materials that I likely wouldn't have obtained otherwise.

While a sincere emphasis on the matter of achieving intersubjectivity with the other will enable researchers to overcome a variety of setbacks and diversions, I also find myself more or less continuously reminded of the virtues of *patience* and *perseverance*. Although one can sometimes move field research along through more intense applications of self, many aspects of the field setting are best appreciated over time, including more detailed understandings, witnessing wider ranges of events, allowing people to become familiar with you (the researcher), and the like. As well, there will be times when things do not happen as quickly or as commonly as researchers might deem desirable. As much as possible, it is important to be attentive to, and accommodative of, the temporal flows in the situation and the importance of letting these develop more naturally. In a related manner, I've found it very useful to make notes on all sorts of things encountered in the field, even when these didn't seem particularly important at the time. On many occasions, it has proved surprisingly valuable to have made these earlier observations, given the ways things worked out in the situations under consideration over time.

The approach taken here is one which attempts to minimize the obtrusiveness of the researcher in the field and in the text eventually produced. It favors an image of a researcher who is more chameleon-like, someone who fits into the situation with a minimum of disruption, and whose work allows the life-worlds of the other to surface in as complete and unencumbered a manner as possible.[15] As someone, though, who has been involved in several, rather diversely situated research projects, the aspect of field research that I like least is the loss of relationships with (ethnographic) others (and the resulting loss of self) that one typically experiences when specific projects are completed. Although I have very much appreciated the interest that the people in each successive setting have taken in the study at hand, in moving from project to project one loses contact with a great many people whose viewpoints, insights, and friendships, have made the earlier studies so viable on both an academic and a more personal level.

Field research can be both immensely interesting and challenging, but this mode of inquiry is also essential for the development of a genuine social science. Not only is there so much that we can learn from others, but there is so much that effectively can be learned only from others involved in a variety of life-worlds (and subcultural pursuits).

In developing this statement on emotionality as a generic social process, I have tried to outline the fundamental social essences of affectivity and to provide an analytical grid (albeit somewhat rudimentary) for synthesizing and fostering ethnographic research in manners that are more attentive to this aspect of human association. While this discussion of emotionality has been presented as a unit unto itself, emotionality seems best appreciated (and demystified) as but one of several interrelated processual subthemes characterizing the life-worlds of the intersubjective other. Thus, in conjunction with the generic social processes outlined in chapter 5, it is hoped that the subthemes outlined in this discussion of emotionality may enable researchers to more effectively conceptualize their ethnographic ventures, as together we move toward a more comprehensive, grounded approximation of the social processes undergirding the dynamics of the human community.

On the surface, chapters 7 and 8, which focus on some of the major debates in the social sciences, would seem to take us some distance from matters pertaining to ethnographic research, generic social processes, and the management of emotional control. However, when we examine these issues a little more closely, it becomes apparent that we are very much submerged in matters pertaining to intersubjectivity, process, and the study of human lived experience.

NOTES

1. For reviews of the literature on emotions more generally, see Denzin (1984), Lutz (1988), Thoits (1989), and Karp (1993, 1994) as well as the Harré (1986), Franks and McCarthy (1989), Franks and Gekas (1992), Wentworth and Ryan (1994) and Flaherty and Ellis (forthcoming) volumes of collected papers. Clearly, not all of these materials are interactionist in nature, but

they do attest to the increased interest in the study of emotionality as a social phenomenon among scholars working in the interactionist tradition.

2. For ethnographic materials pertaining to instances of people learning (sub)cultural notions of emotional frames and understanding, see Waller (1930), Blumer (1933), Blumer and Hauser (1933), Sutherland (1937), Emerson (1970), Bartell (1971), Haas (1972, 1977), Prus and Irini (1980), Haas and Shaffir (1987), Lutz (1988), Prus (1989a), Prus and Sharper (1991), Wolf (1991), Schmid and Jones (1993) and Karp (1993, 1994).

3. The following ethnographies contain materials that highlight the ways in which people develop techniques for expressing and controlling emotional experiences: Sutherland (1937), Emerson (1970), Bartell (1971), Haas (1972, 1977), Prus and Irini (1980), Dietz (1983), Haas and Shaffir (1987), Prus (1989a), Prus and Frisby (1990), Charmaz (1991), Prus and Sharper (1991), Wolf (1991), and Karp (1993, 1994). Much of Goffman's work (especially, 1959, 1961, 1963b) also addresses matters of emotional expression (dramaturgical discipline, expressive control, remedial interchanges).

4. Material pertaining to people's situated involvements in emotional themes can be found in Lemert (1962), Prus (1978), Athens (1980), Prus and Irini (1980), Charmaz (1991), Prus and Sharper (1991), and Wolf (1991). While much of the emotions literature has focused on people experiencing self-feelings as targets, some consideration is also given to those (agents) more explicitly involved in *producing* (attempting to shape) the emotional experiences of others (see Prus and Irini, 1980; Prus, 1989a,b; Stebbins, 1990, 1994; Prus and Sharper, 1991: especially 205–306; and Wolf, 1991).

5. Clearly, stating that more intensive fascinations contribute to sustained solitary involvements does not answer the question of when "attentiveness" becomes heightened. The question of when and how fascinations become intensified is a matter requiring further investigation, as are issues pertaining to the development of acute obligations, the making of commitments, the avoidance and dismissal of discouraging communications from others, and varying assessments of one's options. A fuller appreciation of these subprocesses is central for comprehending the ways in which solitary emotional themes are pursued more intensively on this and that occasion.

6. Some ethnographic material addressing (more) solitary emotional episodes can be found in: Waller (1930), Cressey (1953), Lemert (1962), Lesieur

(1977), Vaughan (1986), Charmaz (1991). Goffman's (1963b) statement on stigma is highly pertinent here as well.

7. Although their work focuses primarily on deviance, I am indebted to Tannenbaum (1937) and Lemert (1951, 1962, 1967) in developing this statement.

8. There is no inference of automatic or unavoidable roles associated with particular labels or typifications. However, as indicated in the discussion of the labeling process (Lemert, 1951, 1967; Becker, 1963) in chapter 3, people's identities and reputations can significantly contribute to the likelihood of continued involvements in situations. This seems particularly likely when there is widespread consensus on the identity in question and when the targets under consideration perceive few viable alternatives in the situation.

9. While many emotional experiences are highly situated occurrences, some have more enduring dimensions. For ethnographic materials depicting continuities of people's involvements in particular emotional themes, see: Waller's (1930) and Vaughan's (1986) considerations of love and disaffection, Davis's (1963) and Charmaz's (1991) examination of long term illnesses, Lemert's (1962) analysis of paranoid relationships, Lesieur's (1977) study of heavy gamblers, Prus's (1989a) work on trust, loyalty, and more enduring enthusiasm in the sales setting, and Karp's (1993, 1994) examinations of depression. A number of sustained emotional experiences may also be seen in more "cultic terms." See Lofland's (1966) study of commitment to a religious cult, Fine's (1983) study of gaming involvements, Prus and Frisby's (1990) account of home party plans; and Wolf's (1991) consideration of violence in biker gangs.

10. For ethnographic materials that more explicitly address the intensification of emotional experiences in group or interactive settings, see Lemert (1962), Lofland (1966), Lesieur (1977), Prus (1978; 1989a), Athens (1980), Prus and Irini (1980), Prus and Frisby (1990), Prus and Sharper (1991), Sanders (1991), and Wolf (1991).

11. Only a small amount of the interactionist literature addresses matters of emotional disengagement or disentanglement. Relevant here are discussions of widowhood and divorce (Waller, 1930; Hunt, 1966; Vaughan, 1968; Lofland, 1985), "cooling out the mark" (Goffman, 1952; Prus and Sharper, 1991), and dealing with troublesome customers in bars (Prus and Irini, 1980) and other marketplace settings (Prus, 1989a). Given the sometimes profound significance of "emotional upsets" for a great many relationships and personal aspirations, the matter (processes and problematics) of

"disengagement from (particular) emotional themes" merits much more attention than it has received to date.

12. Unlike many ethnographers who have had the privilege of learning to do field research under the guidance of a practicing ethnographer, my exposure to this mode of research was somewhat less orthodox. My first experiences in the field involved some graduate student work on parole officers (Prus and Stratton, 1976) and the clergy (Prus, 1976). I had been trained in quantitative research methods at the University of Iowa, and these were rather tentative ventures. In the main, they were guided only by some materials I had read on Chicago-style ethnography.

My major "break" as a field researcher came later, when I met C. R. D. Sharper (Prus and Sharper, 1977), a card and dice hustler. Sharper was a student in a criminology course I taught, but I learned a great deal about people work (and field research) from him. A chance meeting with Styllianoss Irini, who was an undergraduate student (at another university) represented the beginning of another project. Styllianoss had been working in a hotel characterized by a good deal of "underworld activity." Although the ethnographies on which I've since worked generally have also been large undertakings, the study of the hotel community (Prus and Irini, 1980) was by far the most gruelling, demanding, personally unsettling, and precarious project in which I've been involved. In retrospect, I am amazed that we were able to pull so many things together. It's really the study of several subcommunities (hookers, strippers, hotel staff, patrons, rounders [grifters]) that constitute the larger hotel community and of people's interrelationships and activities therein.

Realizing, among other things, that we had just finished studying a number of businesses (entertainment business, bar business, hospitality industry, etc.), I next embarked on an ethnographic study of marketing and sales activity (Prus, 1989a,b). I found that the marketplace (which has been almost totally neglected ethnographically) a fascinating social arena, one in which a great deal might be learned about impression management, influence work, and relationships, as well as ambiguity, gambling, and emotionality. Since then, I've also been working on a sequel study of consumer behavior (Prus and Dawson, 1991; Prus, 1993; 1994a) and have undertaken a field study of economic development. The latter examines the "courtship of corporate investors" on the part of city (mostly), regional, and federal governments (Prus and Fleras, forthcoming). An unexpected call from a magician named Bob Farmer resulted in a smaller, but most interesting, ethnographic study of magic, one that became analytically synthesized with the earlier study of card and dice hustlers (Prus and Sharper, 1991). Some years ago, I had also begun to do a study on illness and wellness, but never pursued it very fully; I found that talking to people about their illnesses simply hurt (empathy) too much.

13. Clearly, there are situations that particular people deem too personally uncomfortable to conduct field research. Insofar as the entire realm of human community life denotes feasible arenas for intersubjectivist inquiry, it seems that one could make substantial contributions to an understanding of the human condition by embarking on field research in settings that are more consistent with one's own "comfort zones." However, when social scientists do venture out into other settings, they have an obligation to respect the moral order of those life-worlds and not use field research settings as fronts for expressing their own emotional frustrations or for promoting particular moral (or political) agendas.

14. The parallels of field research and direct (field) sales work are quite striking. For considerations of the problematics of sustaining enthusiasm in the sales setting, see Prus (especially 1989a:255–286; 1989b:243–276).

15. I am not denying the potential value of ethnographic research that is rooted in deep personal and possibly volatile (emotional) involvements in settings. However, for this research to approach its potential, an exceptional degree of self-reflective detachment will be required of the analyst-ethnographer. Accounts characterized by more extensive moralistic, antagonistic, or even artistic expressive, agendas are apt to have less to contribute to the social sciences than more analytical, comparatively balanced, and presumably still highly detailed, depictions of these same (ethnographic) life-worlds.

7

BETWIXT POSITIVIST PROCLIVITIES AND POSTMODERNIST PROPENSITIES

Pursuing the Pragmatics of Presence
through the Ethnographic Other

So the basic argument is that the higher prestige of a piece of sociological work, the less people in it are sweaty, laughing, ugly or pretty, dull at parties, or have warts on their noses. Field work is the lowest status in methodology, because surprising humans keep popping out and bewildering us by doing things we do not understand; much better to have people answering closed ended questions so that they fall neatly into cross classifications to be analyzed by loglinear methods. (Stinchcombe, 1984:51)

Culture (art, science, philosophy, family or marketplace practices, etc., as well as all forms of communication) is not just a series of linguistic expressions. Culture is a social product and a social process. Even language, which moderates action, exists only, and takes its form, shape or essence, through action. Language is, thus, an ongoing manifestation of human agency and interchange. The preponderant emphasis that postmodernists place on language and metaphors serves to disembody humans from their selves, their actions (and interactions), and the products of their "blood, sweat, and tears." Without these elements, without activity, without the ongoing struggle implied in human lived experience, however, language is nothing more than an empty shell. (Dawson and Prus, 1993a:169)

Although highly compacted in several respects, this chapter locates the quest for an intersubjective social science within the prevailing practices and debates in the social sciences. As will become evident, this statement is neither a criticism of the notion of science nor does it deny the importance of sensory observations for social science inquiry. However, it does attend to the human enterprise and intersubjectivity and argues for a reformulation of the scientific enterprise as this pertains to the study of the human condition.

While the social sciences appear to have derived considerable early impetus from concerns with moral reform and social control, and an emphasis on "appropriate" moral orders continues to define the agenda for the social sciences in some respects (e.g., funding and researcher moralities), this chapter focuses primarily on the problematics of pursuing an intersubjective social science within (a) the context of a deeply entrenched set of positivist paradigms, (b) an emergent postmodernist thrust, and (c) the practical demands of ethnographic inquiry.

Over the past century, the social sciences have been dominated by an overarching set of positivist/structuralist agendas, with the interpretivists providing backbench opposition of sorts. Despite deeply embedded resistance, some significant inroads have been made in the social sciences by those pursuing an intersubjectivist viewpoint, and qualitative orientations have become more accepted overall. Still, there is considerable resistance to interpretive viewpoints in mainstream social science and since the 1980s the situation has become complicated further by the proliferation of "postmodernist" (poststructuralist et al.) thought within the social sciences. Postmodernism shares some affinities with symbolic interaction and other interpretive approaches, but postmodernist skepticism violates essential features of intersubjectivity and the human struggle for existence and thus poses another set of problems for those wishing to build a social science based on human lived experience.

The major obstacles for the intersubjectivist social scientists continue to revolve around positivist notions of social science, but the intersubjectivists now find themselves attempting to pursue the study of human lived experience while maneuvering around and between these two oddly intersecting sets of "minefields." As well, insofar as an intersubjective social science builds on ethnographic inquiry, it introduces another set of demands that can be quite challenging on their own. Heightened attentiveness to some of these issues has been prompted by aspects of positivist and postmodernist critiques, but those embarking on field research face other sets of challenges which are no less formidable than those implied in these debates.

This chapter represents an attempt to situate the pursuit of an intersubjective social science within the context of these developments, being particularly mindful of the sorts of resistances and challenges facing scholars who take seriously the task of studying human lived experience. In pursuing a social science that eludes the epistemological failings of both positivist practices and postmodernist tendencies, the essential objective is that of developing a thoroughly intersubjective orientation that is grounded in the pragmatics of presence or the human struggle for existence.

In contrast to those who might be inclined to blend, assimilate, or synthesize two or three of these approaches in some way, an attempt is made to lay out their root assumptions and assess the relative viability of these epistemologically diverse approaches for attending to human life-worlds in the manners experienced by the participants. Although I have tried to carefully develop and document this statement, the ensuing discussion is rather pointed in essential respects. People desiring a more accommodative or conciliatory stance may find this chapter somewhat polemical or controversial. For my part, I have tried to maintain a rigorous focus on the necessity of respecting the intersubjective essence of the human condition. Attending to this concern, I have found much that is lacking in both positivist and postmodernist approaches to the social sciences. *Intersubjectivity not only represents the central feature to which a genuine social science must attend, but if there is to be any viable syntheses of the social and physical sciences then intersubjectivity represents the vital link to that endeavor.*

POSITIVIST/STRUCTURALIST SOCIAL SCIENCE:
PREMISES, PURSUITS, AND PITFALLS

For the past twenty-odd years, positivism (P) in the natural sciences has been waging a defensive war of survival until today it has few advocates among historians or philosophers of science. On the other hand, in the social sciences and particularly in sociology the conflict between (P) and its critics has continued unabated since at least the publication of Comte's Positive Philosophy *in the 1840s and Mill's* On the Logic of the Moral Sciences *in 1843. (Tibbetts, 1982:184)*

To better appreciate not only the ongoing positivist-intersubjectivist debate in the social sciences but also the very foundations on which the social sciences rest, it is necessary to outline some central features of mainstream positivist social science! While the term, "positivism" has undergone a variety of meanings over the past century, it has also been the target of much criticism over that time as well. As a result, many practicing social scientists have attempted to distance themselves from the term, even though their works may be seen to reflect, if not epitomize, some central and relatively enduring features of a positivist social science.

Attempts to establish a comprehensive and definitive statement on the essence of positivism have proved elusive (see Dawe, 1970; Giddens, 1974, 1976,

1984; Hollis, 1977; Wiley, 1979; Alexander, 1982; Halfpenny, 1982; Tibbetts, 1982; Lemke et. al., 1984; Bryant, 1985; Manicas, 1987; and Dawson, 1985, 1988). Nevertheless, we can establish sets of working parameters that allow us to better approximate shared understandings of the matter at hand. As a first step, it may be instructive to distinguish *positivism as a physical science orientation* from *positivism as a social science orientation*. The latter builds on the former, but the reverse does not seem to have happened.

Positivist Physical Science and Social Science Orientations

Within a physical science orientation context, positivism is contingent on assumptions of the sort following:[2]

1. *Phenomenalism*—The ultimate reality or focus of science is that which is experienced through the senses;[3] metaphysics and morality are irrelevant to the scientific pursuit.
2. *Instrumentalism*—Operationalism or objectivism. Scientific knowledge is based on examination or testing procedures that could be used to make systematic or standardized observations across a range of cases.
3. *Verification*—Scientific knowledge, in principle, is subject to confirmation by independent observers.
4. *Cumulative unity of the sciences*—Science refers to a body of knowledge, which has the potential to achieve coherency with continued inquiry.
5. *Implied causality*—Objects exist in states of relationships with one another, such that one may infer covariation, sequentialism, and determinism through inquiry.
6. *Enabling control*—The purpose of science is to develop a series of factual statements and generalizable principles designed to foster the understanding, prediction, and control of objects.
7. *Methodological unity of the sciences*—The methodology of science is generalizable across the realms of objects involving awareness through the human senses.[4]

As a social science orientation, positivism generally reflects assumptions of the type preceding, but is contingent on one further, vital claim: that humans can and should be studied in ways that approximate the methodological premises and practices of the physical sciences. Ergo, the assumption that human beings can be studied in manners analogous to other objects.

8. *The existence of human analogues*—The essential methodological orientation
    and practices of (positivist) physical sciences should be applied to the study
    of human behavior.[5]

This last point is extremely consequential for those purporting to do "social
science." It is also on this point that the essential features of the positivist—
interpretivist debates hinge. Without attending to the difficulties and debates
revolving around the applicability of the other notions of positivism for those
working in the "natural" or "hard" sciences (for more detail, see Passmore,
1968: v5, 52–57; Feigl and Brodbeck, 1953; Neurath et al., 1955, 1970; Kuhn,
1970), *the more immediate and essential epistemological "rub" for social scientists
revolves around the applicability of the assumptions, conceptual models, and methods
of inquiry developed in the physical sciences for the study of human behavior* (see
Blumer, 1931, 1969; Schutz, 1962, 1964; Berger and Luckmann, 1966; Dilthey
[Ermarth, 1978]; Giddens, 1974, 1976, 1984; Alexander, 1982; Bryant, 1985;
and Dawson, 1988). Indeed, while acknowledging the practical accomplishments
(in the human struggle for existence) that people have made by invoking positivist
assumptions in the physical sciences, one may still question the integrity of
attempts to apply these notions to the human situation as well as the assumption
(see Schutz, 1962:65) commonly made by positivist social scientists that only
the methods of the natural sciences may be defined as "scientific."[6]

   Although positivistically oriented social scientists may emphasize certain
of the preceding assumptions over others, by and large the adoption of a positivist
(structuralist) framework in the contemporary social sciences has meant a heavy
emphasis on (1) restricting the field of inquiry to observable objects, (2) defining
these in reference to structures or antecedent conditions and outcomes or consequences, (3) using standardized methodologies and observations for obtaining
data, (4) ordering observations in manners amenable to quantification and math-
ematical modelling, (5) pursuing hypotheses-testing and reproducibility of results,
and (6) attempting to discern and explicate structural generalizations (and causal
relations).[7] Although more explicit claims regarding prediction and control have
become somewhat muted in recent years, as have concerns with developing
"laws" of human behavior, the emphases on operationalization (instrumentalism), quantitative analysis, and (qualified) structural causation have generally
remained dominant in mainstream social science, as have hopes of developing
a coherent, cumulative social science that reflects a syntheses of data gathered
in these manners.

   Focusing on the operationalization of variables, statistical manipulations,
and analysis of the ensuing "data," a great many social scientists have been

centrally involved in attempts to causally comprehend (to uncover and assess factors thought to account for particular outcomes or conditions of human existence) as well as predict and control particular human conditions.[8] While both the outcomes (end products, dependent variables) emphasized and the structures or forces (independent variables) purported to account for these outcomes vary considerably across and within disciplines, the quantitative thrust with its concurrent emphasis on objectivity and causation has become the methodological nexus of mainstream social science.

Positivist Dilemmas: Epistemological Challenges and Motivated Resistances

Despite the relative prominence of quantitative practices in the social sciences, positivist practices have come under fairly extensive criticism in a number of quarters. It is unclear whether most mainstream social scientists have simply been unaware of, or have disattended to, these critiques, but a great many have continued to act as if these did not exist. A closer examination of the literature reveals that these critiques are intellectually devastating, however, and deserve to be explicitly recognized and addressed by anyone purporting to do social science.

Epistemological Challenges

While the interactionists have long challenged the viability of quantitative social science, the positivist paradigm has been under attack from a number of realms of scholarship. Since the foundations and central dimensions of the interpretive challenge have been dealt with elsewhere (Prus, 1992b) only a summary statement is presented here.

The origins of the interpretive challenge may be most singularly attributed to (1) Wilhelm Dilthey (Ermarth, 1978), but the interpretive critique is apt to be most familiar to sociologists through (2) symbolic interaction (Mead, 1934; Blumer, 1969) and (3) phenomenological sociology via Schutz (1962, 1964), Berger and Luckmann (1966), and Garfinkel (1967). The critique of positivism has become much more broadly based, however. Thus, it also reflects (4) the works of sociologists such as Friedrichs (1970), and Giddens (1974, 1976, 1984), and has also been buttressed centrally by developments in (5) the philosophy of science (and knowledge) [see Winch, 1958; Gadamer, 1960; Kuhn, 1962, 1970; Habermas, 1968, 1970; Hollis, 1977; Lincoln and Guba, 1985; Manicas, 1987], (6) the new (constructionist) sociology of science (see chapter 3), and (7) the emergence of a number of internal disciplinary critiques by practitioners across the social sciences (e.g., Gergen, 1982, 1985; Anderson, 1983, 1986; McCloskey, 1986). Finally, the viability of the interpretive challenge has been further enhanced by (8) a number of central figures in the positivist tradition who have either explicitly acknowledged the centrality of the hermeneutic frame (Campbell, 1986) or who have become openly skeptical of the viability of much of what passes as quantitative research and its potential for relevance, accuracy, coherence and cumulativeness (e.g., Blalock, 1984; Duncan, 1984; Stinchcombe, 1984).[9]

As a set, these critiques—with the partial exception of (8)—posit that those assuming a positivist or structuralist approach to the study of human behavior have neglected or violate essential features of the human condition. *In attempting to model themselves after the physical scientists, these scholars have not only disattended to the human capacities of reflectivity, action, and interaction, but they also have been relatively oblivious to the interpretive and interactive nature of all scientific enterprise.*[10]

People doing research in the physical and social sciences may be seen to engage in somewhat parallel activities, but the hermeneutic subject matter of the human sciences is notably different from the subject matter with which the physical sciences deal. It was on this basis that Dilthey insisted that the study of human lived experience (*Geisteswissenschaften*) required a methodological orientation different from that implied in the study of nonminded objects (*Naturwissenschaften*).[11] Thus, the problem created by positivist social scientists is one of attempting to employ a method used in the study of one type of object to a different type of object; ergo, *the fallacy of methodological reductionism*. The result has been a displacement of human intersubjectivity and activity with the impersonal agency implied in structures, factors, or variables through which some set of overall behavioral effects are produced in the population under consideration. Instead of attending to the life-worlds that people experience from the viewpoints of those who are actively involved in constructing (and maintaining or changing) those life-worlds, those adapting positivist/structuralist approaches, as Blumer (1969) so cogently observed, essentially treat people as "mediums through which alleged forces or factors find expression."

Motivated Resistances[12]

If the interpretive challenge is so viable, why aren't sociologists and other social scientists flocking over to the interpretive paradigm in droves? Most of them are still doing mainstream, quantitative work and appear to have no intention of doing otherwise! (colleague) (Prus, 1990:359)

Despite the formidable challenges represented by the set of critiques just outlined, most social scientists have continued to pursue a positivistically oriented social science, seemingly undaunted by these matters. The statement following attempts to shed light on how this might happen, given the apparently dedicated interest that most of these scholars have in coming to terms with the human condition as an arena of sincere study.

Some social scientists seem inclined to dismiss the interpretive critique as "softheaded" or irrelevant to the pursuit of "real (quantitative) science," but the critique has become so extensive and central that it has become increasingly difficult to dispense with it in this manner. Recognizing, at least particially, the significance of the interpretive frame, some Weberian (see chapter 2) scholars and others such as Denzin (1970) and Collins (1981, 1989) have endeavored to co-opt the interpretive elements within mainstream thought or proposed theoretical or methodological syntheses of sorts. However, these accommodative endeavors ignore the fundamental incompatibility of the assumptions underlying the positivist and the interpretivist approaches. On another level, some researchers have attempted to incorporate aspects of "qualitative research" into their studies on a more situated basis. Typically, this has meant conducting some interviews to facilitate the construction of a questionnaire or to help researchers interpret questionnaire results. Sometimes, too, this material has been used in an antidotal fashion, to add interest to the subject matter being discussed. Generally speaking, however, these endeavors have enabled positivist researchers to move somewhat beyond the realms of "paratheory" (or learned speculation regarding their data analysis) but these efforts have not been widely or fully pursued in the social sciences, and those embarking on these mixed methodological ventures have not given much explicit thought to the epistemological implications of their practices. Consequently, to date, and despite encouragements such as Denzin's (1970) plea for "methodological triangulation," mainstream research has concentrated heavily on structuralist models and quantitative data. Thus, even if one accepts the desirability of a multi-methods thrust, the notion of "motivated resistance" merits much more attention than it has received in the social sciences.

During the past century, notions of a quantitative social science have become deeply entrenched in both academia and the general community at several levels. This has generated a variety of motivated resistances to an intersubjective social science at cultural, organizational, and more individual or personal levels.

First, quantitative research has become highly institutionalized at a cultural level. It has become extensively legitimated or "objectified" (Schutz, 1962; Berger and Luckmann, 1966) through the development of university departments and disciplines in the social sciences whose practices and policies endorse quantitative approaches to teaching, research, and staffing. Ergo, one notes a highly embedded set of institutional practices in the academic community which, while providing a congenial setting for quantification, represent major sources of resistance to the interpretive challenge. In conjunction with this, one notes the formation of numerous professional associations (e.g., American Sociological Association, American Psychological Association, American Marketing Association), which have not only become very large, but which presently also serve as dominant sources of legitimation and control for those endorsing a quantitative social science across a range of disciplines.

It might be noted as well, that this emphasis on quantification has very much been filtered into the society at large via the media and the educational system more generally. Indeed, positivism is typically considered the "natural way" to approach science (and social science) in western society. Additionally, and as a reflection of the enterprise designed to sell outsiders on the (alleged) potential of quantitative social science, one finds that a great many bureaucrats (in government, industry, and other organizations) have become somewhat mystified by, and "habituated" to, this type of information.

Even though it has become increasingly apparent that quantitative analysis is unable to provide effective solutions to social problems and human policy related dilemmas, many decision-makers and members of the general public, persist in the belief that quantitative social science could provide simple answers or "magic formulae" for resolving pressing human problems. Consequently, it is cited as a compelling rationale for people who want "quick fixes" to pressing concerns or at least wish to indicate to others that they are trying to do something about the situation at hand. Regardless of the actual initiator, and regardless of whether projects are encouraged by allure or closure, this source of interest and funding has helped foster and consolidate a quantitative social science.

At a more personal level, a great many scholars have organized their careers around quantitative social science and are dependent on its continued perception of viability for their own notions of prestige, power, and persona. To the extent that people have developed competencies in a field revered by their peers and other gatekeepers, have secured positions, research grants, recognition, and senses of self-accomplishment based on these competencies in their (positivist/ structuralist) work, and are actively engaged in positivist productions at the present, they are not apt to welcome the interpretive critique.

An extensive paradigm shift could generate considerable loss at an individual level, especially among those scholars who have been more productive over the years. Not only do these scholars have vested interests in promoting positivist practices, but they are also the more entrenched and respected gatekeepers in the social sciences. Individually motivated resistances are by no means limited to the more productive scholars in mainstream social science, however, and anyone who anticipates that a paradigm shift would result in unwanted reorientations (ambiguity, extra work, retraining) may exhibit reluctances in these directions. Unfortunately, as well, there is no quick fix substitute to which they can turn. A shift to an intersubjectivist paradigm is much more dramatic and demanding than is incorporating a new statistical procedure into existing quantitative routines, for instance. As well, the computational technology that has been developed over the past several decades makes the use of quantitative data even more alluring than in the past. Thus, even though some of these scholars might be epistemologically concerned about the social science they are producing, they well may find that a continued application of their present practices has immense (albeit commonly recognized as "quick and dirty") short-term appeal. Further, observations that others continue to work in the same traditions is often taken as further indication of the viability of the quantitative paradigm.[13] Consequently, while a greater recognition of the interpretive challenge has become apparent at an intellectual level, it is not evident that much has changed at the level at which the social sciences are practiced on a day-to-day basis. Therein lies the major problem for those concerned about the viability of the interpretive paradigm and the necessity of attending to human lived experience:

> Following Lemert's (1951, 1967) discussions of the difficulties people experience in attempting to disentangle themselves from more extensive involvements in deviant pursuits, we may expect that people who have more fully organized their lives around quantitative routines will have genuine difficulty accepting and approving changes involving the interpretive paradigm even when they themselves are sympathetic or appreciative of these developments. Research is in progress, grants are in midstream, papers are being written or submitted for publication, and textbooks extolling the virtues of quantitative inquiry are being developed. To suggest that people reconceptualize and reorganize so many aspects of their involvements, thus, is to engender resistance on a series of dimensions. (Prus, 1992b:68)

Synthesis and Reconciliations: Feasibilities and Practical Limitations

The term intersubjective *stresses the social nature of the scientific enterprise. If there is to be any "truths" that are accessible only to privileged individuals, such as mystics or visionaries—that is, knowledge-claims which by their very nature cannot be independently checked by anyone else—then such "truths" are not the kind we seek in the sciences. (Feigl, 1953:11)*[14]

In contrast to some earlier proposed syntheses of positivist and interpretivist approaches (e.g., Weber [see chapter 2]; Denzin, 1970; Collins, 1981, 1989), the position taken here is to maintain an integrity of the social sciences by attending in a close, sustained manner to the ongoing lived experiences of people. If a synthesis of positivism and intersubjectivism is be at all epistemologically sound, it requires an entirely different stance than those proposed to date. It will require attentiveness to a (constructionist, sociology of knowledge—Schutz, 1962, 1964; Berger and Luckmann, 1966; Blumer, 1969) viewpoint that ascribes sustained priority to the intersubjective, active, and processual nature of the human condition. This chapter clearly does not purport to provide that synthesis, but does suggest the redirection a synthesis would require if it were to achieve epistemological integrity.

To their credit, Weber, Denzin, and Collins all envision the interpretivist features of human group life as central to their projects, but they were unwilling to consistently subjugate positivist/structuralist tendencies to the interpretive frame. Likewise, they disattended to the ongoing production of action or the enterprise characterizing the human condition. In each case, the emphasis on structural determinism meant a turn away from intersubjectivity, action, and process. *To achieve viability, any syntheses, it seems, must begin with the recognition that science is a thoroughly hermeneutic or intersubjective enterprise.*

While denoting a close, sustained examination of some phenomenon, science is built up or developed as a consequence of a group of scholars communicating with one another regarding their views on and experiences with the phenomenon in question. Regardless of whether one accepts the view that science is beset by more abrupt paradigm revolutions of the sort Kuhn (1970) envisions or wishes to argue for a more consistent, developmental flow (Feigl and Brodbeck, 1953), there seems considerable agreement among those working in the physical sciences that *science represents a negotiated process* in which the integrity of various theories and findings are open to challenge by those providing alternative forms of evidence or developing alternative ways of recasting existing materials.

Within the scientific community, as well, there seems essential agreement on *the centrality of concepts* for the development of a science, *the necessity of examining individual instances of cases in point, the necessity of developing* generalizations or abstract statements regarding the nature of objects and their relationships with one another, and *the necessity of maintaining openness and reassessing one's earlier formations* with respect to the phenomenon being studied.

In more general terms, it should be noted that the practices of developing concepts, encountering instances, developing generalizations, and making ongoing assessments (and adjustments) do not substantially differentiate scientists from the pragmatic orientation of humans at large as they go about developing (collective and more individualized) stocks of knowledge. What appears most distinctive to the scientific enterprise is the sustained attentiveness on the part of an interacting community to the development of knowledge (perspectives, concepts, understandings, technologies, procedures) with respect to some particular category of phenomena. Schutz (1962) makes the case for a further distinction: while citizens at large are essentially concerned about dealing with cases on a "here and now" basis, those adopting a scientific viewpoint tend to assume a stance of "detachment" from practical instances of the here and now; they tend to be concerned with higher level abstractions that transcend a more immediate sense of application.[15]

Clearly, these observations do not invalidate the application of the "scientific method" to the study of human behavior. To the contrary, it might be argued that anyone who actively (*and reflectively*) engages aspects of one's environment may be seen to adapt some minimalist notion of a scientific stance. This presupposes some set of (preliminary) concepts developed through association with others, but suggests that the assumption of a quasi-scientific [anticipation, trial and error, assessment, adjustment, sharing experiences with others] stance has figured prominently in the human struggle for existence. The objective here, then, is not to contest the viability of the scientific enterprise as a matter of human activity, but rather to comment on its fundamentally intersubjective nature.[16]

As Smaling (1992) goes to some length to illustrate, *the concept of intersubjectivity is fundamental to contemporary notions of science* (including mainstream social science, although in a necessarily qualified fashion). Indeed, the practice of science, as we presently know it, would not seem possible without some acknowledgement of intersubjectivity. Consider in this regard what Smaling designates as (1) consensual intersubjectivity, (2) intersubjectivity by regimentation, (3) intersubjectivity by explicitness, and (4) argumentative intersubjectivity.

Consensual intersubjectivity is evidenced by notions such as verifiability, interobserver agreements, repeatability, replicability, and reproducibility. *Intersubjectivity by regimentation* refers to an imposed intersubjectivity of the sort achieved by standardized data collection procedures, whereby one develops a ruler, scale, or other standard or base with which to foster comparisons. *Intersubjectivity by explicitness* addresses the trackability or repeatability of one's procedures, an attempt to more clearly define the experimental procedure or the data collection process so that others might be able to follow its development, assess its integrity, duplicate the procedure, and the like. *Argumentative intersubjectivity* refers to the process of communicative influence that takes place in the scientific community. Thus, what is considered "objective knowledge" in science is a matter of the prevailing (intersubjective) consensus at particular time and community reference points.

In all of these respects, the intersubjective nature of the scientific process seems both indispensable and widely acknowledged. The peculiar problem for the social scientists revolves around what Smaling terms (5) *dialogical intersubjectivity*. This requires an explicit and thorough appreciation of *verstehen* or hermeneutics (Dilthey [Ermarth, 1978]), sympathetic introspection (Cooley, 1909), interpretation (Mead, 1934; Blumer, 1969), an adoption of the standpoint of the other (Schutz, 1962, 1964; Berger and Luckmann, 1966) or "the double hermeneutic" (Giddens, 1976) with respect to one's (human) subject matter.

A recognition of the intersubjective nature of the scientific enterprise suggests that the problems associated with positivism in the social sciences have emerged not because the early positivist social scientists (Comte, Mill, Durkheim, et al.) attempted to study human behavior in a scientific manner, but because these scholars failed to attend to the intersubjective nature of the human condition. The problem was not one of being "scientific" per se, but one of presumption, of acting *as if* people were no different from other objects of study. Unfortunately, as well, since they established the primary agenda for the social sciences, this essential failing has not only been overlooked but has become deeply entrenched both in the academic community and in notions of social science in the community at large. Claiming to study human behavior "scientifically," these scholars were able to objectify (and legitimate) an approach that violated the very essence of what they purported to study.

Consequently, given the inability of positivist social science to adequately incorporate the intersubjective essence of community life either in scientific contexts or the human condition at large, *any hopes for a synthesis should entail an explicit and sustained recognition of the primacy of intersubjectivity*. Positivist social science does not have the ability to absorb the intersubjective viewpoint without violating its own premises. However, by viewing people's involvements in positivist social science in manners paralleling people's participation in other life-worlds or subcultural pursuits, an intersubjective approach such as symbolic interaction can readily absorb positivist notions of the world. This endeavor would largely relegate positivist social science to the status of another life-world to be appreciated (and studied) as a social construction, another instance of an intersubjective pursuit in the human struggle for existence. While this may represent a reasonably viable epistemological means of synthesizing the positivist and intersubjective paradigms, this solution is not apt to be readily welcomed by positivist social scientists.

Rather than a genuine epistemological synthesis, then, we are apt to witness somewhat reluctant tolerances and tentative methodological amalgamations. The tolerances are likely to be expressed through variants of "methodological pluralism." By ignoring epistemological debates (and sidestepping issues that may be intellectually embarrassing for those pursuing positivist research agendas), this tactic may minimize conflict within disciplines. At the same time, however, this posture brings with it an implicit acknowledgement of the viability of intersubjectivist claims and in that sense may represent tentative gains over earlier positions. Some social scientists engaged in structuralist research have also attempted to incorporate ethnographic materials into their studies,[17] but the social sciences are likely to be dominated by positivist/structuralist viewpoints for some time.

Mindful of the disparities between the fundamentally intersubjective nature of the human condition and the present orientation of mainstream social science, it seems entirely appropriate to insist that social scientists become more responsible, epistemologically and in practice, about the ways in which they pursue the study of human group life. It is essential that they strive to achieve a more steadfast emphasis on the manners in which human group life is accomplished by living, thinking, acting, and interacting beings whose behaviors are intersubjectively meaningful only within the community of others.

Although this assessment of positivist/structuralist social science may seem severe to some, it is likely to be seen as excessively light by others, particularly those adopting a postmodernist viewpoint. Professing a skepticism of all forms of scientific endeavor and knowledge, postmodernism has been traversing the humanities and social sciences with surprising rapidity and intensity over the past two decades. While it may be tempting to locate the intersubjectivist or interactionist approach as a midpoint of sorts on a continuum between positivism and postmodernism, a more extended consideration of these three approaches suggests that this would be inaccurate and impractical for a great many purposes (also see Charmaz, 1995). Thus, the discussion following considers the implications of postmodernist thought and enterprise for the development of an intersubjective social science grounded in people's lived experiences.

Postmodernist Propensities: Nietzschean Skepticism, Linguistic Reductionism, and Mixed Agendas

At the heart of postmodernist thought is an extreme or complete skepticism of, or disbelief in, the authenticity of human knowledge and practice. Accordingly, all claims of expertise and science are invalidated or at least are considered no more viable than any other "stories, narratives, fictions, myths or accounts." Partially shaped by the Nietzschean tenet that "Language is the first and great lie," all versions of reality are considered instances of self-perpetuating myths. At best, the postmodernists contend, humans may convince themselves to think that they know something, when in actuality, all that is known is but another version of a myth, another linguistic or textual reality which has no truth value beyond itself. (Dawson and Prus, 1995:107)

In recent years, the interpretive critique of positivist social science has been both supported and confounded by those promoting a "postmodernist" viewpoint.[18] Although the postmodernists (poststructuralists, deconstructionists) may be seen as interpretivists of sorts, postmodernism is characterized by an extreme skepticism in the viability of all forms of knowing (and presumably all interpretation as well!).

As presently used, the term *postmodernist* defies succinct definition. Still, it has become an umbrella term for a great deal of intense dialogue and criticism in academia.[19] While the most singularly unique feature of postmodernist thought revolves around an intense skepticism regarding the authenticity or validity of any knowledge claim, *postmodernist skepticism* has itself often been fused and diffused with, if not displaced by, *postmodernist intellectualism, cynicism, criticism, liberalism, activism, artistic expressionism, emotional experientialism, structural determinism, theoretical textualism, and methodological resurrectionism*. It is tempting, as Rosenau (1992) does, to distinguish "skeptical" from "affirmative" post-modernists, but it may be more advantageous to recognize the highly mixed agendas that have come to characterize postmodernism and to appreciate that individual scholars may adopt any combination of viewpoints and agendas within the context of a single book or article.

Despite the ambiguities and contradictions (and perhaps as a consequence of the elusive, challenging and diffuse formulations) of this "approach," post-modernism has swept across academia in an exceptionally dramatic fashion. Since the 1970s and particularly through the 1980s and 1990s, postmodernism has represented the focal point of considerable intellectual activity in the arts and social sciences. The basis of this popularity is not altogether apparent, but one may note several themes in postmodernism that may appeal to a cross-section of academics.

While some academics may have been attracted to what they envisioned as a new, trendy, or fashionable intellectual development, postmodernism has many other allures. For the philosophically discerning (postmodernist intellectualism), the concept of relativistic skepticism interfused with notions of textually mediated realities and alternative social philosophies may represent highly intriguing conceptual frontiers. As well, the erudite, complex, and abstruse writings of both the "postmodernists" (Foucault, Derrida, Lyotard, and Baudrillard) and those on whose works they have built (Nietzsche, Marx, Heidegger, Freud, Wittgenstein) represent materials that could in themselves provide a lifetime of intellectual reading and dialogue for those caught up in attempts to studiously comprehend these "masters." For those inclined to take viewpoints that might be deemed highly cynical, completely relativist, pervasively despairing, intensely antiscientific or anti-establishmentarian, or pointedly individualistic, postmodernism offers elements that are radical, fatalistic, absurd, and nihilistic in the extreme.

For those concerned with exploitation, power, and empowerment (from a Marxist, "critical" or "culture studies" perspective), postmodernism offers a powerful rhetorical weapon that might be used not only to challenge disfavored situations, practices, and people, but also to change (in activist manners) the prevailing social order.[20]

More generally, since no viewpoints are to be privileged over any others, postmodernist notions also may appeal to those pursuing themes such as liberalism, democratization, egalitarianism, and individualism. Indeed, not only is there the implication that allegedly de-valued groups may have more of a voice in postmodernist reconfigurations of the world but, in (skeptically) rendering the boundaries of science and fiction, philosophy and literature, data and theory inconsequential, there also is the promise (and self-motivated appeal) of a more equal voice across academia for those embarked on postmodernist agendas.

Similarly, in representing freedom from restraint, postmodernism promises opportunities for unlimited artistic and self-expression by implying an immunity from the criticisms associated with conventional practices and disciplinary standards. In like fashion, by allowing for a fuller range of emotional expressionism, some postmodernism may find appeal among those appreciating emotional sensations in the course of academic productions.[21]

In addition to these points of interest, those pursuing (in postmodernist terms) what might be envisioned as "more conventional social science" may find in postmodernism opportunities for theoretical textualism and methodological resurrectionism. Using scholars such as Foucault, Derrida, Baudrillard, and Lyotard as mentors, some scholars have purported to fashion new and compelling "postmodernist social theory," not uncommonly intertwining this with the structural determinism underlying aspects of Marx and Freud.[22] Beyond the forums provided to those interested in theorizing about linguistic representations and the human condition, postmodernist considerations of textually-mediated reality and the poetic license postmodernism implies, have also represented sites for those intending to methodologically resurrect the "social sciences" in this or that manner.

Regardless of the basis of its popularity and its lack of internal philosophical integrity, postmodernism has become one of the recent, "hot" realms of academic enterprise (and debate). Whether postmodernism subsequently will become a fad or a more enduring intellectual fashion, people working in the interpretive tradition are faced with the prospects of making sense of, and coming to terms with, postmodernist thought. Since postmodernism appears to have some affinities with the interpretive paradigm, it is particularly important to locate this development with respect to matters of intersubjectivity and ethnographic research.

To better comprehend the postmodernist phenomenon, it is essential to note that postmodernism is not a highly unique intellectual invention of a magical "postmodernist era" that somehow popped into existence after World War II.[23] More accurately, one might say that "postmodernist" thought is very much inspired by the skepticisms and subjective idealisms of Friedrich Nietzsche, Henri Bergson, Martin Heidegger, and Ludwig Wittgenstein, and to a very large extent represents a popular resurgence (albeit with some new ripples—commonly Marxist or Freudian twists) of the core ideas with which these scholars worked.[24] Unless one acknowledges the conceptual anchorage denoted in these historical roots, it is exceedingly easy to become mesmerized or overwhelmed by what has become a burgeoning intellectual labyrinth of discourse and mixed agendas.

On a more contemporary plane, the term *postmodernism* has generally been used to refer to the writings of Michel Foucault (1967, 1970, 1972), Jacques Derrida (1976, 1978),[25] Jean Baudrillard (1981, 1983a,b, 1988a,b), and Jean-Francois Lyotard (1984). There are substantial differences of viewpoint among these authors (who have also fused their writings variously with aspects of the phenomenology of Husserl, the hermeneutics of Heidegger, images of power and exploitation characterizing Marxist structuralism, and notions of self deception and unconscious motivation associated with Freudian analysis),[26] but all of these commonly acknowledged postmodernist spokespeople are disposed to view knowledge skeptically, as a rather arbitrary form of linguistic expression.

By explicitly emphasizing, dramatizing, and exploiting inconsistencies they've noted (or created) in the human fabric of community life, postmodernist writers have attempted to shock (sometimes embarrassingly, sometimes entertainingly) audiences into a state of disbelief regarding the integrity of human beliefs and practices. In Nietzschean style, they've argued that all human constructions are capricious and arbitrary; none is absolute or correct beyond its own contextual or situational validations. Given the relative, situated nature of human knowledge and practices, no knowledge claims, they argue, should be privileged over any others.[27]

Total relativist skepticism is the insightful and awesome (albeit misfounded) feature of the postmodernist critique,[28] but postmodernism was given a more alluring quality, yet.

What was required to make postmodernism more generally appealing was a peculiar leap in logic—a move from totalizing (and debilitating) cynicism to an "agenda-cized skepticism" that deprivileged others while simultaneously enabling those adopting a postmodernist mantle to presume more prominent roles in forging the present and shaping the future. Since no forms of knowing were to be seen as more viable than any others, then, ostensibly, any postmodernist claims could be made with impunity. Thus, albeit somewhat implicitly, postmodernism promised a panorama of free-flowing expression, of freedom from concerns with bounded disciplines of any sort. While established traditions represent popular targets for the expression of (postmodernist) discontent, the opportunities for pursuing (postmodernist) secondary agendas seem unbounded.

This was the liberating message. Those subscribing to the postmodernist philosophy not only could invoke the compelling skepticisms of relativism to neutralize and disregard prevailing perspectives, practices, and standards, but, simultaneously, they could justify their own productions (regardless of how these might be developed) as being at least equally (relativistically) viable as those that had preceded them. Thus, postmodernist skepticism became fused with what might be termed, *postmodernist expression*:

> *This is particularly apparent in, but is by no means limited to, the realms of art, architecture and literature. Here, one finds a seemingly total disregard for propriety, tradition, convention, prevailing notions of coherence and the like. Indeed, one finds considerable effort directed toward evidencing disharmony, incongruity, irony, and disruptures, as if to indicate that one has somehow transcended more established styles of expression and has developed a flair for displaying irrelevance of form. In practice, however, postmodernist expression in these areas is rather contradictory in itself. The modes of expression are generally limited to the same*

mediums and applications as those of their "modernist" predecessors, and "objects"
are produced with much the same intentions (e.g., to entertain, create interest,
foster sales). As well, the novelty of forms displayed are generally produced by
contrasting (exploiting) different styles already created by others as opposed to
developing more comprehensive forms which are more unique unto themselves.
Ironically, postmodernist skepticism is seldom applied to postmodernist expression.
To do so would be to render these expressions quite banal or no more viable than
any other productions; at best, they would only expand the range of irrelevant
or mundane expressions.

Like those pursuing postmodernist expression in the "art worlds,"
postmodernist expressions in sociology are liable to these same charges. First,
although denying the validity of any claims over others, postmodernists commonly
allege that a fuller appreciation of this approach to genuine understanding can
only be achieved by immersing oneself in the appropriate intellectual climate;
that is, attending in a highly studious fashion to the progenitors (e.g., Michel
Foucault, Jacques Derrida, Jean Baudrillard, Jean-Francois Lyotard) of the
postmodernist movement. Secondly, by denying tradition and authority, those
claiming to adhere to postmodernist sensibilities often claim an exceptional sense
of expressive freedom. They use "postmodernist" ideology to exempt themselves
from the usual restraints and discipline normally associated with academic routines.
Instead of attending to concepts and research in more precise and sustained fashions
or being intellectually accountable to others, many of those adopting postmodernist
stances claim, citing the appropriate (postmodernist) authority figures, that they
have transcended the mundane worlds of modernist mythology and now can
engage in more viable, creative, and personalized productions, unrestrained by
the trappings of modernity. (Prus and Dawson, 1993:2)

Utilized in this way, postmodernism provides avenues for those pursuing
a wide array of agendas in the social sciences. In a more direct sense, postmodernism offers little in the way of "resources" for knowing about people's
experiences in the world. Nevertheless, it has had a particularly strong appeal
among many who have become disaffected with the prevailing versions of social
science. Those invoking postmodernist frames display wide ranges of loyalties
and linkages with earlier theories and methodological practices in the social
sciences and have developed an assortment of postmodernist "hybrids."[29] For
our purposes, though, it may be most instructive to focus on those of the
postmodernist persuasion who have dealt most directly with matters pertaining
to ethnographic research for it is here that notions of intersubjectivity come
most directly into play in the world of human lived experience.

POSTMODERNIST METHODOLOGICAL RESURRECTIONISM:
REPRESENTING AND OBSCURING THE ETHNOGRAPHIC OTHER

My topic is postmodernism, which Richardson (1991, p. 173) describes as a "sensibility," a way of looking at and operating in the world that is alive and open, and not boring. The core of that sensibility is doubt that any discourse has a privileged place, any method or theory a universal and general claim to authoritative knowledge. (Denzin, 1993:179)

If one were genuinely to acknowledge postmodernist skepticism, there would be no incentive for anyone to do ethnographic research or gather any other sort of data or information about anything, since there is no privileged form of knowing (period!). From this viewpoint as well, ethnography would not be privileged over questionnaire or experimental data, or even deliberately constructed misrepresentations. However, in doing ethnography (implying a serious attempt to learn about the life-worlds of the other, through the other), one not only privileges a particular procedure of data collection, but also the life-world of the ethnographic other, and the ethnographer's account of that life-world. To do ethnography is to forego, rather clearly, the essentialist features of postmodernist skepticism. Nevertheless, a number of people have attempted to do exactly this, as "postmodernist ethnographers," "experimental ethnographers," "experiential ethnographers," "new ethnographers," and the like.

Although their affinities to the baseline skepticisms of postmodernism are vague, weak, tenuous, and, perhaps, opportunistic and pretentious, a number of scholars in anthropology and sociology have attempted to extend aspects of postmodernist skepticism and expression to the ethnographic venture. Much of the "postmodernist critique" of ethnography originated in anthropology and has been partially inspired by long-standing awarenesses of (a) the exceptionally complex problems of accessing unfamiliar communities or life-worlds and faithfully representing these to others and (b) the mixed agendas that have often characterized those making contact with other people.

With its emphasis on linguistically constructed worlds or textually mediated reality, postmodern skepticism provided a new intellectual springboard for those concerned with the "crises of representation" in ethnographic research.[30] The concerns expressed (see Clifford and Marcus, 1986; Marcus and Fisher, 1986) are quite sweeping, ranging from allegations that anthropological ethnography represents a form of cultural domination, to questions concerning people's abilities to inform others about their lived experiences, to matters of propriety regarding forms of representation, to explicit calls for poetic license and fiction in the development of ethnographic accounts.[31] While their own writings are fraught with ambiguity and contradiction, the postmodernist critics have drawn heightened attention to some of the problematic features of ethnographic representation. Given a general commitment or openness on the part of anthropologists to cultural relativism and the more erudite (and ambiguous) form these challenges assumed in postmodernist garb, these criticisms have attracted a great deal of attention in anthropological circles.

Interestingly, while these scholars are neither clearly of one mind, nor even consistent "within one mind," they do not seem highly intent on denying the viability of the overall ethnographic enterprise. As Dawson (1995) indicates, those claiming identities as "postmodernist ethnographers" have defined their *raison d'être* with respect to the "crises of representation," but they've also continued to affirm the broader objectives of realist ethnography. Likewise, whereas their criticisms may well have a disabling and confusing effect, they seem to intend their efforts to be constructive in developing more adequate representations of the ethnographic other. Oddly, though, while explicitly encouraging texts that display the limitations and vulnerabilities of the ethnographic enterprise as well as providing fuller textual representation of the ethnographic other, these spokespeople also argue for much greater license in developing poetic (and other attenuating) representations of the other. As well, as Dawson observes, their entire exercise, while seemingly intended to deprivilege ethnographic inquiry, provides a peculiar, ironic testimony to intersubjectivity as an essential (privileging) feature of the human condition that extends beyond any textual representation.

As a consequence of the highly diverse and eclectic sets of agendas, assumptions, and fieldwork styles that have characterized their ethnographies over the years, the anthropologists have been particularly vulnerable (and perhaps unnecessarily sensitive) to "postmodernist" critiques. But beyond the disavowal of nonpostmodernist practices, the postmodernist critique has been relatively inattentive to matters of epistemological restraints or the specification of standards to be invoked in the practical accomplishment of ethnographic research. In the absence of viable guidelines for assessing the integrity or authenticity of ethnography or any knowledge claim, it appears likely that "postmodernist ethnography" (if, feasibly, there can be such a thing) is apt to be subject to more confusion and dismay (given the mixed theoretical viewpoints, assorted methodological practices, diverse cross-cutting agendas, self-enhancing expressions, and fictionalizing endeavors tolerated) than has been the case for more conventional ethnography which, for all of its faults, denotes an essentially sincere attempt to openly learn about and depict the life-worlds of the ethnographic other.

In contrast to their anthropological counterparts, those working in the tradition of symbolic interaction have had a much clearer set of theoretical assumptions and standardized ethnographic practices with which to work.[32] Thus, while many anthropologists have indicated (personal communications) that they feel very comfortable with premises of the sort that Blumer (1969) uses to characterize Meadian interactionism (also see Whittaker, 1994), they've observed that they have had nothing comparable with which to work when they've gone into the field. As well, there is little evidence that those embarking on (postmodernist) critiques of anthropological ethnography are especially familiar with either Blumer's work or Chicago-style ethnography. Quite simply, too, these "postmodernist anthropologists" have no comparable theoretical or methodological resources to offer their colleagues or other ethnographers.

Still, and perhaps wishing to inform their colleagues of other intellectual developments, or to create further license for pursuing their own agendas under the banner of "postmodernist scholarship," some sociologists have levelled critiques of the sort developed in anthropology at those doing interactionist ethnography. However, these sociologists have not used interactionist thought or ethnography to inform those in postmodernist circles of the potential of interactionism for a genuinely intersubjective social science,[33] nor have they carefully sorted out the epistemological foundations of postmodernism, symbolic interactionism, and ethnographic research.[34] Neither, as Snow and Morrill (1993) observe, are they attentive to the differing (and particularly acute) predicaments of anthropological ethnographers as opposed to interactionist ethnographers. Instead, they've seemed more interested in informing symbolic interactionists of "the new thinking in European scholarship" and in chastising them for not being more cosmopolitan, skeptical and artistically entertaining. The (interconnected) writings of Denzin (1988, 1989a,b, 1990a,b, 1994), Richardson (1988, 1991, 1992, 1994a,b), Richardson and Lockridge, 1991), Fontana and Preston (1990), and Clough (1991) are illustrative here.[35] While displaying only some affinities with postmodernist skepticism, their writings have coincided with the "trendy" interest in postmodernism that has been sweeping across the arts and social sciences and, as a result, have attracted considerable attention both within and somewhat beyond the interactionist community. It has taken some time for others in the interactionist community to come to terms with the rather elusive, complex, and contradictory literature on which the postmodernist critique has been founded and to sort out the products, intents, and potential contributions of those promoting postmodernist ethnography, but the reaction has been far from positive.[36]

Although there are certain aspects of postmodernist thought that most interactionists would find congenial, symbolic interactionism (Mead, 1934; Blumer, 1969) is a much more thoroughly *intersubjectivist* approach. Most centrally, while appreciating an attentiveness to notions of linguistically mediated, relativistic human realities, interactionism does not endorse textual or linguistic reductionism or subjective idealism. Interactionism attends fundamentally to human interchange and the ongoing accomplishment of human activity; and neither human activities (and accomplishments) nor human relations are reducible to textuality. Likewise, there may be aspects of postmodernist expressions or other secondary agendas that individual interactionists may find entertaining or politically appealing on more personal levels. However, there is a very basic interactionist concern that these secondary interests, pursuits, or appreciations not interfere with the grounded study of human lived experience or the development of better conceptual understandings of the processes by which people accomplish their routines in conjunction with others.

Utilizing what is probably the clearest and most succinct articulation of the principles of "postmodernist ethnography" (Denzin, 1990a) as a prototype,[37] Dawson and Prus (1993a) dismantled the notion of "postmodernist ethnography" on a point-by-point basis.[38] Insofar as Denzin and other purported "postmodernists" attempt to do careful, thorough ethnography according to agendas of the sort Denzin has outlined, there is, first of all, not much that is uniquely postmodernist about the enterprise. Like those who might follow Denzin's advice on how to be "postmodernist ethnographers," conventional ethnographers have long been concerned with the problematics of accessing, comprehending, and representing the other, and in doing so in manners that are maximally comprehensible to prospective readers (see Palmer, 1928; Waller, 1930). Indeed, while practices vary from ethnographer to ethnographer, a central objective in interactionist ethnography is to provide a careful, balanced, open, and representative voice to the participants.[39] However, the elements that are more uniquely "postmodernist" pose particular problems since these tend to violate matters pertaining to the adequacy of representing the ethnographic other in a thorough, open fashion.

As is more typically the case with others purporting to prescribe or do "postmodernist ethnography" and variants thereof (see Marcus, 1994), Denzin's prescriptions are characterized by mixed agendas. Overall, Denzin's ethnographic orientation is more interactionist than postmodernist in emphasis, but his "postmodernist" work is significantly defined by the adoption of a "cultural studies" (Mills, 1959; Denzin, 1992, 1993) perspective. Thus, within the guise of doing "postmodernist ethnography" Denzin emphasizes, *in both nonpostmodernist and noninteractionist terms*, the centrality of structuralist factors such as class, race, and gender for analyses of the human condition.

With respect to a careful representation of the other, Denzin's model (1990a) offers little, if anything, not already achieved in more conventional ethnographies. However, as a consequence of the sorts of contradictory concerns, structuralist leanings, and poetic licenses embedded in Denzin's proposal (see especially Dawson and Prus, 1993a:159–165) and others of this ilk, postmodernist ventures based on these types of models are likely to distract and distort much more than they depict or illuminate the experiences of the people whose life-worlds are under consideration. When contrasted with more conventional ethnographic endeavors in the social sciences, ethnographies of the sort encouraged by Denzin and other proponents of the postmodernist sensibility are apt to be of limited utility to readers who wish to learn about the life-styles of others in a careful, thorough, reliable, and open manner.

Those claiming to do postmodernist ethnographies, experiential ethnographies, new ethnographies, and the like, may be seen as contributing more directly to an intersubjectively informed study of human lived experience when they: (*a*) advocate turns to the study of the situated, interpretive, interactive, emergent features of human lived experience; (*b*) emphasize the necessity of attending to the other in a thorough, careful, open-ended manner; (*c*) argue for concepts that are built up through sustained encounters with the life-worlds of ethnographic others; and (*d*) are concerned that ethnographic others be accorded fuller participation in representations of their life-worlds.

However, the postmodernistically inclined violate basic notions of an intersubjective/ethnographic social science to the extent that they: (*a*) layer their analysis with secondary agendas, such as emphasizing cultural (Marxist) studies or Freudian structures; (*b*) use ethnography as a basis for moralizing about or reconstituting the life-worlds of the ethnographic other; (*c*) fail to respect the life-worlds (and activities and accomplishments) of the other as instances of paramount reality in the human struggle for existence, and treat these instead as meaningless, valueless fictions and myths; (*d*) ignore, reject, or try to circumvent firsthand observations and interviews with those whose life-worlds they purport to analyze; (*e*) argue that their "deconstructions" of the life-worlds of others are no less viable than the actual accounts of those whose life-worlds they are purporting to analyze;[40] (*f*) use their text to develop self-enchanting representations rather than attempting to represent the other in careful, thorough fashions; (*g*) exploit ethnography to shock, entertain, and dramatize human conditions;

(b) attempt to represent the viewpoint of the other more exclusively through various attenuation devices, such as poems, pictures, artifacts, and contrived or fictionalized accounts;[41] (i) disregard the development of concepts that are central to people's lived experiences; and (j) disclaim or disavow researcher accountability for the task of endeavoring to sincerely, openly, and carefully conveying images provided by the ethnographic other to readers. People engaging in these practices may define their works as postmodernist, artistic, expressive, or in any other terms they desire, but if those in the broader academic community are to maintain a reasonably viable notion of a social science that attends to the study of human lived experience in a careful, thorough manner, then they ought not to feel obligated in any way to define or recognize this type of work as constituting "ethnographic research" or representing contributions to an intersubjective social science.

There are other problems, as well, associated with these postmodernist methodological ventures. In disavowing the integrity of conventional standards for evaluating ethnographic ventures and providing only tentative, experimental, and contradictory alternatives, the "postmodernist methodological resurrectionists" (PMRs) have become caught up in the paradox characterizing the broader "postmodernist sensibility." In the absence of recognized or acknowledged standards, the question, "How are things to be judged?", becomes increasingly consequential.[42] To focus on ethnography more specifically: if one adopts the postmodernist viewpoint that conventional ethnography ought to be rejected because it is (hopelessly) "modernist," does this mean that everything proffered as "postmodernist ethnography" is to be accepted on a par with everything else? Is all postmodernist work more or less equally acceptable, equally viable, equally compelling? Are there no standards of quality for making such judgements? Do the PMRs seriously contend that "anything goes?" And, if not, how might people know if they are moving along the appropriate lines? Is an important theme of postmodernist ethnography, as Laurel Richardson (1991:173) and Norman Denzin (1993:179) argue, that something *not be boring*, but rather (like a "good" movie or joke?) be interesting and entertaining? And, if so, *who* is to be privileged enough to decide if something is boring or entertaining?

To their "realist" credit, perhaps, those promoting postmodernist ethnography seemingly have invoked some standards. Most centrally, they seem to be arguing that ("good"—i.e., postmodernist) ethnography should (a) stress greater representation of the researcher's background and personal experiences throughout the ethnographic text; (b) encourage extensive, open-ended, polyvocal (researcher presence diminished) textual representation of those being studied;

and (*c*) display extensive poetic license and expression on the part of the ethnographer/author (i.e., they advocate [highly attenuating] devices, such as poems and fictionalized accounts, as substitutes for "actual" representations of the other) in the text.

If asked about the ambiguous and potentially contradictory nature of these "standards,"[43] most PMRs would likely assume an evasive stance, suggesting that openness and diversity, and even contradiction are appropriate in developing ethnography, just as one will most assuredly encounter these elements in everyday life. Indeed, some would observe, it is this receptivity to free-flowing creativity and inconsistency that most desirably sets postmodernist ethnography apart from the less creative, more mundane modernist or contemporary ethnography. Some (e.g., Denzin, 1993:182) might further add, "Let many flowers bloom," but even here, in this sagely, receptive context, vital questions arise.

Surely, those claiming to be postmodernist scholars are not saying that they have lost or forfeited their abilities to be critical of other "postmodernist productions." This stance would seem untenable, for presumably, if such openness were pursued or implemented on a more massive scale, the "postmodernist sensibility" would reduce the social sciences to an ill-defined pile of subjectivist, self-enchanting rubble, in which morality and entertainment on the one hand, and deliberate misrepresentation and absurdity on the other, are granted intellectual equality with the more careful, conscientious work normally associated with the social sciences.

Despite their professed openness to postmodernist and other experimental ethnography, this does not seem to be the position that people such as James Clifford, George Marcus, and Norman Denzin, wish to champion.

In a recent statement, Marcus (1994) clearly disavows much of the openness implied in his (Marcus and Cushman, 1982; Marcus and Fischer, 1986) earlier discussions of postmodernist ethnography. He observes that a decade of postmodernist endeavor has produced "messy texts," which are "neither models to follow nor the much awaited products of a new paradigm" (Marcus, 1994: 573). Marcus still values "creativity" (vaguely defined), but now endorses more responsible or accountable conventionalist ethnography and encourages (more conventional) ethnographers not to be intimidated by the postmodernist critique. Beyond this, however, Marcus offers limited methodological guidance.

In contrast to Marcus's more solemn commentary on the lack of progress on the part of postmodernist ethnographers, Richardson (1994) and Denzin (1994) continue with some optimism to endorse "theatrical productions" (my term), the strong undertones of which are to entertain audiences. In a statement that is much more revealing about her own lack of appreciation of the human condition than anything else, Richardson (1994:516–517) says:

> *I have a confession to make. For 30 years, I have yawned my way through numerous supposedly exemplary qualitative studies. Countless numbers of texts I have abandoned half read, half scanned. I'd order a new book with great anticipation—the topic is one I want to read—only to find the text boring. . .*

As a solution, Richardson proposes that readers venture on postmodernist voyages that fashion themselves after Barbara Tuchman's statement in the *New York Times* (February 2, 1989): *The writer's objective is—should be—to hold the reader's attention. . . I want the reader to turn the page and keep on turning to the end.* Working with this manifesto, Richardson's agenda is to foster what she envisions as highly engaging postmodernist text. To this end, she encourages (social scientists?) to be more evocative, to replace conventional ethnography with stories about oneself, fictional representations, poetic representations, drama, and mixed (eclectic literary, artistic, scientific) genres.

Perhaps drawing cues from Richardson, Denzin (1994) recommends that social scientists heed the writing advice provided by Raymond Carver, the short story writer. In Denzin's words:

> *Writing, then relives and reinscribes experience, bringing newly discovered meanings to the reader. No cheap tricks, Carver (1989, p. 23) says, no gimmicks. Writing must bring news of the world to the reader. In writing,* the writer creates this world. He or she fills it with real and fictional people *(Denzin, 1994:504–505; emphasis added).*

On an overall basis, Denzin expresses much more concern with authenticity of representation and academic responsibility than does Richardson, but his emphasis on entertaining the reader and his seeming endorsement (although less pronounced) of various accentuating (and fictionalizing) practices in the quest for readers' attention also falls far short of a viable model for social scientists concerned with depicting the human condition for those who are genuinely interested in the ways in which others come to terms with their life-worlds.

Perhaps somewhat mindful of objections of the sort just raised, but more likely denoting attempts to come to terms with the vast array of conceptual and methodological contradictions of the postmodernist thought that inspired many of the statements assembled in their *Handbook of Qualitative Research*, Denzin (1994), Denzin and Lincoln (1994), and Lincoln and Denzin (1994), have begun promoting the concept of "the social scientist as (intellectual) bricoleur." Although intriguingly cosmopolitan and rustic at the same time, this notion seems intended as a means of maintaining a sense of academic integrity and respectability for those embarked on projects of the sort discussed here:

> A bricoleur *is a "Jack of all trades or a kind of professional do-it-yourself person."* (Lévi-Strauss, 1966, p. 17)... The bricoleur *is adept at performing a large number of diverse tasks, ranging from interviewing to observing, to interpreting personal and historical documents, to intensive self-reflection and introspection. The* bricoleur *reads widely and is knowledgable about the many interpretive paradigms (feminism, Marxism, cultural studies, constructivism) that can be brought to any particular problem. He or she may not, however, feel that paradigms can be mingled or synthesized... The researcher-as-bricoleur-theorist works between and within competing and overlapping perspectives and paradigms.... The product of the* bricoleur's *labor is a bricolage, a complex, dense, reflexive, collagelike creation that represents the researcher's images, understandings, and interpretations of the world or phenomenon under analysis.* (Denzin and Lincoln, 1994:2-3)

Endorsing an image (highly romanticized) of a widely read, tolerant (and obviously not easily bored) scholar who can move across and within intellectual paradigms with exceptional facility and whose research skills are similarly unbounded, Denzin and Lincoln provide another (elusive) mantle that some scholars might eagerly claim as their own. Once again, though, there is minimal direction for social scientists. Vaguely claiming "humanism" as a guiding virtue is of no advantage here. Indeed, Denzin and Lincoln (1994) acknowledge the ambiguity (and ensuing frustration?) that has characterized their efforts both to assemble and then later to appraise (Lincoln and Denzin, 1994) the volume they have produced. In attempting to locate themselves on the "cutting edge" of everything (postmodernist and new), Denzin and Lincoln have retained a commitment to "qualitative research" but have found little in the way of direction to pass on to others:

> The answer to the question, Where have we come to? is unclear, as is the answer to the question, What are the many futures that lie ahead for qualitative research? We are not wandering, for that implies that we have no direction.... And perhaps it is the case that the Handbook itself is the fifth moment. Perhaps it is the particular time in our history to take stock of where we are, to think about where we are going, to try to imagine a new future.... And what remains, throughout, will be the steady, but always changing, commitment of all qualitative researchers—the commitment to study human experience from the ground up

from the point of interacting individuals who, together and alone, make and live histories that have been handed down from the ghosts of the past. (Lincoln and Denzin, 1994:584).

Insofar as Marcus, Denzin, Lincoln, and others remain committed to ethnographic research or qualitative research more generally, they violate the essential skepticism that undergirds postmodernist thought. Even Richardson's and Denzin's "privileging of entertainment" violates postmodernist skepticism.

Even if, in a more genuine postmodernist skeptical stance, one refuses to privilege or endorse particular standards of any sort (the position that Foucault professes to maintain), one may well ask if standards are not implicit in postmodernist criticisms of "modernity." Indeed, can one offer criticisms, or even make observations, without invoking vantage points? Can one act, in a meaningful fashion, without some reference point? Can one purport to do "postmodernist ethnography" without (privileging) some sense of direction? Can one even appreciate postmodernist productions without (privileging) some vantage point? And, in the case of postmodernist academics, does not the question still arise as to when, and by what (privileging) criteria, might one's work be accepted (or rejected) as noteworthy or suitable for publication?

In the absence of intersubjectively defined standards, scholars in a community context become more dependent on the capricious interests of any gatekeepers (who become authorities by default, if not intent) in this and that realm. A broader base of tolerance might please more people (e.g., as authors of prospective publications), but, as editors of journals and other collections of articles (see Denzin and Lincoln [1994:xi], "Tales of the Handbook" for an explicit testimonial along these lines) know from experience, certain decisions must be made when the materials submitted exceed the physical capacities or seem at odds with the vantage points of the publications in question. When decision making is more centralized, then the absence of clearer, intersubjectively defined standards may be seen as resources with which gatekeepers may work to pursue whatever interests they deem most appropriate. Where decision making is more diffuse or widely dispersed, the acceptance of particular productions is likely to reflect marketplace pragmatics, wherein members of the consuming public select from the available options according to their images and interests.

Either way, and in a much broader sense, *whenever someone acts*, whether this be as a consumer, a producer, an editor, an ethnographer, or a critic, a thinker, a daydreamer, or a "mere" observer—*it introduces a pragmatic feature of the human condition which extends beyond the postmodernist emphasis on a linguistically mediated world. Something is given priority over something else.*

It is in the doing or the forging of action that one moves beyond the subjective and the refusal to recognize standards or vantage points. *Intersubjectivity implies not only an interacting community of others, but the ongoing accomplishment of activities and the prioritizing of knowledge claims.* That these claims may be relative to particular cultural (and historical) contexts is not of central importance. What is of primary consequence, instead, is the sense-making practices of the human community, the meaningful linkaging of symbols and activity, that enables people to come to terms with the ongoing struggle for existence.

It is an appreciation of the human struggle for existence, the active engaging of humans with one another and with other aspects of their environment (as they know it) that is the essential missing ingredient in *postmodernism*—which, for all its discourse about discourse, *fails to appreciate that even the existence of "postmodernism" is predicated on intersubjectivity and human enterprise* (i.e., pragmatism by default):

> *Postmodernism . . . might achieve viability in a world where no "knowledge" would be privileged over any other "knowledge" because it is never tested or used to accomplish anything. However, in a world of action or human enterprise, we can speak of intentionality, application, accomplishment, and assessment. In each of these instances, by being invoked, tested, used to perform certain tasks, and being evaluated with respect to other forms of knowing, particular forms of knowing do acquire privilege. People may later decide that they were mistaken in taking this or that tact or they may have experienced doubts along the way, but in order to "do something," people have to privilege certain forms of knowing over others. This human use of knowledge straightforwardly violates what Denzin and others describe as "the postmodernist sensibility." (Dawson and Prus, 1993b: 199)*

In concluding this discussion, a further observation is in order. In contrast to those promoting postmodernist ethnography of sorts, interactionist ethnography offers two additional, very powerful and distinct advantages. First, symbolic interactionism provides a much clearer theoretical and methodological focal point for approaching the study of the ethnographic other (through the study of human activity) than does postmodernism. Secondly, because the interactionists have focused on activity in developing the ethnographic tradition, they have built up an exceedingly valuable base of materials that enable researchers, via the development of generic social processes, to dialogue with research that has been conducted at other times, in different contexts, and by different people. In this way, the interactionists have not only established a vital, transcontextual, privileged base for learning about the generalized other, but they have also created an analytical frame that enables contemporary researchers to actively contribute to, and dialogue with, this literature through their ongoing ethnographic enterprises. In contrast to the textually-mediated realities of the postmodernist, however, this venture takes one into the obdurate reality of human lived experience and a privileging of the ethnographic venture.

NOTES

1. Although I found many sources helpful in tracing the developments of positivism in the social sciences, I would particularly recommend Blumer (1969), Giddens (1974, 1976, 1984), Wiley (1979), Martindale (1981), Alexander (1982), Halfpenny (1982), Bryant (1985), and Dawson (1988) to those interested in more sustained considerations of the positivist tradition and its intersections with the interpretivist tradition.

2. Readers may also wish to examine Bryant's (1985:2–9) appraisal and syntheses of Kolakowski's and Giddens's statements on positivism, as well as Halfpenny's (1982) and Dawson's (1988:36–37) formulations of positivist tendencies. My statement builds on these and other materials.

3. It is essential to distinguish phenomenalism from interpretivism (entailing intersubjectivity and reflectivity). While people use "sense data" in their day-to-day lives as well as in scientific contexts, *things become "sense data" only because people act toward these [objects] in meaningful ways.* Phenomenalism (implying an ability to define things as "objects" [and to develop lines of action toward those actions]) has enabled people to gain control over various features of their environments, but this baseline concept effectively circumvents or overlooks the interpretive process. Meaningful human experience entails an *intersubjective reflectivity* that phenomenalism takes for granted.

4. The most sustained attention to the methodological (and linguistic) unity of the social sciences was generated by the "Vienna circle of logical positivism." For accounts of this set of dialogues and dilemmas pertaining to a unified, sense-based approach to the study of (mainly) the phenomena of the physical sciences, see Feigl and Brodbeck (1953), Passmore (1968), Jorgensen (1970), Halfpenny (1982), and Bryant (1985).

5. Although the history of positivist thought is somewhat synonymous with the development of western philosophy and science (Fletcher, 1971; Rossides, 1978; Martindale, 1981), the development of positivism with respect to the social sciences may be most explicitly rooted (as an intellectual

hybrid) in the works of Comte Henri de Saint-Simon (1760–1825), Auguste Comte (1798–1857), John Stewart Mill (1806–1873), Herbert Spencer (1820–1903), Wilhelm Wundt (1832–1920) and Emile Durkheim (1855–1917). While it is clearly beyond the scope of this chapter to provide a historical overview of the development of positivist social science, readers may also find it instructive to consider the development of instrumental or structuralist positivism in North America and more specifically the roles played by people such as Franklyn Giddings, George Lundberg, William Ogburn, Paul Lazarsfeld, Hans Zetterberg, Arthur Stinchcombe, George Homans, Donald T. Campbell, Herbert Blalock, and O. D. Duncan. The works of Mullins (1973), Wiley (1979), Martindale (1981), Alexander (1982), Halfpenny (1982), and Bryant (1985) are particularly valuable in this respect.

6. Anticipating, in a sense, aspects of what was to become "the new (constructionist) sociology of science," Schutz (1962:66) asks whether the methodological problems of the physical sciences might not be approached as special cases of a more general problem of the possibility of scientific knowledge.

7. Giddens (1974:3–4) envisions positivistically oriented sociology as focusing on three related themes (1) adapting the *methodological* procedures of natural science; (2) formulating the *outcomes* or end results of sociological investigations in terms parallel to those of natural science; and (3) pursuing a *technical* character (or what Alexander [1982:5] describes as "scientific" self-consciousness). In an even more truncated fashion, Wiley (1979:50) uses the terms, "highly quantified," "scientistic," and "social factist," to refer to this positivist practice of trying to model the study of human behavior after images of practices in the physical sciences.

8. While much mainstream (positivist) social science is characterized by quantification and attempts to precisely specify and measure causal factors, most Marxist (and "cultural studies") and Freudian analysts, as well as many postmodernists, feminists, humanists, and historians, who disavow interest in quantification, nevertheless continue to invoke generalized positivist notions of objective conditions and structural causation. Although only some of these scholars may envision themselves as "quantitative" or "scientific" in their analysis of the human condition, many of those taking these approaches may be viewed as positivists or structuralists of sorts.

9. One might also make reference to some (9) humanist (especially the Frankfurt school, see Bryant, 1985; Mills, 1959) and (10) postmodernist

critiques (discussed later) of positivist social science, but these are of a substantially different order and are beset by concerns with moralities and extreme skepticisms, respectively, which take one some distance from the current positivist-interpretivist debate. Readers interested in recent attempts to formulate the tenets of "humanistic sociology" (and the positivist-humanist debate) are referred to Tibbetts (1982), Lemke et al. (1984), Dawson (1985, 1988), and Scimecca (1989). While generally acknowledging (a) human agency and (b) the meaningfulness of human conduct, many self-defined humanists also emphasize (c) the centrality of values in science and all other realms of human enterprise, and (d) display clear preferences for works that purport to provide maximal realization of human potential. As Dawson (1988:37) observes, "Humanistic sociology does not represent a systematic doctrine, but an aggregate of reactions to positivism, derived from sometimes very different sources." Thus, despite its seeming affinities with an intersubjective social science, the term *humanism* has been used to encompass all sorts of viewpoints from Comtean and Durkheimian analysis to Marxism, cultural studies, feminism, Freudianism, and postmodernism/poststructuralism.

10. Those adopting a positivist social science orientation have generally assumed that (physical) science produces truth or knowledge of an objective or immutable nature. They've failed to appreciate that the physical sciences, for all of their accomplishments, are social constructions and ought to be approached as instances of intersubjective accomplishment on the part of beings who, like other people, think, act, interact, and create within a subcultural or community context.

11. Giddens's (1976) depiction of "the double hermeneutic," likewise, is particularly relevant here. While all (physical and social) science may be seen as a hermeneutic exercise, those attempting to do social science are studying objects that are themselves interpretive or hermeneutical in their essence.

12. This discussion of motivated resistances was initially formulated in Prus (1990), but was developed more fully in Prus (1992b).

13. One is here reminded of the observations by Festinger et al. (1956) about the tendency on the part of believers to take renewed confidence in the continued practices of others (believers) in *When Prophecy Fails*. As well, abrupt challenges to the faith may result in intensified proselytization efforts, as existing members attempt to convince newcomers (and themselves in the process?) of the viability of the seemingly discredited viewpoint.

14. Although Feigl (a longstanding spokesperson for the Vienna circle of logical positivism and champion of the notion of a unified methodology for the sciences) does not seem prepared to accord central importance to the hermeneutic essence to members of the human community at large, his observations about science clearly attest to aspects of the intersubjective essence of scientific inquiry.

15. Feigl's (1953:11) claim that, "The criterion of intersubjective testability thus delimits the scientific from the nonscientific activities of man" addresses this theme somewhat, but represents a less compelling position. Since all notions of reality are intersubjectively achieved, all shared conceptions may be subjected to any variety of "tests" (explicitly defined as such or not) and interactive reassessments on a day-to-day basis.

16. To appreciate that both the development of a scientific stance and the human struggle for existence are predicated on the human capacity for intersubjectivity, is not to claim that all instances of human reflectivity and enterprise are scientific in their thrust. Rather, the point is simply that insofar as people attempt to make sense of their life-worlds by reflectively assessing their experiences with the phenomena they encounter, they may be said to embark on (quasi-) scientific ventures of sorts.

17. These efforts are essential if structuralist researchers are to move past meta-speculations (however "learned" these may appear) in their attempts to explain how human group life is accomplished. Still, it is not apparent that efforts such as these represent much hope for either the syntheses of positivist and intersubjectivist paradigms or the fuller development of ethnographic research more generally. Proportionately few structuralist researchers have embarked on these agendas and those who have done so often seem at a loss about the ways in which to manage the ethnographic data. Lacking familiarity with the interactionist literature and ethnographic research practices more generally, they often tend to fall back on the quicker, handier, and more familiar quantitative component.

18. This discussion very much builds on materials that Lorne Dawson and I (Dawson and Prus, 1993a,b; 1995) have published elsewhere. Readers are referred to these statements for (a) more comprehensive reviews of the postmodernist literature, (b) more complete considerations of the affinities and disjunctions of postmodernist thought with an intersubjective social science, and (c) fuller elaborations on the practical limitations of postmodernism for appreciating the human condition.

19. Although neither Madan Sarup (1989) nor Pauline Marie Rosenau (1992) attend significantly to interactionism, pragmatism, ethnography, or the

positivist-interpretive debate more generally, they provide excellent overviews of the central features and key players in the poststructuralist, postmodernist movement.

20. It is worth noting, as do Sarup (1989) and Rosenau (1992) in their reviews of postmodernism, that the primary progenitors of contemporary post-modernist thought are former Marxists who have become disenchanted with the grand materialism of Marxist thought but who continue to retain underlying Marxist affinities (and sympathies). Readers interested in the relationships between postmodernism and Marxism may find Kincheloe and McLaren's (1994) paper especially interesting. Characterized by a great many illusive shifts and turns, this very erudite statement essentially endeavors to salvage a Marxist agenda. While critiquing "ludic postmodernism" (which they describe as denoting playful skepticism, avante-garde academic posturing, and metropolitan criticism), Kincheloe and McLaren use (variously) "oppositional postmodernism," "postmodern education," "resistance postmodernism," "critical ethnography," and "critical postmodernism," as forums, fronts, and facades for promoting Marxist agendas through a renewed emphasis on alleged oppression and political/materialist inter-vention. Thus, while some Marxists, such as Callinicos (1989) clearly deny the intellectual viability or integrity of Marxist-postmodernist syntheses, for others (such as Kincheloe and McLaren), postmodernism becomes another (albeit an intellectually complex) gloss for encouraging Marxist insurgency.

21. See Fontana's endorsement of Freeman's (1992) "Perfect Valentine" and Denzin's tribute to Cunningham's (1993) "Barbie Doll Culture" as cases in point. In both cases, intellectual facades are used to place expressions of sexual fantasies and related disenchantments (and vicarious readings thereof) on a par with scholarly work that is more explicitly and genuinely attentive to the ethnographic other.

22. Agger (1990, 1992), Vittimo (1991), White (1991), Bernstein (1992), and Borgmann (1992) represent instances of postmodernist scholarship along these lines. For an extended debate around matters of theoretical textualism allegedly directed toward a reorientation of the social sciences, see the "symposium on postmodernism" (Steven Seidman, Jeffery C. Alexander, Robert J. Antonio, Charles Lemert, and Laurel Richardson) in *Sociological Theory* 1991:131–190.

23. Despite the postmodernist tendency to dispense with history as irrelevant, it is worthwhile noting that Nietzschean skepticism, on which post-

modernist skepticism is centrally founded, swept across the academic community, in a somewhat parallel fashion, in the late 1800s:

> *In the last decade of the nineteenth century the thought of Nietzsche struck Europe like a thunderbolt.... Perhaps retrospectively his efforts may be aligned with the venerable tradition of Socratic reflection or the Kantian notion of critique of values, but at the time Nietzsche portended rather a radical iconoclasm, a colossal "break" in every sense. In "philosophizing with a hammer" Nietzsche destroyed more than he created, even though, as Dilthey observed, his highest aim was creation. For Dilthey...the much touted "overcoming" of nihilism was at base nothing more than "the great Nietzschean malady of exaggerated subjectivity."... In overturning culture and history, Nietzsche has not enthroned man or the creative self, but merely a gargantuan solipsism (85).... Nietzsche had not uncovered the texture of life, but merely peeled it away to a new set of arbitrary, subjective constructions. (Ermarth, 1978:86)*

Interestingly, especially in light of what recently has been portrayed and trumpeted as the "new, postmodernist tradition," Dilthey and an intellectual contemporary, York, worried that the *modern style of thought was likely to become "Nietzscheanism"—experimental, daring, and anti-historical* (Ermarth, 1978:86). It is perhaps fitting, to remind postmodernists of some virtues of history.

24. Likewise, the debate unfolding here is not without historical parallel. While the present discussion is informed by the development of symbolic interaction and ethnographic research and complicated by the secondary agendas of various postmodernists, Dilthey's (see Ermarth, 1978: especially, 84–89, 282–285, 318–321) critique of Nietzsche and his followers (Henri Bergson, Ludwig Klages, and Stefan George) addresses essential weaknesses of (the allegedly new!) postmodernist thought. In particular, Dilthey argued that Nietzschean skepticism effectively reduced analysts to the status of subjective idealists. Human nature, as Dilthey pointed out nearly a century ago, takes its essence in the relationships of people with one another over time; human nature is bound up in and cannot be separated from ongoing community life. Far from being the great lie, *language*, Dilthey contends, is the essential liberator of the human condition. Only through language (and the interactive other) may one attain a sense of being, of experience, of reality, of self. Even skepticism (as a linguistically informed and mediated viewpoint) presupposes a reflective capacity which develops (intersubjectivity) *through an interactive community of others*. Nietzschean (and postmodernist) skepticism, thus, represents a fallacy of (textual or linguistic) reductionism.

25. While Lamont (1987) focuses primarily on Jacques Derrida, readers may find Lamont's analysis of "how to become a dominant French Philosopher" suggestive more generally.

26. For a compacted overview of some of the essential differences between these four authors, see Dawson and Prus (1993a:152–155). Sarup (1989) and Rosenau (1992) provide more extended review statements.

27. As Giddens (1987:72–108) observes, poststructuralist scholars also appear to have derived some inspiration from (the structuralists) Ferdinand de Saussure and Claude Lévi-Strauss who argued for both (a) the arbitrary linkage of signs and (referent) objects, and (b) the related, "decentering of subjects;" not only is there no necessary linkage of sign or term and the object in question, but the (decentering) emphasis should be on the signifier rather than the signified. From this viewpoint, the author is rendered irrelevant to the interpretation of the text, and the text is seen to derive its meaningful essence from the reader/signifier. In a corrective mode, Giddens contends that the notion of a completely arbitrary sign becomes problematic when one examines the practical use of language in ongoing community life. He also posits that the structuralist/poststructuralist emphasis on the signifier (to the neglect of the signified) in the case of human "text" fails to attend to both human agency and the hermeneutic concern with communicative intent. Those who engage in the practice of decentering the subject in this manner effectively eschew concerns with effective communication. Since the signifiers emerge as the ultimate (and singular) authorities of interpretation, concerns with authentic human interchange are rendered inconsequential; there is no one "to talk back" and there is no basis on which to challenge the signifier.

28. The problem with postmodernism arises not from using relativist insight to illustrate or consider the diverse, situated, often contradictory, and fragile nature of the human condition, but (as will be indicated in greater length later) the problem is one of reducing human lived experience to linguistic or textual reality, of ignoring human accomplishment (including the development of language) and the human struggle for existence (and the products and practices that people develop thereof).

29. Despite a baseline claim that no forms of knowing are to be privileged above any others, postmodernist scholars have not been above criticizing other (nonpostmodernist) forms of knowing and have been quite vocal as well in maintaining the orthodoxy of their own interpretations of things. As two cases in point, readers are referred to the exchanges between (a)

Farberman (1991; 1992) and Clough (1992) and Fee (1992); and (*b*) Dawson
and Prus (1993a,b) and Fontana (1993) and Denzin (1993).

30. For a succinct, but highly informative critique of "the culture and personality writings" that have typified much anthropological ethnography,
see Lindesmith and Strauss (1950). As Lindesmith and Strauss indicate,
as well, several anthropologists writing in the 1930s and 1940s were deeply
concerned about the viability of the practices (and ensuing representations
of other life-worlds on the part) of many of their colleagues who had
ventured into other communities.

31. See Dawson (1995) for a much more fully developed discussion of these
points and an extended review of this literature. Snow and Morrill's (1993)
commentary is also pertinent here.

32. As well, since most ethnographic research conducted by symbolic interactionists has involved people from the same general culture, the interactionists have not had to struggle with more acute obstacles of access,
comprehension, and representation facing those embarking on studies of
more completely unfamiliar life-worlds. Also see Snow and Morrill (1993)
on this point.

33. Interestingly, two French sociologists, Briand and Chapoulie (1991), along
with some other colleagues, have begun to encourage the development
and recognition of participant-observation as a means of extending and
grounding the interpretivist potential of French (postmodernist) sociology.
Perhaps, in expressing both the contradictions and the practical limitations
of postmodernist thought with respect to the study of human lived experience, the present chapter (and chapter 8 following) may likewise
contribute to this overall objective.

34. Although one may attempt to synthesize almost anything, the basic
premises underlying symbolic interaction and ethnographic research on
the one hand and postmodernism on the other seem diametrically opposed
in some essential respects. Whereas *postmodernist thought* is based on a
presumption of relativistic skepticism and linguistic reductionism, fostering
a turn toward analytic subjective idealism, moralistic structuralism, and
self-enchanted expressionism, *symbolic interaction* is based on appreciations
of the human accomplishment of activity, the dynamics of intersubjectivity,
and the ethnographic task of achieving intimate familiarity with the life-
worlds of the other. *Ethnographic research* has assumed a great many
dimensions in anthropology and sociology, but it is premised on the
necessity of attending to the life-worlds of the other as a *privileged arena
of knowledge*.

35. Of these people, Norman Denzin has been by far the most influential spokesperson and gatekeeper. A very capable and highly prolific scholar, Denzin has attempted to synthesize symbolic interaction with a variety of alternative viewpoints over his career. These have ranged from mainstream positivist research (Denzin, 1970), to ethnomethodology (1969), to postmodernism (1986, 1990a,b, 1993), to cultural studies (1992). Given his congenial and charismatic interpersonal style, his own intellectual productivity, his gatekeeping functions, and his embeddedness in a variety of networks, Denzin has been able to pull a number of scholars with him in these ventures. Unfortunately, while Denzin seems committed to an overall interactionist venture, he also seems intent on "theorizing within the historical moment" (Denzin, 1989a:138–139) and as a result has tended to become caught up in a variety of popular (but epistemologically very mixed) trends in the field.

36. In addition to our own work (Dawson and Prus, 1993a,b, 1995), which is clearly skeptical of claims regarding the unique and valuable nature of the postmodernist enterprise for the social sciences, readers may be interested in the instructive criticisms of the postmodernist turn offered by Farberman (1991), Best (1995), Charmaz (1995), and Sanders (1995). Following some initial interest and curiosity about this seemingly new approach, there has been a significant disaffection with this brand of "scholarship" among many of those in the interactionist community.

37. Denzin's (1989a), *Interpretive Interactionism*, provides a much more extended statement on what appears to be his overall message, but this volume represents an attempt to synthesize the larger field of qualitative research and is less readily defined as uniquely postmodernist in thrust.

38. Space simply does not allow an elaboration of this material. See Dawson and Prus (1993a,b) and the Denzin (1993) and Fontana (1993) exchanges for fuller considerations of the practical limitations of "postmodernist ethnography."

39. There have been different styles of representing the other in ethnographic text, but the use of direct and extended quotations from participants has been in effect for several decades among those in the interactionist community. As well, it might be observed that two early Chicago classics (*The Jack-Roller* and *The Professional Thief* were very much "written" by the focal characters (Stanley and Chic Conwell, respectively, in response to the ongoing inquiries of Clifford Shaw and Edwin Sutherland). Nels Anderson's *The Hobo* was written by a graduate student who "gave voice" to his former life-world in the course of developing this study. However

mundane it may sound, a street urchin, a thief, and a hobo who shared aspects of their life-worlds with some academics in sociology played consequential roles not only in shaping notions of ethnographic research, but in fostering an interactionist viewpoint more generally.

40. "Deconstruction" generally refers to the practice of analysts providing or invoking (imposing) analytical frames (external to those used by the participants in the setting whose life-worlds are under consideration) to interpret the products, practices, and other aspects of the life-worlds of others. Most deconstructionism implies Marxist notions of hegemony or false-consciousness pertaining to allegedly oppressive circumstances, whereby analysts purport to inform readers of the underlying structures (class, gender, and race are commonly used in this manner) that "really" determine the social context in which people's behavior is formulated. In the process, those engaged in deconstructionism typically perpetuate the very myths of grand narratives and structural determinism that they purport to deny.

41. The objection, here, is not to the use of these artifacts within the context of ethnographic texts, but to tendencies to substitute these (and other attenuation devices) for fuller ethnographic text. As decontextualized records of human productions, their primary value seems destined to remain obscure and "artistic" rather than ethnographically informative and illustrative of a way of life. Also, see Wolf's (1992) *Thrice-Told Tale* in which she, as a postmodernist oriented ethnographer, retrospectively compares a story she wrote, her field notes, and a published essay. Wolf concluded that, from the viewpoint of comprehending the life-world of the other, that there is no viable substitute for the more thorough, conventional ethnographic version of one's experiences.

42. This discussion is necessarily cryptic and is pointed directly at those who propose to evaluate ethnographic endeavors from a (postmodernist) viewpoint. Readers interested in the broader matter of evaluating qualitative research are referred to a very thoughtful statement developed by Altheide and Johnson (1994). Although attempting to be attentive to matters of "reflexive ethnography," Altheide and Johnson are not prepared to slip into solipsistic relativism nor are they intent on denying what Lorne Dawson and I (Chapter 8) refer to as the "privilege of presence." Somewhat similar points are made by Marcus (1994).

43. For instance, given that everything cannot be adequately represented at once, the question arises: what should have precedence or denote central emphasis in postmodernist ethnography. Should emphasis be placed on

(a) a full accounting of the researcher's personal experiences and reflections; (b) a thorough representation of the actual others in the field; or (c) the development of poems, fictionalized accounts, and the like? And to whom is privilege to make these decisions accorded? Is privilege to be accorded to the ethnographers (authors), the editors and reviewers of journals and other academic outlets, the ethnographic others whose life-worlds are purportedly being examined, the consumers of these products, or those who purport to define the essence of postmodernist productions through their writings?

8

OBDURATE REALITY AND THE INTERSUBJECTIVE OTHER

The Problematics of Representation and the Privilege of Presence

(with Lorne Dawson)

Part of the allure of postmodernism for social scientists appears to revolve around its emphasis on a *textually-mediated reality*. In the process of stressing its centrality for the human condition, however, language has become so reified in postmodernist thought that one can easily lose sight of the people, the action, and the community in which language takes its shape, expression, and very essence. Part of the allure of positivism for social scientists appears to revolve around its emphasis on a *structurally-mediated reality*. In the process of stressing its centrality for the human condition, the forces (external and internal) which are thought to predispose people to act in particular manners have become so reified in positivist thought that one can easily lose sight of the ways in which human behavior is accomplished in practice, by living, acting, interacting minded beings within a community context; the ways in which the human condition takes its shape, expression, and very essence.

Refocusing attention on the necessity of researchers permeating the life-worlds of the (ethnographic) other and examining the ways in which those realities are constituted or accomplished in practice by people acting and inter-acting with others in a community context, this book argues that modes of knowing about people are most appropriately rooted in (*a*) the human struggle for existence and (*b*) the privilege of presence.

In contrast to the postmodernists, who tend to reduce human experience to textual reality, and the positivists, who tend to reduce human lived experience to structuralist reality, it is argued that human existence is predicated on people coming to terms with the day-to-day situations in which they find themselves.

What is required to address the intersubjectively-mediated reality in which and on which human group life is constituted, is a pragmatic appreciation of the human life-world as it is accomplished on a day-to-day, moment-to-moment basis. This active participation "in the world out there" necessitates an acknowledgement of the "obdurate reality" to which Blumer (1969) referred. To this end, a more detailed formulation of Blumer's notion of "obdurate reality" is provided. While in no way discounting the significance of language for human group life, this statement situates human discourse within the context of activity and ongoing community life. It reflects the realms of ambiguity, enterprise, resistance, and readjustment in which humans find themselves. Clearly, human encounters with the "obdurate reality" of which Blumer spoke are centrally mediated through language use, but language takes its shape in the course of human encounters with this same "obdurate reality." Likewise, rather than discounting the significance of objectification as a human tendency, this statement draws attention to the ways in which people go about objectifying their world as they attempt to come to terms with the human struggle for existence.

On the Nature of "Obdurate Reality"[1]

Assuming some interpretive license, we wish to suggest that Blumer's phrase "obdurate character of the empirical world" should be read as referring to four intertwined yet distinguishable features of social life, which methodologically constrain, and hence guide, social research in ways seemingly either not considered or not accepted by postmodernist orientations. The obdurateness of reality exists in the irreducibility of intersubjectivity for the human condition. This is rooted in a pragmatic appreciation of: (1) the most basic resistances to human action experienced daily in the material and the social environments of the human struggle for existence,[2] (2) the objectifying nature of being human, (3) the resultant phenomenon of "culturally motivated resistances" stemming from the ongoing and group nature of human life, and (4) the rudimentary and universal social processes undergirding the ongoing accomplishment of human group life. These four modes or realms of experienced intersubjectivity are interrelated, and each depends on the other for a fuller or more holistic appreciation of its significance.[3]

Blumer's first sense of obdurate reality involves a consideration of the *environment of human action* at the most practical level. In line with the pragmatist philosophic tradition from which it developed, symbolic interactionism frames all aspects of human life against the dialectic nature of people's encounters, as embodied entities, with the environs in which they find themselves. Blumer does not attempt to specify the ways in which people do or should make sense of themselves or their surroundings, nor does he deem it appropriate to use the latest developments in the physical sciences to stipulate the nature of the human environment and hence the constraints on human action. Blumer centrally accepts the pragmatist notion that objects take on meanings by virtue of the ways in which people act toward them. The meanings that people attribute to objects are products of ongoing group life and the ways in which people attempt to incorporate objects into their activities. Hence people may make sense of the world in highly diverse ways. Completing the dialectic, however, he is attentive also to the *resistances of the world that people encounter* when they act toward it in various manners—resistances that account for the tendencies of humans to revise the meanings they attribute to objects. In a strict sense, as we will explicate further, there is nothing "objective" or "definitive" about the resistances in question. But it is difficult to imagine the course of human affairs without their experienced "reality," both as human beings and social researchers. Consequently, Blumer is very much aware of human enterprise in an environment riddled with the problematics of accomplishment, an environment of action that cannot be controlled simply by language, discourse, and related human conceptual developments.

Blumer's second sense of "obdurate reality" involves *the objectification process* that human activity entails; it denotes the more enduring, but recastable, qualities that [objects] acquire by virtue of the ways in which these [things] are delineated, conceptualized, and incorporated into human activity. Like the pragmatists (e.g., William James, 1907; John Dewey, 1938; George Herbert Mead, 1934) and the social constructionists (e.g., Alfred Schutz, 1962, 1964; Peter Berger and Thomas Luckmann, 1966) more generally, Blumer never speaks of "a singular objective or absolute world out-there." He, like them, does recognize "objectified worlds." Indeed, all contend that some objectification is essential if human conduct is to be accomplished. The meaningful pursuit or accomplishment of any task or objective, however, depends on people acting toward the world *as if* something exists and can be approached in this or that manner. The world is or becomes a place of "obdurateness" when people act toward it. Objectivity exists, thus, not as an absolute or inherently meaningful condition to which humans react but as an accomplished aspect of human lived experience. In this sense, the world is a place of resistances, as explicated below.

The third aspect of Blumer's talk of the obdurate nature of social reality is what might be labeled *culturally motivated resistances*. As people develop ways of conceptualizing and acting toward the world, they begin organizing their lives around those particular themes and practices. These "life-worlds," "ways of life," "social worlds," and the like, are important since they entail the stocks of knowledge, frames of reference, and senses of direction that the people constituting this and that community take into account in developing their lines of action. These socially constructed realities, these objectifications, also denote sources of resistance to insiders and outsiders who may represent change in prevailing worldviews and practices. These realities are amenable to disruption and confusion, challenge and alteration. At the same time, however, insofar as people develop and acquire perspectives consistent with this or that social world, recognize and achieve identities in particular settings, perform and coordinate activities with others in meaningful fashions, develop and maintain viable relationships with others, and make commitments of a more enduring and comprehensive nature within certain realms of community life, these objectifications become resistant to challenge and alteration.

While life-worlds vary in the extent to which they are transitory in their existence, as well as in the extensiveness and centrality with which they epitomize particular communities, we must duly appreciate the concrete relevance of these objectifications for understanding human experiences in those settings. We should ask how particular aspects of community life-styles develop, how they achieve prominence to this or that extent, how features of group life are challenged and defended, or fall into disfavor and (possibly) become reestablished. In other words, we should examine the "objectification process" in terms of a subset of existent and resistant social processes (i.e., the emergence, entrenchment, disenchantment and displacement, and reintrenchment of this or that definition of reality). We need to understand how people actually deal with these definitions of reality in the course of ongoing human group life.

As researchers we must guard against abstracting these situated objectifications when conceptualizing the various processes of objectification. Though elicited and recorded as "texts," the objectifications that people develop and experience represent the "means of transacting business with [their] environment" (Blumer, 1969: 163). And the same substantive sets of worldviews and practices that people implement in socializing newcomers, effecting social control with respect to potential and recognized deviants, and conducting other aspects of their here and now situations, provide the essential foundations for participant responses to researcher inquiries or probes. It is from this base of experience that members of the community inform and (hopefully) talk back to ethnographers (and other researchers). This set of ongoing life-world practices (and the motivated resistances they engender) are the intersubjective worlds of others, and these worlds constitute the third sense in which it can be suggested that Blumer argues there is an obdurate character to the empirical world.

The culturally motivated resistances encountered in the course of research with humans (and even experienced by researchers themselves) constitute one partner, so to speak, in the dialogue from which "knowledge" emerges. The other partner is the meta-objectifications of the researcher, which Blumer envisions in terms of generic concepts, or better, *generic social processes*. These meta- or transsituational objectifications are the fourth mode or level of obdurateness encountered by the ethnographer. Past efforts in philosophy and social science have generated a set of generic processual features of human lived experience to which Blumer refers in outlining the very premises of symbolic interactionism (Blumer, 1969:2):

> *The first premise is that human beings act toward things on the basis of the meanings they have for them. . . . The second premise is that the meaning of such things is derived from, or arises out of, the social interaction that one has with one's fellows. The third premise is that these meanings are handled in, and modified through, an interpretative process used by the person in dealing with the things he encounters.*

We are creatures who live in worlds of "action," "interaction," and "interpretation," which means, in Blumerian terms too well known to be rehearsed here, that we develop "selves" and engage in "joint activity." These are some of the most rudimentary generic features of human life, the features that render us "social" in our being. They also indicate that human existence is one of endless "process." Accordingly, in developing the scientific study of human lived experience, Blumer wished to focus on the generic formulation of certain transcontextual processes, from the very development of language and self-conceptualization, to the processes of conflict, cooperation, influence, and so on. By extension, we would call attention to processes of the sort entailed in acquiring perspectives (acquiring and using language, learning and adopting the standpoint of the generalized other, developing meanings for the local world of objects); achieving identity (learning self and other definitions, taking the role of the other, developing a capacity for self reflectivity, managing impressions); doing activity (formulating lines of action, coordinating or fitting lines of action with others, influencing and resisting others' definitions of reality); and developing relationships (initiating, intensifying, severing, renewing associations with others). These generic social processes (see chapter 5), derived admittedly from the very process of ethnographic understanding at the heart of research itself, constitute the fourth experienced mode or level of obdurateness (i.e., of intersubjectivity) guiding the hermeneutics of ethnography.

THE PROBLEMATICS OF REPRESENTATION
AND THE "PRIVILEGE OF PRESENCE"[4]

An acknowledgement of the obdurate nature of social reality (i.e., social-material environmental resistances, the objectifying nature of being human, culturally motivated resistances, and generic social processes) sets the rudimentary parameters of "understanding" for the ethnographer. These parameters may be used by ethnographers, with varying degrees of skill, to warrant a claim to the privilege of presence, with varying degrees of plausibility. The ethnographer's way is rife with difficulties and pitfalls. Consequently, extended sensitivity to the relevant interpretative issues, within these parameters, is essential for achieving sufficient intersubjectivity. Contrary to the "postmodernist sensibility" (Denzin, 1993), however, the difficulties encountered by ethnographers do not justify being skeptical about the very possibility of intersubjectivity.

The complicated process whereby "an ethnography comes into being" involves at least four consequential and analytically distinguishable hermeneutic subprocesses or phases: access, conceptualization, presentation, and comprehension. Although we can only make brief reference to each of these aspects of the representational process, this schematization helps us to do two things: (1) indicate the points at which representation is indeed problematic in producing ethnographic research and hence open to skepticism, and (2) indicate the foundational role played, nevertheless, by the assumption and achievement of intersubjectivity in the method of ethnography.

The first problem of representation in any research inquiry is one of access: whether the researcher is able to examine her or his subject matter at length and in close detail or establish the intimate familiarity with the subject matter recommended by Blumer (1969) and others. While this, presumably, is an objective in all the sciences, it is particularly challenging in the social sciences since our subject matter involves reflective, interactive beings who, like the researcher, are capable of defining and acting toward any object from a plurality of viewpoints. Thus, access would seem to require that researchers open themselves to the viewpoints, practices, and experiences of the other in as full or comprehensive a manner as possible. This process, of opening oneself up to the other, constitutes a part of the first phase of the ethnographic task, which we will term the *hermeneutics of access*. It is an attempt to establish intersubjectivity with the other, an attempt to understand the sense-making activities of the other. It normally entails an ongoing adjustive, interactive process as researchers endeavor to share the "reality" of the other; and in this sense all good (i.e., responsible) observation in the social sciences is to some extent inevitably and importantly "participant" observation.

This initial effort to establish intersubjectivity is complicated by the fact that while participants may be open, sincere, and cooperative, they may also resist and deceive researchers by both concealing and selectively revealing information.[5] As well, participants may unintentionally forget, become confused, and otherwise inadvertently mislead researchers.

The point here is not to reiterate the many detailed discussions of the problems and procedures of gaining "access" to the subjects of ethnographic research. Rather we simply wish to remind the reader of the instrumental role of intersubjectivity, both as a methodological assumption and an experienced development (or perhaps creation) in the doing of ethnographic research from the start. As Giddens (1984:334–343) observed, at issue is the conclusion that a working assumption of "mutual knowledge" between sociological observers and lay members of society (any society) is the *sine qua non* of all social research.

Like those they study, researchers also work from preexisting intersubjective frames of reference and although they may explicitly attempt to put these preexisting notions in suspension in order to maximize openness in their queries and assessments, the material gathered is apt to be guided to some extent by certain aspects of their preconceptualizations. It is this tension between preconceptualization, exploration, examination, and reconceptualization that constitutes the second phase of the ethnographic task: *the hermeneutics of conceptualization*. While this aspect of the larger task is rather pragmatically fused with that of achieving intimate familiarity with one's subject matter, the matter of interpreting the situation of the other with respect to one's own background experiences and conceptual frames is analytically distinguishable. As a conceptually independent process it may both facilitate and interfere with the ethnographer's interpretive practices and hence the achievement of intersubjectivity with the subjects of study.

Beyond the tasks of achieving intimate familiarity with the other and conceptualizing this material within one's existing (and expanding) knowledge base, a third problem in representation is that of presenting the position of the other. Here, the researcher not only assumes the task of "speaking for the other," but also of communicating the position(s) of the other to third parties. This means that researchers are faced not only with the task of selecting and organizing materials that depict in central manners the lived experiences of the other, but also with selecting ways of conveying and contextualizing these to prospective readers so that they find these experiences (transcontextually) meaningful and comprehensible. Typically this is done in reference to the sense of the generalized other (Mead, 1934) of the researchers; their anticipation of how this ambiguous but somewhat informed, linguistically consonant set of others might experience the material being produced. The task of conveying participant experiences and anticipating reader interpretations becomes even more challenging given the researcher's practical constraints concerning both the form and length of the documents they assemble.

In addition, unless researchers are content to provide only supposedly descriptive accounts of the life-worlds of the other, they face the task of contraposing this information with other studies that bear some conceptual relevance to the present inquiry. This latter objective is essential if one is to move past idiographic accounts of the case(s) at hand to the conceptual dimensions on which "science" is founded (Blumer, 1931). Although these comparisons need not suppress the unique features of the situation(s) at hand and typically foster readers' appreciations of various facets of the setting under study, researchers are often faced with the task of balancing allocated space between materials that are more idiographic or more analytical in thrust. The process of making or assessing these decisions is rendered considerably more complicated if the inquiry in question is either explicitly or implicitly associated with other agendas (e.g., moral crusades, government policies). Researchers are differentially attentive to these aspects of representation, but they all struggle with this overall set of undertakings, which we will refer to as *the hermeneutics of presentation*. This phrase signifies the task of conveying the intersubjectivity of the other, through the fashioning of another realm or level of intersubjectivity between researchers and their hypothetical publics.

The fourth point at which representation becomes problematic, then, revolves around *the hermeneutics of comprehension* or the problem of readers achieving intersubjectivity with the (ethnographic) other through the interpretations of the text so presented. Thus, one may ask to what extent eventual readings of texts (books, papers, films, etc.) by third parties fashion an intersubjectivity in correspondence with the foci of the two previous achieved intersubjectivities: (a) the lived experiences of the other, as presented by the researcher and (b) the other objectives pursued by the researcher, as author, in developing the text. Comprehension implies an attentiveness on the part of readers to the intended meanings of these other parties.

In rounding out this discussion, it may be useful to make further reference to Mead's (1934) notion of the "generalized other" as this applies more generally to the hermeneutics of inquiry. Although ethnographers often work alone and face a great many challenges coming to terms with life-worlds of those they encounter at all points in the ethnographic process, it may be counterproductive (despite some postmodernists' encouragement along these lines) for ethnographers to dwell extensively on the more unique features of the researcher's consciousness. As an outreaching activity, ethnographic inquiry may afford perceptions of "self-growth" and edification on the one hand and provide a context for more personalized notions of curiosity and entertainment on the other. However, as with matters of pride, embarrassment, displeasing encounters, and the like, more generally, unless these "self-experiences" are allowed to interfere with the research process by the researcher or are deemed intolerable by the ethnographic other, they may be relatively incidental to the broader ethnographic enterprise. Clearly, personal experiences in the field may run the range from being highly enjoyable to downright disconcerting, even to the extremes of ethnographers "going native" or "becoming abruptly disinvolved from the field." Still, the point remains. The central task of ethnographers in the field is not to provide extended "tourist-like," "voyeuristic," or more dramatic accounts of their personal affections and affrontations, but to represent or embody the generalized other of the (scholarly) home community of which the ethnographers are members. While in the field, the ethnographer has an obligation to think and act with respect to the viewpoint of the generalized other. Information is gathered, observations are made, and questions are asked, mindful of the generalized other. It is incumbent on the ethnographer to adopt a scientific viewpoint, not as a distant party in the situation, but as a conscientious, thorough, curious, information-seeking representative of the scholarly community. Instead of focusing attention on their more peculiar field experiences, ethnographers are better advised to try to assess the nature of these experiences within the context of the ethnographic other and to reframe these experiences in ways that would enable members of the broader home community to better appreciate what they have learned about the ethnographic other. Similarly, in making contact with the ethnographic other, researchers face the task of sorting out *both* the unique aspects of the actual people encountered and the more general features of the life-world being considered. The challenge, in part, for ethnographers is to be able to move past their more personal fascinations with, repulsions of, and even boredom with, particular aspects of the life-world of the other and instead concentrate on what Gadamer (1976) terms "the fusing of horizons." This requires that researchers move past the more idiosyncratic features of the situation and attempt to achieve a more typical member understanding of the worldview(s) of the ethnographic other and, then, recontextualize what were seemingly more unique aspects of the life-worlds of the other. Likewise, in developing a statement of the life-world of the other, the ethnographer is writing for the generalized other. The task is one of enhancing the abilities of those in one's home community to "fuse horizons" with those in the ethnographic setting; to provide one set of the generalized other with a viable appreciation of the life-worlds of the other (as experienced at the level of the generalized other through particular representatives of that community). This task, as well, is fostered, by the ethnographer's explicit willingness both (a) to serve as a representative of the generalized other in the field and (b) to subject oneself to the ethnographic other in the field so that the end product might more openly and honestly enable a greater comprehension of the life-world of that generalized (ethnographic) other.

There are multiple points of slippage in the representation process: some information will be lost and some misunderstandings are likely in all stages of the process (access, conceptualization, presentation, and comprehension), no matter how those involved attempt to be exceedingly thorough, careful, and sincere. Likewise, we know that researchers are not uniformly attentive or skilled in accessing information, nor are they uniformly able to write clearly or present their findings in manners that maximize comprehension for readers in general. Given the diverse backgrounds and interests of those who may eventually examine the texts that researchers produce, some very different interpretations will emerge as well. However, the potential for slippage in these regards is endemic to all communication and it has been the subject of continual pragmatic and theoretical discussion among sociological ethnographers for decades.[6]

As indicated, the activity of ethnographers is necessarily grounded at all times in the tensions of the dialogue of very specific objectifications as well as in the general human experience of objectification. The constraints placed on ethnographic interpretation by this state of affairs are much more "obdurate" than suggested by the postmodernist stress on the linguistical and textual character of social life. The resistance of the lived objectifications encountered by the ethnographer imparts a crucial measure of direction to the conceptualizing practices of ethnographic researchers. In fact, it is an essential impetus to creativity at each of the hermeneutical phases of the ethnographic task. It also provides the substance of the mutuality of experience and hence knowledge that facilitates and guides the comparative assessment and integration of ethnographers' interpretations.

In the broadest sense, the task of the social researcher, especially the ethnographer, is one of delineating the notions of "objectivity" (stemming from the processes of objectification) with which people approach the world of every-day experience (and other researchers approach their subject matters [in achieving "understanding" and in formulating "theory"]). Nevertheless, like other people pursuing other tasks, ethnographers also act *as if* there were something out there to be studied, probed, and analyzed. They make the assumption that there are things to be learned, discovered, understood, tested and assessed about the other. In the process, ethnographers privilege participants (on the basis of their own experience of objectified social life) in the worlds under study with the capacity to share their experiences with the researcher. The world of the other as told by the other thus becomes the "objectified" or paramount reality for the purposes of inquiry. Not only is this life-world seen as a privileged source of information, it is also deemed to be the fundamental testing ground for inferences (and theory) the researcher or other scholars have developed.

At the same time, the objective of the researcher is not to "go native" or become so immersed in that life-world that one loses sight of its "objectified" character. Thus, a second requirement of the ethnographic endeavor is to locate the experiences of the other with respect to some emerging set of concepts about how group life is accomplished—in essence to learn about the complicated thoughts and actions of different patterns of objectification and about objectification itself. Thus, while pursuing intimate familiarity with the life-worlds of the other, one also requires some way of stepping back from each inquiry and developing some more generic appreciations of the phenomenon at hand. One must, in other words, engage in some process of meta-objectification. This is a constituent component of the life-world of ethnography and scholarship in general.[7]

In the quest for attaining a more viable appreciation of ongoing community life, there is still no substitute for ethnographic inquiry. There is no substitute for "being there" (no matter how problematic the expression of being there may be), if we are to grasp the nature of human lived experience. There is no substitute for "attending to actual others," for examining the ambiguity, enterprise, resistance, and readjustments entailed in people's struggles for existence. Full cognizance of the hermeneutics of ethnographic inquiry should not foster increased interpretive license. Rather it should lead to a heightened appreciation of the obdurate realities of human social existence; the "realities" that enable intersubjectivity and the possibility of representation.

Between Scylla and Charybdis[8]

Like the legendary Greek mariners who (in attempting to negotiate a course on the narrow straits of Messina between an extremely hazardous rock formation and a highly treacherous whirlpool) had to maintain a mindful presence of their own objectives and the perils simultaneously facing them on multiple fronts, those interested in developing a social science that is genuinely attentive to the lived experiences of people are faced with the task of achieving the essential features of a pragmatic presence through the ethnographic other, while simultaneously negotiating positions of epistemological integrity with respect to both structuralist social science and postmodernist tendencies. Only in this way, by attending in a highly concerted fashion to the practical accomplishment of action, may we, as a community of scholars, maneuver between positivist proclivities and postmodernist propensities on route to a more complete understanding of the human condition.

NOTES

1. This discussion has been extensively abstracted from Dawson and Prus (1995).

2. Weigert (1991) makes a very interesting case for the necessity of interactionists attending more fully to the ways in which people come to terms with the world of [objects] out there or "the environmental other." This attentiveness to the "world out there" is also evident in Arluke's (1988) and Sander's (1990, 1993, 1994) considerations of the ways in which people develop lines of action toward animals as well as Charmaz's (1991) portrayal of people's attempts to come to terms with disruptive changes in their own bodies.

3. Brief discussion of each mode demonstrates that we do not need to posit a clearly knowable, objective reality "out-there" to make sociological ethnography work. Much more minimally, we just need to recognize that access to and interpretation of human social relations is not subject to the kind of infinite variability implied by the subjective idealism operatively present in most postmodernist critiques of sociology. Rather, our interpretations are methodologically constrained by the experienced resistance of intersubjectivity—as that is encountered and achieved.

4. This discussion of the "privilege of presence" is largely adapted from Prus and Dawson (1993).

5. From the perspective of those being studied, it may be said that the problematics of the hermeneutics of access is experienced in the form of a "hermeneutics of disclosure."

6. It might be acknowledged that the problem of representation (i.e., the hermeneutics of inquiry) is much more acute in anthropological than in interactionist ethnography. Not only do matters of access and language typically pose much more pressing problems for researchers in foreign settings, but the anthropological tradition has been characterized by a great many more conceptual cross-currents (e.g., functionalism, Darwinism, Freudianism, imperialism, Marxism) than has been true of interactionist ethnography. As well, early anthropologists exhibited much less concern about achieving intimate familiarity with their subject matters than was true for those early ethnographers working in the Chicago interactionist tradition. Rather ironically, while anthropological ethnography has been particularly vulnerable to postmodernist criticism because of these practices and eclectic orientations, those encouraging an adoption of postmodernist sensibilities among interactionists appear to be encouraging the same sort of conceptual confusions that have plagued the anthropological literature.

7. Interestingly, ethnographic research is made possible because it is constrained, in a constructive way, by the intersubjective "realities" of both culturally motivated resistances and scientifically motivated generic social processes. The ethnographer must act in the life-worlds of both and this "fact" gives assessable form to one's work.

8. Scylla, *a huge dangerous rock on the coast of Italy, supposed to be the abode of the mythical monster, Scylla, which seized and wrecked passing vessels. Just across the narrow Straits of Messina, near Sicily, was a dangerous whirlpool, thought to be the home of another monster, Charybdis; for a vessel to avoid one meant the great risk of falling into the clutches of the other. (Webster's New Twentieth Century Dictionary, 1964:1633)*

References

Abel, Theodore. 1948. "The Operation Called '*Verstehen.*'" *American Journal of Sociology* 54:11–18.

Adler, Patricia. 1985. *Wheeling and Dealing*. New York: Columbia University Press.

Adler, Patricia, and Peter Adler. 1987. *Membership Roles in Field Research*. Newbury Park, Calif.: Sage.

———. 1991. *Backboards and Blackboards: College Athletes and Role Engulfment*. New York: Columbia University Press.

Agger, Ben. 1990. *The Decline of Discourse: Reading, Writing and Resistance in Postmodern Capitalism*. New York: Falmer Press.

———. 1992. *The Discourse of Domination: From the Frankfurt School to Postmodernism*. Evanston, Illinois: Northwestern University Press.

Albas, Daniel C., and Cheryl Mills Albas. 1984. *Student Life and Exams*. Dubuque, Iowa: Kendall/Hunt.

Alexander, Jeffrey C. 1982. *Positivism, Presuppositions, and Current Controversies*. Berkeley, Calif.: University of California Press.

———. 1983. *The Classical Attempt at Theoretical Synthesis: Max Weber*. Berkeley, Calif.: University of California Press.

Altheide, David L., and John M. Johnson. 1994. "Criteria for Assessing Interpretive Validity in Qualitative Research." Pp. 485–99 in Norman K. Denzin and Yvonna S. Lincoln (eds.) *Handbook of Qualitative Research*. Thousand Oaks, Calif.: Sage.

Anderson, Nels. 1923. *The Hobo* (1961). Chicago: University of Chicago Press.

———. 1983. "A Stranger at the Gate: Reflections on the Chicago School of Sociology." *Urban Life* 11:396–406.

Anderson, Paul. 1983. "Marketing, Scientific Progress, and Scientific Method." *Journal of Marketing* 47(4):18–31.

———. 1986. "On Method in Consumer Research: A Critical Relativist Position." *Journal of Consumer Research* 13:155–73.

Arluke, Arnold. 1988. "Sacrificial Symbolism in Animal Experimentation: Object or Pet." *Anthrozoos* 4:88–112.

Athens, Lonnie. 1980. *Violent Criminal Acts and Actors: A Symbolic Interactionist Study*. Boston: Oxford University Press.

Baker, Paul J. 1973. "The Life Histories of W. I. Thomas and Robert E. Park." *American Journal of Sociology* 79:243–60.

Baldwin, James Mark. 1906. *Social and Ethical Interpretations in Mental Development: A Study in Social Psychology* (1897). Fourth Edition. New York: Macmillan.

Barnes, Barry. 1974. *Scientific Knowledge and Social Theory*. London: Routledge and Kegan Paul.

Barnes, Barry, and David Edge. 1982. *Science in Context: Readings in the Sociology of Science*. Cambridge: MIT Press.

Bartell, Gilbert. 1971. *Group Sex*. New York: Signet.

Baudrillard, Jean. 1981. *For a Critique of the Political Economy of the Sign*. St. Louis: Telos Press.

———. 1983a. *Simulations*. New York: Semiotext(e).

———. 1983b. *In the Shadow of the Silent Majorities*. New York: Semiotext(e).

———. 1988a. *Jean Baudrillard: Selected Writings*. Edited and Introduction by Mark Poster. Stanford, Calif.: Stanford University Press.

———. 1988b. *America*. (Trans. Chris Turner) London: Verso.

Becker, Howard S. 1963. *Outsiders*. New York: Free Press.

———. 1970. *Sociological Work: Method and Substance*. Chicago: Aldine.

Becker, Howard, Everett Hughes, and Blanche Geer. 1968. *Making the Grade: The Academic Side of Student Life*. New York: Wiley.

Becker, Howard, Everett Hughes, Blanche Geer, and Anselm Strauss. 1961. *The Boys in White*. Chicago: University of Chicago Press.

Becker, Howard S., Blanche Geer, David Reisman, and Robert Weiss. 1968. *Institutions and the Person*. Chicago: Aldine.

Bendix, Rhinehard. 1960. *Max Weber: An Intellectual Portrait*. New York: Doubleday-Anchor.

Bennett, John. 1948. "The Study of Cultures: A Survey of Technique and Method in Field Work." *American Sociological Review* 13:672–89.

Berger, Peter and Thomas Luckmann. 1966. *The Social Construction of Reality*. New York: Anchor.

Bernstein, Richard J. 1992. *The New Constellation: The Ethical Political Horizons of Modernity*. Cambridge: MIT Press.

Best, Joel. 1989. *Images of Issues: Typifying Contemporary Social Problems*. New York: Aldine de Gruyter.

————. 1990. *Threatened Children: Rhetoric and Concerns*. Chicago: University of Chicago Press.

————. 1995. "Lost in the Ozone Again: The Postmodernist Fad and Interactionist Foibles." Pp. 125–130 in Norman K. Denzin (ed.) *Studies in Symbolic Interaction* 17. Greenwich, Conn.: JAI Press.

Bieder, Robert E. 1986. *Science Encounters the Indian, 1820–1880*. Norman, Okla.: University of Oklahoma Press.

Bigus, O. E., S. C. Hadden, and B. G. Glaser. 1982. "Basic Social Processes." Pp. 251–72 in R. B. Smith and P. K. Manning (eds.) *Qualitative Methods*. Vol. 2, *Handbook of Social Science Methods*. Cambridge: Ballinger.

Blalock, Hubert. 1984. *Dilemmas in the Social Sciences*. Beverly Hills: Sage.

Blumer, Herbert. 1928. *Method in Social Psychology*. Doctoral Dissertation. University of Chicago.

————. 1931. "Science Without Concepts." *American Journal of Sociology* 36:515–33.

————. 1933. *Movies and Conduct*. New York: Macmillan (Reprinted 1970. New York: Arno Press).

————. 1937a. "Social Disorganization and Personal Disorganization." *American Journal of Sociology* 42:871–77.

————. 1937b. "Social Psychology." Pp. 144–98 in Emerson P. Schmidt (editor), *Man and Society*. New York: Prentice-Hall.

————. 1939. *Critiques of Research in the Social Sciences: An Appraisal of Thomas and Znaniecki's "The Polish Peasant in America."* New York: Social Science Research Council, Bulletin 44.

————. 1940. "The Problem of the Concept in Social Psychology." *American Journal of Sociology* 45:707–19.

————. 1947. "Sociological Theory in Industrial Relations." *American Sociological Review* 12:271–78.

————. 1948. "Public Opinion and Public Opinion Polling." *American Sociological Review* 13:542–54.

————. 1953. "Psychological Import of the Human Group." Pp. 185–202 in Muzafer Sherif and M. O. Wilson (eds.), *Group Relations at the Crossroads*. New York: Harper and Row.

————. 1954. "What's Wrong with Social Theory?" *American Sociological Review* 19:3–10.

————. 1955. "Attitudes and the Social Act." *Social Problems* 3:59–65.

————. 1956. "Sociological Analysis and the 'Variable' " *American Sociological Review* 21:683–90.

———. 1958. *The Rationale of Labor-Management Relations*. Rio Piedras, Puerto Rico: University of Puerto Rico.

———. 1960. "Early Industrialization and the Laboring Class." *Sociological Quarterly* 1:5–14.

———. 1962. "Society as Symbolic Interaction." Pp. 169–92 in Arnold Rose (editor), *Human Behavior and Social Process*. Boston: Houghton-Mifflin.

———. 1964. "Industrialization and the Traditional Order." *Sociology and Social Research* 48:129–38.

———. 1966. "Sociological Implications of the Thought of George Herbert Mead." *American Journal of Sociology* 71:535–48.

———. 1969. *Symbolic Interactionism*. Berkeley, Calif.: University of California Press (1986).

———. 1971. "Social Problems as Collective Behavior." *Social Problems* 18:298–306.

———. 1972. "Action vs. Interaction: Relations in Public: Microstudies of the Public Order by Erving Goffman." *Society* 9 (6):50–53.

———. 1980. "Mead and Blumer: The Convergent Methodological Perspectives of Social Behaviorism and Symbolic Interactionism." *American Sociological Review* 45:409–19.

———. 1990. *Industrialization as an Agent of Social Change* (Edited by David R. Maines and Thomas J. Morrione). New York: Aldine de Gruyter.

Blumer, Herbert, and Troy Duster. 1980. "Theories of Race and Social Action." Pp. 211–38 in *Sociological Theories: Race and Colonialism*. Paris: United Nations Educational, Scientific and Cultural Organization.

Blumer, Herbert, and Philip Hauser. 1933. *Movies, Delinquency and Crime*. New York: Macmillan (Reprinted 1970. New York: Arno Press).

Bogdan, Robert, and Steven J. Taylor. 1975. *Introduction to Qualitative Research Methods: A Phenomenological Approach to the Social Sciences*. New York: Wiley Interscience.

Borgmann, Albert. 1992. *Crossing the Postmodern Divide*. Chicago: University of Chicago Press.

Bosanquet, Helen. 1898. *The Standard of Life and Other Studies*. London: Macmillan.

Bowden, Henry Warner. 1981. *American Indians and Christian Missions: Studies in Cultural Conflict*. Chicago: University of Chicago Press.

Brannigan, Augustine. 1981. *The Social Basis of Scientific Discoveries*. New York: Cambridge University Press.

Briand, Jean-Pierre, and Jean Michel Chapoulie. 1991. "The Uses of Observation in French Sociology." *Symbolic Interaction* 14:449–69.

Brisset, Dennis, and Robert P. Snow. 1993. "Boredom: Where the Future Isn't." *Symbolic Interaction* 16:237–56.

Bryant, Christopher G. A. 1985. *Positivism in Social Theory and Research*. London: Macmillan.

Buban, Steven. 1986. "Studying Social Processes: The Chicago and Iowa Schools Revisited." Pp. 25–38 in C. J. Couch, S. L. Saxton, and M. A. Katovich (eds.). *Studies In Symbolic Interactionism: The Iowa School*. Greenwich, Conn.: JAI Press.

Bulmer, Martin. 1984. *The Chicago School of Sociology: Institutionalization, Diversity, and the Rise of Sociological Research*. Chicago: University of Chicago Press.

Callinicos, Alex. 1989. *Against Postmodernism: A Marxist Critique*. Cambridge, UK: Polity Press.

Campbell, Donald T. 1986. "Science's Social System of Validity Enhancing Collective Belief Change and the Problems of the Social Sciences." In Donald W. Fiske and Ricard A. Shweder (eds.) *Metatheory in Social Sciences*, Pp. 108–35. Chicago: University of Chicago Press.

Carlson, Rae. 1984. "What's Social About Social Psychology? Where's the Person in Personality Research?" *Journal of Personality and Social Psychology* 47:1304–9.

Carnap, Rudoloph. 1938. "Logical Foundations of the Unity of Science." Pp. 42–62 in O. Neurath et al. (eds.) *Foundations of the Unity of Science*. Vol. 1. Chicago: University of Chicago Press.

Cavan, Ruth Shonle. 1928. *Suicide*. Chicago: University of Chicago Press (New York: Russell and Russell, 1965).

———. 1983. "The Chicago School of Sociology, 1918–1933." *Urban Life* 11:407–20.

Chapin, F. Stuart. 1920. *Field Work and Social Science*. New York: Century.

Charmaz, Kathy. 1991. *Good Days and Bad Days: The Self In Chronic Illness*. New Brunswick, N.J.: Rutgers University Press.

———. 1995. "Between Positivism and Postmodernism: Implications for Methods." Pp. 43–72 in Norman K. Denzin (ed.) *Studies in Symbolic Interaction* 17. Greenwich, Conn.: JAI Press.

Charon, Joel. 1979. *Symbolic Interactionism*. Englewood Cliffs, N.J.: Prentice-Hall.

Christakes, George. 1978. *Albion W. Small*. Boston: Twayne.

Clarke, Adele, and Elihu Gerson. 1990. "Symbolic Interactionism in Social Studies of Science." Pp. 179–214 in Howard S. Becker and Michal M.

McCall (eds.) *Symbolic Interaction and Cultural Studies*. Chicago: University of Chicago.

Clarke, Adele, and Joan H. Fujimura. 1992. *The Right Tools for the Job: At Work in Twentieth Century Life Sciences*. Princeton, N.J.: Princeton University Press.

Clifford, James. 1983. "On Ethnographic Authority." *Representations* 1:118–46.

Clifford, James, and George E. Marcus (eds.) 1986. *Writing Culture: The Poetics and Politics of Ethnography*. Berkeley: University of California Press.

Clough, Patricia. 1991. *The End(s) of Ethnography*. Newbury Park, Calif.: Sage.

———. 1992. "A Response to Farberman's Distinguished Lecture: A Close Encounter with Postmodernism." *Symbolic Interaction* 15(3):359–66.

Cole, Jonathan, and Stephen Cole. 1973. *Social Stratification in Science*. Chicago: University of Chicago Press.

Cole, Stephen. 1992. *Making Science: Between Nature and Society*. Cambridge: Harvard University Press.

Collins, H. M., and T. J. Pinch. 1982. *Frames of Meaning: The Social Construction of an Extraordinary Science*. London: Routledge and Kegan Paul.

———. 1993. *The Golem: What Everyone Should Know about Science*. New York: Cambridge University Press.

Collins, Randall. 1981. "On the Microfoundations of Macrosociology." *American Journal of Sociology* 86(5):984–1014.

———. 1989. "Sociology: Proscience or Antiscience?" *American Sociological Review* 54:124–39.

Comte, Auguste. 1853. *The Positive Philosophy of Auguste Comte* (from Cours de Philosophie Positive, 1830–1842; translated by Harriet Martineau). London: John Chapman.

Cooley, Charles Horton. 1909. *Social Organization: A Study of the Larger Mind*. New York: Shocken.

———. 1922. *Human Nature and the Social Order* (1902). New York: Shocken.

———. 1926. "The Roots of Social Knowledge." *American Journal of Sociology* 32:59–79.

———. 1928. "Case Study of Small Institutions as a Method of Research." *American Sociological Review* 22:123–32.

Coser, Lewis. 1970. *Masters of Sociological Thought* (Second edition). New York: Harcourt, Brace.

Couch, Carl. 1968. "Collective Behavior: An Examination of Some Stereotypes." *Social Problems* 15:310–22.

———. 1975. "Obdurate Features of Group Life." Pp. 237–54 in C. J. Couch and R. Hintz (eds.) *Constructing Social Life: Readings in Behavioral Sociology from the Iowa School*. Champaign, Ill.: Stipes.

————. 1984. "Symbolic Interaction and Generic Sociological Principles." *Symbolic Interaction* 7:1–14.

Couch, Carl J., and Robert A. Hintz. 1975. *Constructing Social Life: Readings in Behavioral Sociology from the Iowa School.* Champaign, Ill.: Stipes.

Couch, Carl J., Michael A. Katovich, and Steven Buban. 1994. "Beyond Blumer and Kuhn: Researching and Studying Across-Time Data Through the Use of Point-in-Space Laboratory Procedures." Pp. 121–38 in Nancy J. Herman and Larry T. Reynolds (editors), *Symbolic Interaction: An Introduction to Social Psychology.* Dix Hills, N.Y.: General Hall.

Couch, Carl J., Stanley L. Saxton, and Michael A. Katovich. 1986a. *Studies in Symbolic Interaction: The Iowa School.* Part A. Greenwich, Conn.: JAI Press.

————. 1986b. *Studies in Symbolic Interaction: The Iowa School.* Part B. Greenwich, Conn.: JAI Press.

Cressey, Paul G. 1932. *The Taxi-Dance Hall.* Chicago: University of Chicago Press.

————. 1983. "A Comparison of the Roles of 'Sociological Stranger' and the 'Anonymous Stranger in Field Research." (Circa 1927) *Urban Life* 12:102–120.

Cunningham, Kamy. 1993. "Barbie Doll Culture and the American Waistland." *Symbolic Interaction* 16:79–83.

Cushing, Frank. 1979. *Zuni: Selected Writings of Frank Hamilton Cushing* (J. Brown, ed.). Lincoln: University of Nebraska Press.

Davis, Fred. 1961. "Deviance Disavowal: The Management of Strained Interaction by the Visibly Physically Handicapped." *Social Problems* 9:120–32.

————. 1963. *Passage Through Crises: Polio Victims and Their Families.* Indianapolis: Bobbs-Merrill.

Dawe, Alan. 1970. "The Two Sociologies." *British Journal of Sociology* 21:207–18.

Dawson, Lorne. 1985. " 'Free-Will Talk' and Sociology." *Sociological Inquiry* 55:348–62.

————. 1988. *Reason, Freedom and Religion: Closing the Gap Between the Humanistic and Scientific Study of Religion.* New York: Peter Lang.

————. 1995. "Postmodern Ethnography and the Sociology of Religion." In M. Lynn and D. Moberg (eds.) *Research in the Social Scientific Study of Religion*, vol. 7. Greenwich, Ct.: JAI Press (in press).

Dawson, Lorne, and Robert A. Campbell. 1994. "Generic Social Processes and Ethnographic Studies in Science." Paper presented at Symbolic Interaction and Ethnographic Research Conference, University of Waterloo, Waterloo, Ontario, May, 1994.

Dawson, Lorne, and Robert Prus. 1993a. "Interactionist Ethnography and Postmodernist Discourse: Affinities and Disjunctures in Approaching Human Lived Experiences." Pp. 147–77 in Norman K. Denzin (ed.) *Studies in Symbolic Interaction* 15. Greenwich, Conn.: JAI Press.

———. 1993b. "Human Enterprise, Intersubjectivity, and the Ethnographic Other: A Reply to Denzin and Fontana." Pp. 193–200 in Norman K. Denzin (ed.) *Studies in Symbolic Interaction* 15. Greenwich, Conn.: JAI Press.

———. 1995. "Postmodernism and Linguistic Reality Versus Symbolic Interactionism and Obdurate Reality." Pp. 105–124 in Norman K. Denzin (ed.) *Studies in Symbolic Interaction* 17. Greenwich, Conn.: JAI Press.

Denzin, Norman K. 1969. "Symbolic Interactionism and Ethnomethodology: A Proposed Synthesis." *American Sociological Review* 34:922–34.

———. 1970. *The Research Act: A Theoretical Introduction to Research Methods.* Chicago: Aldine.

———. 1984. *On Understanding Emotion.* San Francisco: Jossey-Bass.

———. 1985. "Emotion as Lived Experience." *Symbolic Interaction* 8:223–40.

———. 1986. "Postmodern Social Theory." *Sociological Theory* 4:194–204.

———. 1988. "Blue Velvet: Postmodern Contradictions." *Theory, Culture and Society* 5:461–73.

———. 1989a. *Interpretive Interactionism.* Newbury Park, Calif.: Sage.

———. 1989b. *Interpretive Biography.* Newbury Park, Calif.: Sage.

———. 1990a. "Researching Alcoholics and Alcoholism in American Society." Pp. 81–101 in N.K. Denzin (ed.) *Studies in Symbolic Interaction* 11. Greenwich, Conn.: JAI Press.

———. 1990b. "The Sociological Imagination Revisited." *The Sociological Quarterly* 31:1–22.

———. 1992. *Symbolic Interactionism and Cultural Studies: The Politics of Interpretation.* Cambridge, Mass.: Blackwell.

———. 1993. "The Postmodern Sensibility." Pp. 179–88 in Norman K. Denzin (ed.) *Studies in Symbolic Interaction* 15. Greenwich, Conn.: JAI Press.

———. 1994. "The Art and Politics of Interpretation." Pp. 500–15 in Norman K. Denzin and Yvonna S. Lincoln (eds.) *Handbook of Qualitative Research.* Thousand Oaks, Calif.: Sage.

Denzin, Norman K. and Yvonna S. Lincoln. 1994. *Handbook of Qualitative Research.* Thousand Oaks, Calif.: Sage.

Derrida, Jacques. 1976. *Of Grammatology.* Translated by G. Spivak. Baltimore: John Hopkins University Press.

———. 1978. *Writing and Difference.* Translated by A. Bass. London: Routledge and Kegan Paul.

Dewey, John. 1931. "George Herbert Mead." *Journal of Philosophy* 28:309–14.

————. *The Logic of Inquiry*. New York: Henry Holt.

Dietz, Mary Lorenz. 1983. *Killing for Profit: The Social Organization of Felony Homicide*. Chicago: Nelson-Hall.

Dietz, Mary Lorenz, Robert Prus, and William Shaffir. 1994. *Doing Everyday Life: Ethnography as Human Lived Experience*. Toronto, Ontario: Copp Clark Longman.

Ditton, James. 1977. *Part-Time Crime: An Ethnography of Fiddling and Pilferage*. London: Macmillan.

————. 1980. *The View from Goffman*. London: Macmillan.

Dix, Dorothy. 1939. *How to Win and Hold a Husband*. New York: Doubleday (Reprint 1974, New York: Arno).

Donovan, Frances. 1920. *The Woman Who Waits*. Boston: Gorham (Reprint 1974, New York: Arno).

————. 1929. *The Saleslady*. Chicago: University of Chicago Press.

————. 1939. *The Schoolma'am*. New York: Stokes (Reprint 1974, New York: Arno).

Dubin, Steven C. 1983. "The Moral Continuum of Deviancy Research." *Urban Life* 12:75–94.

Duncan, Otis. 1984. *Notes on Social Measurement*. New York: Russell Sage.

Durkheim, Emile. 1895. *The Rules of the Sociological Method*. Eighth edition. Trans. S. A. Solvay and John Mueller, and edited by E. G. Catlin, 1938; 1958. New York: Free Press.

————. 1897. *Suicide*. J. A. Spaulding and G. Simpson, trans. 1951. New York: Free Press.

————. 1983. *Pragmatism and Sociology* (1955) J. C. Whitehouse and John B. Allcock, trans. New York: Cambridge University Press.

Ebaugh, Helen Rose Fuchs. 1988. *Becoming an Ex*. Chicago: University of Chicago Press.

Ebihara, May. 1985. "American Ethnology in the 1930's: Contexts and Currents." Pp. 101–21 in June Helm (ed.) *Social Contexts of American Ethnography 1840–1984*. Washington, D.C.: American Ethnology Society.

Edgerton, Robert. 1967. *The Cloak of Competence: Stigma in the Lives of the Mentally Retarded*. Berkeley: University of California Press.

Edgerton, Robert and L. L. Langness. 1974. *Methods and Styles in the Study of Culture*. San Francisco: Chandler and Sharp.

Ellen, R. F. 1984. *Ethnographic Research*. London: Academic Press.

Ellis, Carolyn. 1991. "Sociological Introspection and Emotional Experience." *Symbolic Interaction*: 14:23–50.

Emerson, Joan. 1970. "Behavior in Private Places: Sustaining Definitions of Reality in Gynaecological Examinations." Pp. 74–97 in Hans Peter Dreitzel (ed.) *Recent Sociology no. 2.* New York: Macmillan.

Emerson, Robert M. 1969. *Judging Delinquents.* Chicago: Aldine.

Ermarth, Michael. 1978. *Wilhelm Dilthey: The Critique of Historical Reason.* Chicago: University of Chicago Press.

Evans, Donald. 1987. "Institutionally Developed Identities: An Ethnographic Account of Reality Construction in a Residential School for the Deaf." Pp. 161–84 in *Sociological Studies of Child Development.* Greenwich, Conn.: JAI Press.

———. 1988. "Strange Bedfellows: Deafness, Language and the Sociology of Knowledge." *Symbolic Interaction* 11:235–55.

———. 1994. "Socialization into Deafness." Pp. 129–42 in Mary Lorenz Dietz, Robert Prus, and William Shaffir (eds.) *Doing Everyday Life: Ethnography as Human Lived Experience.* Toronto: Copp Clark Longman.

Evans, Donald, and W. W. Falk. 1986. *Learning to be Deaf.* Berlin: De Gruyter.

Evans-Pritchard, E. E. 1951. *Social Anthropology.* London: Cohen and West.

Farberman, Harvey. 1991. "Symbolic Interaction and Postmodernism: Close Encounters of a Dubious Kind." *Symbolic Interaction* 14:471–88.

———. 1992. "The Grounds of Critique: A Choice among Metaphysics, Power, and Communicative Action: A Reply to Fee and Clough." *Symbolic Interaction* 15:375–79.

Faris, Ellsworth. 1936. "Review of Mind, Self and Society." *American Journal of Sociology* 41:809–13.

———. 1937a. *The Nature of Human Nature.* New York: McGraw-Hill.

———. 1937b. "The Social Psychology of George Mead." *American Journal of Sociology* 43:391–403.

Faris, Robert E. L. 1967. *Chicago Sociology 1920–1932.* Chicago: University of Chicago Press.

Fee, Dwight. 1992. "Symbolic Interaction and Postmodernist Possibilities: A Comment on Harvey Farberman's Distinguished Lecture." *Symbolic Interaction* 15:367–74.

Feigl, Herbert. 1953. "The Scientific Outlook: Naturalism and Humanism." Pp. 8–18 in Herbert Feigl and May Brodbeck (eds.) *Readings in The Philosophy of Science.* New York: Appleton-Century-Crofts.

Feigl, Herbert, and May Brodbeck. 1953. *Readings in The Philosophy of Science.* New York: Appleton-Century-Crofts.

Festinger, Leon, Henry Riecken, and Stanley Schacter. 1956. *When Prophecy Fails.* New York: Harper and Row.

Fine, Gary A. 1983. *Shared Fantasy: Role Playing Games as Social Worlds*. Chicago: University of Chicago Press.

———. 1993. "Ten Lies of Ethnography." *Journal of Contemporary Ethnography* 22:267–94.

Finestone, Harold. 1957. "Cats, Kicks and Color." *Social Problems* 5:3–13.

Flaherty, Michael G., and Carolyn Ellis. Forthcoming. *Social Perspectives on Emotions*, Vol. 3. Greenwich, Conn.: JAI Press.

Fleck, Ludwig. 1979. *Genesis and Development of a Scientific Fact* (1935). Translated by F. Bradley and T.J. Trenn. Chicago: University of Chicago Press.

Fletcher, Ronald. 1971. *The Making of Sociology* Vol. 1. London: Michael Joseph.

Fontana, Andrea. 1993. "Interactionist Ethnography and Postmodern Discourse Revisited." Pp. 189–92 in Norman K. Denzin (ed.) *Studies in Symbolic Interaction* 15. Greenwich, Conn.: JAI Press.

Foucault, Michel. 1967. *Madness and Civilizations*. London: Tavistock.

———. 1970. *The Order of Things*. London: Tavistock.

———. 1972. *The Archaeology of Knowledge*. London: Tavistock.

Franks, David D., and E. Doyle McCarthy. 1989. *The Sociology of Emotions*. Greenwich, Conn.: JAI Press.

Franks, David D., and Viktor Grecas. 1992. *Social Perspectives on Emotions*, Vol. 1. Greenwich, Conn.: JAI Press.

Freeman, Jennifer A. 1992. "The Perfect Valentine." *Journal of Contemporary Ethnography* 2:478–83.

Freilich, Morris. 1970. *Marginal Natives: Anthropologists at Work*. New York: Harper and Row.

Friedrichs, Robert W. 1970. *A Sociology of Sociology*. New York: Free Press.

Frisby, David. 1984. *Georg Simmel*. London: Tavistock.

Gadamer, Hans-Georg. 1976. *Philosophical Hermeneutics* (translated and edited by David E. Linge). Berkeley, Calif.: University of California Press.

———. 1986. *Truth and Method* (1960). New York: Crossroad Publishing.

Garbarino, Merwyn. 1983. *Sociocultural Theory in Anthropology*. Prospect Heights, Ill.: Waveland.

Garfinkel, Harold. 1956. "Conditions of Successful Degradation Ceremonies." *American Journal of Sociology* 61:420–24.

———. 1967. *Studies in Ethnomethodology*. Englewood Cliffs, N.J.: Prentice-Hall.

Gergen, Kenneth. 1982. *Toward Transformation in Social Knowledge*. New York: Springer-Verlag.

———. 1985. "The Social Constructionist Movement in Modern Psychology." *American Psychologist* 40:266–75.

Giddens, Anthony. 1974. *Positivism and Sociology.* London: Heinemann.

———. 1976. *New Rules of the Sociological Method: A Positive Critique of Interpretive Sociology.* London: Hutchinson.

———. 1981. *A Contemporary Critique of Historical Materialism.* London: Macmillan.

———. 1984. *The Constitution of Society: Outline of the Theory of Structuration.* Cambridge: Polity.

———. 1987. *Social Theory and Modern Sociology.* Stanford, Calif.: Stanford University Press.

Glaser, Barney, and Anselm Strauss. 1967. *The Discovery of Grounded Theory: Strategies for Qualitative Research.* Chicago: Aldine.

Glick, Ira. 1957. A Social Psychological Study of Futures Marketing. University of Chicago: Doctoral Dissertation (Sociology).

Goffman, Erving. 1952. "On Cooling Out the Mark." *Psychiatry* 14:451–63.

———. 1959. *The Presentation of Self in Everyday Life.* New York: Anchor.

———. 1961. *Asylums.* New York: Anchor.

———. 1963a. *Behavior in Public Places.* New York: Free Press.

———. 1963b. *Stigma.* Englewood Cliffs, N.J.: Spectrum.

———. 1971. *Relations in Public.* New York: Harper Colophon.

———. 1974. *Frame Analysis.* New York: Harper Colophon.

Grills, Scott. 1994. "Recruitment Practices of the Christian Heritage Party." Pp. 96–108 in Mary Lorenz Dietz, Robert Prus, and William Shaffir (eds.) *Doing Everyday Life: Ethnography as Human Lived Experience.* Toronto: Copp Clark Longman.

Gubrium, Jaber, 1975. *Living and Dying at Murray Manor.* New York: St. Martin's.

Gusfield, Joseph R. 1955. "Social Structure and Moral Reform: A Study of the Women's Christian Temperance Union." *American Journal of Sociology* 61:221–32.

———. 1963. *Symbolic Crusade: Status Politics and the American Temperance Movement.* Urbana: University of Illinois Press.

———. 1981. *The Culture of Public Problems.* Chicago: University of Chicago Press.

———. 1984. "On the Side: Practical Action and the Social Constructionism in Social Problems Theory." Pp. 31–51 in Joseph W. Schneider and John I. Kitsuse (eds.) *Studies in the Sociology of Social Problems.* Norwood, N.J.: Ablex.

———. 1989. "Constructing the Ownership of Social Problems: Fun and Profit in the Welfare State." *Social Problems* 26:431–41.

Haas, Jack. 1972. "Binging: Educational Control among High Steel Iron-workers." *The American Behavioral Scientist* 16:27–34.

———. 1977. "Learning Real Feelings: A Study of High Steel Ironworkers' Reactions to Fear and Danger." *Sociology of Work and Occupations* 4:147–70.

Haas, Jack and William Shaffir. 1987. *Becoming Doctors: The Adaption of a Cloak of Competence*. Greenwich, Conn.: JAI Press.

Habermas, Jürgen. 1968. *Knowledge and Human Interests* (translated by Jeremy J. Shapiro). Boston: Beacon Press.

———. 1988. *On the Logic of the Social Sciences* (1970) (translated by S. N. Nicholson and J. A. Stark).

Haddon, Alfred C. 1934. *History of Anthropology*. London: Watts and Co.

Halfpenny, Peter. 1982. *Positivism and Sociology: Explaining Social Life*. London: George Allen and Unwin.

Hall, Ian. 1983. Playing For Keeps: The Careers of Front-Line Workers for Developmentally Handicapped Persons. University of Waterloo: M.A. Thesis.

Hammersley, Martyn. 1989. *The Dilemma of Qualitative Method*. London: Routledge.

———. 1992. *What's Wrong with Ethnography?* London: Routledge.

Hargreaves, David, Stephen Hestor, and Frank Melor. 1975. *Deviance in Classrooms*. London: Routledge and Kegan Paul.

Harré, Rom. 1986. *The Social Construction of Emotions*. Oxford, UK: Basil Blackwell.

Harré, Rom, and Paul Secord. 1975. *The Explanation of Social Behavior*. Oxford, UK: Basil Blackwell.

Hayner, Norman. 1936. *Hotel Life*. College Park, Md.: McGrath (1969).

Hearn, H. L., and Patricia Stoll. 1975. "Continuance Commitments in Low-Status Occupations: The Cocktail Waitress." *Sociological Quarterly* 16: 105–14.

Heelas, Paul. 1986. "Emotion Talk Across Cultures." Pp. 234–66 in Rom Harré (ed.) *The Social Construction of Emotions*. Oxford, UK: Basil Blackwell.

Helmes-Hayes, Richard. forthcoming. " 'I Have Trod the Ecological Path': Everett Hughes' Interpretive Institutional Ecology." in Luigi Tomasi (editor) *The Tradition of the Chicago School*. (work in progress).

Henry, Frances, and Satish Saberwal. 1969. *Stress and Response in Fieldwork*. New York: Holt.

Herskovits, Melville. 1953. *Frans Boas: The Science of Man in the Making*. New York: Charles Scribner.

Hickman, C. Addison, and Manford Kuhn. 1956. *Individuals, Groups, and Economic Behavior.* New York: Dryden.

Hiller, E. T. 1928. *The Strike.* Chicago: University of Chicago Press.

Hochschild, Arlie Russell. 1979. "Emotion Work, Feeling Rules, and Social Structure." *American Journal of Sociology.* 85:551–75.

Hollis, Martin. 1977. *Models of Man: Philosophical Thoughts on Social Action.* New York: Cambridge University Press.

Holy, Ladislav. 1987. *Comparative Anthropology.* Oxford, England: Basil Blackwell.

Homans, George C. 1958. "Social Behavior as Exchange." *American Journal of Sociology* 63:597–606.

Hopper, Joseph. 1993. "Oppositional Identities and Rhetoric in Divorce." *Qualitative Sociology* 16:133–56.

Hughes, Everett. 1928. A Study of a Secular Institution: The Chicago Real Estate Board. University of Chicago: Doctoral Dissertation (Sociology).

———. 1943. *French Canada in Transition.* Chicago: University of Chicago Press.

———. 1961. "Introduction: The Place of Fieldwork in the Social Sciences." Pp. v–xiv in Buford H. Junker. *Fieldwork: An Introduction to the Social Sciences.* Chicago: University of Chicago Press.

———. 1971. *The Sociological Eye: Selected papers on Work, Self, and the Study of Society (Books One and Two).* Chicago: Aldine-Atherone.

Hunt, Morton. 1966. *The World of the Formerly Married.* New York: McGraw Hill.

James, William. 1907. *Pragmatism, A New Name for Some Old Ways of Thinking.* New York: Longmans, Green, and Co.

———. 1977. *The Writings of William James,* edited by John J. McDermott. Chicago: University of Chicago Press.

Joas, Hans. 1985. *G.H. Mead: A Contemporary Reexamination of His Thought.* Cambridge: Polity.

Johnson, John M. and David L. Altheide. 1991. "Text Without Context and the Problem of Author-ity in Ethnographic Research." Pp. 53–57 in N. K. Denzin (ed.) *Studies in Symbolic Interaction* Vol. 12. Greenwich, Conn.: JAI Press.

Jorgensen, Danny. 1989. *Participant Observation.* Newbury Park, Calif.: Sage.

Jorgensen, Joergen. 1970. "The Development of Logical Empiricism." Pp. 845–946 in Otto Neurath, Rudolf Carnap, and Charles Morris (eds.) *Foundations of the Unity of Science* Vol. II. Chicago: University of Chicago Press.

Junker, Buford. 1960. *Field Work: An Introduction to the Social Sciences*. Chicago: University of Chicago Press.

Karp, David A. 1993. "Taking Anti-Depressant Medications: Resistance, Trial Commitment, Conversion, and Disenchantment." *Qualitative Sociology* 16:337–59.

———. 1994. "The Dialectics of Depression." *Symbolic Interaction* 17:341–366.

Karp, David A. and William Yoels. 1979. *Symbols, Selves, and Society: Understanding Interaction*. New York: Lippincott/Harper & Row.

Karsh, Bernard, Joel Seidman, and Daisy M. Lilienthal. 1953. "The Union Organizer and His Tactics: A Case Study." *American Journal of Sociology* 59:113–22.

Kincheloe, Joe L., and Peter L. McLaren. 1994. "Rethinking Critical Theory and Qualitative Research." Pp. 138–57 in Norman K. Denzin and Yvonna S. Lincoln (eds.) *Handbook of Qualitative Research*. Thousand Oaks: Sage.

Kivisto, Peter, and William H. Swatos. 1990. "Weber and Interpretive Sociology in America." *Sociological Quarterly* 31:149–63.

Klapp, Orrin. 1962. *Heroes, Villains and Fools*. San Diego, Calif.: Aegis.

———. 1964. *Symbolic Leaders*. Chicago: Aldine.

———. 1969. *The Collective Search for Identity*. New York: Holt.

———. 1971. *Social Types: Process, Structure and Ethos*. San Diego, Calif.: Aegis.

Kleinman, Sherryl. 1984. *Equals before God: Seminarians as Humanistic Professionals*. Chicago: University of Chicago Press.

Kluckhohn, Florence. 1941. "The Participant-Observer Technique in Small Communities." *American Journal of Sociology* 46:331–43.

Knorr-Cetina, Karin. 1981. *The Manufacture of Knowledge: An Essay on the Constructivist and Contextual Nature of Science*. Oxford, England: Permagon.

———. 1983. "New Developments in Science Studies: The Ethnographic Challenge." *Canadian Journal of Sociology* 8:153–77.

Konvitz, Milton, and Gail Kennedy. 1960. *The American Pragmatists*. Cleveland: Meridan.

Kroeber, Alfred Louis. 1952. *The Nature of Culture*. Chicago: University of Chicago Press.

Kuhn, Manford. 1954. "Kinsey's View on Human Behavior." *Social Problems* 1:119–25.

———. 1964. "Major Trends in Symbolic Interaction Theory in the Past Twenty-five Years." *The Sociological Quarterly* 5:61–84.

Kuhn, Thomas S. 1962. *The Structure of Scientific Revolutions* (Revised edition, 1970). Chicago: University of Chicago Press.

Kurtz, Lester. 1984. *Evaluating Chicago Sociology: A Guide to the Literature, with an Annotated Bibliography*. Chicago: University of Chicago Press.

LaBarre, Weston. 1947. "The Language of Emotions and Gestures." *Journal of Personality* 16:49–68.

Lamont, Michele. 1987. "How to Become a Dominant French Philosopher: The Case of Jacques Derrida." *American Journal of Sociology* 93:584–622.

Latour, Bruno. 1987. *Science in Action*. Cambridge, Mass.: Harvard University Press.

Lauer, Robert H., and Warren H. Handel. 1977. *The Theory and Application of Symbolic Interaction*. Boston: Houghton-Mifflin.

Lemert, Edwin. 1951. *Social Pathology*. New York: McGraw-Hill.

———. 1962. "Paranoia and the Dynamics of Exclusion." *Sociometry* 25:2–25.

———. 1967. *Human Deviance, Social Problems and Social Control*. Englewood Cliffs, NJ: Prentice-Hall.

Lemke, James, David Shevach, and Richard H. Wells. 1984. "The Humanism-Positivism Debate in Sociology: A Comment on Tibbetts' Reconsideration." *Sociological Inquiry* 54:89–97.

Lesieur, Henry. 1977. *The Chase*. New York: Anchor.

Lester, Marilyn, and Stuart C. Hadden. 1980. "Ethnomethodology and Grounded Theory Methodology." *Urban Life* 9:3–33.

Levine, Donald. 1971. *Georg Simmel: On Individuality and Social Forms*. Chicago: University of Chicago Press.

Lincoln, Yvonna S., and Egon Guba. 1985. *Naturalistic Inquiry*. London: Sage.

Lincoln, Yvonna S., and Norman K. Denzin. 1994. "The Fifth Moment." Pp. 575–86 in Norman K. Denzin and Yvonna S. Lincoln (eds.) *Handbook of Qualitative Research*. Thousand Oaks, Calif.: Sage.

Lindesmith, Alfred R. 1959. "Federal Law and Drug Addiction." *Social Problems* 7:48–57.

Lindesmith, Alfred R. and Anselm R. Strauss. 1950. "A Critique of Culture and Personality Writings." *American Sociological Review* 15:587–600.

Lindgren, E. J. 1939. "The Collection and Analysis of Folk-lore." Pp. 328–74 in F. C. Bartlett, M. Ginsberg, E. J. Lindgren, and R. H. Thoules (eds.) *The Study of Society*. New York: The Macmillan Company.

Lofland, John. 1966. *The Doomsday Cult*. Englewood Cliffs, N.J.: Prentice-Hall.

———. 1969. *Deviance and Identity*. Englewood Cliffs, N.J.: Prentice-Hall.

———. 1970. "Interactionist Imagery and Analytic Interruptus." Pp. 35–45 in Tamotsu Shibutani (ed.), *Human Nature and Collective Behavior: Papers in Honor of Herbert Blumer*. Englewood Cliffs, N.J.: Prentice-Hall.

———. 1976. *Doing Social Life*. New York: Wiley.

————. 1984. "Erving Goffman's Sociological Legacies." *Urban Life* 13:7–34.

Lofland, John, and Lyn Lofland. 1984. *Analyzing Social Settings*. Belmont, California: Wadsworth.

Lofland, Lyn. 1980. "Reminiscences of Classic Chicago: The Blumer-Hughes Talk." *Urban Life* 9:251–81.

————. 1985. "The Social Shaping of Emotion: The Case of Grief." *Symbolic Interaction* 8:171–90.

Lowie, Robert H. 1937. *The History of Ethnological Theory*. New York: Holt, Rinehart and Winston.

Lutz, Catherine A. 1988. *Unatural Emotions*. Chicago: University of Chicago Press.

Lyman, Stanford, and Marvin Scott. 1970. *Sociology of the Absurd*. New York: Appleton-Century-Crofts.

Lyman, Stanford, and Arthur Vidich. 1988. *Social Order and the Public Philosophy: An Analysis and Interpretation of the Work of Herbert Blumer*. Fayetteville, Arkansas: University of Arkansas Press.

Lynd, Robert S., and Helen Murell Lynd. 1929. *Middletown: A Study in Modern American Culture*. New York: Harcourt, Brace (1956).

————. 1937. *Middletown in Transition: A Study in Cultural Contrast*. New York: Harcourt, Brace.

Lyotard, Jean Francois. 1984. *The Postmodern Condition*. Translated by Geoff Bennington and Brian Massumi. Minneapolis: University of Minnesota Press.

Lyotard, Jean Francois and F. Thebaud. 1985. *Just Gaming*. Minneapolis: University of Minnesota Press.

MacAndrew, Craig, and Robert Edgerton. 1969. *Drunken Comportment*. Chicago: Aldine.

Maines, David. 1986. "Researching Form and Process in the Iowa Tradition." Pp. 415–29 in Carl Couch, Stanley Saxton, and Michael Katovich (eds.) *Studies in Symbolic Interaction* (The Iowa School, Supplement 2, Part B). Greenwich, Conn.: JAI Press.

————. 1989. "Repackaging Blumer: The Myth of Herbert Blumer's Astructural Bias." *Studies in Symbolic Interaction* 10:383–413.

Makkreel, Rudolph A. 1975. *Dilthey: Philosopher of the Human Studies*. Princeton, N.J.: Princeton University Press.

Malinowski, Bronsilaw. 1922. *Argonauts of the Western Pacific*. London: Routledge and Kegan Paul.

————. 1967. *A Diary in the Strict Sense of the Term*. New York: Harcourt, Brace and World.

Manicas, Peter T. 1987. *A History and Philosophy of the Social Sciences*. New York: Basil Blackwell.

Marcus, George E., and Dick Cushman. 1982. "Ethnographies as Texts." *Annual Review of Ethnography* 11:25–69.

Marcus, George E., and Michael Fischer. 1986. *Anthropology as Cultural Critique*. Chicago: University of Chicago Press.

Martindale, Don. 1981. *The Nature and Types of Sociological Theory*. Boston: Houghton Mifflin.

Matthews, Fred H. 1977. *Quest for an American Sociology: Robert Park and the Chicago School*. Montreal: McGill-Queen's University Press.

McCarthy, E. Doyle. 1989. "Emotions are Social Things: An Essay in the Sociology of Emotions." Pp. 51–72 in David D. Franks and E. Doyle McCarthy (eds.) *The Sociology of Emotions*. Greenwich, Conn.: JAI Press.

McCloskey, Donald N. 1986. *The Rhetoric of Economics*. Madison, Wis.: University of Wisconsin Press.

McKinney, John. 1966. *Constructive Typologies and Social Theory*. New York: Appleton-Century-Crofts.

McPhail, Clark, and Cynthia Rexroat. 1979. "Mead vs. Blumer: The Divergent Methodological Perspectives of Social Behaviorism and Symbolic Interactionism." *American Sociological Review* 44:449–67.

———. 1980. *"Ex Cathedra* Blumer or *Ex Libris* Mead?" *American Sociological Review* 45:420–30.

Mead, George H. 1904. "The Relations of Psychology and Philology." *The Psychological Bulletin* 1:375–91.

———. 1906. "The Imagination in Wundt's Treatment of Myth and Religion." *The Psychological Bulletin* 3:393–99.

———. 1909. "Social Psychology as a Counterpart to Physiological Psychology." *The Psychological Bulletin* 6:401–8.

———. 1910. "Social Consciousness and the Consciousness of Meaning." *The Psychological Bulletin* 8:397–405.

———. 1932. *The Philosophy of the Present*. Edited by Arthur E. Murray. Lasalle, Ill.: Open Court.

———. 1934. *Mind, Self and Society*. Edited by Charles W. Morris. Chicago: University of Chicago Press.

———. 1936. *Movements of Thought in the Nineteenth Century*. Edited by Merritt A. Moore. Chicago: University of Chicago Press.

———. 1938. *The Philosophy of the Act*. Edited by Charles W. Morris. Chicago: University of Chicago Press.

————. 1956. *On Social Psychology: Selected Papers*. Edited by Anselm Strauss. Chicago: University of Chicago Press.

Mehan, Hugh, and Houston Wood. 1975. *The Reality of Ethnomethodology*. New York: Wiley.

Meltzer, Bernard, and John Petras. 1972. "The Chicago and Iowa Schools of Symbolic Interactionism." Pp. 43–57 in Jerome G. Manis and Bernard N. Meltzer (eds.) *Symbolic Interactionism* (Second edition). Boston: Allyn and Bacon.

Meltzer, Bernard, John W. Petras, and Larry T. Reynolds. 1975. *Symbolic Interactionism: Genesis, Varieties and Criticism*. London: Routledge and Kegan Paul.

————. 1978. "Varieties of Symbolic Interactionism." Pp. 41–58 in Jerome G. Manis and Bernard N. Meltzer (eds.) *Symbolic Interactionism* (Second edition). Boston: Allyn and Bacon.

Merton, Robert K. 1957. *Social Theory and Social Structure*. New York: Free Press.

————. 1973. *The Sociology of Science*. Chicago, Ill.: University of Chicago Press.

Mill, John Stuart. 1959. *System of Logic*. (1843) London: Longmans.

Miller, David L. 1973. *George Herbert Mead*. Chicago: University of Chicago Press.

Mills, C. Wright. 1959. *The Sociological Imagination*. New York: Oxford University Press.

————. 1969. *Sociology and Pragmatism*. New York: Oxford University Press.

Mitchell, Richard G. Jr. 1983. *Mountain Experience*. Chicago: University of Chicago Press.

————. 1993. *Secrecy and Fieldwork*. Newbury Park, Calif.: Sage.

Miyamato, Frank. 1959. "The Social Act: Re-examination of a Concept." *Pacific Sociological Review* 2:51–55.

Molseed, Mari J. 1994. "Naturalistic Observation in the Laboratory." *Symbolic Interaction* 17:239–51.

Mooney, James. 1965. *The Ghost-Dance Religion and the Sioux Outbreak of 1890*. (1896) Chicago: University of Chicago Press.

Moore, Sally Falk. 1975. "Epilogue" Pp. 210–238 in *Symbol and Politics in Communal Ideology*. Sally Falk Moore and Barbara Myerhoff (eds.) Ithaca, N.Y.: Cornell University Press.

Morgan, Lewis Henry. 1901. *The League of the Ho-de-no-sau-nee, or Iroquois*. [1851] New York: Burt Franklin (1964 reprint).

————. 1959. *The Indian Journals 1859–1862*. Leslie A. White (editor). Ann Arbor: The University of Michigan Press.

Morrione, Thomas. forthcoming. *The Collected Papers of Herbert Blumer: Fundamentals of Symbolic Interaction.* Berekely, Calif.: University of California Press.

Morris, Charles. 1970. *The Pragmatic Movement in American Philosophy.* New York: Braziller.

Mueller-Vollmer, Kurt. 1989. *The Hermeneutics Reader: Texts of the German Tradition from the Enlightenment to the Present.* New York: Continuum.

Mulkay, Michael. 1979. *Science and the Sociology of Knowledge.* London: George Allen and Unwin.

Mullins, Nicholas C. 1973. *Theories and Theory Groups in Contemporary American Sociology.* New York: Harper and Row.

Neurath, Otto, Rudolf Carnap, and Charles Morris. 1969. *Foundations of the Unity of Science Vol. I.* Chicago: University of Chicago Press.

―――. 1970. *Foundations of the Unity of Science Vol. II.* Chicago: University of Chicago Press.

Nietzsche, Friedrich. 1986. *Human, All too Human* (1878, 1886). Translated by R. J. Hollingdale. Cambridge, UK: Cambridge University Press.

Noblit, George W., and R. Dewight Hare. 1988. *Meta-Ethnography: Synthesizing Qualitative Studies.* Newbury Park, Calif.: Sage.

Oakes, Guy. 1980. *Georg Simmel: Essays on Interpretation in Social Science.* Totawa, N.J.: Rowman and Littlefield.

Oberschall, Anthony. 1965. *Empirical Social Research in Germany 1848–1914.* The Hague: Mouton.

Oleson, Virginia. 1994. "Feminisms and Models of Qualitative Research." Pp. 158–74 in Norman K. Denzin and Yvonna S. Lincoln (eds.) *Handbook of Qualitative Research.* Thousand Oaks, Calif.: Sage.

Palmer, Vivian. 1928. *Field Studies in Sociology.* Chicago: University of Chicago Press.

Park, Robert E., and Ernest Burgess. 1921. *Introduction to the Science of Sociology.* Chicago: University of Chicago Press (second edition 1924).

Park, Robert, Herbert A. Miller, and W. I. Thomas. 1921. *Old World Traits Transplanted.* New York: Harper and Row.

Parsons, Talcott. 1951. *Toward a General Theory of Action.* New York: Harper and Row.

Passmore, John. 1968. "Logical Positivism." *The Encyclopedia of Philosophy.* New York: Macmillan. Vol. 5:52–57.

Paul, Benjamin. 1953. "Interview Techniques and Field Relationships." Pp. 430–51 in Alfred L. Kroeber (ed.) *Anthropology Today: An Encyclopedia Inventory.* Chicago: University of Chicago Press.

Pickering, Andrew. 1990. "Knowledge, Practice and Mere Construction." *Social Studies of Science* 20:682–729.

———. 1992. *Science as Practice and Culture*. Chicago: University of Chicago Press.

———. 1993. "The Mangle of Practice: Agency and Emergence in the Sociology of Science." *American Journal of Sociology* 99:559–89.

———. In press. *The Mangle of Practice*. Chicago: University of Chicago Press.

Plantinga, Theodore. 1980. *Historical Understanding in the Thought of Wilhelm Dilthey*. Toronto: University of Toronto Press.

Platt, Jennifer. 1985. "Weber's *Verstehen* and the History of Qualitative Research." *British Journal of Sociology* 36:448–67.

Powell, Walter. 1985. *Getting Into Press*. Chicago: University of Chicago Press.

Prus, Robert. 1975a. "Labeling Theory: A Reconceptualization and A Propositional Statement on Typing." *Sociological Focus* 8:79–96.

———. 1975b. "Resisting Designations: An Extension of Attribution Theory into a Negotiated Context." *Sociological Inquiry* 45:3–14.

———. 1976. "Religious Recruitment and the Management of Dissonance: A Sociological Perspective." *Sociological Inquiry* 46:127–34.

———. 1978. "From Barrooms to Bedrooms: Towards a Theory of Interpersonal Violence." Pp. 51–73 in M. A. B. Gammon (ed.) *Violence in Canada*. Toronto: Methuen.

———. 1982. "Designating Discretion and Openness: The Problematics of Truthfulness in Everyday Life." *The Canadian Review of Sociology and Anthropology* 18:70–91.

———. 1984. "Career Contingencies: Examining Patterns of Involvement." Pp. 297–317 in N. Theberge and P. Donnelly (eds.) *Sport and the Sociological Imagination*. Fort Worth, Tex.: Texas Christian University Press.

———. 1987. "Generic Social Processes: Maximizing Conceptual Development in Ethnographic Research." *Journal of Contemporary Ethnography* 16:250–91.

———. 1989a. *Making Sales: Influence as Interpersonal Accomplishment*. Newbury Park, California: Sage.

———. 1989b. *Pursuing Customers: An Ethnography of Marketing Activities*. Newbury Park, Calif.: Sage.

———. 1990. "The Interpretive Challenge: The Impending Crisis in Sociology." *Canadian Journal of Sociology* 15(3): 355–63.

———. 1992. "Producing Social Science: Knowledge as a Social Problem in Academia." Pp. 57–78 in Gale Miller and James Holstein (eds.), *Perspectives in Social Problems*, Vol. 3. Greenwich, Conn.: JAI Press.

———. 1993. "Shopping with Companions: Images, Influences, and Interpersonal Dilemmas." *Qualitative Sociology* 16:87–110.

———. 1994a. "Consumers as Targets: Autonomy, Accountability, and Anticipation of the Influence Process." *Qualitative Sociology* 17:243–62.

———. 1994b. "Generic Social Processes: Intersubjectivity and Transcontextuality." Pp. 393–412 in Mary Lorenz Dietz, Robert Prus and William Shaffir (editors), *Doing Everyday Life: Ethnography as Human Lived Experience*. Toronto: Copp Clark Longman.

———. 1994c. "Generic Social Processes and the Study of Human Lived Experience: Achieving Transcontextuality in Ethnographic Research." Pp. 436–50 in Nancy J. Herman and Larry T. Reynolds (eds.), *Symbolic Interaction: An Introduction to Social Psychology*. Dix Hills, N.Y.: General Hall.

Prus, Robert, and Lorne Dawson. 1991. "Shop 'til You Drop: Shopping as Recreational and Laborious Activity." *Canadian Journal of Sociology* 16:145–64.

———. 1993. "Postmodernism and Linguistic Reality Versus Symbolic Interaction and the Human Struggle for Existence: Toward a Synergistic Social Science." Paper presented at the Society for the Study of Symbolic Interaction Meetings, Miami, Florida.

Prus, Robert, and Augie Fleras. forthcoming. "'Pitching' Images to the Generalized Other: Promotional Strategies of Economic Development Officers." In Helena Znaniecki Lopata (editor), *Current Research on Occupations and Professions: Societal Influences*, Vol. 9. Greenwich, Conn.: JAI Press.

Prus, Robert, and Wendy Frisby. 1990. "Persuasion as Practical Accomplishment: Tactical Manoeuverings at Home Party Plans." Pp. 133–62 in Helena Znaniecki Lopata (editor), *Current Research on Occupations and Professions: Societal Influences*. Vol. 5. Greenwich, Conn.: JAI Press.

Prus, Robert, and Styllianoss Irini. 1980. *Hookers, Rounders, and Desk Clerks: The Social Organization of the Hotel Community*. Salem, Wis.: Sheffield (1988).

Prus, Robert, and C. R. D. Sharper. 1977. *Road Hustler: The Career Contingencies of Professional Card and Dice Hustlers*. Lexington, Mass.: Lexington Books.

———. 1991. *Road Hustler: Hustlers, Magic and the Thief Subculture*. New York: Kaufman and Greenberg.

Prus, Robert, and John R. Stratton. 1976. "Parole Revocation Decision-Making: Private Typings and Official Designations." *Federal Probation* 40:48–53.

Radcliffe-Brown, A. R. 1958. *Method in Social Anthropology*. Edited by M. N. Srinivas. Chicago: University of Chicago Press.

Radin, Paul. 1920. *The Autobiography of a Winnebago Indian*. University of California Publications in American Archaeology and Ethnology 16: 381–473.

———. 1966. *The Method and Theory of Ethnology: An Essay in Criticism* (1933). New York: Basic Books.

Ray, Marsh. 1961. "The Cycle of Abstinence and Relapse among Heroin Addicts." *Social Problems* 9:132–40.

Reinharz, Shulamit. 1992. *Feminist Methods in Social Research*. New York: Oxford University Press.

Reynolds, Larry T. 1993. *Interactionism: Exposition and Critique* (third edition). New York: General Hall.

Richards, Audrey I. 1939. "The Development of Field Work Methods in Social Anthropology." Pp. 272–316 in F. C. Bartlett, M. Ginsberg, E. J. Lindgren, and R. H. Thoules (eds.) *The Study of Society*. New York: Macmillan.

Richardson, Laurel. 1988. "The Collective Story: Postmodernism and the Writing of Sociology." *Sociological Focus* 21:199–208.

———. 1991. "Postmodern Social Theory: Representational Practices." *Sociological Theory* 9:173–80.

———. 1992. "Resisting Resistance Narratives: A Representation for Communication." *Studies in Symbolic Interaction* 13:77–82.

———. 1994a. "Nine Poems: Marriage and the Family." *Journal of Contemporary Ethnography* 23:3–13.

———. 1994b. "Writing: A Method of Inquiry." Pp. 516–29 in Norman K. Denzin and Yvonna S. Lincoln (eds.) *Handbook of Qualitative Research*. Thousand Oaks, Calif.: Sage.

Richardson, Laurel, and Ernest Lockridge. 1991. "The Sea Monster: An Ethnographic Drama." *Symbolic Interaction* 14:335–40.

Richmond, Mary E. 1917. *Social Diagnoses*. New York: Russell Sage.

Rickman, H. P. 1976. *W. Dilthey: Selected Writings*. New York: Cambridge University Press.

———. 1988. *Dilthey Today: A Critical Appraisal of the Contemporary Relevance of His Work*. Westport, Conn.: Greenwood.

Rosenau, Pauline Marie. 1992. *Post-Modernism and the Social Sciences: Insights, Inroads, and Intrusions*. Princeton, NJ: Princeton University Press.

Ross, H. Lawrence. 1980. *Settled Out of Court*. New York: Aldine.

Rossides, Daniel. 1978. *The History and Nature of Sociological Theory*. Boston: Houghton Mifflin.

Rubington, Earl. 1968. "Variations in Bottle-Gang Controls." Pp. 308–16 in E. Rubington and M. Weinberg (eds.), *Deviance: The Interactionist Perspective*. New York: Macmillan.

Rubington, Earl, and Martin Weinberg. 1973. *"Deviance: The Interactionist Perspective"* (Second edition). New York: Macmillan.

Rucker, Darnell. 1969. *The Chicago Pragmatists*. Minneapolis: University of Minnesota Press.

Sandelowski, Margarete, Betty G. Harris, and Diane Holditch-Davis. 1991. " 'The Clock has been Ticking, the Calendar Pages Turning, and We Are Still Waiting': Infertile Couples' Encounters with Time in the Adoption Waiting Period." *Qualitative Sociology* 14:147–73.

Sanders, Clinton. 1990. "Excusing Tactics: Social Responses to the Public Misbehavior of Companion Animals." *Anthrozoos* 4 (2):82–90.

———. 1991. *Customizing the Body: The Art and Culture of Tattooing*. Philadelphia: Temple University Press.

———. 1993. "Understanding Dogs: Caretakers' Attributions of Mindedness in Canine-Human Relationships." *Journal of Contemporary Ethnography* 22:205–26.

———. 1994. "Annoying Owners: Routine Interactions with Problematic Clients in a General Veterinary Practice. *Qualitative Sociology* 17:159–70.

———. 1995. "Stranger Than Fiction: Insights and Pitfalls in Post-Modern Ethnography." Pp. 89–104 in Norman K. Denzin (ed.) *Studies in Symbolic Interaction* 17. Greenwich, Conn.: JAI Press.

Sarup, Madan. 1989. *An Introductory Guide to Post-Structuralism and Postmodernism*. Athens, Georgia: University of Georgia Press.

Scheff, Thomas J. 1963. "Decision Rules, Types of Error, and Their Consequences in Medical Diagnoses." *Behavioral Science* 8:97–107.

———. 1990. *Microsociology: Discourse, Emotion, and Social Structure*. Chicago: University of Chicago Press.

Scheffler, Israel. 1974. *Four Pragmatists: A Critical Introduction to Peirce, James, Mead, and Dewey*. New York: Humanities.

Schmid, Thomas J., and Richard S. Jones. 1993. "Ambivalent Actions: Prison Adaptation Strategies of First-Time, Short-Term Inmates." *Journal of Contemporary Ethnography* 21:439–63.

Schneider, Joseph W., and Peter Conrad. 1983. *Having Epilepsy*. Philadelphia: Temple University Press.

Schoolcraft, Henry R. 1978. *Personal Memoirs of a Residence of Thirty Years with the Indian Tribes on the American Frontiers: With Brief Notices of Passing Events, Facts, and Opinions, A.D. 1812–A.D. 1842* [1851]. New York: AMS.

Schutz, Alfred. 1962. *Collected Papers I: The Problem of Social Reality.* The Hague: Martinus Nijhoff.

———. 1964. *Collected Papers II: Studies in Social Theory.* The Hague: Martinus Nijhoff.

———. 1967. *The Phenomenology of the Social World.* Translated by George Walsh and Fredich Lehnert. Evanston, Illinois: Northwestern University.

Schutz, Alfred, and Thomas Luckmann. 1973. *The Structures of the Life-world.* Evanston, Ill.: Northwestern University Press.

Scimecca, Joseph A. 1989. "The Philosophical Foundations of Humanist Sociology." *Current Perspectives in Social Theory* 9:223–38.

Scott, Lois. 1981. *Being Somebody: The Negotiation of Identities in a Community Context.* University of Waterloo: M.Sc. Thesis (Kinesiology).

Scott, Marvin. 1968. *The Racing Game.* Chicago: Aldine.

Shaffir, William, and Robert Stebbins. 1991. *Experiencing Fieldwork: An Inside View of Qualitative Methods.* Newbury Park: Sage.

Shalin, Demetri. 1986. "Pragmatism and Social Interactionism." *American Sociological Review* 51:9–29.

Shaw, Clifford. 1930. *The Jack-Roller: A Delinquent Boy's Own Story* [1961]. Chicago: University of Chicago Press.

Shaw, Clifford, and M. E. Moore. 1931. *The Natural History of a Delinquent Career.* Chicago: University of Chicago Press.

Shaw, Clifford, Henry McKay, and James McDonald. 1938. *Brothers in Crime.* Chicago: University of Chicago Press.

Shibutani, Tamotsu. 1961. *Society and Personality.* Englewood Cliffs, N.J.: Prentice-Hall.

Shott, Susan. 1979. "Emotion and Social Life: A Symbolic Interactionist Analysis." *American Journal of Sociology* 84:1317–34.

Simmel, Georg. 1950. *The Sociology of George Simmel.* Translated and edited by Kurt H. Wolff. New York: Free Press.

———. 1955. *Conflict and the Web of Group Affiliations.* Translated by Kurt Wolff and Reinhard Bendix. London: The Free Press of Glencoe.

———. 1978. *The Philosophy of Money* (1907). Translated by Tom Bottomore and David Frisby. Boston: Routledge and Kegan Paul.

Simmons, J. L. 1969. *Deviants.* Berkeley, California: Glendessary Press.

Smaling, Adri. 1992. "Varieties of Methodological Intersubjectivity—the Relations with Qualitative and Quantitative Research, and with Objectivity." *Quality and Quantity* 26:169–80.

Snodgrass, Jon. 1983. "The Jack-Roller: A Fifty Year Follow-Up." *Urban Life* 11:440–60.

Snodgrass, Jon, and The Jack-Roller. 1982. *The Jack-Roller at Seventy: A Fifty-Year Follow-Up.* Lexington, Ma.: Lexington Books.

Snow, David A., and Calvin Morrill. 1993. "Reflections on Anthropology's Ethnographic Crisis of Faith." *Contemporary Sociology* 22:8–11.

Sorokin, Pitirim. 1937–1941. *Social and Cultural Dynamics* (4 vols.) New York: American Book Company.

Spitzer, Stephan, Carl Couch, and John Stratton. 1994. "Kuhn's Formulation of the Self." Pp. 70–75 in Nancy J. Herman and Larry T. Reynolds (eds.), *Symbolic Interaction: An Introduction to Social Psychology.* New York: General Hall.

Spradley, James P. 1979. *The Ethnographic Interview.* New York: Holt, Rinehart, Winston.

———. 1980. *Participant Observation.* New York: Holt, Rinehart, Winston.

Star, Susan Leigh. 1989. *Regions of the Mind: Brain Research and the Quest for Scientific Certainty.* Stanford, Calif.: Stanford University Press.

Stebbins, Robert. 1990. *The Laugh-Makers.* Montreal: McGill-Queens University Press.

———. 1994. "Doing Stand Up: Comedians on Stage." Pp. 245–59 in Mary Lorenz Dietz, Robert Prus, and William Shaffir (editors), *Doing Everyday Life: Ethnography as Human Lived Experience.* Toronto: Copp Clark Longman.

Steffensmeier, Darrell J. 1986. *The Fence: In the Shadow of Two Worlds.* Totowa, N.J.: Rowman and Littlefield.

Stinchcombe, Arthur L. 1984. "The Origins of Sociology as a Discipline." *Acta Sociologica* 27(1): 51–61.

Stocking, George. 1974. *The Shaping of American Anthropology 1883–1911: A Frans Boas Reader.* New York: Basic Books.

———. 1979. *Anthropology at Chicago: Tradition, Discipline, Department.* Chicago: Joseph Regenstein Library.

Stone, Gregory, and Harvey A. Farberman. 1967. "On the Edge of Rapprochement: Was Durkheim Moving Toward the Perspective of Symbolic Interaction?" *Sociological Quarterly* 8:149–64.

Strauss, Anselm. 1970. "Discovering New Theory From Previous Theory." Pp. 46–53 in T. Shibutani (ed.), *Human Nature and Collective Behavior: Papers in Honor of Herbert Blumer.* Englewood Cliffs, N.J.: Prentice-Hall.

Stryker, Sheldon. 1980. *Symbolic Interactionism: A Social Structural Version.* Menlo Park: Benjamin/Cummings.

Sutherland, Edwin. 1937. *The Professional Thief.* Chicago: University of Chicago Press.

———. 1950. "The Diffusion of Sexual Psychopath Laws." *American Journal of Sociology* 56:142–48.

Szasz, Thomas S. 1961. *The Myth of Mental Illness.* New York: Hoeber-Harper.

———. 1970. *The Manufacture of Madness.* New York: Delta.

Tannenbaum, Frank. 1938. *Crime and the Community.* New York: Columbia University Press.

Thoits, Peggy A. 1989. "The Sociology of Emotions." *Annual Review of Sociology* 15:317–42.

Thomas, William I. 1896. "The Scope and Method of Folk-Psychology." *American Journal of Sociology* 1:434–45.

———. 1923. *The Unadjusted Girl: With Cases and Standpoint for Behavioral Analysis.* Boston: Little, Brown.

———. 1966. *On Social Organization and Social Personality.* Edited by Morris Janowitz. Chicago: University of Chicago Press.

———. 1973. "Life-History" (Paul Baker, ed.) *American Journal of Sociology* 79:243–60.

Thomas, William I., and Florian Znaniecki. 1918–1920. *The Polish Peasant in Europe and America* (Volumes I–V). Boston: Richard Badger.

Thrasher, Frederick M. 1927. *The Gang.* Chicago: University of Chicago Press.

Tibbetts, Paul. 1982. "The Positivism-Humanism Debate in Sociology: A Reconsideration." *Sociological Inquiry* 52:184–99.

Turner, Victor. 1985. *On the Edge of the Bush: Anthropology as Experience.* Tucson, Arizona: University of Arizona Press.

———. 1986. "Dewey, Dilthey, and Drama: An Essay in the Anthropology of Experience." Pp. 33–44 in Victor W. Turner and Edward M. Bruner (eds.), *The Anthropology of Experience.* Urbana: University of Illinois.

Urry, James. 1984. "A History of Field Methods." Pp. 35–61 in R.F. Ellen (ed.), *Ethnographic Research: A Guide to General Conduct.* London: Academic Press.

Vaughan, Diane. 1986. *Uncoupling: Turning Points in Intimate Relationships.* New York: Oxford.

Vidich, Arthur J., and Stanford Lyman. 1994. "Qualitative Methods: Their History in Sociology and Anthropology." Pp. 23–59 in Norman Denzin and Yvonna S. Lincoln (eds.) *Handbook of Qualitative Research.* Thousand Oaks, Calif.: Sage.

Vittimo, Gianni. 1991. *The End of Modernity: Nibilism and Hermeneutics in Postmodern Culture.* Baltimore: John Hopkins University Press.

Vold, George. 1951. "Edwin Hardwin Sutherland: Sociological Criminologist." *American Sociological Review* 16:3–9.

Waller, Willard. 1930. *The Old Love and the New*. Carbondale, Ill.: Southern Illinois University Press (1967).

———. 1932. *The Sociology of Teaching*. New York: Russel and Russel (1961).

Warner, W. Lloyd, and Paul S. Lunt. 1941. *The Social Life of a Modern Community*. New Haven, Conn.: Yale University Press.

Wasielewski, Patricia L. 1985. "The Emotional Basis of Charisma." *Symbolic Interaction* 8:207–22.

Wax, Rosalie. 1971. *Doing Fieldwork*. Chicago: University of Chicago Press.

Weber, Max. 1947. *The Theory of Social and Economic Organization*, edited by A. M. Henderson and Talcott Parsons. New York: Free Press.

———. 1971. *On Interpretation of Social Reality*, edited by J. E. T. Eldridge. London: Michael Joseph.

Weger, Katarina. 1992. "The Sociological Significance of Ambivalence: An Example from Adoption Research." *Qualitative Sociology* 15:87–103.

Weigert, Andrew J. 1991. "Transverse Interaction: A Pragmatic Perspective on Environment as Other." *Symbolic Interaction* 14:353–63.

Wentworth, William, and John Ryan. 1994. *Social Perspectives on Emotions*, Vol. 2. Greenwich, Conn.: JAI Press.

White, Stephen K. 1991. *Political Theory and Postmodernism*. Cambridge: Cambridge University Press.

Whittaker, Elvi. 1994. "The Contribution of Herbert Blumer to Anthropology." Pp. 379–92 in Mary Lorenz Dietz, Robert Prus, and William Shaffir (eds.) *Doing Everyday Life: Ethnography as Human Lived Experience*. Toronto: Copp Clark Longman.

Whyte, William Foote. 1943. *Street Corner Society* (1955 enlarged edition). Chicago: University of Chicago Press.

Wiley, Norbert. 1979. "The Rise and Fall of Dominating Theories in American Sociology." Pp. 47–79 in W. E. Snizek, E. R. Fuhrman, M. K. Miller (eds.) *Contemporary Issues in Theory and Research*. Westport, Conn.: Greenwood.

Winch, Peter. 1958. *The Idea of a Social Science and Its Relation to Philosophy*. London: Routledge and Kegan Paul.

Wirth, Louis. 1928. *The Ghetto*. Chicago: University of Chicago Press.

Wiseman, Jacqueline. 1970. *Stations of the Lost: The Treatment of Skid Row Alcoholics*. Englewood Cliffs, NJ: Prentice-Hall.

———. 1987. "In Memoriam: Herbert Blumer (1900–1987)." *Journal of Contemporary Ethnography* 16:243–349.

Wolf, Charlotte. 1994. "Conversion into Feminism." Pp. 143–57 in Mary Lorenz Dietz, Robert Prus, and William Shaffir (eds.) *Doing Everyday Life: Ethnography as Human Lived Experience.* Toronto: Copp Clark Longman.

Wolf, Daniel. 1991. *The Rebels: A Brotherhood of Outlaw Bikers.* Toronto: University of Toronto Press.

Wolf, Marjorie. 1992. *A Thrice-Told Tale: Feminism, Postmodernism, and Ethnographic Responsibility.* Stanford, Calif.: Stanford University Press.

Wundt, Wilhelm. 1916. *Elements of Folk Psychology*, translated by Edward L. Schaub. New York: Macmillan.

Young, Michael. 1979. *The Ethnography of Malinowski: The Trobriand Islands 1915–1918.* London: Kegan Paul.

Zerubabel, Eviatar 1981. "If Simmel were a Fieldworker: On Formal Sociological Theory and Analytical Field Research." *Symbolic Interaction* 3(2):25–33.

Zimmerman, Don H. 1978. "Ethnomethodology." *The American Sociologist* 13:6–15.

Zorbaugh, Harvey. 1929. *The Gold Coast and the Slum.* Chicago: University of Chicago Press.

Zuckerman, Harriet. 1988. "The Sociology of Science" Pp. 511–74 in Neil Smelser (ed.) *Handbook of Sociology.* Newbury Park, Calif.: Sage.

Index of Names

Index of Terms